FUNDAMENTALS
OF BEHAVIORAL
RESEARCH

FUNDAMENTALS OF BEHAVIORAL RESEARCH

PIETRO BADIA
Bowling Green State University
AND
RICHARD P. RUNYON

Addison-Wesley Publishing Company

Reading, Massachusetts • Menlo Park, California
London • Amsterdam • Don Mills, Ontario • Sydney

Library of Congress Cataloging in Publication Data

Badia, Pietro, 1930–
   Fundamentals of behavioral research.

   Bibliography: p.
   Includes index.
   1. Psychological research.   I. Runyon, Richard P.
II. Title.
BF76.5.B3157   150′.72   81-14863
ISBN 0-201-06378-6   AACR2

ISBN 0-201-06378-6
ABCDEFGHIJ-DO-8987654321

This book is dedicated to
Rita, Debra, and Patricia Jo,
and to Maribeth, Thomas, Richard,
Nancy, and Amy

CONTENTS

PREFACE

Courses in undergraduate research methods vary in content, in the order of presenting material, and in the laboratory opportunities provided for the student. Therefore the "core" of material considered to be fundamental and necessary for the student to master may differ across instructors, colleges, and universities.

We have written a book that focuses on fundamental research methods and procedures that we feel are common to most courses. It does not deal with content from any particular area of psychology such as perception, learning, etc. Our emphasis throughout is on methodology—from the initiation of the research (planning stages) to its completion (writing up the report). The intention is to provide students with the necessary knowledge to evaluate research, to do research, and to appreciate its importance.

For the most part, each chapter is a unit in itself covering what we consider to be important, fundamental information. Within limits, this should provide instructors with flexibility in selecting the chapters they wish to assign and in choosing a sequence of chapters to their liking. Some may choose to follow the sequence of chapters that we have provided; others may want to follow a different one.

In addition to the traditional concepts, methods, and procedures found in many good texts, we have included material on important developments. These developments are reflected in the chapter headings such as Single-Subject Research, Observational Procedures and Inter-Observer Agreement, Program Evaluation, Different Designs and Different Laws. While the chapter titles provide a general idea of the contents of the text, within each chapter can be found detailed treatment of specific issues. We have consistently included in each chapter concrete examples to illustrate the conceptual points that are made.

It is unusual to begin a text with a chapter devoted to ethical considerations. This decision was carefully considered and deliberately made. It is an affirmation that, although science is dedicated to advancing knowledge, its primary mission is to serve humanity. Students should be aware that ethical concerns are not tangential matters that are given consideration only after "more important" aspects of research design have been resolved. Rather, we are asserting the primacy of ethical concerns. They are as much a part of designing research as the selection of independent and dependent variables. To this end, we begin the book with ethical issues involving both human (adults, children) and nonhuman subjects. In addition, we discuss the controversial issues involving the use of deception. While information on these ethical issues is important for all students taking research courses, it is especially so for those who undertake individual research projects and for those assisting faculty in their professional research efforts.

We also give prominence to ethical issues for another reason. There are many who have expressed strong reservations about research done on living organisms. These reservations are based on what is perceived as past and present insensitivities on the part of researchers concerning the welfare of their subjects. There are, unfortunately, examples of insensitivities that can be pointed to using both human and nonhuman subjects. We describe some of these instances but others, equally serious, could also be described. These occurrences have led to the formation of lobby organizations seeking legislation that places constraints on research beyond the ethical guidelines imposed by professional and governmental agencies. We feel that additional constraints are unnecessary and that full awareness along with strict adherence to current ethical guidelines will lessen future problems considerably. Addressing ethical issues in the first chapter is one way of giving prominence to ethical concerns and indicating to others that behavioral scientists are not only fully committed to these concerns in their research but that they are also fully committed to teaching them.

The other chapters follow more traditional lines. Some main concerns in these chapters are as follows. Chapter 2 deals with a description of science, how it differs from common sense and from technology. The value of basic and applied research is described and we present reasons why it is important to support basic research. In Chapter 3 we distinguish between data and inference and include material on theories, empirical generalizations, confirmation bias, scaling, and measurement. Chapter 4 deals with research methods with a special emphasis on both correlational and experimental methods. We describe how to distinguish between the two methods in those instances when the distinction is not obvious, and why a distinction should be made. Our particular concern is that students know the permissible conclusions allowed by each method and why this is so. After reading this chapter students should be better able to evaluate the validity of conclusions drawn by researchers and by writers for popular magazines and other mass media sources.

Chapter 5 describes the necessary characteristics of a good dependent variable and also provides some useful guidelines for choosing values of an independent variable. Dependent variables based on observational data are discussed in Chapter 6. Since much of the behavior in which psychologists are interested cannot be automatically recorded, rules for making observations, ways of recording observations, and the necessity for inter-observer reliability are described.

In Chapter 7 we deal with the necessary procedures that must be followed when attempting to isolate the effects of the independent variable. We describe why control groups are necessary and what happens when they are not used. We also describe several specific procedures that should be followed in trying to isolate the effects of the independent variable. Great emphasis is placed on the meaning and value of random assignment. Chapter 8 is a continuation of the issues described in Chapter 7 but it deals specifically with the many different types of confounding by pointing to variables often "entangled" with the independent variable. Chapter 9 deals with sampling and we start the chapter by distinguishing random assignment procedures from random sampling ones. Among other topics we describe simple random sampling, stratified random sampling, and convenience sampling. We place emphasis on why it is necessary to identify the population from which the sample is drawn. We also describe why many researchers cannot identify the population from which the sample was drawn because a convenience sampling procedure was used.

Chapters 10, 11, and 12 deal with analyzing variability and with research designs. We contrast the differences between independent group designs and repeated measures designs. The possibility that these different research designs may produce different kinds of lawful relations is discussed at length. We also discuss in some detail the circumstances under which each may be properly used and we also discuss their advantages and disadvantages.

A conceptual description of the rationale for statistical decision making is given in Chapter 13. In doing so, we focus on the overall research process and show that research methods, specific procedures, experimental design, and statistical evaluation form an integral whole. We believe that this approach provides students with a better perspective and a fuller understanding of how the various important aspects of research relate. The conceptual approach to statistics is supplemented by worked examples placed in the appendices. In addition to enhancing overall understanding, this combined approach should also serve as a useful review for many.

A relatively full account of the single-subject approach is presented in Chapter 14. This chapter allows the student to contrast the earlier inferential statistical approach to research with a descriptive, nonstatistical (i.e., noninferential statistics) approach to research. The contrast should be beneficial to students generally for illustrating the importance of both approaches. It should be a particularly interesting chapter for those with more applied interests.

Chapter 15 deals with program evaluation and with some of the problems associated with evaluation in "real-life" settings. Both formative and summative evaluation are discussed. We include in this chapter both longitudinal and cross-sectional approaches. In addition, further examples are given of how the phenomena of regression to the mean can affect evaluation, particularly some types of program evaluation.

Our last chapter deals with writing of the manuscript as a final product of the research effort. We devoted considerable effort to writing a chapter that would be truly useful to students with limited writing experience and to those preparing a manuscript for the first time. Some of the topics include: how to begin writing, materials that each of the early paragraphs should contain, writing mechanics, writing style, and APA format. Additional material related to writing style and nonsexist language is included in the appendices. Also included here is a checklist for evaluating research reports and examples of two reports, written by students, that received either a grade of "A" or a grade of "C."

We are grateful to the Literary Executor of the late Sir Ronald A. Fisher, F.R.S. and to Dr. Frank Yates, F.R.S. and to Longman Group Ltd. London, for permission to reprint Table B.2 from their book, *Statistical Tables for Biological, Agricultural and Medical Research* (6th edition, 1974).

We would also like to thank the following individuals for their indirect but valuable contributions to many aspects of this book: Paul Lewis, R. H. Defran, Stuart Culbertson, Preston Harley, Charles Coker, Caroline Fisher, Marlene Goldberg, James Freeman, Bruce Abbott, Kathy Ryan, Larry Schoen, and particularly John Harsh.

CHAPTER ONE

ETHICAL PRINCIPLES OF RESEARCH

1.1 VIOLATIONS OF ETHICAL PRINCIPLES

Syphilis is a venereal disease caused by the invasion of the body by a spirochete, *Treponema pallidum*. In its early stages, the infection is usualiy be-
nign. A painless lesion develops at the site of the infection with secondary
inflammatory lesions erupting elsewhere as the tissues react to the presence
of the spirochetes. If untreated, an early syphilitic infection characteristic-
ally undergoes a secondary stage, during which lesions may develop in any
organ or tissue throughout the body, although it shows a preference for the
skin. Then, in many individuals, the disease goes underground, so to speak.
During this latent phase, the spirochete may establish a foothold in an
organ, bone, muscle, or any other part of the anatomy. It may be years
later before the blight it has inflicted upon the individual becomes evident.
If the spirochete settles in the heart, it leads to severe and debilitating
cardiovascular disorders. In the spinal cord, it may destroy the ascending
sensory neurons in a disorder known as *tabes dorsalis*. An individual so
affected literally loses touch with his or her own legs—all muscle sense is
lost—and walking becomes possible only by watching the feet. When the
cerebral cortex is attacked, the victim suffers impaired memory, fatigues
easily, and undergoes profound and pervasive personality changes. Moreover, many symptoms mimic those of mental disorders. The psychological
symptoms of the paretic patient may resemble the slovenliness of the simple
schizophrenic, the euphoria of the manic complete with delusions of
grandeur, the persecutory delusions of the paranoid schizophrenic, or the
suicidal tendencies of the depressive.

In 1932, a group of researchers undertook a long-term evaluation of the
effects of untreated syphilis. Known as the Tuskegee study on syphilis, it was
sponsored by the Venereal Disease Division of the U.S. Public Health Service.
The study involved 399 Blacks from Macon County, Alabama, and began in
1932. All were twenty-five years of age or older and were selected because they
had the venereal disease of syphilis and had not been treated. There were also
two control groups. One consisted of 201 Blacks without syphilis and the other
of 275 Blacks previously treated. At the time the study was begun penicillin
was unknown but less effective treatment compounds were available. The interest in the study was in the natural progression of the disease if left untreated. Earlier observations suggested that some individuals left untreated
apparently recovered from the disease spontaneously. Therefore, some physicians felt it might be better not to use drugs known to be hazardous. The latter
was apparently the justification for the study. However, with the advent of
penicillin in the early 1940s, an effective cure for syphilis had been found. This
cure was withheld from the subjects in order to complete the research findings.
The public became aware of the study in a story printed by the *New York
Times,* July 26, 1972. People were outraged. Four months later the study was
terminated. As of the early 1980s, a publication on the research has not yet
appeared. (See Box 1.1.)

BOX 1.1   PRISONERS AND MEDICAL RESEARCH

The Food and Drug Administration (FDA) issued a new rule in 1980 that in effect halted the use of prisoners in drug and medical research. In substance the rule states that the FDA will not accept findings for drug marketing based on prison populations. Since FDA approval is necessary before a drug can be marketed, it is unlikely that drug companies will continue to use one of its favorite populations. Earlier the former Department of Health, Education, and Welfare (now Health and Human Services) barred the use of federal funds for conducting research with prisoners. The issue of using prisoners in research appeared in 1976. During this and preceding years the widespread use of prisoners for medical research was essentially unregulated by government agencies. A lawsuit in 1976 by the American Civil Liberties Union revealed some questionable research practices that took place in prison. These included injecting informed volunteers with viruses to test new drugs. A national study followed the ACLU suit and, among other things, revealed that money was the major incentive for participating. However, since prisoners were locked up it was believed that they were more available for the imposition of burdens that others would not bear simply for money. As expected, drug companies were unhappy with the rules since the prison offered a population whose life style and diet were relatively controlled. However, strong objections were also made by prisoners and prison groups. The new rules deprived them of two strong incentives. In addition to depriving them of an opportunity to make money, it also deprived them of a way of repaying society for their crimes against it. Drug companies have turned to a new population of volunteers—they are advertising on college campuses.

In a study undertaken in a hospital in New York during the 1960s, twenty-two seriously ill elderly patients were injected with live cancer cells. None was informed of the fact.

Another series of investigations was initiated in the 1960s by a couple of Harvard University researchers who experimented freely on the effects of LSD. Many serious investigators felt that these studies were undertaken without adequate safeguards against potentially dangerous side effects, which included suicidal tendencies, psychotic episodes, and chromosomal damage.

Times change and views are relative. Today scientists do not take pride in these studies. They represent research inquiry gone rogue. No matter how honorable the underlying motives, the plain truth is that the investigators forgot or ignored their obligation to their subjects. Before describing some consequences that followed disclosures of the sort above, we want to describe two additional behavioral studies that have generated considerable controversy.

1.1.1   The Milgram and Zimbardo Studies

Social and behavioral scientists have also had their share of controversy concerning ethical issues in research. Two controversial ones, among others, are Stanley Milgram's study dealing with obedience to authority, and Philip

Zimbardo's simulated prison experiment. These studies reveal that difficult to resolve ethical issues often emerge in research. While important information may have been provided by these studies, the issues raised by them seem to involve a cost/benefit analysis. The studies also reveal that attitudes related to ethical concerns sometimes change. Both Milgram and Zimbardo are highly respected, ethical scientists, yet many individuals objected to their studies when they were published. We would guess that it is unlikely that either of these studies would be undertaken with today's ethical standards. Concerning the latter, it is interesting to note that the year his study was published (1964), Stanley Milgram received the American Association for the Advancement of Science award for social psychology.

We will give a brief description of each study and some of the ethical issues raised by them.

Milgram's study dealt with obedience to authority and it was his belief that it would contribute to avoiding another "holocaust" similar to that which took place in Nazi Germany (Milgram, 1965). However, subjects were not told the true purpose of the experiment until it was over. In essence, Milgram told volunteer subjects that they were participating in a learning-memory task that required them (the "teacher") to shock another individual (the "learner") when the "learner" made an error. (The "learner" was out of view in another room.) Unknown to the subjects was that the "learner" was an accomplice (collaborator) of the researcher and that even though cries of pain were heard, no shock was ever presented. Thirty switches identifying the level of supposed shock intensity were clearly marked and ranged from 15 to 450 volts (labels ranged from "Slight Shock" to "Danger: Severe Shock"). Subjects were instructed to increase the shock intensity one step for each error made. The "learner," according to the plan, was to provide periodic wrong answers and, as shock supposedly increased, was to demand that the experiment be stopped, cry out, or moan. The situation was convincing to subjects; as shock intensity "increased," and cries from the adjoining room became louder, some subjects wanted to quit the experiment. At this point the researcher simply instructed the subjects that they were required to go on. The real purpose of the experiment was to determine how high a "shock intensity" subjects would "deliver" to others on orders from the researcher. Many subjects continued in the experiment and delivered the highest shock intensity, while others defied the experimenter's order to continue. For some subjects the experience was a very intense, emotional one, filled with conflict. It should be noted that Milgram took precautions to debrief each subject and to follow up on their well being after the experiment was concluded. We will discuss the ethical issues below.

Another behavioral science study raising ethical issues was conducted by Zimbardo. Philip Zimbardo was interested in investigating the psychological effects of imprisonment (Zimbardo, 1969). He conducted his research with college students in a setting designed to achieve similar psychological effects found in prisons. Newspaper ads were placed asking students to volunteer for a two-week study of prison life at fifteen dollars a day. Only emotionally stable volunteers were chosen and they were randomly assigned to a condition of "guard" or "prisoner." The basement of the Stanford University psychology building served as the "prison" where three small rooms were converted to prison cells with three beds and barred doors. The experiment began without warning when the students were picked up in a surprise mass arrest one Sunday morning by real police with siren's screeching. They were charged with a felony, searched, handcuffed, given their constitutional rights, and then taken to the police station for booking and fingerprinting. After this they were blindfolded and taken to the Stanford basement prison where they were stripped, searched again, and given uniforms, bedding, etc. For purposes of group identity, prisoners wore a white smock, a nylon stocking cap, and a chain around one ankle. Guards wore khaki uniforms, sunglasses with silver reflectors, and carried clubs, whistles, and handcuffs. The reaction to this simulated environment by both "prisoners" and "guards" was very strong. In a short time a distorted relationship developed with the prisoners becoming passive and the guards aggressive, abusive, and authoritarian. The experiment had to be stopped much earlier than planned because of the "intensity" of the behavior and the consequences that followed. According to Zimbardo, the first of the nine prisoners had to be released by the second day because of crying, fits of rage, and a severe depression. Three others on the third and fourth days developed similar symptoms, and a fifth prisoner had to be released because of a rash over his entire body.

Were ethical issues involved in the Milgram and Zimbardo studies? Many researchers feel that there were. Some deceit was involved in both studies and subjects were not fully informed. There was also the possibility of psychological or physical damage to the participants. Behavioral scientists have expressed concern about the possible negative psychological effects that may have resulted to subjects from unsought, involuntary self-knowledge of an uncomplimentary nature. The unsought self-knowledge that they were capable of participating in such an unsavory act may have affected subjects adversely. However, we might note in passing that there is no evidence of this in either study and also that a sizable number of Milgram's subjects felt that they had benefited from their participation.

Largely as a result of disclosures of the preceding sort, federal and state governments as well as a number of scientific and professional societies have taken a long, hard look at the ethics of research. Included in their scrutiny are such issues as the professional behavior of the researcher, the treatment of human subjects, research with children, and research using nonhuman subjects. We shall be examining each of these issues in this chapter and attempt to summarize policies that have evolved to date. Before doing so we want to note that many ethical questions arise in the course of doing research for which answers are not readily available. In this chapter we deliberately stress the rights of subjects, but keep in mind that researchers are obligated to push forward the frontiers of science and to provide new knowledge for the citizens of the world. Therefore, while we justifiably show increasing concern for human and animal welfare, the ethical questions are more a risk (cost)/benefit dilemma; that is, the risk (cost) of research in terms of side effects, money, time, inconvenience, etc., versus the benefits to human kind in the long run. It is appropriate to note at this point that the quality of research in itself can be an ethical issue. Poorly designed and poorly conducted studies do not permit unambiguous conclusions to be drawn. Thus, such studies are also unlikely to provide any benefits. If benefits cannot be derived from the research, then only risk remains in the risk/benefit ratio. It would surely be unethical to ask subjects to participate in a study where risk existed without possible benefits.

Not all ethical issues encountered by researchers are of the magnitude of those we have just described. Many involve far less risk or harm, yet they involve ethical concerns. The next section illustrates this point.

1.2   PROFESSIONAL BEHAVIOR OF THE INVESTIGATOR

What is wrong in the following scenario?

Fred M. and Margot T. are engaged in a joint research project. Prior to collecting data, they spent many hours together designing the study, rounding up and installing the appropriate apparatus, preparing forms on which to record data, and locating subjects and assigning them at random to the experimental conditions. In order to familiarize themselves with the experimental procedures, they ran each other as a subject. Based on their preliminary findings, they estimated it would take approximately twenty-five minutes to run each subject. Accordingly, they scheduled their subjects to arrive every thirty minutes. Reasoning that some subjects might have difficulty remembering their appointment times, they scheduled each subject on the hour and the half hour.

On the day they were to begin running subjects, they misjudged the time it would take to get from class to their experimental laboratory. Consequently, they arrived five minutes late. After apologizing for their tardiness, they proceeded to conduct the experiment. The first subject was somewhat slower than expected. She finished thirty-five minutes later. As she prepared to leave, she turned to Margot and asked, "Could you tell me what the experiment was about? I found the task very interesting. Did it tell you anything about me?"

Margot noticed that the next subject was already getting a little restive. He had arrived a few minutes early and had been waiting almost a quarter hour. She turned to her first subject and said, "I'm sorry, there isn't enough time to explain things right now. The next subject is already here, we are running behind, and I'm afraid we may get backlogged. Why don't you look up Fred or me in a week or two?"

Things did not get better. During the briefing period prior to running the second subject, many questions were asked. He wanted to know how the apparatus worked, whether there was any possible danger, what the experimenters hoped to find out, and whether his performance would be kept confidential. He emerged from the laboratory fifty minutes later. By now the waiting room was beginning to look like a medical doctor's office. One subject was visibly upset. "I thought you told me it would only take a half hour, at the most. I've been here that long already. I'm sorry but I've got a class in thirty minutes." With this he turned on his heels and departed abruptly.

Many aspects of Fred and Margot's preparation are commendable. They designed this study in advance, prepared data collection forms, checked out the apparatus, and made an effort to estimate how long the experimental sessions would last.

However, they made two big mistakes. They failed to take into account the convenience and comfort of the subjects and to schedule a debriefing period at the end of the experiment. It was correct to run each other as experimental subjects since it gives them a subject's eye view of the proceedings, but they should have recognized that they were not typical subjects. Presumably they knew what was going on. They were not entering an unfamiliar situation, a cause of apprehension in many subjects. Some fear the possibility of physical discomfort (e.g., electric shock) and others experience threats to their self-esteem (e.g., not measuring up to the performance standards of other subjects). Since anxiety and tension frequently provoke an outpouring of questions, it may take a considerable time to get some subjects underway. Moreover, the completion of the experimental session often opens a floodgate of questions. Therefore, it is important to build into the experiment a debriefing period. Such a period is essential to relieve anxiety, for giving as full an account of the purposes of the experiment as permissible, and for answering questions. "What was the experiment all about? How did I do? Are you going to publish the results?"

If you are conducting a research study you should schedule adequate time for each subject so that you are not forced to give him or her the "bum's rush" after each session. Inform the subjects as much as possible about the nature of the experiment without compromising it. In some instances, of course, it will not be possible to provide much information until all subjects have been run. If this is the case, subjects should be told this and a mechanism should be set up to provide detailed information at a later date. Once you have set up this mechanism, it is imperative that you follow through. Perhaps you could send the subjects a preliminary report, a preprint of a publication, or an abstract of the research. Your efforts should be directed to making participation a pleasant educational experience. Research psychologists want to establish a reputation of trust. When this is not achieved, rumors and folklore develop, particularly on college campuses, which tend to establish local reputations of various departments. Once established, deserved or undeserved, there is a considerable inertia, making it difficult to change the reputation.

There are related behaviors that distinguish between an "amateur" and a "professional" or between an incompetent and competent investigator. Competent investigators show up on time, they are well prepared, and the equipment has been checked beforehand and is working well. Moreover, they are familiar with the apparatus, with the procedure, and with the instructions. All the necessary secondary equipment is at hand, e.g., data sheets with names, dates, conditions, experiment number, and biographical sketch. A checklist of necessary steps and equipment should be used if the experiment is complex. By being well prepared and competent, you inspire confidence on the part of subjects.

Keep in mind our earlier observation that subjects are often nervous or anxious about participating in psychological experiments. Do not forget the amenities—be thoughtful and courteous. Bluntly telling subjects to do something may appear as though you are ordering them to do it.

If they respond according to **reactance theory** (Brehm, 1966), they will regard the order as a threat to their personal freedom. They may then assert their freedom by becoming negative or uncooperative. However, a request coupled with words like "please," "thank you," and "you are welcome" is less likely to arouse negative reactions.

REACTANCE THEORY   When people find their freedom threatened, they attempt to restore the threatened freedom.

Remember that data gathered in an experiment are confidential. Individuals are sometimes very sensitive about their performance in experimental tasks. It is imperative that the experimenter refrain from discussing the performance of individual subjects with anyone. Where possible, code the data sheets to preserve the anonymity of subjects. If follow-up information is not needed, you may be able to eliminate the subject's name entirely from the data sheet.

One final word. The experimental setting should be used strictly for research purposes. It should not be a hangout for friends or a place for "bull sessions." More than one experiment has been compromised by distractions arising from a heated argument in the waiting room. In closing this section, we should note that how we conduct ourselves as experimenters can influence the subject in significant ways and can introduce unwanted bias into the experiment. (See Chapter 8.)

1.3   TREATMENT OF HUMAN SUBJECTS: ETHICAL STANDARDS OF PSYCHOLOGISTS

Recall the three research studies cited earlier in the chapter—the syphilis patients to whom treatment was denied over a period of forty years, the elderly patients injected with live cancer cells, and the administration of LSD to subjects without apparent safeguards against possible serious side effects.

Disclosures of these and other abuses have sensitized researchers and their professional organizations to the need for guidelines dealing with the ethics of research with human subjects. Few, if any, students are likely to inject a sub-ject with cancer cells or administer LSD, but other potentially abusive prob-lems may arise in their research. The use of deception, the induction of anxi-ety, or subtle manipulations that may affect the subject's self-esteem can all create ethical concerns. The American Psychological Association has been a leader in the establishment of such guidelines. Today, no investigator should undertake research with human subjects without intimate familiarity with these guidelines. It should be noted that writing guidelines is a difficult task. They must be written in a manner that places limits or restrictions on certain research activities without stifling the activities. Moreover, they are not fixed and immutable. In fact, they continue to change and evolve, reflecting largely the current views and experiences of laypersons and professional organizations regarding the freedom to obtain knowledge and the rights of the subject.

For psychologists, guidelines can be found in APA publications entitled *Ethical Principles in the Conduct of Research with Human Participants* (1973) and *The Revised Code, Ethical Standards of Psychologists* (1977). (See APA references at end of chapter.) Both are being revised and should be available in 1982. In Box 1.2 are the Preamble to the Revised Ethical Standards of Psy-chologists and the guidelines for human research of the ten ethical principles agreed on by APA. These principles are greatly elaborated in the booklet.

BOX 1.2   REVISED ETHICAL STANDARDS OF PSYCHOLOGISTS
As adopted by APA Council of Representatives, January 1977

PREAMBLE

Psychologists respect the dignity and worth of the individual and honor the pre-servation and protection of fundamental human rights. They are committed to increasing knowledge of human behavior and of people's understanding of them-selves and others and to the utilization of such knowledge for the promotion of human welfare. While pursuing these endeavors, they make every effort to pro-tect the welfare of those who seek their services or of any human being or animal that may be the object of study. They use their skills only for purposes consistent with these values and do not knowingly permit their misuse by others. While de-manding for themselves freedom of inquiry and communication, psychologists accept the responsibility this freedom requires: competence, objectivity in the application of skills, and concern for the best interests of clients, colleagues, and society in general. In the pursuit of these ideals, psychologists subscribe to princi-ples in the following areas: (1) Responsibility, (2) Competence, (3) Moral and Legal Standards, (4) Public Statements, (5) Confidentiality, (6) Welfare of the Consumer, (7) Professional Relationships, (8) Utilization of Assessment Tech-niques, and (9) Pursuit of Research Activities.

GUIDELINES: THE TEN ETHICAL PRINCIPLES

The decision to undertake research should rest upon a considered judgment by the individual psychologist about how best to contribute to psychological science and to human welfare. The responsible psychologist weighs alternative directions in which personal energies and resources might be invested. Having made the decision to conduct research, psychologists must carry out their investigations with respect for the people who participate and with concern for their dignity and welfare. The Principles that follow make explicit the investigator's ethical responsibilities toward participants over the course of research, from the initial decision to pursue a study to the steps necessary to protect the confidentiality of research data. These Principles should be interpreted in terms of the context provided in the complete document offered as a supplement to these Principles.

1. *Ethical evaluation*   In planning a study, the investigator has the personal responsibility to make a careful evaluation of its ethical acceptability, taking into account these Principles for research with human beings. To the extent that this appraisal, weighing scientific and humane values, suggests a deviation from any Principle, the investigator incurs an increasingly serious obligation to seek ethical advice and to observe more stringent safeguards to protect the rights of the human research participant.

2. *Ethical practice*   Responsibility for the establishment and maintenance of acceptable ethical practice in research always remains with the individual investigator. The investigator is also responsible for the ethical treatment of research participants by collaborators, assistants, students, and employees, all of whom, however, incur parallel obligations.

3. *Informed consent*   Ethical practice requires the investigator to inform the participant of all features of the research that reasonably might be expected to influence willingness to participate and to explain all other aspects of the research about which the participant inquires. Failure to make full disclosure gives added emphasis to the investigator's responsibility to protect the welfare and dignity of the research participant.

4. *Openness and honesty*   Openness and honesty are essential characteristics of the relationship between investigator and research participant. When the methodological requirements of a study necessitate concealment or deception, the investigator is required to ensure the participant's understanding of the reasons for this action and to restore the quality of the relationship with the investigator.

5. *Right to decline or discontinue*   Ethical research practice requires the investigator to respect the individual's freedom to decline to participate in research or to discontinue participation at any time. The obligation to protect this freedom requires special vigilance when the investigator is in a position of power over the participant. The decision to limit this freedom increases the investigator's responsibility to protect the participant's dignity and welfare.

6. *Investigator and participant responsibilities*   Ethically acceptable research begins with the establishment of a clear and fair agreement between the investigator and the research participant that clarifies the responsibilities of each. The investigator has the obligation to honor all promises and commitments included in that agreement.

7. *Protection from physical and mental harm*   The ethical investigator protects participants from physical and mental discomfort, harm, and danger. If the

risk of such consequences exists, the investigator is required to inform the participant of that fact, secure consent before proceeding, and take all possible measures to minimize distress. A research procedure may not be used if it is likely to cause serious and lasting harm to participants.

8. *Debriefing participants* After the data are collected, ethical practice requires the investigator to provide the participant with a full clarification of the nature of the study and to remove any misconceptions that may have arisen. Where scientific or humane values justify delaying or withholding information, the investigator acquires a special responsibility to assure that there are no damaging consequences for the participant.

9. *Correct undesirable consequences* Where research procedures may result in undesirable consequences for the participant, the investigator has the responsibility to detect and remove or correct these consequences, including, where relevant, long-term aftereffects.

10. *Information confidentiality* Information obtained about the research participants during the course of an investigation is confidential. When the possibility exists that others may obtain access to such information, ethical research practice requires that this possibility, together with the plans for protecting confidentiality, be explained to the participants as a part of the procedure for obtaining informed consent.

Although these guidelines attempt to safeguard the rights of research participants, the participants must still often rely on the judgments of the researcher. Researchers must remain vigilant and concerned about human rights, the invasion of privacy, and the possibility of physiological and psychological damage.

There is one further legal matter about which you should be aware. Unlike physicians, lawyers, and members of the clergy, researchers are not protected by laws concerning privileged communications. While highly unlikely, it is possible that subjects admitting to crimes on questionnaires (stealing, using, or selling controlled substances, etc.) could result in arrest and prosecution. Consequently, it would be a risk for subjects to admit to a researcher that they have participated in a crime. When questionnaires are used and such information is required to achieve the goals of the study, it would be wise to avoid the problem completely by omitting all forms of identification from the questionnaire. When mailed questionnaires are used, you can keep track of which subjects have participated and still maintain their anonymity by having each one mail in a separate card indicating that the questionnaire has been completed.

1.3.1   Informed Consent—The Right to Know

The ethical principles make it clear that informed consent is fundamental (Principle 3). Subjects must be informed of the nature of the experiment, the degree of detail depending upon potentially harmful effects. When the potential is high (such as in drug research when undesirable side effects may occur), the subject is entitled to a careful assessment of the risks.

Federally funded research *requires* that informed consent be obtained. Subjects must indicate *in writing* that they understand the nature of the experiment and that they agree to participation in it. A sample consent form is given in Box 1.3.

BOX 1.3 SAMPLE CONSENT FORM
Bowling Green State University, Bowling Green, Ohio

CONSENT TO SERVE AS A SUBJECT IN RESEARCH

I consent to serve as a subject in the research investigation entitled:_____
_____
_____.

    The nature and general purpose of the experimental procedure and the known risks involved have been explained to me by_____.
The investigator is authorized to proceed on the understanding that I may terminate my service as a subject in this research at anytime I so desire.
    I understand the known risks are:_____
_____
_____.

    I understand also that it is not possible to identify all potential risks in an experimental procedure, and I believe that reasonable safeguards have been taken to minimize both the known and the potential but unknown risks.

Witness_____   Signed_____
                                                      (subject)

                                         Date_____

To be retained by the principal investigator.

The subject agrees to participation in an experiment on the basis of a verbal description. Obviously, a verbal description of an experiment is far less informative than actual participation in the study. Principle 3 supports Principle 5 which, among other things, states that subjects may freely decide to discontinue in their participation in a study at any time. Then, if the experiment is different from what the subject expected, consent is revoked by merely withdrawing from the experiment.

Incidentally, Principle 5 may have an added value in the experimental setting. We previously noted that many subjects approach an experiment with some degree of apprehension—they fear something will happen to them or they are anxious about whether their performance will be satisfactory. An impressive body of recent research indicates that subjects are more tolerant of stressors when they believe they have some control in a situation (e.g., Glass and Singer, 1972). For example, when subjects in a crowded room believed they were free (vs. not free) to leave the room whenever they desired, they exhibited fewer negative aftereffects (Sherrod, 1974).

Further protection of the subject is provided at most colleges and universities. Many faculties have set up committees dealing with the treatment of human subjects. Typically, such committees review research designs and procedures before the experiment is conducted. They may also have developed their own set of ethical principles with which the experimenter is required to comply.

1.3.2   On the Use of Deception

The APA guidelines make clear that researchers must assume personal responsibility for assuring the moral acceptability of their research. Providing this assurance can create a conflict situation for the experimenter, particularly as it relates to informed consent. Fully informing a subject about the nature of the research may alter the kind of findings a researcher obtains. In some cases, subjects who are fully informed of the nature of the experiment, the procedure, and the hypothesis may try either to help or to hinder the research. (See Chapter 8.) In other cases, realism can only be achieved by misinforming or misleading the subject. Under these circumstances the behavioral scientist may be faced with a dilemma. On the one hand the researcher wants to be open and honest but on the other to do so may reduce the validity of the findings (see Rosenthal and Rosnow, 1975).

Some psychologists have resolved this dilemma by misinforming or misleading their subjects about the true purposes of the research. Subjects are fully informed of the true purposes only *after* the experiment is completed. This is usually what is meant by the term *deception*. A major problem with this procedure is that it deprives the individuals of information that could influence their decision to participate in the research (i.e., the individuals are not fully informed). The use of deception is a very controversial one and we will not resolve the issues here. However, few psychologists feel that deception can be entirely eliminated. The kind and the degree of deception vary greatly across experiments. Some forms of deception are completely harmless (withholding certain information concerning words to be recalled in a memory task) while other forms are potentially harmful (failure to specify the risks of participation when potential risks exist). It is usually the latter that pose significant problems. The researcher must decide when the potentially harmful effects of the experiment are worth the potentially beneficial effects of the knowledge to be gained (Ethical Principles 3, 4, 7). Under these circumstances researchers often consult with those less personally involved (colleagues-peers) to help evaluate the merits of the research. Although APA guidelines recommend against deception, its use is increasing slightly. In 1968 about 40 percent of the research appearing in the *Journal of Personality* and the *Journal of Abnormal and Social Psychology* used deception (Seeman, 1969). In 1974 this increased to 42 percent and 62 percent (Levenson, Gray, and Ingram, 1975).

Satisfying solutions to the ethical problems created by the use of deception are not yet available but it is important to express concern about its use. Deception was once routinely accepted; unfortunately in some cases even when it was unneeded. Today it is still used but with greater concern and always accompanied with elaborate justification and careful **debriefing.** Alternatives to deception have been tried. One is referred to as "role playing." With this procedure the subjects are fully informed about the nature of the experiment and then asked to play a role. That is, they are instructed to act as if they were actually a subject under the conditions described. In other instances an experiment is "simulated." The subjects are asked to imagine certain conditions and then specify how they would perform. For some experiments these techniques have worked out but for others they have not. Many psychologists feel that these alternatives to deception are too limited to be useful. Others have tried to avoid some of the ethical issues by abandoning laboratory research in favor of field research. However, as we describe in this chapter, disguised research in a field setting has its own problems. As we noted earlier, while satisfying solutions to deception are not yet available, efforts to seek them should continue and a major effort to reduce the use of deception should be made. For those interested in reading more on alternatives to deception, articles by Rubin (1973) and Berscheid et al. (1973) will be of great interest.

> **DEBRIEFING** A period, usually at the conclusion of a study, during which the subject is informed of the goals of the study, receives reassurances, if needed, and is given the opportunity to answer questions.

1.3.3 FIELD EXPERIMENTATION AND ETHICS

For a variety of reasons, which we will examine later, some researchers have become disenchanted with laboratory experiments. Not least among these reasons are the stringent requirements necessary to achieve and maintain ethical standards. Field experimentation is a possible alternative to laboratory methods. Individuals are observed in a natural setting, experimental variables are manipulated, and behavior is recorded without the subjects' knowledge. In fact, individuals are not aware that they are serving as subjects. The behavioral measures recorded under these circumstances are referred to as **nonreactive** or unobtrusive measures. It is believed by those using nonreactive measures that the behavior is more natural or representative than are reactive measures.*

---

*With reactive measurement, subjects are aware that they are being observed and that their behavior is being recorded. Some researchers have expressed concern that the very act of observing changes that which is being observed. And, instead of behaving as they normally would, individuals may behave in ways considered more socially desirable.

Since most field experiments fall within the public domain (i.e., the observations made by the experimenter can be made by anyone, experimenter or not), it has been argued that permission of the subjects is not required (Bickman and Henchy, 1972). Nevertheless, in some instances there are considerable intrusions into the private lives of some individuals. (See Table 1.1 for examples of field research.) Consequently, the issue is far from settled. Indeed, the legal aspects of field research pose a problem. Do the observations of subjects and the manipulation of variables without their knowledge violate any civil or criminal laws? Sharp disagreement exists among legal experts (Silverman, 1975). Moreover, the reaction of the general public to the type of research illustrated in Table 1.1 is mixed (Wilson and Donnerstein, 1976). Some types of research elicited few negative reactions, whereas others were found objectionable. Although the many ethical issues involved in field research have yet to be resolved, it would appear undeniable that the public's attitudes toward this research must be taken into account.

NONREACTIVE MEASURES   Measures taken on subjects without their awareness.

**Table 1.1
Summaries of nonreactive methods.***

1. Experimenters, walking singly or in pairs, ask politely for either 10 cents or 20 cents from passersby, sometimes offering an explanation for why they need the money (Latané, 1970).

2. The experimenter comes to a home, says that he has misplaced the address of a friend who lives nearby, and asks to use the phone. If the party admits him, he pretends to make the call (Milgram, 1970).

3. Automobiles, parked on streets, look as if they were abandoned. (License plates are removed and hoods are raised.) Experimenters hide in nearby buildings and film people who have any contact with the cars (Zimbardo, 1969).

4. A female and a confederate experimenter visit shoe stores at times when there are more customers than salespersons. One of them is wearing a shoe with a broken heel. She rejects whatever the salesperson shows her. The confederate, posing as a friend of the customer, surreptitiously takes notes on the salesperson's behavior (Schaps, 1972).

5. Housewives are phoned. The caller names a fictitious consumers' group that he claims to represent and interviews them about the soap products they use for a report in a "public service publication," which is also given a fictitious name. Several days later the experimenter calls again and asks if the housewives would allow five or six men into their homes to "enumerate and classify" all of their

*Taken from I. Silverman, "Nonreactive Measures and the Law," *American Psychologist* 30 (1975): 764–769.

Table 1.1
(Cont.)

household products for another report in the same publication. If the party
agrees, the caller says he is just collecting names of willing people at present and
that she will be contacted if it is decided to use her in the survey. No one is
contacted again (Freedman & Fraser, 1966).

6. People sitting alone on park benches are asked to be interviewed by an experi-
    menter who gives the name of a fictitious survey research organization that he
    claims to represent. At the beginning of the interview, the experimenter asks a per-
    son sitting nearby, who is actually a confederate, if he would mind answering the
    questions at the same time. The confederate responds with opinions that are
    clearly opposite those of the subject and makes demeaning remarks about the sub-
    ject's answers; for example, "that's ridiculous," or "that's just the sort of thing
    you'd expect to hear in this park" (Abelson & Miller, 1967).

7. A person walking with a cane pretends to collapse in a subway car. "Stage blood"
    trickles from his mouth. If someone approaches the victim, he allows the party to
    help him to his feet. If no one approaches before the train slows to a stop, another
    experimenter, posing as a passenger, pretends to do so and both leave the train
    (Piliavin & Piliavin, 1972).

8. Letters, stamped and addressed to fictitious organizations at the same post office
    box number, are dropped in various locations, as if they were lost on the way to
    being mailed. Some are placed under automobile windshield wipers with a pen-
    ciled note saying "found near car" (Milgram, 1969).

1.3.4   Regulation of Human Research

As you might imagine, it is much more difficult to conduct human research today. Before human research can be undertaken at any institution receiving any
federal funds (i.e., funds for research, education, scholarship, development,
etc.) it is necessary that the research be approved by an institutional review
board (IRB) at that institution. This is the case for all research whether it takes
place in a research setting, educational institution, hospital, prison, etc. The
same is true whether the research is done by a single individual or by groups,
and whether it is financed by private funds or government funds. In the case of
federally funded research, failure to comply with these guidelines could mean
that the entire institution could lose all forms of federal support (e.g., scholarship money, veterans' benefits, development, building, etc.). The federal agency assuming the major responsibility for establishing guidelines related to research with human subjects is the Department of Health and Human Services
(HHS).

The local IRB evaluates and weighs the risk to subjects, whether informed
consent is planned, the nature of the experiment, and provisions for debriefing. If the researcher plans to request federal funds then the proposed research
is evaluated by a panel of nationally recognized scientists (peer review). After

the research proposal is passed upon by the appropriate review boards then the researcher must obtain subjects based upon informed consent who are willing to participate in the study. In some cases signed informed consent forms are used to assure that the participant has been fully informed. There are now many legal and ethical considerations involved in research with humans. As a result, a new periodical by the Hastings Center in New York began publication in March of 1979. The Center plans to publish ten annual issues dealing with ethical dilemmas, government regulations, and difficult questions related to behavioral and medical research. We should note that researchers have been unhappy with some of the regulations first issued in 1974 because the rules needlessly interfered with risk-free projects. Their opposition resulted in a revision (1981) of these rules. They are noted in Table 1.2. Previously these studies were under the guidelines noted earlier.

Table 1.2
Department of Health and Human Services revised regulations for research with human subjects

The revised guidelines exempt many projects from regulation by HHS. Below is a list of projects now free of the guidelines.

1. Research conducted in educational settings, such as instructional strategy research or studies on the effectiveness of educational techniques, curricula, or classroom management methods.

2. Research using educational tests (cognitive, diagnostic aptitude and achievement) provided that subjects remain anonymous.

3. Survey or interview procedures, except where all of the following conditions prevail:
   a) participants could be identified;
   b) participants' responses, if they became public, could place the subject at risk on criminal or civil charges, or could effect the subjects' financial or occupational standing;
   c) research involving "sensitive aspects" of the participant's behavior, such as illegal conduct, drug use, sexual behavior, or alcohol use.

4. Observation of public behavior (including observation by participants), except where all three of the conditions listed in #3 above are applicable.

5. The collection or study of documents, records, existing data, pathological specimens, or diagnostic specimens if these sources are available to the public or if the information obtained from the sources remains anonymous.

The regulations apply to studies funded by HHS and institutional review boards are responsible for deciding which studies qualify for exemption.

1.4   RESEARCH WITH CHILDREN: ETHICAL GUIDELINES

We have been looking at ethical problems when human adults are used as subjects. Try for a moment to apply the ten principles to the study of children. How do you obtain informed consent when the child may not yet have acquired language ability? Even if the child is capable of language, how can we be sure that he or she understands the purpose of the study? Will the child understand Principle 5, which permits withdrawal from the study at any time? What about occasions when the children are unaware of the fact that they are participants, e.g., research done in nursery school settings when observations are made under natural conditions?

Clearly, special provisions must be made to protect the interests of children. To illustrate, informed consent of the parents or guardian is generally obtained. Therefore, it is important that the researcher carefully and fully inform the parent or guardian of the nature of the research. The latter includes information about deception if it is to be used.

While investigators must be concerned with the health and welfare of all research participants, they must be especially concerned and cautious when using children as participants. Only mild forms of arousal or stimulation should be used. Obviously the experiment should be terminated if signs of distress become apparent. When using children as participants, careful observations of the children must occur at all times. Box 1.4 lists guidelines to follow when the research project involves children.

BOX 1.4   ETHICAL GUIDELINES FOR RESEARCH WITH CHILDREN

A large portion of the most recent (1968) APA statement of ethical standards for developmental psychologists is set forth below for the edification and advice of persons interested in the pursuit of information advances in child psychology.

Children as research subjects present problems for the investigator different from those of adult subjects. Our culture is marked by a tenderness of concern for the young. The young are viewed as more vulnerable to distress (even though evidence may suggest that they are actually more resilient in recovery from stress). Because the young have less knowledge and less experience, they also may be less able to evaluate what participation in research means. And, consent of the parent for the study of his child is the prerequisite to obtaining consent from the child. These characteristics outline the major differences between research with children and research with adults.

From Newsletter, American Psychological Association, Division on Developmental Psychology, 1968, pp. 1–3. Quoted by permission.

1. *Child's rights supersede investigator's rights*   No matter how young the subject, he has rights that supersede the rights of the investigator of his behavior. In the conduct of his research the investigator measures each operation he proposes against this principle and is prepared to justify his decision.

2. *No physical or psychological harm*   The investigator uses no research operation that may harm the child either physically or psychologically. Psychological harm, to be sure, is difficult to define; nevertheless, its definition remains a responsibility of the investigator.

3. *Informed consent of caretakers*   The informed consent of parents or of those legally designated to act *in loco parentis* is obtained, preferably in writing. Informed consent requires that the parent be given accurate information on the profession and institutional affiliation of the investigator, and on the purpose and operations of the research, albeit in layman's terms. The consent of parents is not solicited by any claims of benefit to the child. Not only is the right of parents to refuse consent respected, but parents must be given the opportunity to refuse.

4. *No coercion to participate*   The investigator does not coerce a child into participating in a study. The child has the right to refuse and he, too, should be given the opportunity to refuse.

5. *Submit plan to colleagues when in doubt*   When the investigator is in doubt about possible harmful effects of his efforts or when he decides that the nature of his research requires deception, he submits his plan to an *ad hoc* group of his colleagues for review. It is the group's responsibility to suggest other feasible means of obtaining the information. Every psychologist has a responsibility to maintain not only his own ethical standards but also those of his colleagues.

6. *Anonymity protected*   The child's identity is concealed in written and verbal reports of the results, as well as in informal discussions with students and colleagues.

7. *Investigator is not diagnostician or counselor*   The investigator does not assume the role of diagnostician or counselor in reporting his observations to parents or those in *loco parentis*. He does not report test scores or information given by a child in confidence, although he recognizes a duty to report general findings to parents and others.

8. *Respect ethical principles of caretakers*   The investigator respects the ethical standards of those who act *in loco parentis* (e.g., teachers, superintendents of institutions).

9. *Standards apply to control and experimental subjects*   The same ethical standards apply to children who are control subjects, and to their parents, as to those who are experimental subjects. When the experimental treatment is believed to benefit the child, the investigator considers an alternative treatment for the control group instead of no treatment.

10. *Principles apply even if subjects are paid*   Payment in money, gifts, or services for the child's participation does not annul any of the above principles.

11. *Responsibilities of teachers of developmental psychology*   Teachers of developmental psychology present the ethical standards of conducting research on human beings to both their undergraduate and graduate students. Like the university committees on the use of human subjects, professors share responsibility for the study of children on their campuses.

12. *Responsibilities of editors of professional journals*   Editors of psychological journals reporting investigations of children have certain responsibilities to the authors of studies they review: they provide space for the investigator to justify his procedures where necessary and to report the precautions he has taken. When the procedures seem questionable, editors ask for such information.

13. *Responsibility of Division of developmental psychology to continue updating standards*   The Division and its members have a continuing responsibility to question, amend, and revise the standards.

Shown in Box 1.5 is a sample research form authorizing a minor to serve as a subject in research.

BOX 1.5   SAMPLE CONSENT FORM FOR A MINOR
Bowling Green State University, Bowling Green, Ohio

Authorization for a Minor to Serve as a Subject in Research

I authorize the service of _____ as a subject
in the research investigation entitled: _____
_____
_____.

The nature and general purpose of the experimental procedure and the known risks have been explained to me. I understand that _____
(name of minor)

will be given a preservice explanation of the research and that he/she may decline to serve. Further I understand that he/she may terminate his/her service in this research at any time he/she so desires.

I understand the known risks are: _____
_____
_____.

I understand also that it is not possible to identify all potential risks in an experimental procedure, and I believe that reasonable safeguards have been taken to minimize both the known and the potential but unknown risks.

I agree further to indemnify and hold harmless Bowling Green State University and its agents and employees from any and all liability, actions, or causes of actions that may accrue to the subject minor as a result of his activities for which this consent is granted.

Witness _____   Signed _____
                                                      (parent or guardian)

                                        Dated _____

             To be retained by the principal investigator.

1.5   USING NONHUMAN SUBJECTS: GUIDELINES

Not too long ago, experimental psychologists were often referred to as "rat psychologists." This was not a term of derision but merely reflected the fact that many experimental psychologists chose to conduct laboratory research with nonhuman subjects. Their interest, however, was not confined to the rat. They have used such diverse organisms as worms, snakes, fish, cockroaches, birds, bees, mice, rats, dogs, sheep, horses, elephants, pigs, and an assortment of nonhuman primates, to name a few. The reasons for selecting infra-human organisms are as diverse as the organisms selected. Suffice it for the moment to note that we have greater control over nonhuman subjects—they are generally available twenty-four hours a day over days, weeks, months, or years. Moreover, we may subject them to conditions that would be clearly unethical with human subjects. Yet these experiments ultimately are important in promoting human welfare. Experiments of this nature must be carefully assessed and evaluated even though lower animals are used. Important ethical questions are clearly involved. (See Box 1.6.) Experiments inflicting irreversible physical and psychological damage, and/or intense pain or stress must be evaluated in terms of promised scientific gains versus the cost in terms of damage to the subject. If the experiment is undertaken, it must be conducted in a way that avoids unnecessary suffering and injury to the animal. Further, post-experimental care of the subjects must attempt to minimize discomfort and the consequences of any disability resulting from the experiment. Finally, if it is necessary to sacrifice the animal, it must be done in such a way that ensures immediate death. State and federal guidelines and guidelines from professional organizations insist that researchers make the lives of experimental subjects as pleasant as possible and their deaths as painless as possible.

Anyone considering research using nonhuman subjects should obtain guidelines from state and federal agencies and from professional organizations. These agencies have responded to pressures brought forth by the growing strength of antivivisectionist movements. The American Psychological Association has guidelines for the treatment and care of laboratory animals. (See Box 1.7.) There is also a recent revision of the booklet produced by the National Institute of Health (NIH) entitled *Guide for Laboratory Animal Facilities and Care* (DHEW publication #(NIH) 78–23, Revised, 1978). The NIH guidelines are complete, covering topics such as housing, sanitation, husbandry, veterinary care, animal diseases, anesthesia, analgesia, surgery, euthanasia, and other topics. Moreover, the appendices describe programs related to animal technology programs, locations, and training programs in laboratory animal medicine. Table 1.3. presents the guidelines for the use of animals in school projects.

BOX 1.6   ISSUES IN ANIMAL RESEARCH

Often, published experiments using nonhumans as subjects expose them to unpleasant or painful conditions. Monkeys, dogs, rats, and other animals have been given shock or some other form of painful stimulation. At times, animals have been deprived of food or water for long periods, while still others have been deprived of their mothers. In some cases, even the lives of animals have been sacrificed for research purposes. A number of individuals consider these experiments to be cruel and ethically unjustifiable. They argue that the animals are confined to cages, denied their freedom, and exposed to suffering without their consent. Further, they argue that this research with animals does little to help us understand human behavior and to relieve human misery. In short, the suffering by these animals is needless. Others argue that animal research has been beneficial to both humans and nonhumans. They point to research on animals that has helped contribute to the elimination of diseases such as polio and small pox. They also note that animal research has aided us in understanding behavioral problems such as depression, fears, phobias, drug addiction, brain functioning, psychosomatic ailments, and others. From their view, more animal research is needed.

Those against animal research argue that suffering in animals should be eliminated, while those favoring more animal research argue that eliminating suffering in animals is virtually impossible. To do so would require that we ban many activities that humans now engage in. Gallup and Suarez (1980) deal with the topic in some depth. Fishing might be banned since worms are "impaled on hooks" and fish suffocate on the bottom of a boat. Are we willing to change our life styles because of animals suffering? For example, our food habits require that livestock be crowded into holding pens ". . . to be slaughtered, castrated, branded, dehorned, caponized, or decapitated without the benefit of painkillers or anesthesia." (Gallup and Suarez, 1980). These authors also point out that pesticides and insecticides are used freely to eliminate unwanted animal life. The problem of eliminating suffering in animals is a very complex one that requires philosophical and practical considerations and perhaps more knowledge of what constitutes suffering in different animals.

BOX 1.7   PRINCIPLES FOR THE CARE AND USE OF ANIMALS*

An investigator of animal behavior strives to advance our understanding of basic behavioral principles and to contribute to the improvement of human health and welfare. In seeking these ends, the investigator should insure the welfare of the

*These Principles were written by APA's Committee on Animal Research and Experimentation and were approved by the Council of Representatives in September 1979. They supercede the 1971 Principles for the Care and Use of Animals. Copies are available from the APA Scientific Affairs Office, 1200 Seventeenth St., N.W., Washington, D.C. 20036. Reprinted here by Permission.

animals and should treat them humanely. Laws and regulations notwithstanding, the animal's immediate protection depends upon the scientist's own conscience. For this reason, the American Psychological Association has adopted the following Principles to guide individuals in their use of animals in research, teaching, and practical applications. All research conducted by members of the American Psychological Association or published in its journals must conform to these Principles:

1. The acquisition, care, use, and disposal of all animals shall be in compliance with current federal, state or provincial, and local laws and regulations.

2. A scientist trained in research methods and experienced in the care of laboratory animals shall closely supervise all procedures involving animals and be responsible for insuring appropriate consideration of their comfort, health, and humane treatment.

3. Scientists shall insure that all individuals using animals under their supervision have received explicit instruction in experimental methods and in the care, maintenance, and handling of the species being used. Responsibilities and activities of individuals shall be consistent with their respective competencies.

4. Scientists shall make every effort to minimize discomfort, illness, and pain to the animals. A procedure subjecting animals to pain, stress, or privation shall be used only when an alternative procedure is unavailable and the goal is justified by its prospective scientific, educational, or applied value. Surgical procedures shall be performed under appropriate anesthesia; techniques to avoid infection and minimize pain must be followed during and after surgery. Euthanasia shall be prompt and humane.

5. Investigators are strongly urged to consult with the Committee on Animal Research and Experimentation at any stage preparatory to or during a research project for advice about the appropriateness of research procedures or ethical issues related to experiments involving animals. Concerned individuals with any questions concerning adherence to the Principles should consult with the Committee.

6. Apparent violations of these Principles shall be reported immediately to the facility supervisor. If a satisfactory resolution is not achieved, a report should be made to the responsible institutional authority. Unresolved allegations of serious or repeated violations should be referred to the APA Committee on Animal Research and Experimentation.

7. These Principles shall be conspicuously posted in every laboratory, teaching facility, and applied setting where animals are being used. All persons in each laboratory, classroom, or applied facility shall indicate by signature and date that they have read these Principles.

Table 1.3
Guidelines for the use of animals in school science behavior projects committee on animal research and experimentation.

With today's emphasis on the advancement of science, more and more intermediate and secondary students are participating in classroom and science fair projects with live animals. Although new knowledge may result from classroom research, the guidelines that follow are predicated on the assumption that the main objective of using animals in such projects is educational. Such projects should not only teach research procedures but should also introduce students to ethical issues in animal care and animal research. Since the resources available in schools will rarely be comparable to those of an established research facility, these guidelines are more restrictive than those for research settings. They do not apply to supervised student work in research laboratories, which comes under the provisions of the APA *Principles for the Care and Use of Animals.*

1. In the selection of science behavior projects, students should be urged to select animals that are small and easy to maintain as subjects for research.

2. All projects *must* be pre-planned and conducted with humane considerations and respect for animal life. Projects intended for science fair exhibition must comply with these guidelines as well as with additional requirements of the sponsor.

3. Each student undertaking a school science project using animals *must have a qualified supervisor.* Such a supervisor shall be a person who has had training and experience in the proper care of the species and the research techniques to be used in the project. The supervisor *must* assume the primary responsibility for all conditions of the project, and must insure that the student is trained in the care and handling of the animals as well as in the methods to be used.

4. The student shall do relevant reading about previous work in the area. The student's specific purpose, plan of action, justification of the methodology, and anticipated outcome for the science project shall be submitted, and approved by a qualified person. Teachers shall maintain these on file for future reference.

5. No student shall inflict pain, severe deprivation or high stress levels or use invasive procedures such as surgery, the administration of drugs, ionizing radiation or toxic agents *unless* facilities are suitable both for the study and for the care and housing of the animals and *unless* the research is carried out under the extremely close and rigorous supervision of a person with training in the specific area of study. These projects must be conducted in accordance with the APA *Principles for the Care and Use of Animals.*

6. Students, teachers, and supervisors *must* be cognizant of current federal and state legislation and guidelines for specific care and handling of their animals (e.g., the Animal Welfare Act). Copies of humane laws are available from local or national humane organizations. A recommended reference is the *Guide for the Care and Use of Laboratory Animals,* available from the Superintendent of documents

Table 1.3
(Cont.)

U.S. Government Printing Office, Washington, D.C. 20402, Stock Number
017-040-00427-3.

7. The basic daily needs of each animal shall be of prime concern. Students *must* insure the proper housing, food, water, exercise, cleanliness, and gentle handling of
their animals. Special arrangements *must* be made for care during weekends, holi-
days, and vacations. Students must protect their animals from sources of distur-
bance or harm, including teasing by other students.

8. When the research project has been completed, the supervisor is responsible for
proper disposition of the animals. If it is appropriate that the animal's life be
terminated, it shall be rapid and painless. *Under no circumstances should students
be allowed to experiment with such procedures.*

9. Teachers and students are encouraged to consult with the Committee on Animal
Research and Experimentation of the American Psychological Association for
advice on adherence to the Guidelines. In cases where facilities for advanced research by qualified students are not available, the Committee on Animal Research
and Experimentation will try and make suitable arrangements for the student.

10. A copy of these Guidelines shall be posted conspicuously wherever animals are
kept and projects carried out, including displays at science fairs.

1.6 REFERENCES CONCERNING ETHICAL STANDARDS:
APA PUBLICATIONS

American Association of University Professors. Statement on Principles on Academic
Freedom and Tenure. *Policy Documents & Report,* 1977, 1–4.

American Psychological Association. *Guidelines for Psychologists for the Use of Drugs
in Research.* Washington, D.C. 1971.

American Psychological Association. *Principles for the Care and Use of Animals.*
Washington, D.C. 1979.

American Psychological Association. Guidelines for conditions of employment of psychologists. *American Psychologist,* 1972, *27,* 331–334.

American Psychological Association. Guidelines for psychologists conducting growth
groups. *American Psychologist,* 1973, *28,* 933.

American Psychological Association. *Ethical Principles in the Conduct of Research
with Human Participants.* Washington, D.C. 1973.

American Psychological Association. *Publication Manual of APA.* 2nd ed. Washington, D.C. 1974.

American Psychological Association. *Standards for Educational and Psychological
Tests.* Washington, D.C. 1974.

American Psychological Association. *Standards for Providers of Psychological Services.* Washington, D.C. 1977.

American Psychological Association. *The Revised Code, Ethical Standards of Psychologists,* 1977.

American Psychological Association. *Ethical Principles of Psychologists,* 1981.

American Psychological Association. *Casebook on Ethical Standards of Psychologists,* 1967 (updated, 1974).

Committee on Scientific and Professional Ethics and Conduct. Guidelines for telephone directory listings. *American Psychologist,* 1969, *24,* 70–71.

Available from: American Psychological Assoc.
                   1200 Seventeenth St., N.W.
                   Washington, D.C., 20036

WHAT IS SCIENCE?

2.1 WHAT IS SCIENCE?

Almost every moment of our waking lives we are confronted with situations that require us to make choices. Shall we obey the strident summons of the morning alarm or turn off the infernal machine in favor of another forty winks? Should we go to the aid of a friend who is in the throes of an emotional "down" even though doing so means breaking other commitments we have made? Should we buy the latest recording of our favorite musical group even though it precipitates a temporary financial crisis? How many times a day do questions like this race through our thoughts? How often are we required to assess situations, make decisions, predict actions, and draw conclusions?

Whether we are scientists or laypeople, the ways in which we carry out these activities are of profound significance. They determine the quality of our decisions and, ultimately, the quality of our lives. In the hustle and bustle of daily living, we are rarely aware of the assumptions we make as we seek solutions to problems. Nor do we take much time to reflect over the variety of approaches we take. At times we are intuitive, relying upon a hunch or some vague feeling. At other times we examine questions in a rational manner. On yet other occasions we become empirical, basing our actions on our prior experiences or on the experiences of others. Often we rely on authority, looking toward experts to fill gaps in our own backgrounds.

Let's take a closer look at these approaches to knowing.

2.2 APPROACHES TO KNOWING

In science, we are interested in making observations, discovering laws, deriving predictions, and improving our understanding of ourselves and the world about us. To these ends, we are interested in improving theory, developing better analytical and measuring methods, and providing a broader data base (information) for future development.

2.2.1 Authority

Information or rules are derived from accepted authority figures. Religious leaders, teachers, parents, and judges may dictate the "truth" as they believe it. Or "truth" may be found in authoritarian works such as the Bible or encyclopedia. The method of authority is dogmatic and, if wrong, can hinder the development of science. In the past, some scientists have believed so firmly in their theories that they asserted, dogmatically, that they were true. When false, these beliefs resulted in faulty knowledge and hindered the development of these disciplines.

For example, a Russian geneticist and agronomist by the name of Lysenko was involved with the science and economics of crop production. Based on faulty research, Lysenko announced that crop characteristics, as a result of environmental changes, could be transmitted genetically. Since the view of genetics was compatible with the political doctrine of the USSR, his position was forced upon all geneticists conducting research within the Soviet Union. Lysenko's view was later repudiated but not before it considerably set back the science of agriculture in Russia. Ivan Pavlov also noted that each generation of dogs conditioned faster than the preceding generation. This was also accepted within the Soviet Union as evidence of the genetic transmission of acquired traits, in this case, learning. The truth of the matter is that the dogs were conditioning faster because the researchers were getting better at their trade, so to speak. Improved conditioning techniques and better control over extraneous variables were responsible for the generational improvement rather than genetic coding. Thus, Soviet genetic research suffered from several decades of allegiance to an erroneous theory.

2.2.2   Literary-Artistic-Intuitive-Metaphorical

Some individuals (e.g., writers, artists) have insights derived from their experiences and observations unique to them. They attempt to communicate their insights and intuitions to others through writing and works of art. They try to communicate, through their work, general truths with which those familiar with their work can identify. To illustrate, who has read Shakespeare's *As You Like It* and failed to respond to the lines, "All the world's a stage, and all the men and women merely players. They have their exits and their entrances; and one man in his time plays many parts. . . ."?

2.2.3   Rationalist

Experience is not emphasized, but reasoning and logic are. Propositions are not empirically tested, but are accepted as self-evident. Thus, if we accept the proposition that the sin of Adam and Eve in the Garden of Eden corrupted all creatures born of man and woman, it follows that all human infants are sinful at birth. The rational approach will often deny the relevance of observation and experience in a search for universal truths, pointing out that our senses are faulty and incomplete.

2.2.4   Empirical

Unlike rationalism, which tends to seek universal truths, the goals of empiricism are more modest. The empiricist stresses the importance of observation experience as the basis for understanding our past and present and predicting those that will come in the future. Recognizing the fallibility of experience, the empiricist does not search after universal or absolute truth. Statistics and probability, which are tools for dealing with uncertainty, are key weapons in the arsenal of the scientist. All four approaches to knowledge are important, and we use them. The scientists emphasize the rational and empirical approaches, but also make use of authority on occasion.

2.3 DEFINING SCIENCE

What is science? Most people, including scientists, find it difficult to answer this question. Why? Mainly because there is no simple, straightforward definition. We might try to break the ice by defining science as an organized body of knowledge that has been collected by use of the scientific method. We should then state what we mean by the scientific method, being careful to state the assumptions and goals fundamental to science. Therefore, to define the term *science* adequately, we must state the goals that are sought, the assumptions that are made, and the characteristics of the method.

2.3.1 Goals

Most scientists, but not all, are interested in three goals: *prediction, control,* and *understanding.* Of these three goals, two of them, prediction and understanding, are sought by all scientists. The third goal, control, is sought only by those scientists who can manipulate the phenomena they study. One of the most rigorous and precise disciplines in terms of prediction is astronomy, but it is unlikely that astronomers will ever acquire sufficient control over their subject matter to manipulate events.

Sometimes description and explanation are used synonymously with understanding when stating the goals of science. While there is a similarity of meaning among the three concepts, there are also subtle differences. Description of things and events appears first. We must know the "what" of what we are studying. It is important to give an accurate description, identifying the factors and conditions that exist and also the extent to which they exist. As the description becomes more complete, as we identify more factors or conditions affecting the events we are studying, the better our understanding of the event. A complete description of the event would constitute an explanation. We would then be able to state clearly and accurately the conditions under which a phenomenon occurs.

Some have argued that prediction is the ultimate goal that sciences seek. To a degree, we know that we understand (at some level) an event when we can predict the occurrence of that event. Prediction may also permit a substantial amount of control. When events can be predicted accurately, preparation in anticipation of the event can occur. However, we should be careful not to fully equate prediction with understanding. Based on past experience, we may correctly predict that some manic depressives will evidence a remission of symptoms following electro-convulsive shock. However, we may have little understanding why this is so.

Considerable research has taken place in countries throughout the world concerning natural disasters such as earthquakes, hurricanes, droughts, epidemics, etc. Imagine, in terms of human welfare, the impact of acquiring an understanding sufficient to predict these natural disasters. Timely preparation of those threatened could save lives and dramatically reduce injuries and human suffering. But the next step—achieving control of the environmental conditions leading to these events—would permit us to alter the time, place, and intensity of their occurrence or prevent them altogether. The prospects of control over disordered behavior is also exciting to contemplate. When sufficient knowledge is acquired, perhaps we will be able to eliminate psychosis and neurosis, minimize depression, maximize a sense of well being, enhance learning, etc.

Ultimately, science seeks to explain, through the development of theory, the phenomena that exist in the universe. Scientists try to arrive at general statements that link together the basic events being studied. If this is accomplished, understanding, prediction, and control follow.

2.3.2   Assumptions

There are two fundamental assumptions that all scientists make. One is that the events in the universe, including behavior, are lawful or orderly. The second assumption is that this lawfulness is discoverable. These two assumptions are frequently lumped together and referred to as *determinism*. We shall treat the two as different assumptions. In other words, we can assume that behavior is lawful without presuming that we will discover this lawfulness.

To say that behavior is lawful is to say that behavior is a function of antecedent events. More loosely, we could say that there is a cause-effect relationship between the past and the present, a continuity between before and after. According to this view that behavior is orderly i.e., lawful, individuals do not behave randomly or capriciously. Even behavior that appears to be random is assumed to follow some underlying lawfulness.

The assumption that behavior is lawful is justified by everyday experiences. Everytime we place ourselves behind the steering wheel of our car, we implicitly assume that the behavior of hundreds of other motorists on the road will be orderly. They will not suddenly veer off the road into our path, brake the car without cause, or try to play rumple fender. Similarly, when traveling by air, we assume the pilots will take a course that minimizes air turbulence and maximizes the comfort of passengers. We feel assured that they will not commit any act on a whim, such as doing loop-to-loops at forty thousand feet.

The assumption of lawfulness is very important for several reasons. One major reason is that it determines our own behavior as scientists. If we were to assume that behavior is free of causes or determiners, it wouldn't make much sense for us to study it. By definition, if an individual's behavior is free of causes, then there is no lawfulness. There is no pattern to it, no connection with the past. It simply would not make good sense to study a phenomenon assumed to be unlawful or unorderly.

It is important to note that these assumptions are not thought of as true or false, provable or unprovable. As scientists, we make certain assumptions to see where they take us in terms of achieving our goals. If we achieve our goals of prediction, control, and understanding, we feel more confident about the assumptions we have made. But we do not assert that we have proved determinism or that free will does not exist. These assumptions may be thought of as the rules of the games in which scientists engage. We stick by these rules as long as they prove to be useful. When no longer useful, we discard them and adopt others that promise to carry us further in our quest for understanding.

The history of science is replete with instances in which major advances occurred only when one set of assumptions was replaced by a different set. To illustrate, we presently regard astronomy as one of the most accurate sciences. However, a few centuries ago, astronomy was in chaos. Astronomers labored under the assumption that the sun revolves about the earth (Ptolemy). Even though this assumption nicely corresponded with everyday experiences (the sun *does* look as if it revolves about the earth; the earth does *not* appear to be moving), little progress was made in astronomy until it was discarded. Many conflicting observations simply could not be resolved within the Ptolemaic framework. Ironically, astronomy emerged as a vibrant science only when it adopted an assumption that ran counter to casual observation. Copernicus posed the startling hypothesis that the earth revolves around the sun. Only with this assumption did many confusing observations about the "behavior" of the stars and the planets become coherent. The Copernican assumption ultimately prevailed because it has proved more useful in predicting and understanding celestial events.

2.3.3   The Scientific Method

Just a few decades ago, many members of the scientific community raised questions concerning the characteristics of the opposite side of the moon. Although it was generally agreed that at some future date the entire moon would be accessible to scientific inquiry, the existing state of technology precluded answering the questions at the time. In a sense, then, the questions were useless as long as there was no way of answering them. The advent of lunar probes and orbiting satellites have, of course, altered this state of affairs. Unanswerable questions of yesterday are the facts of today.

There are a couple of lessons to be learned from this example. Not all events are subject to scientific inquiry. Some are inaccessible because of technological limitations—the state-of-the-art—as was the case with the far side of the moon prior to the space age. Others are inaccessible because there is no **empirical referent** to the presumed event (e.g., ghosts, evil spirits). By empirical we mean that it is capable of being experienced; that the event will stimulate one of our many senses. We must be able to feel it, taste it, see it, smell it, or hear it, or we must be able to sense a record it makes. In other words, an event must be observable or measurable, either directly or indirectly. For example, no one has seen a subatomic particle, but some scientists have seen and measured a trace it leaves on a photographic plate. No one has ever seen gravity, but its effects are observable and measurable all around us. Similarly, in psychology the construct of "learning" is never observed directly, but is measured in terms of its effects on some aspect of behavior.

EMPIRICAL REFERENT   an object, person, or event of which we are capable of having a direct experience.

To say that an event must have an empirical referent implies that the event is a public one, not a private one. It also implies that the observations are objective and not subjective. As noted, there are events that cannot be studied since they do not have an empirical referent. For example, the question "Is there a God?" cannot be answered scientifically. The subject matter is not empirical and therefore cannot be subjected to scientific study. Questions such as this require faith on the part of the believer, and the faith one has is derived from authority figures, i.e., clergy, bible. However, a related question can be asked that would allow us to study religious beliefs. We could ask, "What are the effects of religious beliefs on behavior?" We could study these effects scientifically because the presence or absence of religious beliefs in a person can be determined empirically (verbal reports, questionnaires, etc.), and the effects of these beliefs on behavior can also be determined. Both the beliefs and the behavior are directly or indirectly measurable. They are empirical events.

The second essential requirement for the scientific study of events is that the observations must be *repeatable,* thereby permitting one investigator to verify the work of another. Insisting on repeatability allows the *self-correcting* feature (the third essential requirement) found in all science to operate. The scientific method is, perhaps, the only one that has a built-in self-correcting procedure. Since events are empirical and repeatable, research conducted in one place can generally be repeated in any other part of the world to either confirm or cast doubt on the reliability of published findings.

Students are sometimes distressed to learn that an event must be repeatable if it is to be studied scientifically. What about unique events? Aren't they as important and shouldn't they be studied? My birth is unique! My death will be unique! As a person I am unique! Indeed, all people are unique and important. How can scientists ignore these unique events?

In a word, *they do not.* Scientists are well aware of the problem. The solution is to deal with classes of events. While your birth is unique, births in general are not. The same is usually true for other unique events. We study the class of events, e.g., births, deaths, personality, etc., and then bring our understanding to bear on particular events. On occasion, however, some important events may occur so infrequently that you cannot study a class of these events. There is no happy solution to this problem. Often the best that we can do is to have multiple observers on the scene at the time of occurrence (e.g., Mt. Saint Helens volcano). Although the event may not itself be repeatable, a number of observations can be made independently and the results compared. Fortunately, the rare, important event does not appear with sufficient frequency to pose a serious problem for science at the present state-of-the-art.

2.3.4   Distinguishing Observation from Inference—Examples of Faulty Inference

Of the many activities that scientists undertake, two of the most important are making accurate observations of the phenomena under study and drawing inferences* from these observations. While both are important, the first, accurate observation, is critical. Our scientific enterprise begins here. The usefulness or goodness of our interpretation is dependent upon the accuracy of our observations. As we shall see in the following chapters, there are many factors that can affect our observations. However, even though we may begin with accurate observations it does not follow automatically that our interpretations will be correct. They may still be wrong. In other words, the observations that we record may occur for reasons other than what we give. (See also "Construct Validity," Chapter 3.)

It is important that we distinguish between observing an event and making inferences based on those observations. As the following anecdotes illustrate, the observations may be objective and repeatable but the inferences can be wrong.

This story has appeared in many guises and it is a humorous example of faulty inference or logic. Imagine, if you will, a well-trained cockroach capable of responding to verbal commands. Whenever the trainer said, "Jump!" the cockroach immediately did so. A researcher became interested in the behavior of the cockroach and decided to study the jumping behavior. After a few observation sessions, he pulled a leg off the cockroach and gave the command, "Jump!" Again the roach jumped. The process of systematically removing legs continued until all legs were removed. Again the researcher gave the command, "Jump!" but the roach did not move. The results were written up in an experimental report with the conclusion that "when a cockroach loses all of its legs, it becomes stone deaf."

There is another humorous example of faulty logic. Imagine a young woman born and raised in a small isolated community without any form of outside communication. One day, she hears of the wonders of other places and

---

*The activity of "drawing inferences" includes such things as providing interpretations of the data, "explaining" the data, theorizing or guessing about the underlying processes responsible for the observations, creating new concepts to explain the observations, etc.

decides to visit them. She travels to one of our large cosmopolitan cities. The sights and sounds of the city are fascinating experiences, but the most fascinating of all are her experiences interacting with the citizens in the ethnic parts of the city. She notes that some of the people speak very smooth and fluent English, but others have strong accents. She also accurately observes that it is usually the much older members of the community who have these accents. After thinking about this observation for a while, our visitor concludes, "As people grow older, they develop accents."

2.3.5 Systematic Nature of Science

We have noted the three major characteristics of the scientific method (empirical referent, repeatability, self-correcting). There is an additional characteristic that is important and distinguishes knowledge gained using the scientific method from that gained through our daily experiences. The point is that science is *systematic*. For example, in psychology, whether scientists or laypeople, we all have some familiarity with the subject matter. Major portions each day of our lives are spent interacting with others, observing others, evaluating people, and considering our own behavior. Everyone has learned something about human behavior without studying it scientifically. Also, philosophers, poets, and literary people often have insights into behavior that exceed those of psychologists. Based on our daily experiences we arrive at many conclusions. Unfortunately not all of our conclusions derived from daily experiences are accurate. Many, in fact, are false. To avoid arriving at conclusions that appear intuitively correct, but that are in fact false, we need a systematic approach to the study of behavior. A systematic approach allows us to collect data under clearly specified and controlled conditions that can be repeated, measured and evaluated. Considerable emphasis is placed on evaluating and ruling out alternative explanations (hypotheses) for the phenomena being studied. In addition, a special effort is made to identify relations among phenomena. Much of this book is devoted to teaching you how to perform these activities.

Let's summarize the characteristics of the scientific method. As we have seen, science cannot be defined simply. An adequate definition requires a statement of the assumptions, goals, and methods. The following is a summarizing definition that many, but not all, scientists would agree with.

Goals	Prediction Control Understanding	Many believe that these goals are best achieved by improving theories, developing better analyzing and measuring instruments, and providing a broader data base (information).
Characteristics of Methods	Empirical Referents-Objective-Observable-Public Events	

Deals with Repeatable Events

Self-Correcting

Systematic

Assumptions   The universe (for psychologists, behavior) is lawful or orderly.

The lawfulness or orderliness is discoverable.

2.3.6   Common Sense and Science

When it comes to human behavior some have argued that common sense produces the same conclusions that psychological research does. Implied in this comment is that scientific research is a waste of time and effort since common sense would provide the same answers. Indeed, as Senator Proxmire at times has argued, psychological research is also a waste of the taxpayers' money. What is meant by common sense? It is usually taken to mean the accumulation of knowledge through our experiences that allows us to develop generalizations (statements, conclusions, hypotheses) about the world in which we live. These generalizations simplify complex situations by drawing conclusions that are absolute, i.e., without qualifications.

It is not unusual for the conclusions of common sense to agree with the findings of science, but the conclusions of common sense may also conflict with those of science. Principles derived with the methods of science are based upon careful, **systematic observation** of empirical events often in controlled settings. The observations are then carefully evaluated and precisely communicated to others where further evaluation takes place. (See text for other important features of the scientific method.) Usually the principle (generalization, conclusion) derived from this research predicts behavior consistently. If it does not, further research is undertaken and additional principles are derived. Often the derived principles are stated in a qualified form such as "given these conditions then this behavior is expected to occur." The latter is not the case with common sense, particularly those found in proverbs of generalized "truths." Proverbs based on common sense often conflict with each other. For example, the proverb "Look before you leap" is contradicted by the proverb "He who hesitates is lost." Yet, given the proper set of circumstances (unspecified by the proverb), both proverbs may be correct. There are other examples. "Two heads are better than one" is not consistent with "Too many cooks spoil the broth." Is it true that "Absence makes the heart grow fonder" or is it the case that "Out of sight, out of mind"? How often have you heard that you are "Never too old to learn" and also that "You can't teach an old dog new tricks"? Should parents rely on the proverb "Spare the rod and spoil the child" or instead "You catch more flies with honey than with vinegar"?

When stated in absolute terms such as our common sense proverbs above, the proverbs appear inconsistent and contradictory. It may well be that "Out of sight, out of mind" is an accurate conclusion *under certain conditions* and

---

SYSTEMATIC OBSERVATION   observations planned and prepared well in advance, including control over conditions under which observations are made.

---

that "Absence makes the heart grow fonder" is an accurate conclusion under other conditions, *but these conditions remain unspecified.* Scientific knowledge improves over common sense proverbs by specifying the conditions necessary for the principles to be applied.

We should note that while we recognize the serious weaknesses of a strictly common sense approach to knowledge, we also recognize the contributions made to our understanding of behavior by nonscientists such as poets, playwrites, novelists, and philosophers. Such individuals can provide us with great insights into human behavior, which serve as a creative source for our research.

2.3.7   Molecular-Molar Levels of Analysis and Explanation

The molecular-molar distinction illustrates that the evolution of various disciplines did not occur arbitrarily. Generally, as knowledge accumulated, different questions were asked requiring different units of measurement. For example, physicists are generally interested in the level of analysis emphasizing atomic and subatomic particles. (See Figure 2.1.) This currently is the most

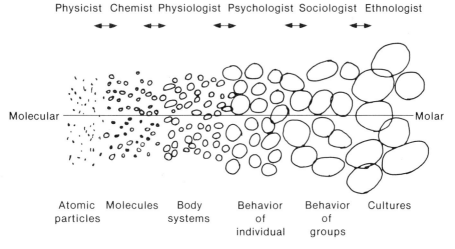

Fig. 2.1   The molecular-molar continuum. The level of analysis is extremely small in nuclear physics (molecular) and extremely large in ethnology (molar). The arrows indicate that the boundaries among the various sciences are not rigid and fixed. At times, a psychologist may operate at the level of analysis of a physiologist and, at other times, at the level of a sociologist.

molecular level of analysis. Atoms combine and form the basis for molecules, and molecules are the domain of the chemist. The questions usually asked by chemists, therefore, deal with molecules as the unit of analysis. Molecules combine to make up systems such as the circulatory system, glandular system, muscular system, etc. Physiologists are generally concerned about questions that relate to these systems. These systems combine to give us the next level of analysis, which is the behaving organism. This is the domain of the psychologist. Psychologists are interested in the behavior of individual organisms. We can easily continue this molar-molecular development. Individual organisms combine into groups, and the study of group behavior defines sociology. Groups combine into larger units to make up cultures. The study of cultures defines ethnology. Obviously, these are not competing disciplines; they are usually complementary, each with its own level of analysis. When these disciplines are looked upon along a molecular-molar continuum, their origin and development do not have to be arbitrary. They apparently developed as the unit of analysis became obvious and as the need to provide answers to different questions arose.

Controversies have arisen from time to time concerning the kind of theory that scientists should develop. At what level should we attempt to theorize about and explain behavior? What would our unit of analysis (level of analysis) be? In psychology, should the unit of analysis be the atom? The molecule? Perhaps it should be a physiological system? What about intact behavior? Could it not also be group behavior or the entire culture?

Some psychologists have argued that the level of analysis and theory construction in their dicipline should be at the physiological level (molecular). Such individuals have been referred to as **reductionists** since they seek to explain complex behaviors in terms of relatively simple structures and functions. Others have argued that the unit of measurement and theory construction should be at the behavioral (molar) level. Obviously, molecular and molar are relative terms. (See Figure 2.1.) Psychology, with its emphasis on the physiology of the organism or on the observable behavior of the organism, is molecular relative to sociology where the emphasis is on group behavior. Yet, relative to chemistry, the unit of analysis in psychology is molar.

REDUCTIONIST a person who seeks to explain complex phenomena in terms of relatively simple and basic building blocks.

Most scientists feel that theorizing at different levels is necessary and can be complementary. Perhaps at some future time we may be able to be reductionistic (molecular) and interpret the phenomena of all sciences in the language of physics. Clearly, we cannot come close to doing so at this time.

2.4 IMPORTANCE OF BASIC RESEARCH—
SEEKING NEW KNOWLEDGE AND UNDERSTANDING VS. SOLUTIONS TO
IMMEDIATE PROBLEMS

Basic research is not easy to define, and, unfortunately, it is often unappreci-
ated by those political leaders who control considerable sums of money for research. In fact, one senator (Proxmire) has created an award referred to as the
"Golden Fleece Award." The recipient of this award is usually a scientist engaged in basic research whom the senator feels is squandering or wasting
(fleecing) the public funds on worthless or silly (trivial) research projects. Unfortunately, the senator does not provide any criteria for, or definition of,
triviality. Further, the research projects chosen to receive the "Golden Fleece
Award" often appear to be selected solely on the basis of the title of the research project. To an uninformed reader, the research taken out of context
and specified by title only, may appear trivial, silly, and unimportant. We discuss below why it may be a serious mistake to trivialize basic research.

BASIC RESEARCH   research engaged in for the purpose of increasing knowledge of
fundamental processes. May have no immediate goals or applications.

It is our opinion that awards intended to disparage basic research, because
the immediate practicality of the research is not obvious, result in a serious in-
justice to scientists dedicated to improving the world in which we live. To
some, the research may seem frivolous. Surely, we are indulging scientists by
supporting their pet hobbies, such as their studies of sexual behavior of moths,
communication among bees, and sexual attractance among insects. But in each
instance, as is often the case with basic research, the results of these studies
eventually have had and are having important implications related to agricultural practices, to the world's food supply system, and to the economy. To illustrate, insects cause crop damage in the multimillion dollar range annually,
but *chemical control* of these insects has created their own serious problems.
New and safer techniques of *biological control* have been made possible because of basic research on the behavior and physiology of insects. This research is often ridiculed or criticized.

One further comment before describing basic research more fully: Political leaders controlling research funds may not appreciate the value of basic research for many reasons. At times they consider it unimportant, but at other
times they reject it because of their own bias, prejudice, or moral values rather
than on the scientific merit of the research. Whatever their basis for not ap-
preciating its value, the fault, at times, rests with the scientists. Scientists too
often consider the value of basic research as self-evident. They have not always

made a strong argument in its defense. More care must be devoted to doing this by scientists and by educated laypeople. We now turn to a defense of basic research.

2.4.1   A Defense of Basic Research

It is often difficult to see the relationship between basic research done years ago and the present application of sophisticated technology to current problems. Basic research provides the foundation (data base) for the resolution of present and future problems, for the development of technology, and for a better understanding of all aspects of the world in which we live.

Basic research is research directed to the understanding of nature, of all aspects of the universe, of natural processes. It is not research directed toward the solving of specific social problems. It is not mission oriented, i.e., it is not involved in the mission of "curing" or "correcting" a specific illness or problem or in developing a specific technology. Basic research has no immediate regard for practical application; paradoxically, however, it is probably the most effective way of solving many of our current and future problems. It has been a critical component in virtually every approach to our major problems. In the late 1960s, the National Science Foundation released the results of a study (TRACES) showing the importance of basic research (*Science,* 1969). They looked at technological innovations of wide importance and diverse application. Research was traced back to 1850. It was concluded that about 70 percent of the key and critical events were from basic research. Another excellent source for describing the important contributions of basic research can be found in Comroe and Dripps (1976).

Some examples may provide us with a better appreciation of the virtues of basic research. X-ray photography was not developed by physicians as an aid in the diagnosis of disease. Rather, medical use of X-rays followed the pioneering research of Wilhelm Roentgen who was "only" interested in basic problems dealing with the physics of rays. A few decades ago, poliomyelitis (infantile paralysis) was a dreaded disease that left many of its survivors permanently paralyzed. We are all familiar with the applied research of Drs. Salk and Sabin which culminated in vaccines that immunized against the disease. But how many of us have heard about the basic research of John Enders, who was "merely" interested in studying viruses? To accomplish his goal, he needed to devise a means of growing viruses in culture. When he finally succeeded, he opened the sluice gates for a veritable flood of practical applications of his techniques. The Salk and Sabin vaccines are but two of many monumental advances that found their underpinning in the laboratory of John Enders. George Cotzias was not pursuing a treatment for Parkinson's disease, but because of his interest in trace metals and body metabolism, the drug L-Dopa was developed for treating the disease. Similarly, the drug that has nearly eradicated tuberculosis, streptomycin, was discovered by a soil biologist.

It is very difficult to appreciate the importance of basic research at the time it is being conducted. How important was the effect of current flow on magnetic needles at the time of Faraday? Today, induction coils in the field of transportation are incredibly important. People interested in transportation didn't discover induction coils (this would have been mission-oriented research). The discovery of induction coils gave rise to a transportation industry. IBM, Control Data, and other computer giants did not set out to discover basic circuits for computers. Physicists in the 1930s interested in nuclear physics discovered them. At the time of Boyle (gas laws), how important were the properties of vacuum tubes? Who could have anticipated transistors, printed circuits, computer chips? With the discovery of the atom, who could have anticipated the electronic industry (Weisskopf, 1972)?

Basic research continues today to produce exciting and promising findings. As a result of recombinant DNA research, relatively pure forms of insulin can be produced. The latter is a marked improvement over current insulin derived from animals. In addition, the discovery and now production of the substance interferon holds promise for the treatment of certain ailments. A discovery that has excited both scientists and technicians is the identification and production of monoclonal antibodies. This discovery should allow specific antibodies (monoclonal) to be developed that attack specifically targeted bacteria, virus, or other material foreign to the body. Important discoveries have also occurred for behavioral scientists. One of these is the use of biofeedback procedures to "teach" individuals to control their blood pressure, heart rate, brain waves, and other response systems. In addition, we are now beginning to understand the effects of peptides (compounds formed by groups of amino acids) on social behavior, development, perception of pain, etc.

We could continue with examples of the kind above. Clearly, basic research is important, and its full impact is not felt for many years. We do not mean to suggest that the value of basic research be determined solely by its practical significance. Basic research can be justified on the basis that the production of knowledge is, in itself, of great value. It is our firm belief that knowledge has inherent value of its own and that it is strongly preferred to ignorance. In this sense, practical significance is a bonus.

2.4.2 Two Important Reasons for Supporting Basic Research

After reviewing the history of discovering important events and also observing the problems experienced by each succeeding generation, we conclude that there are two fundamental reasons for fully supporting basic research: (1) *we cannot determine today what discoveries will prove important for tomorrow,* and (2) *we cannot determine today what problems we (the world) will experience tomorrow.* Regarding the latter, we have not become much better over the years at predicting what important problems we will experience in the future. We do not know today what will be important tomorrow. We must be prepared for any eventuality. Our sights must not be narrow in terms of specific missions or focusing solely on today's problems. Change is so incredibly fast and sure that we must be in a position to move in many directions—we must have a solid data base in all areas. New problems continue to appear that require more basic knowledge: Legionnaire's Disease, carcinogins, ozone layer, nutrition and cell health, pollution, energy supplies, and toxic shock syndrome are but a few examples.

It is understandable, to some extent, that some members of society insist that scientists do their work on more relevant social problems. This emphasis reflects the genuine belief that by addressing the problems directly, the problems will be solved more quickly. Unfortunately, an excessive effort to make science more productive in terms of directing its efforts toward specific but unsolved problems may make it less productive. The war on cancer may be an example. Nature is not yet ready to reveal its secrets. Scientists within the Institute of Cancer have essentially acknowledged, after years of trying to find cures, that much more basic research is needed on cell physiology before suc-

---

BOX 2.1   BASIC BEHAVIORAL RESEARCH AND PRACTICAL BENEFITS

The following is an excellent example of basic research resulting in important practical benefits. Much research has taken place since the late 1960s dealing with whether chimpanzees and gorillas can learn to communicate using a true language. Earlier attempts to teach apes to speak were unsuccessful because the animals are physiologically incapable of producing the sounds needed for speaking. However, later attempts suggested that apes were capable of using sign language similar to that used by the deaf (Ameslan). In other instances, investigators have constructed their own artificial language and have used objects differing in size, shape, and color to represent words. There is no question concerning whether apes can communicate with humans or with other apes. They do in fact use ''words'' as symbols the way we do. The controversy concerns whether this type of communication involves the use of a true language. A true language has two elements: (1) words must be symbols for something, and (2) words must be combined with one another to form novel phrases or sentences that are understandable to others. Whatever the case turns out to be, communication between ape and humans is well established. An important practical benefit has occurred from this ape research on language. Based upon this work, methods have been developed for teaching severely retarded human beings; in some cases, working with individuals with IQ's of 20. Many severely retarded persons do not have the ability to communicate. They simply cannot speak. Without this ability there is very little they can do. This is now changing. Investigators are applying the lessons learned studying communication with apes to the mentally retarded and with apparently great success. What works with chimps also works with the retarded. In fact, some investigators working with the retarded have reported that ''despite their severe behavioral and linguistic problems, the people are still much easier to teach than chimps.''

cess is achieved. To insist that scientists solve the problems before the basic research data are in may be wasteful of highly trained researchers and other resources of money and personnel. (See Box 2.1.)

2.5   SCIENCE AND TECHNOLOGY

Science is generally thought of as seeking information or discovering basic phenomena in a systematic way and then organizing this information into general explanatory principles. Technology is usually thought of as the application of these scientific discoveries and principles to existing practical problems. As noted earlier, at times the basic principles are discovered by scientists many years before they are applied in the form of technology. Computers are one example, and immunization techniques in medicine are another. Before technology develops, the principles must be available; but at times, a technology must be developed before the principles can be applied. Examples of the latter can be related to the space program and to atomic weaponry.

Too frequently scientists are blamed for the problems created by the technology that followed from scientific discoveries. Knowledge in itself is neither good nor bad; it is the use to which knowledge is put that is either good or bad. The stereotype of the "mad scientist" often should be called the "mad technologist." Again, we use computers as an example. Scientists cannot be blamed for the abuses (e.g., invasion of privacy) occurring in today's society. Similarly, the automobile is a technical achievement, and the problems created by it (pollution) cannot be blamed on scientists. The discoveries related to genetics are leading to a technology of genetic engineering over which scientists may have little control.

What we are attempting to do here is to urge everyone to think critically about the distinction between science and technology as we ponder the problems besetting society. However, we must recognize that there is an interplay between science and technology such that the distinction between them may be blurred. It is unfortunate that scientists often are blamed for problems and are not recognized for their contributions that benefit society. Technologists are usually given praise for the latter contributions. For example, there is the technology of medicine based on the sciences of physiology and chemistry. There is the technology of engineering based on the science of physics. Similarly, there is the technology of education based on the science of learning. Most people wrongly attribute achievement in medicine, engineering, and education to the technologists and not to the scientists. (See Box 2.2.)

2.6   SCIENCE-TECHNOLOGY-POLITICS-PHILOSOPHY-ECONOMICS

Sometimes the public is unhappy with the progress that societies make toward the resolution of problems. Science is often implicitly accused. You have heard many times that "if scientists can put a man on the moon, they can do any-

---

BOX 2.2   SCIENCE AND TECHNOLOGY—BLEEDING THE VAMPIRE BATS

Vampire bats are a serious problem in some Latin American countries. At night these bats silently attack sleeping animals by painlessly scooping out a piece of skin and then taking some of their blood. Some cattle receive bites from as many as fifteen bats in a single night. Because of an anticoagulant in the bat's saliva, the blood flows freely most of the night. Some of the bitten cattle are infected with rabies carried by the vampire bats. In other cases, the wounds become infected resulting in lower weight gains and lower milk production. The solution to this problem illustrates the complementary nature of science and technology in solving problems.

Various previous attempts had been made to destroy the vampire bats. These included shooting, netting, and electrocuting bats in flight. A major problem with these procedures was that it killed beneficial insect-eating bats without reducing the loss due to vampires. Biologists from the Denver Wildlife Research Center began working on the problem in 1968. Since only some of these bats attacked cattle, they wanted to devise a method that would control only vampires that attacked farm animals. The biologists brought bats into their Denver laboratories and discovered that the vampires suffered fatal bleeding if an anticoagulant was added to their blood. Question: How do you get additional anticoagulant into free-flying bats? The biologists tried several techniques but unsuccessfully. They then tried injecting the anticoagulant into the first stomach of cattle in doses harmless to the cattle. It was not harmless to the vampires attacking cattle. Bats feeding on the blood of treated cattle received sufficient amounts of the antocoagulant to kill them. Cattle could be treated twice a year at thirty or forty cents per animal. The method resulted in a 91-percent reduction in vampire bat bites and resulted in an increase of milk and beef production. (*Science 80*, Nov./Dec., 1979).

---

thing.'' They should be able to cure diseases, clear up pollution, end drug and discrimination problems, and eliminate the food supply problem. Some of these problems are technological, some scientific, but all are also political-philosophical-economical. Problems of society must be dealt with at several levels. In addition to the scientific laws and basic principles, we also need the technology. Equally important is that philosophical-political-economical decisions must be made in terms of what problems are to be dealt with, and political support must be given to implement the decisions. We must decide philosophically the priorities of goals that are to be pursued. Our economic system must be sufficiently robust to provide necessary wealth. Politically, legislatures must pass forms of legislation and provide funding to implement these goals. Many of the problems of the world are not scientific or technological, but instead philosophical-political-economical.

CHAPTER THREE

LOGIC DEFINITIONS MEASUREMENT

3.1 INDUCTIVE AND DEDUCTIVE RESEARCH STRATEGIES

Much has been written about the methods of science. At times, the scientific method is portrayed as a thing apart from the ordinary affairs of our species. It is seen as mysterious, secretive, and requiring prodigious intelligence to put into practice. Nothing could be farther from the truth. There are countless occasions in our daily lives when we are called upon to make judgments and decisions that require the same thought processes as those in which scientists engage. Take the process of induction, from which we move from specific facts to general formulations:

Today's the day of the picnic and family reunion. Do we hold it outdoors, as planned, or move it indoors because of the threatening weather? You have noted previously that overcast skies, accompanied by a falling barometer are likely to bring rain within hours. Generalizing from past experience, you decide to hold it indoors.

Your apartment is overrun with cockroaches. Previous attempts at exterminating them have ended up in frustration and defeat. You decide to observe their behavior in hopes of discovering a point of vulnerability. You note that time after time, the cockroaches follow the same paths. Indeed, on close examination, you discover cockroach trails in the dust of your kitchen cabinets. When you sprinkle poisonous roach bait along these trails, the cockroaches are finally eliminated.

What do these routine examples have in common with science? The development of any science begins with observations. These observations lead to lawful relations (empirical laws) and as they accumulate, empirical generalizations are made. These, in turn, become organized, categorized, and accompanied by interpretations or inferences referred to as theory. In other words, specific facts (empirical laws) build upward toward general statements (empirical generalizations), which in turn invite inferences or interpretation (theory). The preceding reveals, in part, the process of **induction,** a very important component of science. With induction, the direction of movement is from specific facts to general statements or theories. Obviously there is more to theory development than this, some of which we describe below.

INDUCTION   reasoning from a particular fact to a general statement.

A concrete example of this direction of movement from empirical law, to empirical generalization, to theory development may be helpful. It is now well established (Badia, Harsh, and Abbott, 1979) that many organisms prefer a situation in which painful electric shock is made predictable (signaled) to one in which it is not. We can refer to this as an **empirical relationship** or *empirical law.* If we now generalized the finding dealing with the specific stimulus of painful shock to all painful stimuli, we would be dealing with an *empirical generalization.* In this generalized case we would state "Organisms prefer a situation in which painful stimuli (of any kind) are made predictable to one in which they are not.'' Our empirical generalization extends (generalizes) the finding dealing with a single painful event (electric shock) to an entire class of events (all painful events such as intense pressure, heat, cold, noise, etc.). At this point we might ask, ''Why do organisms prefer this predictability?'' Our answer would be theoretical. Our *theoretical statements* would speculate about the mechanism or reasons for organisms preferring predictable events. A number of reasons (theories) could be offered, each of which could adequately account for the data. One such theory might state that predictable events are preferred to unpredictable ones because predictability permits organisms to prepare to receive painful stimulation. Preparation for this stimulation, in turn, would minimize the painfulness of the stimulation. As we describe later, our theory would best be considered provisional and subject to change as new findings are obtained.

EMPIRICAL RELATIONSHIP   one based on experience and observation.

Another important component of the scientific method, **deduction,** is used frequently by both laypeople and scientists. In contrast with induction, we start at the ''top'' with the general statement or theory and work downward to a specific prediction (hypothesis) or consequence of the theory. In this case, we go from the general statement to the specific one. With this process, new data are generated, which allows us to verify, modify, or discard our initial general statements or theory. Deductive reasoning includes statements such as, ''If this is true (premise) then this should follow (conclusion).'' (See Box 3.1.)

DEDUCTION   reasoning from the general to the particular: if all animals are air-breathing, so is a particular animal.

We have simplified inductive and deductive reasoning considerably, and deliberately avoided some controversial issues surrounding their role in the development of scientific theory.

BOX 3.1   DEDUCTIVE AND INDUCTIVE REASONING

Deductive conclusions follow logically from the premises. For example:

All Xs are Ys,	(premise)
All Ys are Zs,	(premise)
Therefore, all Xs are Zs	(conclusion)

The same reasoning in concrete terms would be the following:

> All dogs (Xs) are mammals (Ys),
> All mammals (Ys) are warm blooded (Zs),
> Therefore, all dogs (Xs) are warm blooded (Zs).

Logical validity is not the same as empirical truth. An argument can be logically valid but empirically false. For example, the premises can be true or false, the reasoning still follows logically to a valid conclusion. In this sense, we can logically prove a conclusion that is *not* empirically true. For example, the following is a valid conclusion, but does not conform to experience since the second premise is false.

> All dogs (Xs) are mammals (Ys)   (premise)
> All mammals (Ys) have horns (Zs)   (premise)
> Therefore, all dogs have horns   (conclusion)

Induction contrasts sharply with deduction. Since induction does not follow logically, we can never prove our conclusion. A commonly used example can be given here. We observe a white swan on one occasion, then again on a second, third, fourth, etc., occasion. We conclude that all swans are white, based upon our observations. This is an inductive leap. We cannot prove logically that this is the case. We can never be sure that we have observed all swans everywhere in existence. We may have considerable confidence in our hypothesis since we repeatedly experience this, but inductive conclusions lack the logical certainty that characterize deductive conclusions. Inductive reasoning is also referred to as "affirming the consequent."

3.2 INTERPLAY BETWEEN THEORY AND RESEARCH

As we noted, development of theory is one important method we use for making understandable the subject matter that we are studying. While everyone agrees that theories are important, still the question "What is a theory?" is difficult to answer. There is often disagreement about the meaning of the term and much has been written on the topic. However, some agreement does exist. A theory is a system of ideas or a set of principles often dealing with mechanisms or underlying reasons for behavior and which help us to organize and to assimilate the empirical relationships (observations) that we discover. This is an important function since without theory to aid us in organizing our observations we would soon be overwhelmed by the accumulation of huge numbers of isolated facts. As we have seen, in addition to accounting for already available observations, a theory provides guidance for discovering new ones, i.e., predicting new relationships. The latter is done through the testing of hypotheses derived from the theory. Hypotheses can also be less formal and based upon one's own experience. When this is the case they are usually not much better than a guess.

Theories are evaluated through research. There is an interplay between theory and research in that theories guide research and the research findings are then used to revise or modify the theory. The worth of a theory is determined by how well it accounts for the observed relationships, its precision in making the prediction, its **parsimony** (accounting for the largest number of observations with the fewest number of principles), and its internal consistency. (Is the theory testable or falsifiable or can it account for any kind of outcome?) Theories, when tested, are not judged to be true or false, proven or unproven. Instead we describe them as being supported or unsupported, confirmed or unconfirmed. To say that a theory is supported or confirmed means only that the evidence is consistent with prediction. It does not suggest that the theory is true. Indeed, other theories dealing with the same phenomenon may predict correctly and it may turn out that the other theories are the better ones. (See Confirmation Bias.) It is, after all, possible to predict an outcome correctly but for the wrong reasons. For a full discussion of these issues, see Mahoney (1976).

PARSIMONY   accounting for the largest number of observations with the fewest assumptions or principles.

3.3 BOUNDARY CONDITIONS AND THEORY

Establishing boundary conditions simply means specifying the conditions or limits within which the theory applies. For example, it may be that the theory was developed to deal with nonhuman subjects. If so, then it would be inappropriate to test the theory using humans. Similarly, a theory could be constructed to apply only to adults, therefore it would be an unfair test of the theory if children were used. The boundary conditions of a theory may change over the life-time of the theory. Initially a theory may have restrictive boundary conditions and deal only with a narrow range of behavior. As the theory is further developed its boundary conditions may expand, provided, of course, that it was able to account well for the behavioral observations under the more narrow boundary conditions. Conversely, a theory may be stated broadly initially only to find that it cannot be usefully applied in certain situations. Since theorists are reluctant to discard their theories, they would most likely consider those conditions where the theory is least useful as conditions beyond the boundaries of the theory.

3.4 CONFIRMATION BIAS

We may think that we are always logical in our thinking but errors of reasoning occur. Let's start out by posing a problem for you to solve. We're going to provide you with a series of three numbers. It is your task to discover the rule by which we generated the three numbers. You are to do this in as few trials as possible. We will now give you some numbers generated by our rule, i.e., an example of our rule—the series, 2, 4, 6. Please generate a further series using what you think our rule is. Tell us when you think you know the rule. We will say "yes" if your series agrees with our rule and "no" if it does not. Begin.

If you behave as most people, you will say something similar to "8, 10, 12." Our answer is "yes." You may then say "7, 9, 11" and again, our answer is "yes." Perhaps you may attempt one more series before you state the rule, such as "14, 16, 18." Most likely, you have concluded that the rule is "numbers increasing by twos." If so, you are incorrect! You could go on indefinitely generating numbers increasing by twos and never discover that your hypothesis of "two" was incorrect! If you followed a procedure similar to the one described, you were illustrating confirmation bias (Wason, 1960, Wason and Johnson-Laird, 1972). You were repeatedly attempting to confirm your hypothesis of "increasing by twos" rather than disconfirming (falsifying) it by considering alternative rules. In each case, you gave examples increasing by twos. There seems to be a general tendency among individuals to emphasize positive confirming outcomes rather than negative or disconfirming ones.

What if your second reply had been "5, 8, 11" and we responded "yes"? At this point, you would have disconfirmed the rule, "increasing by twos." You still wouldn't know the rule but you would have eliminated one hypothesis. Perhaps your next thought is that the rule is "equal intervals between numbers." If you now try 5, 10, 15 you would again receive a "yes," indicating the series is compatible with our rule, but you would again be illustrating confirmation bias. To test the "equal interval" hypothesis would require that you try to disconfirm (falsify) it by testing "not equal intervals" such as 5, 8, 15. If we say "no" then your hypothesis of equal intervals may be correct. If we say, "yes" then you know immediately that it is incorrect and you go on to another hypothesis, such as "any series of three increasing numbers." The point is that the fastest way to test this hypothesis (identify a false theory) is to try to disconfirm it. To disconfirm the hypothesis, a series of three decreasing numbers might be chosen, such as 8, 5, 2. We would give you a "no" since 8, 5, 2 is not compatible with our rule. This information suggests that your last hypothesis of "three increasing numbers" may be correct. In fact, this was the rule that we wanted you to try to discover.

This example illustrates an important point. We can now return to some points made earlier. Any number of theories or hypotheses can be supported, even if incorrect, by a continuing run of positive instances (successful predictions). You could have continued using inductive reasoning and generalizing the "twos" hypothesis endlessly, thinking it was correct. (See Box 3.1.) This behavioral strategy is what we referred to earlier as affirming the consequent. It is a strategy often used by scientists but, as our illustration shows, there are shortcomings to it of which we should be aware. We can never establish that a theory is correct with this strategy, but as the number of positive instances increase (instances of support or confirmation), so does our confidence in the theory. But sometimes this confidence is misplaced.

The other strategy we described is referred to as *disconfirmation* or *falsification*. Earlier we referred to this strategy as deductive reasoning (also referred to as *Modus tollens*). It is a powerful way of proving logically the conclusions derived from our theories. A falsification strategy allows us to quickly identify a false theory.

3.5 DEFINITIONS OF KEY TERMS

Here's a thought problem that stirred a great deal of philosophical interest around the turn of the present century.

Imagine you are standing at the base of a tree looking at a squirrel that is peering at you from behind the tree. To get a better look at the squirrel, you slowly circle the tree. But true to its nature, the squirrel moves in such a way that it is always facing you on the opposite side of the tree. When you have completed one circle of the tree, have you also gone around the squirrel?

The answer to the question depends on the definition of "go around." If it means "stand in front of the squirrel, to the left of, to the rear of, to the right of, and again to the front of the squirrel," you have not gone around the squirrel. On the other hand, if "go around" means "to walk around the circumference of the circle in which the squirrel is included," you have walked around the squirrel.

How often have you been in an argument with a friend, only to find out after much debate that you are using key words in different ways. The argument is one of *semantics* rather than of issues. You defined the word one way, and your friend defined it a different way. This experience is more common among laypersons than among scientists, but it still occurs. Before the merits of an issue or a position can be discussed, there must be agreement about the meaning of the important terms. The same is true in science. If we are to avoid confusion and misinterpretation, we must be able to communicate unambiguously the meaning of such terms as: intelligence, anxiety, altruism, hostility, love, alienation, aggression, guilt, reinforcement, frustration, memory, information. These terms have all been used scientifically and in a very precise way.

Each of these terms could be given a *dictionary definition*. Dictionary definitions are usually referred to as *literary* or *conceptual* definitions. Dictionary definitions are not sufficiently precise for many of our scientific terms because they are too general and often too ambiguous. When a word is to be used scientifically or technically, its precise meaning must be conveyed—it must be clear and unambiguous. We achieve this clarity of meaning by operationally defining the term. To state the operations for a term means to make the term observable by pointing to how it is measured. **Operational definitions,** then, make the term or word observable by stating the operations for measuring it. For example, anxiety could be defined in dictionary terms as "a state of being uneasy, apprehensive, or worried." An operational definition of the term could include: sweating palms (observable as sweat gland activity), increased heart rate (observable with heartbeat recording), dilated pupils (observable), and other observable physiological changes. We could in each case also specify the precise amounts of each measure necessary for our operational definition of anxiety. Box 3.2 contains both dictionary definitions and operational definitions of some common terms. Note that in each case, the operational definition refers to events that are observable or events that can easily be made observable. Note further that the definition is very specific rather than general.

OPERATIONAL DEFINITION   a definition of terms or concepts by the way in which they are measured, i.e., making the term observable.

A point that is sometimes very difficult to grasp is that the researcher's specific operational definition of a term may be very different from the common use of the term. For example, many people doing research on intelligence start with a dictionary definition and then translate it into operations. One operational definition of intelligence is simply "a score on a specific intelligence test." Some individuals recoil at this definition. They are free to do so. They may reject it, but they will certainly understand the meaning since "a

---

BOX 3.2   DICTIONARY AND OPERATIONAL DEFINITIONS OF SEVERAL ITEMS COMMONLY USED BY PSYCHOLOGISTS.
For each concept other operational definitions are possible.

Dictionary Definition	Operational Definition
Punishment: harsh or injurious treatment for an offense	Presentation of 3 milliamp shock for .5 second following certain (specified) behavior
Learning: acquiring knowledge or skill.	Change in behavior (specify kind of behavior) as a function of practice
Anxiety: state of being uneasy, apprehensive, or worried	Sweat gland activity (amount), heart rate (amount), physiological changes (specify)
Intelligence: ability to learn or understand from experience.	A score on the Stanford-Binet Intelligence Test
Thirst: distressful feeling caused by a desire or need for water.	Eighteen hours (or other value) without access to water
Sleep: recurring condition of rest, no conscious thought, eyes closed, etc.	Specific brain wave frequencies (EEG) for different sleep stages
Guilt: a painful feeling of self reproach	A score on Personality Inventory

score on an intelligence test" is observable. We will say more about what determines the value of any given operational definition. Keep in mind that definitions when used by researchers are somewhat arbitrary. They are neither right nor wrong, nor are they true or false. They are simply definitions related by the experimenter to observable events.

As we shall see in Chapter 5, it is especially important to define operationally the independent and dependent variables. Any ambiguity in the definition of these terms could impede the discovery of lawful relations between them. If we are interested in studying the lawful relation between the effects of punishment (independent variable) on disruptive classroom behavior (dependent variable), we would have to carefully define specifically what we mean by punishment and what we mean by disruptive behavior. Punishment could be presenting an aversive event (defined) to the student. Disruptive behavior could be talking, leaving one's seat (unauthorized), giggling, etc.

Sometimes the same term (constructs) are defined differently by different investigators, i.e., by different measuring operations. For example, an operational definition of reward may take several forms:

Construct	Operation	Operational Definition
Reward	Presenting money	State specific amount of money
Reward	Presenting praise	State specific kinds of praise
Reward	Presenting food	Specify amount
Reward	Presenting sweet solution	Specify concentration

Similarly, anxiety could be operationally defined as change in the physiology of the subject or as a score on an anxiety test scale, such as the Taylor Manifest Anxiety Scale (Taylor, 1951). The feature that determines whether a particular definition is more useful than another is whether it allows us to discover meaningful laws about behavior. Some will and some will not. Those that do will be retained; those that do not will be discarded. The first step in the life of a concept is to define it in clearly unambiguous, observable terms. It then may or may not be useful. If the concept of intelligence were defined as "the distance between the ears," its meaning would be clear but it is very doubtful that it would ever become useful.

Operational definitions restrict the meaning of a concept to the narrowly described operations used for measuring it. Also, as we have shown with the concept of reward, the same name for a concept may be defined by different operations. Another example may be helpful. Researchers interested in memory or retention operationally define the concept in different ways. *Retention* can be measured (defined) by the operation of *recognition* where initially learned items are identified from a larger set of learned and unlearned items. A practical example of this is the use of multiple choice items on exams. Retention can also be measured by the operation of a straight *recall* where the individual is required to produce material without external aids. Exams using fill-in items would be an example of the latter. A third way of measuring retention is by the operation of *relearning*. This method involves assessing the difference in the number of trials to learn material initially and the number of trials it takes to relearn the same material after a time period has elapsed. Each of these measures of retention has its own distinct operation (way) of being defined (measured). This permits the researcher to ascertain objectively whether the different operations lead to different results. If they do lead to different lawful relations, then the operations represent different concepts and it may be necessary to relate them to each other through a series of coordinating statements.

Let's look at one additional point before leaving the topic of definitions. An operational definition or any other kind of definition is not an explanation. When definitions are unintentionally used as explanations, we label them as *circular reasoning* or as *tautological arguments*. Circular reasoning has little value. A definition doesn't explain behavior or provide you with any information that will, in and of its self, help in understanding behavior. It is a necessary step in discovering lawful relations but it is only one side of a two-sided law. To explain behavior, two independent (different) types of observation are necessary—one is observations that relate to the independent variable (variable manipulated by the experimenter) and the second is observations that relate to the dependent variable (behavior of subject). When the relationship between the independent and dependent variable is predictable, we say that we have a lawful relationship. A circular argument uses only one side of the relationship, i.e., only one of these observations. For example, suppose we observe two children fighting (body contact with intent to harm) with each other. We may be tempted to say they are fighting because they are hostile children, since hostility leads to fighting. To this point, we have not "explained" anything. All we have is an operational definition of hostility as fighting behavior. Our argument would be a tautology (circular) if we said that the children are fighting because they are hostile and then said that we know that they are hostile because they are fighting.

Tautologies do not add anything to our understanding. To advance our understanding we need an empirical relationship, i.e., two or more independent observations that are related. To provide one we would have to identify the conditions that preceded (led to) the fighting. We could then say that the children fight because of conditions 1, 2, 3, and 4. Our concept of "hostility" would now be defined independently in terms of conditions 1, 2, 3, and 4 on the one hand, and fighting on the other. We have now explained behavior in

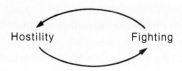

Hostility   Fighting

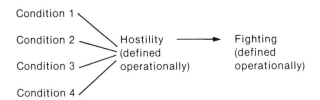

the sense that we can state that people fight because they are hostile, and they are hostile because they previously experienced conditions 1, 2, 3, and 4. The concept of "hostility" is a shorthand way for expressing the relationship between the antecedent conditions (conditions 1, 2, 3, and 4) and consequent conditions (fighting).

Tautological reasoning occurs with a higher frequency than it should. For example, it is not uncommon to hear the statement, "Individuals who commit suicide are mentally ill." When asked, "How do you know they are mentally ill?" the response often is, "Because they committed suicide." Another common tautology refers to musical ability. For example, it is said, "Individuals who play the piano well do so because they have musical ability." When asked, "How do you know they have musical ability?" the response is, "Because they play the piano well." We repeat, tautological arguments do not advance our knowledge.

TAUTOLOGICAL REASONING Circular reasoning, eg., they are fighting because they are hostile. I know they are hostile because they are fighting.

3.6 MEASUREMENT

Measurement is so common and taken for granted that we seldom ask why we measure things or worry about the different forms it may take. It is often not sufficient to describe a runner as "fast," a basketball player as "tall," a wrestler as "strong," or a baseball hitter as "good." If coaches recruited potential team members on the basis of these imprecise words, they would have difficulty holding down a job. Coaches want to know how fast the runner runs the forty- or one-hundred-yard dash, or the mile, etc. They want to know exactly how tall the basketball player is, the strength of the wrestler, the batting average of the hitter. Measurement is a way of refining our ordinary observations. It allows us to go beyond simply describing the presence or absence of an event or thing to specifying "how much," "how long," "how intense," the event. With measurement, our observations become more accurate and more reliable. Precision is important in all areas of our lives, especially in the sciences and technologies, and we look to ways of increasing it.

Measurement is so important and we are so dependent upon it that many countries have an agency whose primary responsibility is to specify the units of measurement and provide precise standards for comparisons. The National Bureau of Standards is the agency responsible for setting the standards of measurement of the United States. This agency also serves the purpose of calibrating some measuring instruments (or recalibrating them) used by large technical industries. There is considerable agreement and cooperation on an international level concerning standards of measurement.

3.6.1 Numbers and Precision

Measurement scales are important because they allow us to transform or substitute numbers for words. We are restricted in what we can do with words but less so with numbers. Numbers permit us to perform certain activities and operations that words do not. In many instances numbers permit us to add, multiply, divide, or subtract. They also permit the use of various statistical procedures. These, in turn, result in greater precision and objectivity in describing behavior or other phenomena. At a minimum we know that the numbers 1, 2, 3, 4, and so on, when applied to frequency of occurrence of any event, means that 4 instances is greater than 3, which in turn is greater than 2, etc. Contrast numbers with words such as *frequently, often,* or *many times.* Does an event occurring *frequently* occur a greater or fewer number of times than an event occurring *often*? It may be true that for a given individual the two terms *frequently* and *often* may be used consistently across situations, other individuals may use the two terms consistently but in reverse order. Confusion would result if this occurred.

The use of numbers rather than words increases our precision in communicating in other ways also. Finer distinctions (discriminations) can often be achieved with numbers if the distinctions can be made reliably. Instead of saying certain behavior was either present or absent, or occurred with high, medium, or low frequency, numbers would permit us to say, more precisely, how frequently the behavior occurred. Words are often too few in number to allow us to express finer distinctions.

Our number system is an abstract system of symbols that has little meaning in and of itself. It becomes meaningful when it becomes involved in measurement. Measurement is the process of assigning numbers to objects and events in accordance with a set of rules. To grasp the full impact of measurement, it is necessary to describe the concept of a measurement scale. There are several different kinds of scales: nominal, ordinal, interval, and ratio. The distinction among scales becomes of particular importance when we conduct statistical analyses of data. Underlying statistical tests are various assumptions, including those relating to the scale of measurement.

3.6.2 Nominal Scales

There has been some disagreement among experts whether the term **nominal scale** should be described as a scale. Most would agree that it does. The fact is that we do name things and this permits us to do other things as a result. The word *nominal* is derived from the latin word *name*. With a nominal scale, numbers are assigned to objects or events simply for identification purposes. For example, participants in various sports have numbers on their jerseys that quickly allow spectators, referees, and commentators to identify them. This is the sole purpose of these numbers. Performing arithmetic operations on these numbers, such as addition, subtraction, multiplication, or division would not make any sense. The numbers do not indicate more or less of any quantity. A baseball player with the number 7 on his back does not necessarily have more of something than a player identified by number 1. Other examples include your social security number, your driver's license number, or your credit card number. Labeling or naming allows us to make **qualitative distinctions** or to categorize and then count the frequency of persons, objects, or things in each category. This activity can be very useful. For example, in any given voting year, we could label or name individuals as Democrat or Republican, Liberal or Conservative, and then count their frequency for purposes of predicting voting outcomes. Other examples of nominal scales used for identifying and categorizing are male-female, neurotic-psychotic, punishment-reward, etc.

NOMINAL SCALES   scales in which numbers are assigned to objects or events for identification purposes.

QUALITATIVE DISTINCTION   distinction made on the basis of differences in kind rather than in "how much."

3.6.3 Ordinal Scales

This scale allows us to rank order events and things. Original numbers are assigned to the order such as first, second, third, etc. For example, we might determine that runners in a race finished in a particular order and this would provide us with useful information. We would know that the runner finishing first ran the distance faster than the runner finishing second, and that the second place finisher ran faster than the third place finisher, and so on. However, we would not know how much faster the first runner was over the second place runner, and the second over the third. The difference between the first and second place runner may have been a fraction of a second or it could have been several seconds. Similarly, the difference between the second and third place runners could have been very small or very large. Precise quantitative information is not conveyed with an **ordinal scale**. Therefore, with an ordinal scale, we know the rank order but we do not have any idea of the distance between the rankings. Some other examples of an ordinal scale are: grades such as "A," "B," "C," etc.; scores given in terms of high, medium, and low; birth order in terms of first born, second born, third born, etc.; examination scores from highest to lowest; list of job candidates ranked high to low; ten best dressed persons; etc. While most psychological scales are probably ordinal, psychologists assume that many of the scales have equal intervals and act accordingly. (See Interval Scales.) It is believed by many that these scales do approximate equality of intervals reasonably well and it is unlikely that this assumption will lead to serious difficulties in interpreting our findings.

> ORDINAL SCALES   scales in which the relationship between classes is expressed by the algebra of inequalities (i.e., greater than, less than).

3.6.4 Interval Scales

When we can specify both the order of events *and* the distance between events, we have an **interval scale.** A given distance between any two intervals on this type scale is equal throughout the scale. The central shortcoming of an interval scale is its lack of an absolute zero point—a location where the user can say that there is a complete absence of a thing. This type of scale has an arbitrary zero point sometimes called an *anchor point.* An example may make clear the difference between an arbitrary zero point and an absolute zero point. Scores on intelligence tests are considered to be on an interval scale. With intelligence test scores, the anchor point is set at an IQ value of 100 (average) and the interval between points is set at 10 (one standard deviation). (See Chapters 10 and 11.) A score of 110 is just as far above the mean (one S.D.) as a score of 90 (one S.D.) is below the mean. Since we have a relative zero point and not an absolute one, we cannot say that an intelligence test score of 100 is twice that of 50. It is simply not meaningful to do so. The distinction between a relative and absolute zero point is also seen clearly when describing historical time periods. We cannot say that the time period up to year 1000 A.D. is one-half as long as the time period up to the year 2000 A.D. We do not know when time began. History began before the year 1 A.D. and is referred to as B.C. Therefore, the time period up to the year 1000 A.D. includes all the A.D. years and the B.C. years of recorded history.

> INTERVAL SCALES   quantitative scales expressing "how much." Do not have true zero point.

Some additional examples of interval scales are: both the centigrade and Fahrenheit scales of temperature, altitude (i.e., zero is sea level rather than the center of the earth), and barometric pressure.

3.6.5   Ratio Scales

Scales of this nature have a number of properties that the others do not. With **ratio scales,** we can identify rank order, equal intervals, and equal ratios, i.e., two times as much, one-half as much. The latter can be determined because the zero point is absolute or a true anchor meaning the complete absence of a property. Zero weight or height means the complete absence of weight or height. A 100-pound person is one-half the weight of a 200-pound person and twice the weight of a 50-pound person. We can say these things because we know that the starting points for these dimensions or measures begins at zero. Seldom do psychologists have ratio scales available.

> RATIO SCALES same as interval scales but, since zero is true, ratios between quantities can be expressed.

Some researchers have argued that the type of measurement scale used in the research is an important consideration in choosing the proper statistic for the analysis of the findings. They would argue that t-tests or F-tests require either interval or ratio scales. However, others would extend the use of these tests to ordinal scales as well.

3.7   PROBLEMS OF MEASUREMENT: VALIDITY

There are two important concepts that relate to the measuring instruments that we use: validity and reliability. In a general sense, **validity** refers to whether the measuring instrument does what it is intended to do, and **reliability** refers to how consistently it does so.

> VALIDITY   a valid instrument measures what it purports to measure.
> RELIABILITY   the consistency of the measuring instrument.

The validity and reliability of a test is established by evidence. Does the SAT (Scholastic Aptitude Test) measure the student's ability to do academic work (question of validity) and, if so, how consistently does it do so (question of reliability)? Do those students scoring high on the SAT perform predictably better in college than those scoring low (validity)? If a student took the SAT today and then again six months from today, would the score on the two performances be similar (reliability)? We should note that a test may be highly reliable, but if it does not relate to our behavior of interest (validity), it is useless for predicting that behavior. The length of the big toe may be measured with a high degree of consistency but it is unlikely to be a valid predictor of academic success. Thus, we can achieve reliability without having validity. However, the reverse is not possible. In order to be valid, a test must be reli-

Table 3.1
Relationship between reliability and validity.

| | | Degree of reliability | |
		Low	High
Degree of validity	High	Cannot have high validity with low reliability	Ideal for predicting from a test to behavior
	Low	A test low in reliability must be low in validity	Test measures consistently but not what it purports to measure

Note that it is not possible to have a test of high validity and low reliability. However, a test may be reliable without being valid.

able. These relationships between reliability and validity are summarized in Table 3.1.

Let us look at four types of validity that are commonly distinguished: Content validity, face validity, predictive validity, and construct validity. Content validity and face validity relate to tests of current knowledge and skills, while predictive validity relates to future performance on a job or task. Construct validity deals with evaluating theoretical terms.

3.7.1   Content Validity

With **content validity,** we are interested in assessing current performance rather than predicting future performance. A test is constructed to measure whether participants in a program have mastered the contents of the program. Course examinations deal with content validity whether midterm, finals, or some other kind. Developers of social programs that require training who are concerned over the effectiveness of the training frequently rely on content validity. *Content validity is achieved by constructing a test drawn directly from material in a program or course.* There can be disagreements regarding the representativeness of the test materials. For example, students taking an exam sometimes complain that it did not cover the material they were required to read. If this were true, the exam would be low in content validity. Although not always possible, we could assure representativeness by constructing a complete listing of the content for the program or course and then selecting test items randomly from the material. Thus, content validity is based on prior considerations about what content will be included.

> **CONTENT VALIDITY**   measuring material is drawn directly from the content of the course or training program.

3.7.2   Face Validity

Face validity is similar to content validity but it is determined *after* the test is constructed. We ask ourselves whether or not the test appears on the face of it to be appropriate. If the test is known to have content validity, face validity can be assumed. However, it does not work in reverse direction; that is, face validity does not ensure content validity. The face validity of an exam in research methods would be high if the questions appeared to deal with research methods. However, without actual knowledge of the course materials, there would be no assurance that the questions would be representative of the actual course material.

> FACE VALIDITY   a judgment made after the test is constructed about whether the test instrument appears to measure the content of the course.

3.7.3   Predictive Validity

Predictive validity, also called criterion validity, is often used in program evaluation studies and is very suitable for applied research. Essentially, a test is constructed and developed for the purpose of predicting some form of behavior. For example, academic performance in college (the criterion) is moderately correlated with scores on the SAT (the predictor). Knowing this relationship and an individual's score gives us a better idea of how a student will perform in college than in the absence of this information. The higher the correlation, the greater the predictive validity. Indeed, if the correlation is perfect (1.00), the prediction is also perfect. (A more detailed description of correlational procedures appears in Chapter 4.) However, most of the time correlations are only modest, somewhere between .30 and .60. Nevertheless, they are considered useful. It is very difficult to construct a good predictor measure; it is also very difficult to obtain a good criterion measure. Both are necessary for program evaluation. (See Chapter 15.)

> PREDICTIVE VALIDITY   validity established by how well the test predicts relevant aspects of behavior.

3.7.4   Construct Validity

Construct validity is one of the most important and also the most difficult to understand. We can only touch upon it here. A much fuller discussion of construct validity can be found in Nunnally and Durham (1975). Construct validity is especially important for the construction of theories and was first introduced by Cronbach and Meehl (1955).

CONSTRUCT VALIDITY an instrument is considered to have construct validity if it assists in understanding and predicting operationally defined behavior.

Theoretical constructs are created by researchers to help predict and understand behavior. Examples of some constructs are frustration, aggression, motivation, learning, fear, hopelessness, creativity, and intelligence. Constructs are created by describing the procedures for measuring them. (See operational definitions.) If the instrument for measuring them assists us in understanding and predicting behavior, they are considered valid. If they do not serve these purposes, their validity is rejected.

There are several steps in establishing construct validity. Generally, the researcher or theorist constructs a test and specifies what it is intended to measure. The test is then tied to or related to the relevant theory. Then predictions are made that relate behavior to the test scores. Finally, data are gathered to ascertain whether the predictions are confirmed. Let's look at an example. Imagine that we constructed a test to measure impaired learning and motivation. We call our test "learned helplessness." We relate our test to the hypothesis (theory) that lack of control over environmental events can be debilitating, both cognitively and physiologically. When individuals are subjected to aversive environmental events over which they have no control, it results in learned helplessness, which is reflected by impaired learning, reduced levels of motivation, poor performance, and physiological deterioration. Our expectations are that individuals scoring high on this test will show these deficits, while individuals scoring low will not. We then give the test (predictor) to a group of individuals and independently collect behavioral evidences of impaired learning, motivation, etc. (criterion). The greater the correlation between the predictor and the criterion, the higher the construct validity. The concept of scholastic aptitude as measured by a test would have construct validity if the test could reliably identify individual differences and then successfully predict future performance.

What we are saying with our example is that constructs reflect basic behavioral processes. If learned helplessness exists, then certain behaviors should follow. If our expectations are confirmed a number of times in a variety of settings, our construct is useful, i.e., valid. Usually many studies are necessary to demonstrate construct validity. With time and continued research, both the construct and the theory usually undergo a series of modifications and become more refined.

3.8   PROBLEMS OF MEASUREMENT: RELIABILITY

A measuring instrument is reliable if its measurements are repeatable. Obviously, we would not want to use a measuring instrument if it did not give similar results under similar circumstances. A test is reliable if it is consistent. As we have previously noted, reliability is a necessary but not a sufficient condition for validity. Information concerning test reliability should be available for every test. This information should specify the extent of the reliability, the type, the conditions under which it was obtained, and the conditions under which the test was given. Reliability estimates are expressed in terms of the coefficient of correlation.

The upper limits of a test of reliability are established by the similarity of items in terms of what they have in common (inter-item correlation) and the number of items on the test. Other things equal, the larger the number of items on a test, the more reliable the test. This notion is found in the way many championship sporting events are determined. Instead of a single game, several games are often scheduled (e.g., baseball, basketball, hockey). On any given day a weaker team may defeat a stronger team but it is unlikely that a weaker team would consistently beat a stronger team. Similarly, witness the Olympic decathlon. It is a contest in which an athlete must take part in ten events. Consider another example. A course in psychology at the end of the term may have available 1,000 questions that could be used on the final exam. The final exam would be constructed by sampling these items. A sample of only five items would be too few for reliability purposes. As we added items, our reliability would increase rapidly but beyond a certain point, reached rather quickly, adding more items would add very little to our reliability. Therefore, a fifty-item test would be considerably more reliable than a five-item test. For those interested in pursuing this notion further, an estimate of reliability that considers both inter-item correlation and the number of items on a test is referred to as the *coefficient alpha* or the *Kuder-Richardson* method. Among other things, this method will allow you to determine the number of items needed to achieve a given value of reliability.

3.8.1   Test-Retest Reliability

One obvious way to determine the reliability of a test is to administer the same test twice to the same individual. With the test-retest procedure, the identical test is administered a second time, usually after a two-week interval. A coefficient of correlation is then calculated for the first and second test scores. The time interval between the tests must be specified since retest correlations decrease as the time interval between tests increases. Some problems with this procedure relate to possible practice effects. Also, if the interval between the tests is very short, the individual may be able to remember previous answers and the scores between the two sets of test scores would not be independent.

While high test-retest reliability suggests that the measuring instrument is relatively free of measurement error, care should be taken in interpreting it. High reliability does not mean that an individual's first and second score are nearly the same. This may or may not be so. Since test-retest reliability is derived through a correlational analysis, the strength of the relationship depends upon the similarity in rank order on the first and second test distributions, i.e., whether the individual was first, second, third, etc., on the two distributions of test scores. In this regard, test-retest reliability is a relative measure. It is very possible to have high test-retest reliability and yet have different absolute scores on the first and second testing.

We also want to comment on low test-retest reliability. Low reliability does not always suggest a faulty measuring instrument. If a marked change in the individual's condition occurs between the first and second testing, then low test-retest reliability may result. For example, a therapy or training program for a reading disability may take place between the first and second testing period. If those with the greatest disability showed the greatest improvement, then this would lower test-retest reliability. On the other hand, if no deliberate effort to change the condition of the individual was made and only a short period of time intervened between the first and second test, then low test-retest reliability is most likely due to a faulty measuring instrument.

3.8.2   Alternate Form Reliability

Some of the difficulties with the test-retest procedure can be avoided with the alternate form method. With this method, an individual is tested on one form of the test (Form A) and then again on a comparable second form (Form B). Again, a correlation coefficient is computed between the scores on Forms A and B. The period of time between the two tests is usually two weeks, although this varies considerably. Usually the two forms contain the same number of items and cover similar content. Alternate form reliability is used more frequently than test-retest reliability because it has fewer associated problems.

3.8.3   Split-Half Reliability

Only a single test session is involved when using this method. Two scores for each individual are obtained by splitting the test into comparable halves. This is usually achieved by assigning odd-numbered items to one form and even-numbered items to the other (odd-even split). Generally, this method is not preferred over others because the scores in both halves are not independent. To illustrate, if a testee is "spaced-out" while taking the test, both scores will be depressed. With a sufficient number of instances of this sort, a spuriously high correlation will result and the reliability will appear to be higher than it really is.

3.9 FACTORS INFLUENCING RELIABILITY

3.9.1 Factors Reducing Test-Retest or Alternate Form Reliability

There are a number of factors that can lower the reliability of a test. These can be divided into two categories of "within" a test session and "between" test sessions. Within a testing period, individuals may become upset or ill, or they may misread the question, or make a clerical error when recording an answer, or may guess at the answer. Between testing sessions an individual may change; there may be differences between two tests (alternate form), or scoring criteria may change. These can affect the reliability of measurement.

3.9.2 Improving Reliability

Measurement "error" can be reduced and reliability improved by carefully writing the items. A standardized procedure for giving the test should be carefully followed so that testing conditions are very similar. Instructions should be clearly stated so that they are easily understood. Finally, objective scoring procedures should be used to avoid error due to subjectivity and changing criteria. We should also restate that longer tests (given the same inter-item correlation) are more reliable than shorter tests. Obviously, when new tests are being constructed, considerable "pilot work" (preliminary selection of items, testing, revising) is necessary before a useful instrument can be developed.

3.9.3 Satisfactory Reliability

Acceptable reliability levels depend upon what the test is used for. For basic research purposes, reliabilities of approximately .70 are not uncommon but correlations of .80 or higher are considered desirable. To obtain higher estimates of reliability requires considerable effort in selecting items, standardizing the procedure, and administering and scoring the test. For applied problems dealing with social issues such as placement in a retraining program, in a special class, or for awards, etc., measurement error must be minimized. Under these and other similar circumstances, reliability coefficients less than .90 are usually *not* acceptable.

CHAPTER FOUR

RESEARCH METHODS

4.1   WHEN IS AN EXPERIMENT AN EXPERIMENT?

It was recently reported that ownership of a dog may be therapeutic. One-year, follow-up studies were conducted on a group of ninety-two coronary patients following their release from the hospital. They were divided into two groups: patients who were dog owners and patients who were not. When the death rates of the two groups were compared, a surprising difference emerged. Fifty of fifty-three dog owners survived at least a year, whereas only twenty-eight of thirty-nine dog nonowners enjoyed a one-year survival record. The appropriate statistical analysis revealed that the difference is statistically significant. It could rightfully be concluded that patients with coronary heart disease who owned dogs enjoyed a better survival record than those who did not. But should we conclude that some sort of *causal* relationship exists between dog ownership and the probability of survival of coronary patients? We should not. Causal relationships can only be clearly established by a properly conducted **true experiment.** The research reported above is not a true experiment but is, instead, **ex post facto research** (after the fact), i.e., correlational research. It lacks two fundamental characteristics of a true experiment: **random assignment** of subjects to conditions and manipulation of the independent variable[1] (dog ownership). Neither random assignment of subjects to conditions nor manipulation of the independent variable could be used in this case since the problem dealt with those who *previously* had dogs and those who did not. Dog ownership was a matter of *history* and the information was obtained from *record files.*

TRUE EXPERIMENT   research in which subjects are assigned at random to conditions and the independent variable is manipulated by the experimenter.
EX POST FACTO RESEARCH   research done on past records in which "independent" and "dependent" variables are ascertained "after the fact."
RANDOM ASSIGNMENT   assigning the subjects to experimental conditions in such a way that each subject is equally likely to be assigned to any given condition.

We shall see in this chapter that many studies closely mimic a true experiment. In some cases the investigator may manipulate the independent variable but be unable to randomly assign subjects to conditions (quasi-experiments). **Quasi-experiments** are very similar to true experiments except for the important feature of random assignment. In other instances, as in our previous illustration, neither random assignment of subjects to conditions nor manipulation of the independent variable are present. In this case, the variables or conditions have *already occurred naturally* and comparisons are made between these

---

1. We discuss independent and dependent variables in detail in Chapter 5. An independent variable is the condition directly manipulated by the experimenter and which affects the behavior we want to measure. The behavior that it affects is referred to as the dependent variable.

naturally formed groups ("treatments"), i.e., variables are not deliberately manipulated by the investigator. We shall see in this chapter that the degree of risk in inferring causal relationships with these three methods can be ordered with correlational (*ex post facto*) methods the highest, quasi-experiments intermediate, and true experiments the lowest.

> **QUASI-EXPERIMENT**   similar to true experiment except that random assignment of subjects is not used.

The concept of "cause" is much discussed. Both the criteria for establishing a cause and for classifying a cause may vary. (See Box 4.1.) An understanding of what constitutes the concept of "cause" will give you a fuller understanding of the strengths and limitations of different research strategies.

BOX 4.1   IDENTIFYING AND CLASSIFYING "CAUSE" AND "CAUSAL RELATIONSHIPS"

The concept of "cause" is a controversial one. Some scientists and philosophers of science feel it is an unnecessary concept, while others argue that it is important. The arguments on this issue are beyond the scope of this text, but others deal with them in detail. For our purpose, we can state the criteria necessary to infer a cause-effect relationship (Cook and Campbell, 1979). These are:

1. A closeness in time (contiguity) between events considered to be causes and events considered to be effects;

2. The order of the relationship in that causes must precede effects; the relationship is asymmetrical in that if X is a cause of Y, then X must always precede Y; Y cannot precede X;

3. Consistency in that causes must be present whenever the effects occur, i.e., a high correlation between the events;

4. Isolation of the events thought to be causes (independent variables; see Chapter 7) through proper experimental procedures such as random assignment, proper control groups, sensitive measuring instruments, control, etc. Isolation is necessary to rule out causes due to some unknown factors that vary with factors manipulated. (See also Third Variable Problem.)

Some researchers find it useful to classify causal relationships. Although several classificatory systems exist, one that is commonly used is shown below.

A *necessary* and *sufficient* causal relationship means that a condition (e.g., Condition A) is both necessary and sufficient to produce an effect (e.g., Event B). Event B occurs only if Condition A is present. Condition A *must* be present (necessary) and when present it alone is capable (sufficient) of producing Event B. Necessary and sufficient causal relationships are unusual in psychology.

A *necessary but not sufficient* causal relationship means that a condition (Condition A) is necessary to produce an effect (Event B) but in itself it is not sufficient to do so. Relationships such as this are common in psychology. The presence of Condition A is necessary to produce Event B but Event B will *not* occur unless other conditions are also present. For example, to play tennis it is necessary to have a racket but not sufficient. A ball, court, and adversary are also needed. A *sufficient but not necessary* causal relationship means that a condition (Condition A) *alone* is sufficient to produce an effect (Event B). However, it is not a necessary condition since other conditions can independently produce the same event. Relationships such as this are also very common. For example, increases in heart rate (Event B) can be produced by exercise, fear, or pain (Conditions A, B, or C).

Contributory conditions.   There are instances when a condition contributes to a causal relationship but it is neither necessary nor sufficient to produce an effect. For example, toxic shock syndrome (TSS) in females has been linked to the use of certain makes of tampons. The tampons most troublesome have been those consisting of material that is most highly absorbent. These tampons have resulted in excessive drying of tissue and the rupturing of skin, thus contributing to conditions favorable for a serious bacterial infection. Thus, the use of tampons may not cause TSS but their use may be a contributing factor for it to occur.

4.2 CHARACTERISTICS OF AN EXPERIMENT

Whenever we observe behavior in a natural setting and we raise a question about the conditions responsible for what we see, we are usually at no loss to provide any number of possible "explanations." In other words, the question has more than one possible answer, i.e., there are usually several rival explanations or alternative hypotheses that can be advanced. For example, the Personalized System of Instruction (PSI) has been shown to produce superior test scores when compared with the traditional lecture system. PSI is characterized by having a clear statement of both objectives and what constitutes success, many small study units, conditions that permit the study units to be completed at the individual's own pace, mastery of each unit before going on to the next, frequent testing, immediate feedback concerning degree of success, and interaction with proctors. Which of these factors is responsible for the success of PSI? Is it one factor or a combination of several?

Research to date combines these factors in such a way that it is not possible to tease out those that produce behavioral changes. This is not a criticism of the research since the objectives are quite frankly applied. Instructors want to produce better learners. However, many experimental psychologists would like to rise to the challenge of identifying the factor or factors that are important for the success of PSI as well as those that are unimportant. We could do this by systematically manipulating a single variable while holding others constant. By combining this procedure with other features we'll be describing in this section, we would be using a method known as systematic laboratory research. This is only one of many different types of research. Most often it takes place under controlled laboratory conditions. When certain criteria are met, we refer to the research as a "true experiment" (see Campbell & Stanley, 1963; Cook & Campbell, 1979) in contrast to either a quasi-experiment or ex post facto research.

On the surface, it might seem relatively simple to design an experiment in which we obtain straightforward answers to our questions. This is not usually the case. In the broadest sense, designing an experiment involves selecting treatment and control conditions (values of the independent variable), choosing the proper behavioral measure for comparisons (dependent variable), selecting and assigning subjects, and applying the proper statistical analyses. In short, **research design** describes the structure of our research. A good research design will allow us to collect and organize data in a systematic way, and draw conclusions that are relevant to the questions we ask.

RESEARCH DESIGN   the structure of the research.

4.2.1   Illustrative example

Let's look at an example of a "true" experiment and use it to illustrate some problems encountered in designing an experiment.

Let us say that we are interested in the effects of marijuana ("grass") on reaction time in college students. We decide to do an experiment to determine if there are any effects. The question we wish to answer is simple but finding an answer requires a surprising amount of preparation, skill, and research knowledge.

Before we collect any data, numerous decisions and preparations must be undertaken. One of the first decisions relates to the population of college students that we should use. Do we want to use college students from all levels? Do we want to use both males and females? Since marijuana is a drug having measurable effects on the physiology of the organism, should we screen subjects and exclude subjects based on the results of a physical exam? Another important question relates to users and nonusers of "grass." Perhaps the results will depend on prior experience with the drug. Moreover, if a person is a user, then duration or frequency of use may be an important factor.

Having decided what subjects to use, getting them to participate might constitute a problem. We would have to rely on fully-informed volunteers and then randomly assign them to the conditions we decide upon. This method of assignment maximizes the likelihood of approaching equality in the makeup of subjects in the various conditions. Other problems must also be addressed. Minimally we would require at least two groups—an experimental treatment (marijuana) group and a control/comparison (no marijuana) group.

And what about the treatment? We would have to assure ourselves that the marijuana would have uniform purity or potency. This would preclude using "street grass." Since the active ingredient in marijuana has been identified as tetrahydrocannabinol (THC), we could manufacture cigarettes highly uniform in THC and thus assure ourselves of a constant potency for each subject (as well as constant amount or quantity). We would still not be ready to begin the experiment. It is essential that the treatment required by the experimental and control groups differ in one way only so that observed changes in our dependent measure, if they occur, may be attributed to this difference. If more than one factor differs, it would be difficult to conclude which factor was responsible for the change or difference. Imagine that we gave the experimental group a cigarette with the proper amount of THC and then tested them. Imagine further that the control group received no cigarette with THC but were tested in the same manner as the experimental group. Any difference obtained could be a result of two things: The experimental group might differ because of the THC or they might differ because they expected to be affected by the THC. Expectancies have been shown to have powerful effects on behavior. Therefore, either the drug or expectancies or the combination of the two may be responsible for any observed differences between the experimental and control groups. When the effects of one or more variables are so intertwined that we are unable to separate them, we speak of the variables as being **confounded.** Without appropriate controls, the effects of marijuana are confounded with subject expectancies in the THC study.

CONFOUNDING   when the effects of two or more variables are so intertwined that we are unable to separate them out.

In many research studies, particularly those dealing with instructional techniques, the effects of many variables are confounded. However, this confounding is deliberate since the interest is in improving learning by any legitimate means available to the investigators. There is usually no interest in separately assessing the effects of each variable. However, in the THC study, the entire thrust of the experiment is to assess marijuana's effects on reaction time. Consequently, confounding THC's effects with expectancies must be avoided. To correct this problem we would have to give both groups the same kind of "treatment" and only one group the drug. Later, we will discuss this as a **placebo** control. With this procedure both groups would get a cigarette identical in all respects, including taste and smell, except for one thing—only one of the "joints" would contain THC. It should be apparent that the conditions under which the experimental and placebo control groups smoked their "joints" were as similar as possible.

PLACEBO   an inactive substance used in place of an active substance it resembles. Group receiving placebo called placebo control.

Many other decisions would have to be made, such as the duration of the experiment, number of test trials, kinds of statistical analyses, etc. The number of experimental groups could be expanded to include different potencies (strengths) of THC. We might also be interested in assessing the effects of THC on several behaviors. Whatever the case, considerable planning must occur before data collection.

One final consideration is necessary prior to beginning our experiment. In the experiment to this point we have controlled almost everything except possible bias that may occur on the part of the experimenter. Since the experimenter knows which subjects are in the experimental group (groups) and which are in the control group, it is possible that he or she may treat them differently. For example, the experimenter may show more concern about the experimental subjects, spend more time with them, observe them more carefully, etc. If this, in fact, occurred, then we would be varying more than one factor. Any observed differences could be a result of either the drug, the additional attention, or both. As we shall see later on, in more detail, the way to avoid this problem is to use a **double blind procedure.** Both the experimenter and the subject are "blind" as to which subjects are experimental and which are controls.

DOUBLE BLIND PROCEDURE neither the subjects nor the experimenters know which subjects receive the experimental treatment and which the placebo.

4.2.2 A Summary of Considerations for the THC Experiment

1. Type of college student to use (age, health, sex, grade)

2. Volunteers—random assignment essential

3. Number of groups—experimental/control

4. User or nonuser subjects

5. Purity and potency of marijuana—THC

6. Amount to be used—frequency and use of tests

7. Consideration of a placebo condition

8. Consideration of double blind procedures

9. Consideration and preparation for measuring dependent variables

10. Holding all conditions as constant as possible, varying only THC.

The example contains many features that characterize sound, competent research practices. The two that identify it as a true experiment are: (1) random assignment, and (2) control over the independent variable. This contrasts with quasi-experiments where random assignment is absent but control over the independent variable is present, and with ex post facto research where neither random assignment nor control is possible. Again, as noted, with random assignment, each subject has an equal opportunity to be assigned to any group (condition) in the experiment, a method of assignment that results in the least bias. It allows us to assume equality of groups, assuring us that any differences in assignment will be due to chance. This is precisely what our statistical tests are designed to do, i.e., compare the results that we obtain with those expected on the basis of chance. Moreover, in our example of a true experiment, we can actively manipulate the independent variable by introducing it or withdrawing it, and we can treat different groups in different ways. It may appear to you that we are making a considerable fuss in distinguishing between true experiments, quasi-experiments, and ex post facto research. We are, in fact. As we shall see, there are sound reasons for making the distinctions.

4.3 QUASI-EXPERIMENTAL RESEARCH

Sometimes research is reported that appears to have all the ingredients of an experiment, yet it is not. It is not an experiment for the simple reason that random assignment is lacking. It is important to distinguish between a true experiment and a quasi-experiment because the conclusions that may be drawn from the research depend upon this distinction. Both in this chapter and in later chapters, we will give examples of some difficulties encountered in drawing conclusions from quasi-experimental research.

Let's look at an example of a quasi-experiment that resembles a true experiment. In this example, active manipulation of that independent variable occurs but random assignment is absent. Active manipulation of a variable is the same as that of a true experiment—treatments are presented and comparisons are made. Also, when put into a tabular form the design appears the same as that of a true experiment. To illustrate, the design of our THC experiment could be represented in the following manner. As you recall, both random assignment and active manipulation of the independent variable was used. The actively manipulated treatment is referred to in the design below as Group I and the placebo condition (comparison) is referred to as Group 2.

THC True Experiment	Random Assignment and Manipulation of Independent Variable	
Group 1	Treatment (THC)	Dependent Variable
Group 2	Placebo control	Dependent Variable

The dependent variables are the same for all groups. Since random assignment was used and all other conditions were held constant, strong and confident statements can be made if statistically reliable differences in the average values of the dependent variable are found between the two groups. Our conclusions could take several very similar forms, e.g., we could say the relationship between THC and behavior is such and such; or if THC, then certain behavior; or THC causes individuals to behave in certain ways. However we say it, we would feel comfortable about being correct since random assignment and all other necessary controls were used. Therefore, no differences should exist between the groups other than the treatment—to which the difference in results can be attributed. But would we feel as comfortable if our subjects were not assigned randomly to the THC treatment condition and to the placebo control condition? Not at all. If this were the case, any observed differences obtained in the experiment could be due to possible differences in the group make-up independent of the THC treatment condition.

Let us contrast the THC study with an example in which random assignment is missing. Suppose that we are interested in evaluating the effects of different test frequencies during the school term on final exam performance. Our research hypothesis is that the more examinations given in a course during the school term, the better the performance. Without going into all the many details, we will simply assume that all possible controls have been used and that the research on test frequency is done rigorously. The design is illustrated as follows:

Quasi-Experiment	Nonrandom Assignment and Manipulation of Independent Variable	
Group 1	10-Exam Treatment	Final exam scores
Group 2	5-Exam Treatment	Final exam scores

In this case, there were two actively manipulated treatment conditions: Group 1 refers to ten exams during the school term, and Group 2 refers to five exams. The dependent variable was performance on the final exam. Two intact introductory psychology sections composed the two experimental groups and numbered 200 students per section. Each section met at the same time of day. However, Group 1 was comprised of students identified by the admissions office as "special." Let us assume that the study was run, the results analyzed, and that marked differences in performance on the final exam were found. The class receiving ten exams performed better than the class receiving five exams. Would we feel as confident about drawing conclusions from this study as we did from the one involving THC? On the face of it, both the THC experiment and the test frequency study appear to be highly similar. But there is one major difference: Random assignment was used in the THC experiment but not in the test frequency study. Since the latter does not meet our criteria for a true experiment, we would be less confident about our conclusions. Since random assignment was not used, the groups (classes) may have differed in their composition independent of the differences in test frequency. Any number of possible differences in students labelled "special" and those attending regular classes may be responsible for the differences found on the final exam. They may have differed in age, experience, maturation, SAT scores, etc. It is, of course, possible that the "special" label was trivial and that the class composition was equal. In this case, the obtained differences may have been a direct result of manipulating the independent variable (test frequency). Unfortunately, we cannot choose between these two alternative interpretations. On the other hand, if this study had used random assignment of subjects, these alternative interpretations would have been eliminated and strong confident conclusions could have been drawn.

When quasi-experiments are conducted using an experimental group and a comparison group, there is always concern about the equality of the two groups since random assignment is absent. Any differences between the two groups could be due to the treatment that only the experimental group received or to differences between subjects in the two groups (brighter, healthier, more motivated, etc.). Researchers conducting quasi-experiments may try to minimize subject differences by selecting subjects as similar as possible for the two groups, but this is very difficult. (See Matching.) Also, there is no way to be sure that the composition of subjects in the two groups will be equal; a random assignment procedure comes closest to doing this.

4.4 CORRELATIONAL RESEARCH (EX POST FACTO)

We have seen that research may be subscribed under three broad classes: experimental, quasi-experimental, and correlational. Recall that, in contrast to true experiments, quasi-experiments lack random assignment of subjects. **Correlational research** involves searching out records of a specified population and ascertaining the relationships among the variables of interest. Such research involves neither random assignment nor manipulation of an experimental variable.

CORRELATIONAL RESEARCH   Selecting a population and ascertaining the relationship among variables of interest; does not use random assignment nor manipulation of conditions.

The two research procedures encountered most frequently, and also most sharply contrasted with each other, are the experimental and correlational ones. Again, we repeat the important differences between them. The experimental approach studies the relationship between manipulated variables and uses random assignment, while the correlational approach studies the relationship between unmanipulated variables and does not use random assignment. We view these research methods, and others discussed in this chapter, as complementary techniques rather than competing ones. As you shall see, they often serve different purposes and provide answers to different questions.

Random assignment of subjects and the manipulation of variables are absent in correlational research because the events of interest are naturally occurring. The interest is in determining how naturally occurring measures on one variable are related to naturally occurring measures on another variable. Often, in psychology, the two naturally occurring variables are behavioral measures.

The correlational approach is sometimes referred to as the study of individual differences because emphasis is placed on differences among individuals. For example, assume that we have a distribution of individual scores on one measure (Intelligence Test Scores—Test 1) and a distribution of individual scores on another measure (Final Exam Scores—Test 2). The question asked of these data by a correlational approach is whether differences among individual scores on one variable (Test 1) are related to differences among individual scores on the other variable (Test 2).

A statistical procedure called *correlational analysis* is used to ascertain the extent of the relationship among individual scores on the two variables (tests). This emphasis on individual differences contrasts with an experimental approach where interest is in comparing the *average* performance of a group in one condition with the *average* performance of a group in another condition.

As you may recall from your introductory statistics course, calculating a correlation between two distributions of scores (scores on Test 1 and scores on Test 2) results in a number called a **correlation coefficient.** The strength of the relationship is indicated by the numerical value of the coefficient and its direction is indicated by a + or − sign. If the individual scores are unrelated (no relationship), the numerical value of the coefficient is 0; if the scores are perfectly related on the two distributions, the numerical value is either a −1.0 or a +1.0. Thus the numerical value of the correlation coefficient may range from a −1.0 to 0 or from 0 to a +1.0, with variations in between. A positive relationship indicates that individuals scoring high on one distribution also tend to score high on the other distribution and that those scoring low on one tend to score low on the other. Put more simply, as individual scores on one distribution increase, their scores on the other increases. If the relationship is negative, then individuals scoring high on one distribution tend to score low on the other and those scoring low on one tend to score high on the other. Again, put simply, as individual scores on one distribution increases, their scores on the other decreases.

CORRELATION COEFFICIENT   a quantitative expression of the degree of relationship between variables.

A curvilinear relationship is also possible. In this case, it indicates that as individual scores increase on one distribution they tend also to increase on the other up to a point; beyond this point, further increases in scores on one distribution are associated with decreases in scores on the other. When measures on two variables are unrelated, i.e., correlation coefficient = 0, knowing an individual's score on one variable is not at all helpful in predicting his or her score on the other variable. As the correlation becomes greater than zero, the accuracy of predicting the individual's score on one variable, simply by knowing his or her score on the other, increases. And when the correlation is perfect, i.e., +1.0 or −1.0, prediction of an individual's score on one variable from knowing his or her score on the other can be made without error.

There are many different correlational techniques available for researchers to choose, each appropriate for different kinds of data. The most common technique is the product-moment correlation where each variable is represented by a continuum of scores. But other correlational procedures are available that deal with variables that are represented by ranks, true dichotomies, artificial dichotomies, or categories. We do not intend to describe these procedures further. However, for those interested in pursuing the topic, there are several excellent books that provide a detailed description of the procedures along with ways to calculate them (e.g., McNemar, 1969). Correlational methods are used in virtually every scientific and professional discipline and they serve many purposes. As we noted in Chapter 3, these methods are excellent for assessing the reliability of measuring instruments (tests). This is the case whether dealing with internal consistency, test-retest reliability, or alternate-form reliability. In studies requiring that different observers rate various aspects of behavior (see Chapter 6), correlational methods are used to establish the extent of agreement among observers, i.e., "How reliably do they make their observations?"

Correlational methods are also used in answering questions concerning test validity. For example, when we ask, "How well does performance on a test (predictor) account for performance on a job?" we are using a correlational method. Regarding the latter, it is often the case that our interests are in prediction rather than in a cause-effect analysis. Once we know the correlation between two measures, we are able to predict one form of behavior from knowledge of the other. For example, there is a correlation between IQ test scores and success, as measured by grades, in school. Over the years considerable data have been gathered on this relationship and it is quite well established. With a quantitative measure of the relationship (i.e., correlation coefficient), we can predict with some accuracy success in school simply by knowing a person's score on the IQ test.

Similar examples emphasizing prediction occur when test scores are used as screening devices for selecting those students most likely to succeed in graduate school, medical school, law school, etc. In the latter cases, individuals take examinations over certain specified material; their scores are obtained and prediction formulas then applied. Thus, predictions can be made on large numbers of individuals almost immediately after obtaining their score. As we have noted, the accuracy of the prediction depends upon the strength of the relationship between the two forms of behavior. The stronger (higher) the correlation, the better the prediction.

Discovering the relationship between two variables can be very valuable, especially if one behavior that can be easily and inexpensively measured permits us to predict behavior that is difficult, inaccessible, and expensive to measure. Knowing the relationship may also be of great practical value, especially for educational systems. For example, special programs may be instituted to prevent problems from occurring among those in need of help and to enrich those who are in need of challenge.

Another example of correlational research that has proven useful relates to diagnostic purposes. Once a disorder is observed, a search can be made for other behaviors or conditions that may vary (correlate) with it. The latter is especially the case if the disorder is difficult to detect or to diagnose accurately. If the search is successful and the correlation strong, then both the speed and accuracy of identifying the disorder may be substantially increased.

While working on this chapter, a number of articles appeared in newspaper accounts and in popular magazines dealing with correlational research. Some of these accounts are found in Table 4.1. They give an idea of the variety of problems that can be studied using correlational procedures. We do not describe the results of these reports since we have not read the primary source from which they came, nor have we evaluated the care with which the studies were conducted. After reading the section on Third Variable Problems and Directionality, you may want to return to this table to evaluate the extent to which these two problems may be present in the description found in Table 4.1. You will most likely conclude that many alternative explanations may be offered for the observed relationships.

Table 4.1
Examples of some recent correlational research finding a relationship between variables.

Type of criminal offense and probability of skipping bail

Marijuana and body tissue damage

Education and political attitude

Behavior problems and time spent in prison

Body weight and longevity and health

Male/Female and scores on standardized mathematics exam

Schizophrenia and chemical substance in body liquid

Tonsillectomy and the development of other illness

Dietary factors and the amount of high density lipoprotein in the blood

Frequency of advertising and gross sales

Coffee consumption and pancreatic cancer

Age and creativity

Alcohol consumed and longevity

Aggression and television viewing

The usefulness and value of a correlational approach are most apparent when studying the effects of naturally occurring events that simply cannot be studied in laboratory settings. This approach may be the only available method when ethical considerations prevent manipulating the phenomena (e.g., abortion, drug use, sexual practices, serious illness, suicide), when the phenomena are impossible to manipulate (e.g., male/female, black/white, temperament), or when studying the effects of natural disasters such as earthquakes, fires, violent storms, etc.

While correlational research allows lawful relationships to be discovered that can lead to precise predictions, causal statements can be made only with great risk since they lack random assignment, active manipulation, and rigorous control over extraneous factors. With all ex post facto research, the "independent" and "dependent" variables have already occurred. Such things as gender, group membership, racial characteristics, birth place, and age are historical events over which researchers have little control. They are determined before the researcher arrives on the scene. The measures that are correlated are often personality variables or variables related to the characteristics of people. These variables generally cannot be manipulated. There are exceptions, of course. Some behavioral measures may be manipulated but only with great difficulty. As we have seen, a question of ethics often arises, e.g., cigarette smoking and lung cancer or cardiovascular disease, exercise and cardiovascular problems. We will give more details of this research in later chapters.

4.4.1 Importance of Correlational Research

Stating that a causal relationship cannot be established by correlational research is not intended to devalue the great importance of this type of research. It is often extraordinarily important both in a practical and in a theoretical way. Research with this method has had a marked influence on the lives of many people and on policy formulations of legislatures, decisions of the judiciary, and actions of private enterprise. A few well known examples are: correlation of smoking habits with lung cancer led to a warning on cigarette packs; the relation between exercise and lowered rates of cardiovascular problems has stimulated increases in jogging, swimming, tennis, bicycling; correlations between socioeconomic conditions and educational proficiency provided a rationale for decisions involving equality in education and school busing; and correlations between particulate matter in the air (pollution) and morbidity rates provided the impetus for clean air legislation.

4.4.2 Direction of Control and Third Variable Problems

Discussion of these problems will illustrate the difficulties of inferring cause-effect when dealing with correlational data. With correlational research, we usually refer to **predictor** and criterion measures rather than independent and dependent variables. The measure (or behavior) being predicted is the criterion variable, and the measure (or behavior) from which the prediction is made is the predictor variable. The use of this terminology emphasizes prediction rather than suggesting a cause-effect relationship. However, there are occasions when individuals, be they scientists, writers, or laypeople, come to cause-effect conclusions based on correlational data. They face a risk of drawing false conclusions when doing so. In effect, they must deal with two different problems: the direction of control problem and the third variable problem. We will give examples of both.

PREDICTOR   the measure used to predict the criterion measure in correlational research.

To infer a cause-effect relationship requires that we specify the direction of control. Assume that variable X and variable Y are highly correlated such that increases in one are associated with increases in the other. Does variable X cause variable Y to vary, or does variable Y cause variable X to vary? With some relationships the answer concerning the direction of control seems obvious but in other instances it can be difficult to specify. Take the often-noted positive relationship between physical activity and cardiovascular health. Regularly active individuals appear to have fewer circulatory problems. On the surface, it would seem that exercise causes better cardiovascular health. However, is this necessarily the case? Is it not possible that individuals with better cardiovascular health engage in more frequent exercise because they are better able to do so than people with heart and circulatory problems?

We will give another example of the "direction of control" problem. Let us say that a high, positive correlation exists between frequency of drug use (variable X) and difficulties in school (variable Y). We could say that the use of drugs were the cause of experiencing difficulties in school. On the other hand, an equally plausible conclusion is that having difficulties in school caused the individual to use drugs.

The fact that in both of these examples we have a high correlation between variable X and variable Y does not help at all in our determining the direction of control. Our risk of coming to a wrong causal conclusion is not reduced. The only way to reduce the risk is to bring additional information to bear on the issue or, when permitted, to attempt an experimental approach and manipulate the important variables.

Our problem is intensified in that the risk of error is even greater when we consider possible "third variable problems" that may be present. In our last illustration, instead of drug use causing school problems, or school problems causing drug use, a third factor (fourth, fifth, etc.) could have caused increases in both drug use and school problems. For example, anxiety, depression, low self-esteem, or conflict within the home could give rise to both increases in drug use and increases in school problems. In this case, then, variables X and Y are related only through some "third" variable.

It is sometimes difficult to avoid a causal conclusion and to maintain the proper perspective when viewing correlational data. The consistent, highly publicized, positive correlation between cigarette smoking and cancer seems causal. The more cigarettes smoked, the higher the incidence of cancer. This relationship seems to suggest that the smoking of cigarettes controls whether or not cancer will occur. Yet, strictly speaking, we cannot say this. A third factor may be involved. (See Box 4.2 for additional examples.) It is possible that only certain people with this factor smoke and that these people would contract the disease whether or not they did so. The more of this factor present the greater would be smoking and the possibility of contracting the disease. If this were so, then increases in both smoking and cancer result from this unspecified third factor. The latter is very unlikely and, in fact, the few recent experimental studies that have been done suggest that it is certain ingredients in tobacco that may cause cancer. Third variable problems are sometimes very difficult to detect and to deal with. Further, you can never be sure that they are absent when using correlational designs. However, some techniques are available for addressing the problem.

4.4.3   Addressing Directionality and Third Variable Problems

There are several methods available that attempt to deal with the problems of directionality and third variables. While these methods are sometimes useful they do not solve the preceding two problems. Each has its problems. A full description of these methods is beyond the scope of this text. We mention them here for those of you who would like to pursue the problems further. A procedure that is sometimes useful for addressing the directionality problem is a *time-lagged correlational design*. The essential aspect of this procedure is to determine a correlation between two variables at Time 1 and again later at Time 2. This technique is also referred to as *cross-lagged panel correlation*. A full description can be found in Kenny (1979). The third variable problem has been addressed by some using a correlational procedure referred to as *partial correlation*. In this case, if a third variable is thought to be a factor affecting the correlation between variables X and Y, then the partial correlation technique can be used to eliminate its effects (Nunnally, 1967). The result of this procedure is a correlation between X and Y uninfluenced by the third variable. Another procedure that is sometimes used to eliminate the third variable problem is **matching**. In this case only data from subjects matched (who are the same) on the third variable are analyzed.

MATCHING   pairing subjects according to their similarity on a predictor variable.

At first glance, matching as a technique for ruling out third variable interpretations seems like an attractive solution. That is, if only individuals who were the same or highly similar on these third variables were assessed, and if the relationship between the two variables of interest still existed, then the third variable considerations could be dispensed with. The thought is a good one, but in practice problems exist; also, matching can be difficult to achieve. One problem is that researchers cannot be sure they have considered the relevant third variables. Some may exist that have not been considered. Another problem is that matching on one variable can sometimes unmatch individuals on other variables. There are other problems also. An article of Meehl (1970) describes some of these for those of you wanting to pursue the issue further. A more serious problem is faced by researchers when they attempt to match on several variables (e.g., brightness, education, motivation, class). The problem is simply in getting a sufficiently large sample. To select a sample of less than fifty cases, matched on several variables, an initial sample of over 2,000 individuals was required by one researcher (Chapin, 1955)! Some of the major drawbacks of matching are discussed in later chapters. Finally, we must mention that some promising procedures that deal systematically with the issues of correlation and causality are available in a recent book by Kenny (1979).

4.4.4 Correlational Ruling Out Factors

The correlation between cigarette smoking and cancer (and heart disease) can be used to illustrate an important aspect of correlational research. Had *no relationship* been found, we could have *ruled out causal factors* and there would be little interest in pursuing the problem further. Therefore, an important contribution of correlational methods may be in a negative sense: In the absence of a relationship, there is no need to devote time to an experimental analysis of the problem to identify the controlling or causal factor.

Perhaps an example contrasting the correlational method with the experimental method would be helpful in illustrating why a causal relationship can be made with an experimental approach and not a correlational one. As noted, in a correlational study involving cigarette consumption and incidence of cancer, a positive relationship was found. While most people of sound mind would be alerted to a possible causal link between the two, a strong relationship regarding cause cannot be made.* We indicated that it is possible that a third factor may be the cause, e.g., people susceptible to cancer also smoke, but the disease would occur whether or not they smoked. Or we could argue that individuals who smoke also engage in other activities that may be related to cancer and that smoking is not the problem. Or, we could say that individ-

---

*While the majority of data between smoking and cancer are correlational, some are not. Also, belief in a causal relationship is enhanced when the correlation between illness and smoking is high for those who continue to smoke but lower for those who stop.

uals with certain dietary habits are susceptible to both smoking and cancer, etc.

The tobacco industry today argues that a causal link has not been clearly established in humans. To decide the question, an experiment is necessary. It would not be difficult to design a research project to answer the question of smoking as a cause for illness. However, serious problems of ethics and practicality prevent its implementation. We would randomly select a large number of twelve- to fourteen-year-old male and female students from different geographic areas. We could then randomly assign them to conditions A, B, C, D, and E—corresponding to levels 0, ½, 1, 2, and 3 packs of cigarettes a day. We would then follow them up over the years with annual physical examinations and also record specific measures known to be related to tissue problems. We could then determine whether there was a systematic relationship between our independent variable (smoking) and our dependent variable (measures of illness, etc.). Obviously, the study cannot and should not be done. However, experimental studies have been conducted with nonhuman species.

Mice, rats, and dogs have been used to study the relationship between the exposure to tobacco ingredients and cancer. A variety of procedures have been used, such as "painting" the substances in tobacco on the skin, confining the animals to enclosed rooms where controlled amount of cigarette smoke may be dispersed, and teaching animals to smoke. These studies have established that tobacco is hazardous to a laboratory animal's health. We have stated several times that it is improper to draw cause-effect conclusions from correlational data. To say this is not to say that such a relationship does not exist. It may. To determine its existence requires other research strategies.

BOX 4.2   SOME EXAMPLES OF THE "THIRD" VARIABLE PROBLEM
Ex Post Facto Research

The "third" variable problem is not intended to imply that there is another third variable that must be considered. The intention is to emphasize that there may be other unspecified variables (third, fourth, or fifth) that must be considered. Again, examples will be helpful.

An example of the "third variable" problem relates to educational level. There are statistics available that suggest that there is a correlation between average income and those who complete high school and college. Those completing high school earn more than those that do not and those that complete college earn more than those who do not. The conclusion that is generally drawn from these correlations is that a high school or college degree is responsible for the higher income. Again, this research (ex post facto) does not permit such a conclusion. Other alternative explanations are equally compelling. It may very well be that there is a substantial correlation between being bright and the income earned. One could then argue that only the brighter students complete high school or college. Therefore in our example the observed relationship is not really between education and income; instead, it is a result of brightness being related to both factors. Those who are brighter are most likely to finish their schooling and most likely to get better paying jobs.

High density lipoproteins (HDL) have captured the interest of the medical profession. Research literature is growing to suggest that high levels of HDL protect against athrosclerosis and heart attack. Most of the research comes from epidemiological studies linking increased concentration of HDL in the blood to decreased risk of heart attacks. In contrast, high levels of low density lipoproteins (LDL) are linked to increased risk. Researchers are now looking for ways of increasing HDL and decreasing LDL to further test the notion that HDL are good for you and LDL are not. A researcher at Stanford University was interested in whether running/jogging might increase HDL. He compared lipoprotein patterns of runners/joggers between the ages of thirty-five and fifty-nine with sedentary nonrunners in the same age group, and he found substantially higher HDL levels in runners. These findings were made public and national publications touted jogging as a way of increasing HDL levels and thus decreasing health risks. This may be the case, i.e., physical activity may be helpful, but the research noted does not permit these conclusions to be drawn. As you probably noted, since neither random assignment nor manipulation was present, the research is considered to be ex post facto. There are other variables or factors that could be used to interpret the relationship between jogging and HDL. One is that runners are leaner, often weighing far less than sedentary individuals. Second, runners smoke less than nonrunners and this too could be a factor. Third, dietary factors may be markedly different between runners and nonrunners. There may also be other factors involving life style. These "third" variable factors could be the important consideration.

Comparisons between vegetarians and nonvegetarians also illustrate the third variable problem. Some reports indicate that vegetarians enjoy a longer, healthier life than nonvegetarians. The question is whether vegetarianism is responsible for this. Vegetarians may live longer but for other reasons. They generally weigh less and it may be "thinness" that relates to longevity. Also, thinness is associated with lower blood pressure and it may be the latter that is the important factor, and not whether you are a vegetarian or if you are thin. Other factors must be considered. It may be that vegetarians are more health conscious and eat a more balanced diet, exercise regularly, avoid smoking, etc.

The third variable problem found with ex post facto research places restrictions on the kind of conclusions that are permitted. Obviously, cause-effect interpretations are hazardous. The "treatments" in our examples had already been applied to previously formed groups. Random assignment of subjects to conditions or groups and manipulation of the independent variable were absent.

4.5   RETROSPECTIVE AND PROSPECTIVE STUDIES

Closely related to ex post facto experiments are retrospective studies. Both are directed backward in time and focus on events that have already taken place. However, in ex post facto research, the investigator usually "digs out" data from the past based upon available records. In **retrospective research,** the subjects are actively involved in the data collection process. For example, considerable research has been directed to assessing the role of stressful life events as factors in various diseases. Social stresses such as marriage, divorce, loss of job, death of a loved one, etc., are observed to be related to cardiac deaths, myocardial infarctions, diabetes, leukemia, accidents, etc. In retrospective studies of this problem, large numbers of people are asked to report their life changes (past events) and histories of illness during a previous period, e.g., the last ten years. They are also asked to complete a social adjustment scale of some kind. Based on this information, a relationship is looked for between life stresses and subsequent illness. The obtained relationships are usually very small (Rabkin and Struening, 1976). Unfortunately, several important sources of error in the measurement of life events can be found in retrospective studies. These errors include selective memory, denial of certain events, and over-reporting.

RETROSPECTIVE RESEARCH   subjects are asked to compile records on life changes over a specified *prior* period.

A different approach is used in **prospective research.** Again, a large sample is used, but the time period is oriented to future events. A period of time is selected, e.g., one year, two years, etc., and investigators look for an association between number and intensity of life events and the probability of specific illnesses in the immediate future. An advantage of prospective studies over retrospective is that such factors as selective memory and denial are less of a problem. With this approach, again, only a modest relationship is observed (Rabkin and Struening, 1976).

PROSPECTIVE RESEARCH   subjects keep ongoing records of life changes over a specified *future* period.

4.6   CORRELATIONAL METHOD—THE EX POST FACTO "EXPERIMENT"

At times, caution must be exercised in deciding whether a study is correlational or experimental. If the determination is not made, an erroneous conclusion may result. A type of study that can masquerade as a genuine experiment is the ex post facto "experiment." It is essentially the same as the correlational research we discussed earlier except that the techniques of analysis are different. It derives its name from the fact that the data are obtained from past records (i.e., after the fact). It mimics an experiment in that comparisons are made between two or more groups of individuals with similar backgrounds who were exposed to different conditions as a result of their natural histories. We then measure the subjects on a dependent variable of interest to determine whether or not statistically meaningful differences exist between the experimental groups. If reliable differences are found, should we conclude that they were due to the historical differences we found in the past records? The answer is no.

Note that the ex post facto experiment uses neither random assignment nor active manipulation of the independent variable. However, the intent of this type of research is precisely that of a true experiment but the problems encountered in drawing conclusions are very different. A concrete example will illustrate our point.

An instructor in a college math course thinks that she sees a relationship between performance in college math courses and whether students had the "old math" or "new math" techniques in grade school. She decides to do a study to determine whether her observations are indeed accurate ones. She looks up the grade school records of a large number of college students taking her college math course. On the basis of these records she selects fifty students who received "new math" and another fifty students who received "old math" techniques. She then gathers the two groups of students together and gives them a college math proficiency test. Her experimental design would look no different from that of a true experiment.

Treatment Condition	Dependent Variable
Group 1—Students with new math	Math Proficiency Test
Group 2—Students with old math	Math Proficiency Test

We have a "treatment" condition and a comparison or control group (old math)—in this case both of which have already occurred. The treatment versus comparison group is the same thing that makes up a true experiment. But any conclusions drawn from our example must be guarded and weak. Why? Obviously, our subjects were not assigned randomly, nor did we manipulate the conditions. They were derived from past records.

The groups may be biased in different and unknown ways. It is quite possible that those who received new math in grade school are very different from those who received the old math. They may have been chosen because of their skills (or lack of skills) in mathematics. It is also possible that new math programs were offered only by wealthy and progressive school districts. Thus, it is quite possible differences existed in the student populations from which the treatment groups were drawn. Perhaps only urban-industrialized communities had new math programs but rural-suburban communities did not. The point is that this is all idle speculation. We simply do not know the many reasons that some students received new math and some old math. Because we could not randomly assign our students to the two groups, systematic subject bias is a distinct possibility. Our two student groups could have differed in their average math proficiency score for any number of reasons other than "new" or "old" math. (A true experiment would have required that we previously randomly assign a number of students from the same school district to new math and approximately an equal number to old math classes, holding other factors constant. Then, years later, we would administer a math proficiency test in college.)

Two questions, if asked, could quickly and accurately allow you to identify whether the experiment is an ex post facto one: (1) Did the researcher have control over assigning subjects randomly? i.e., did the researcher assign subjects randomly to groups? (2) Second, did the researcher actively manipulate the independent variable or had it already occurred? If random assignments was not used then it was not a true experiment. Now the choice is deciding between a quasi-experiment or an ex post facto one. If a variable was not actively manipulated at the time of the research, then the experiment is an ex post facto one and the conclusions must be much weaker. Keep in mind that in ex post facto research those that make up the groups in itself constitute the "treatments." There is no treatment other than membership in a group, e.g., male versus female, heavy versus thin, tall versus short, joggers versus nonjoggers, dogmatic versus nondogmatic, etc. A quasi-experiment, in contrast, has independent groups with no known differences that receive different treatment conditions manipulated by the experimenter. (See Box 4.3 for an additional example of an ex post facto "experiment.")

BOX 4.3   THE EX POST FACTO "EXPERIMENT"

Another example of an ex post facto experiment will help you to discriminate between it and experiments in which the independent variable is, in fact, manipulated. In this example our interests are in the reactions of anxious and nonanxious subjects to a loud noise. Do not confuse the loud noise with the "treatment" condition. It is not a treatment or independent variable, since both groups receive it. The noise and the reaction to it are our dependent variable measures, i.e., the task that all subjects perform. The treatment consists of membership in a group based on whatever characteristics the researcher may be interested in. In the present example these characteristics are anxious and nonanxious subjects. Let's get on with the example.

We could give a personality test (e.g., the Taylor Manifest Anxiety Scale) to a large population of students and then select participants on the basis of their scores. We might select ten students who score very high and ten students who score very low on the anxiety scale. Since high anxious and low anxious subjects are our interest and, as it were, our treatment, they cannot be randomly assigned to different groups. Therefore, our "independent" variable is high versus low anxiety. Our "dependent" variable is the startle reaction to loud noise. Assume that we find our high anxious subjects respond to noise more strongly than do our low anxious subjects. Can we conclude that they did so because of anxiety? No, we cannot. We are again plagued by the "third variable" problem. Since we could not consider random assignment because our interest is in the groups as constituted, it is possible that our subject groups differ in many ways other than anxiety. Their responses could be related to how well they sleep. It may be that high anxious subjects sleep less well than others and that *any* subject, regardless of anxiety, who did not get adequate sleep would perform like high anxious subjects. Perhaps it is the case that high anxious subjects drink much more coffee

than do low anxious subjects. If we assume that coffee affects the startle response, then *any* subjects who drink much coffee, anxious or nonanxious, would
perform in similar ways. There are any number of other alternative interpretations allowed by this ex post facto "experiment" that would not be possible if the
research was either a quasi- or a true experiment.

4.6.1   Summing Up—Why Use Correlational Designs?

We have said much about true experiments and we have described their
strength in drawing strong, confident conclusions. A word of caution is advisable. An experiment may use random assignment and involve manipulating
the treatment variable and still be essentially worthless as a basis for drawing
conclusions. It is essential that rigorous controls, careful execution, planning,
thoughtfulness, etc., accompany a valid design.

Experimental or manipulative research is a very powerful tool for generating a scientific data base for drawing cause-effect conclusions, for testing hypotheses and evaluating theory, for answering questions and satisfying our intellectual curiosity, for systematic manipulation of variables, and, at times, for
discovering principles that may be relevant to everyday life. This being the
case, you may ask, "In view of its limitations, why use correlational designs or
engage in ex post facto experimentation?" The answer is relatively straightforward. Many variables of interest simply cannot be randomly assigned to subjects. If we wish to study the effects of a dependent measure on such naturally
occurring variables as gender, ethnic background, intelligence, temperament,
or body size, we cannot say to the subjects, "For the purposes of this experiment, I am going to declare you a female, or a black, or a person with an IQ of
130. Shazam! You're a black!" On the other hand, some variables may be subject to experimental manipulation but such factors as opportunity, economics,
or ethical concerns may rule out their use. Thus, we may ask, "Do individuals
who have left hemispheric brain damage show greater verbal impairment than
those who have comparable damage to the right hemisphere?" Obviously, we
are not going to conduct brain surgery on human subjects to answer this question. However, if we are to shed any light on the question, we are forced to
look into the histories of people who have suffered brain damage as a result of
adverse circumstances. Similarly, we might look at drug addicts, after the fact,
in hopes of finding some leads to "how they got that way."

4.7   ADVANTAGES AND DISADVANTAGES OF
LABORATORY EXPERIMENTS

4.7.1   Some Advantages

As we have emphasized, one of the defining characteristics of true experiments
is the random assignment of subjects. The procedure allows us to rule out alternative hypotheses that relate to possible bias in the makeup of treatment

groups. Furthermore, with a true experiment, we can specify precisely the independent variable and firmly establish control over the amount of it that we will use. We can introduce, withdraw, or otherwise manipulate the independent variable as we see fit. It can be manipulated individually or in combination with other factors that we consider important. Secondary variables can also be rigorously controlled, thus reducing the prospects of confounding. Having rigorous control over the experimental situation allows us to study relatively "pure" relationships, thus permitting stronger, less ambiguous causal conclusions to be drawn. Most investigators agree that, to establish the reliability of a relationship, more than a single study is necessary. (See Section 8.7, Converging Operations.) Experiments can be replicated (repeated) either literally or with systematic variations from the original. Several different types of replications permit us to assess the reliability of our findings (Lykken, 1968; Sidman, 1960).

Finally, laboratory experiments permit better prior preparation, thereby reducing errors of measurement. In fact, a number of dependent variables routinely used in the laboratory are not readily available for use in the field or outside of the laboratory, e.g., electroencephalograph (EEG), electromyograph (EMG), heart rate (HR), blood pressure (BP), and galvanic skin response (GSR).

4.7.2 Some Disadvantages

To a large extent, whether or not a feature of laboratory experimentation is considered a disadvantage depends upon our goals as researchers. If we are seeking theoretical development, then the features listed here may not constitute disadvantages. On the other hand, if our goal is to generalize our findings to practical situations, then the disadvantages we list are likely to be important.

Because of humane considerations, a major disadvantage of true experiments relates to ethical constraints. In laboratory research involving noxious stimulation or threats, the strength of the independent variable is limited to weak values. This is especially the case with human subjects; to a lesser extent it also pertains to nonhuman subjects. The point can be brought into sharp focus simply by contrasting the laboratory research with studies of some of our recent natural disasters—fires, floods, tornadoes, earthquakes. Clearly, some things can be studied only under natural conditions since these conditions cannot be imposed ethically in research subjects.

Some writers have pointed an accusing finger at the generality (**external validity**) of the findings of laboratory research. They argue that such laboratory research is often trivial in the sense that it does not readily generalize to important "real-life" situations. The findings are restricted to the narrow interests of the laboratory. The implication is that other forms of research would solve "real-life" problems more rapidly and better. This position may be correct but this is an empirical issue and it remains to be seen. As we noted in Chapter 2, the Comroe and Dripps study and the National Science Foundation study (TRACES) gave very high marks to basic research, much of which is laboratory research. In fact, basic research ultimately played a far greater role in advancing our knowledge in applied areas than did applied research. We should also note that the extent to which results from the laboratory can be generalized to other situations, species, etc., relates to the phenomena studied. Since considerable physiological similarity exists across many species, findings dealing with the physiology of organisms may be very generalizable. One final comment: In some cases researchers have striven to create laboratory conditions that, to a remarkable degree, resemble natural conditions. When they are successful in achieving this end, generalizability of the findings should be high.

EXTERNAL VALIDITY   the extent to which research findings can be generalized to other levels of the variable, other settings, and to the broader population.

4.8 OTHER RESEARCH METHODS COMMONLY USED IN PSYCHOLOGY

As you know from your experience with the psychological literature, psychologists are interested in asking many different kinds of questions. Furthermore, some psychologists are strongly oriented toward answering practical questions, whereas others direct their energies toward strong theoretical issues. Those that are practically oriented attempt to answer these questions in a way that will permit them to generalize to "real-life" situations. Thus, both the "type" of questions they ask and the "type" of answer they wish to provide often dictates the research methods they will use. This is true also for those interested more in theoretical development. With these considerations in mind, let us look at some other research methods commonly used in psychology.

4.8.1 Naturalistic Observations

Naturalistic observations take place under natural conditions or under "real-life" conditions. Such observations contrast with those in experimental settings where considerable prior control is possible, where events can be manipulated, and the observations may be repeated. When using naturalistic observation, we observe nature without imposing change. However, the observations are carefully planned and systematized. Consequently, the data can be organized in a meaningful way to permit analysis and interpretation.

Naturalistic observation is the oldest method for the study of behavior or other phenomenon. One of the most accurate sciences (in terms of prediction) is restricted largely to observation (astronomy). Ethologists are people who study animal behavior under natural conditions and use natural observation almost exclusively. Jane Goodall's work with primates in Africa has resulted in some fascinating observations regarding their social interactions. Development and personality psychologists have published extremely informative observational studies of children interacting under natural conditions. Jean Piaget's theory of cognitive development in children was based on naturalistic observation. We have been able to identify migration patterns in fish, fowl, and mammals by "tagging" studies. Naturalistic observation of primitive cultures has given us insight into the range of variation in human institutions. It must be emphasized that natural observation is not anecdotal and casual but, instead, systematic and carefully planned. The observer must be sufficiently skilled to distinguish between an observation and an interpretation.

4.8.2   Case Histories

With this method, one or more individuals are carefully examined over time. Biographical data, interviews, or psychological tests may be components of the case histories. Some examples of case histories are prepared by reconstructing the biography of the individual from memory and records (retrospective). On occasion, a case history may be prospective. It does not rely on memory or records since measurement is taken at periodically planned intervals.

There are two important considerations in a case history approach. One is to search for some regularity or patterning to behavior that might suggest some principle around which it is organized. The second involves additional case studies to confirm the previously observed regularity or pattern. Such information may permit generalization to other situations or persons.

Case studies often arise when it is impossible or unethical to conduct an experiment. At other times, they are closely related to naturalistic observations. Freud's insights into behavior problems were largely based on case studies of his patients. Piaget's theory of intellectual development stems from his intensive observations of his own three children. Case studies of individuals suffering brain damage have been undertaken to assess the extent to which functions are regained.

4.8.3   Survey Research

Survey is a broad term that often includes interviews, questionnaires, and public records. We will discuss both questionnaires and interviews but first let us make a few general comments regarding surveys in the broad sense. A survey is an attempt to estimate opinions, attitudes, and characteristics of a population based on a sample. The Kinsey Reports in 1948 and 1953 provide a well known example. Kinsey and his group interviewed over 10,000 men and women concerning sexual behavior and attitudes. Unfortunately, the participants were not chosen randomly. It is therefore debatable whether the findings can be generalized to the general population. Others, surveying sexual beliefs and practices, have started with a sample of individuals representative of the population. However, only about 20 percent of those contacted were willing to share their beliefs and practices. The latter can hardly be regarded as representative of the population. Individuals who are willing to divulge intimate information are probably different in important ways from those who are not. If survey results are to apply to a population, the sample chosen must be representative. (See Chapter 9.) When this principle is violated, serious problems can occur and risk of error is high. For example, in the presidential election of 1936 between Alf Landon and F.D. Roosevelt, the *Literary Digest* conducted a poll concerning voting preferences. Based on the results of their poll, the *Literary Digest* predicted a Landon (Republican) victory. The outcome of the election? Roosevelt by a landslide. This survey is a classic case of the unrepresentative sample. The magazine polled only those whose names appeared on lists of telephone subscribers and automobile owners. Since 1936 was a depression year, only the wealthier had cars and telephones—hardly a representative group. Affluent people tend to favor more conservative politics. Thus, if only the wealthier citizens had been allowed to vote, the Republican candidate would have won by a landslide. (See Box 9.3 for additional examples.)

Surveys, under different guises, have been used to obtain information on political opinions, consumer preferences, health care needs, attitudes toward the draft, abortion, ERA, etc. The four most familiar are the U.S. Census, the Gallup Poll, the Roper Poll, and the Harris Poll.

Questionnaires   The questionnaire is more than simply a list of questions or forms to be filled out. (See Sellitz, Wrightsman, and Cook, 1976.) When properly constructed, a questionnaire can be used as a scientific instrument to obtain data from large numbers of individuals. Construction of a useful questionnaire that minimizes interfering problems requires experience, skill, thoughtfulness, and time. A major advantage of the questionnaire is that data can be obtained on large numbers of subjects quickly and relatively inexpensively. Further, the sample can be very large and geographically representative. If necessary, anonymity can be easily maintained. When constructed properly, the data can be organized easily, tabulated, and analyzed. Because of these apparent advantages, the use of the questionnaire is a popular method.

There are two broad classes of questionnaires: descriptive and analytical. *Descriptive questionnaires* are usually restricted to factual information, often biographical, which is usually accessible by other means. Job application forms and U.S. Census questionnaires are typically of this type. *Analytical questionnaires* deal more with information related to attitudes or opinions, e.g., "Do you favor a Proposition 13 type of amendment for our state?"

The results of a questionnaire are about as useful as the care and thought that went into their preparation and dissemination. Just as in normal social intercourse, the way questions are formulated and posed may present problems. They may be ambiguous; they may suggest the answer that the researcher "wants"; and they may contain loaded words. Ambiguity is relatively easy to eliminate. A pilot project, limited to a small number of respondents, will usually uncover sources of ambiguity of which the researcher was unaware. These may then be corrected.

As much as we might wish it to be, completing questionnaires is not a neutral task, devoid of feelings and emotions. Often respondents are somewhat apprehensive about how they will appear in the researcher's eye. They want to look good and do well. Consequently, their responses may reflect more their interpretations of the investigator's desires than their own beliefs, feelings, or opinions. This is referred to as *demand characteristics*. We will say more about this later. Obviously questions should be stated in a neutral way and not in a way that suggests a particular response. A fundamental requirement is that the question should be answerable. If respondents are given answers from which to choose, the options should be clear and independent. Also, different results can occur when open-ended or closed-ended questions are used. In some cases the questionnaire is sensitive to position effects. Respondents are more likely to skip items placed toward the end of a questionnaire and the answers are also slightly different when answered.

More attention has been given to response bias than to other sources of possible bias and contamination. As we noted earlier, results can be markedly affected by the sample on which they are based. The problem of sampling bias is compounded in mailed surveys because of the low return rates. The actual sample on which the data analyses are based is generally a subsample of the original sample. Low returns make it difficult to assess the representativeness of the final sample. It is safe to assume that it is biased and that those participating in the survey are different in some way from those who did not. How important is this difference? It may be considerable or it may be trivial. Since the importance cannot be assessed, any generalizations based on low returns must be restricted. For this reason, it is important to know the return rate on survey research. Unfortunately, some studies fail to provide this information. Other things being equal, the higher the return rate, the better the survey.

There are a number of factors that affect return rates. Some are quite costly, so that economic factors must be balanced against the greater generality permitted by higher rates of return. Methods to increase return rate include: follow-up reports, general delivery and pick-up, use of closed-ended rather than open-ended questions wherever possible, use of rewards for participation, and limiting the length of time requested to complete the survey.

Interviews   The interview may be regarded as either an alternative to other survey methods or as a supplementary source of information. Although it is more costly in both time and money than the questionnaire, it is also more flexible. Additional information over and above initial plans can be readily obtained and ambiguity and misunderstanding eliminated immediately.

One of the greatest strengths of the interview—direct verbal communication—is also a source of weakness since variability is so common in social interactions. For an interview to be successful, rapport is generally required. It is most readily established when the interviewer is nonjudgmental, supportive, and understanding. However, these very characteristics lead to variability in social intercourse among those interviewed. We could achieve sufficient control over social interactions so that the interviews are more homogeneous. However, this would inevitably lead to a sterile interview situation. This, in turn, would result in less rapport which, we have noted, is important for a good interview.

Other problems beset the interview, especially when there is more than one interviewer. Different interviewers may vary in the way they ask questions, interpret responses, or in the way respondents react to them. Interviewer differences are common.

How do we assess the comparability of the interviewers? If you reflect a moment, you'll realize that the situation is similar to using several raters in noninterview settings and determining the inter-rater reliability. (See Section 6.8.2.) In the present case, we are asking whether there is inter-interviewer reliability.

One way to achieve greater inter-interviewer reliability is to standardize the interview procedures. While this standardization increases the interview reliability, it decreases its flexibility. Because of these weaknesses, the interview might best be reserved as an exploratory method to generate ideas and hypotheses that can later be tested by the use of other methods.

4.8.4   Field Research

How does the following differ from a true experiment? A car was stopped at a traffic signal. However, when the light turned green, the car did not move. The dependent variable was the time it took before someone honked. The independent variable was the age of the car. Are people more likely to honk sooner at an old "stalled" car than at a new one (Doob and Gross, 1968)? As you can see, this study incorporates many features of a true experiment. There is an independent variable that is under the control of and is manipulated by the investigator, and there are "experimental" (new car) and control (old car) conditions. The response measure is objective. Finally, the subjects are in a sense "randomly assigned" to the experimental condition. That is, it is left to chance to determine which motorists wind up behind either the old car or the new car. Although a study of this sort lacks the precise control over extraneous variables that laboratory experiments permit, many researchers would agree that field experiments can be true experiments.

This is but one example of a type of investigation known as field research. As we previously noted, field research takes place under "natural" conditions or in "real-life" settings. Generally, the subjects are unaware of their participation in the study and, if a variable is manipulated, they are oblivious to this fact.

There are two broad classes of field research. One involves the manipulation of independent variables, as in the stalling car experiment just described.

This type of research is the field analogue to the laboratory experiment. The other category involves no active manipulation of an experimental variable. Rather, as in the ex post facto experiment, the independent variable occurs naturally. Some of the classic studies in social psychology used this latter technique. For example, following a particularly rough game between Princeton and Dartmouth, student spectators at the two schools were asked to indicate which team was responsible for the rough play (Hastorf and Cantril, 1954). In this field research the two "experimental" conditions were: Group A, spectators attending Princeton University; Group B, spectators attending Dartmouth College. The dependent variable consisted of a judgment, e.g., Princeton was responsible versus Dartmouth was responsible.

In each of these types of field research, the dependent measure may be subjective (describe your feelings, attitudes, or whatever went through your mind) or objective (a behavioral measure, such as honking a car horn.) This leads to a four-fold classification of field studies. (See Table 4.2.)

A major reason for using field experiments is that they increase substantially the external validity or generalizability of the findings. If we are interested in generalizing or applying our experimental findings to practical problems or to social issues, then external validity is essential. Further, if we are interested in understanding and predicting human or nonhuman behavior in situations other than those studied in the laboratory, then our research

Table 4.2
Four types of field studies. An example using the relationship between TV watching and aggression.

Independent variable	Subjective report	Objective measure (behavior)
Manipulated	*Independent variable:* Manipulation of how violent TV watched	*Independent variable:* Manipulation of how much violent TV watched
	Dependent variable: Report of anger at sibling	*Dependent variable:* Hitting sibling
Varies freely	*Independent variable:* Measure how much violent TV watched	*Independent variable:* Measure how much violent TV watched
	Dependent variable: Report of anger at sibling	*Dependent variable:* Hitting sibling

Note that only when the IV is manipulated is the study a true experiment. When the IV is "free to vary," the investigation is analogous to a quasi-experiment. (Adapted with permission from D. F. Schneider, *Social Psychology* (Reading, Mass.: Addison-Wesley Publishing Co., 1976), Table 1.1.)

methods should be more representative of these situations. Some examples will clarify the distinction between laboratory and field experiments.

Social psychologists have used field experiments frequently and successfully; they also, of course, use laboratory experiments. An excellent film entitled, *Bystander Intervention: When Will People Help?* depicts both types. Bystander intervention is one area where both field and laboratory experiments exist.

In the typical field experiment on bystander intervention, a person suddenly collapses in full view of other pedestrians. The researchers are usually interested in the numbers of people coming to the aid of the distressed person. A number of factors may be systematically varied in order to assess their effects on "helping behavior," e.g., age, race, gender, appearance of the individual, location in the city, time of day, etc. Observers stationed nearby can unobtrusively collect different kinds of data, such as the proportion who offer aid, the time it takes before aid is offered, who offers aid, and so forth. In fact, followup questionnaires or interviews may be used to pinpoint more precisely the differences among those who offered aid versus those who did not.

Another example of a field experiment is the "lost letter routine." The investigator writes a letter addressed to himself, complete with necessary postage. The letters are then dropped ("lost") at various locations. The dependent variable is the number of letters returned. The independent variable may be any number of different factors. For example, the address could be a political party, a religious group, a political candidate, section of the city, a government agency, etc. Individuals finding a "lost letter" must decide what to do with it, i.e., return it, open it, ignore it, discard it. Dependent measures noted in the last two paragraphs are referred to as *unobtrusive measures* since individuals are unaware that they are being measured.

Are field experiments experiments?   Our illustrations of field experiments suggest their considerable scope. Do they qualify as true experiments or are they quasi-experiments? There is general agreement that to qualify as an experiment, the researcher should have sufficient control to assign subjects randomly to the conditions or treatments. Both the independent and dependent variables must be precisely specified and other variables fully controlled (confounding minimized.) When the preceding exist, then causal conclusions concerning the relationship may be made. Field experiments often approximate these conditions but at times they fall far short. Therefore, there are times when a study is described as a true experiment when it should not be. When this is the case, considerable care should be taken when formulating conclusions.

Field experiments have many attractive features. They use unobtrusive measures that do not require the cooperation of others; they generally take place in natural real-life settings, thus increasing their external validity or the generalizability of the results; and they add new and interesting procedures to the collection of data. They also pose some problems.

For example, a degree of control may be lost in selecting the participating subjects. The extent to which this may be a problem varies considerably from study to study. It is also sometimes difficult to control or systematically manipulate additional components of field experiments. This may make it difficult to explore detailed aspects of the field experiment that may be important. The laboratory permits this. In contrast to the systematic and often exhaustive explorations found in laboratory research, field experiments appear as isolated events with little meaningful correlation among them. On the other hand, field experiments are often addressed to some practical problems of considerable contemporary importance. Given this, systematic accumulation of information may be unnecessary. The applied nature of field experiments can be seen by identifying those who favor the procedure—sociologists, social psychologists, clinical psychologists, and educators. In contrast, systematic research is essential when the interest is in developing a powerful theoretical system. In the long run, such a system may allow many diverse data to be organized into a few simple statements. Ultimately this should, in turn, be capable of application to practical problems.

Then there is the ethical problem. Subjects (or participants) are unwittingly involved in research without their consent. In some instances, their participation is active. As a result, informed consent is not obtained in some studies where perhaps it should be. Obviously, not all field studies should be criticized on this basis.

Ethical difficulties may also arise whenever the field experiment has potential benefits for those in the experimental conditions. If individuals are randomly assigned to different psychotherapy treatment conditions or educational methods, and some are found superior to others, subjects in the "inferior" treatment groups may have cause for complaint. Parents may object, therapists may object, etc. A similar problem occurs in medical research in evaluating a vaccine or a drug that may be beneficial to numbers of people but, for purposes of rigorous evaluation, it must be withheld from some (control group). Clearly then, the use of random assignment in some instances becomes a practical problem of ethics.

Some partial solutions to these problems can be obtained by designing the study differently. In some cases the experimental and control conditions can be reversed after a fixed period of time (cross-over design). This would assure that both groups receive the effective treatment (if it turns out to be so.) Another procedure might be to use several different treatments thought to be nearly equal in effectiveness. This procedure has a distinct disadvantage of failing to include "no treatment" control conditions. Even so, relative comparisons to other treatment conditions can be made. In some cases investigators have provided the control group with a treatment irrelevant to the problem at hand, but designed to enhance other aspects of performance. Sometimes it is simply impossible to reconcile the ethical problems with rigorous experimental procedure prior to and during the experiment, but the problems can be reconciled after the experiment is completed. See Section 7.6.2 for a description of some possible ethical issues when using a placebo control group procedure.

CHAPTER FIVE

INDEPENDENT AND DEPENDENT VARIABLES

5.1 ON DOING GOOD RESEARCH

In the next chapters we describe in detail the many difficulties encountered when doing laboratory research. Our goal is to provide you with the necessary knowledge to plan and conduct well designed experiments. There are many problems that must be anticipated when planning research. Some of the problems can be easily corrected, others not so easily. Our critical attitude toward research and the many problems that we describe may give you the impression that it is impossible to perform "good", "solid", research. This is far from the case.

You are in the process of becoming a knowledgeable researcher. Once some general research principles are learned, designing "tight," "rigorous", or "elegant" experiments will become challenging and enjoyable. You will experience "the thrill of victory" in your attempts to design research that will provide a "clean" answer to the questions you have asked. *You will learn first hand that the better the experiment is planned, the less effort will be required to interpret the results.* Also, you will read the psychological literature with a new enthusiasm and with a greater understanding and appreciation.

As you become more familiar with basic principles of research, you may be baffled as to why some research was published in respected scientific journals. Not all research that is published in reputable scientific journals is well designed, well controlled, and well executed. Some of it is obviously flawed. There are several reasons why a "flawed" study may have been published. One possibility is that the editor and the journal consultants reviewing the report for publication, and the investigator submitting the report, may not have detected the problem at the time of publication. The report managed to "slip by" in spite of being evaluated carefully by reviewers. In other instances, research reports considered as "flawed" by today's standards were not judged so by past standards. Standards of excellence often change and evolve with the introduction of new concepts, methods, techniques, tools, and measuring devices. Finally, we should note, in some cases, even though a study may have methodological problems, it may also be thought to have great potential value, either theoretical or practical. Given this, a judgment is made that there is more to gain than to lose by publishing the report.

5.2 QUESTIONS TO ANSWER DURING THE PLANNING STAGE OF THE STUDY

In this chapter we deal with the problems of selecting dependent and independent variables. However, these decisions are only two among many that must be made. Prior to collecting data, we must raise and answer the following questions. Why are we doing the research? What do we hope to accomplish? What precisely is the research question? Then we might ask: How do we provide an answer to the question? All of these questions relate to the design of the experiment. *Before* we run the first subject in our experiment proper we must answer several other questions: Will **pilot research** (preliminary research) be needed to resolve methodological questions? Will we use independent groups of subjects for each condition or will we use the same subjects? How many subjects shall we use? Will subjects be selected and assigned randomly or will we use only random assignment? What independent variables will we use? Having decided on the independent variable, what values of the variable will be manipulated? What dependent variables will we record? How long will the study continue? What are the proper control groups? What variables must be controlled? How do we analyze our data? Do our research design and statistical analyses provide an answer to our research question? We must have answers to these questions before our first subject is run. Otherwise, serious problems are likely to be encountered in the course of our research that diminish the likelihood of finding an answer to our research question. If this happens, the time and effort we invested in the research project turns out to be an exercise in futility. This we must avoid. Information related to many of these principles is provided in the chapters that follow.

PILOT RESEARCH   preliminary research usually aimed at resolving methodological and procedural problems.

5.3   SELECTING A RESEARCH PROBLEM

Scientists select a research problem for any of several reasons. Some studies are undertaken to evaluate or to advance a particular theory. Others may be undertaken for the purpose of comparing the adequacy of two or more theories. In these cases such terms as *pure* or *basic* research is often used to describe the research since often no immediate practical application of the results is intended. (See Chapter 2, Basic Research.) In contrast, some research is undertaken because of its applied, practical nature. A social problem exists and questions related to the problem are in need of answering. Is the smoking of marijuana a health hazard? Will certain changes in our educational system reverse the downward trend in scores on the American College Test or Student Achievement Test?

Others undertake studies to resolve inconsistencies or contradictory findings. If some research indicated that sleep following learning aided memory (which it does) and other research found that sleep hindered memory (which it doesn't), then the findings would be contradictory. If so, then little could be said concerning sleep and memory without additional research. The additional research would be directed to resolving the inconsistent findings. It would begin with a careful assessment of the two studies to determine in what ways they were similar and in what ways they were different. If important differences in procedure were found between the studies, then the contradictory findings may be due to these differences. In this case a study could be undertaken to determine whether procedural differences were important. In fact, an exact replication of one or both studies could be undertaken. An exact replication involves repeating the study in a manner as close to or exactly as the original study. Replicating both studies should answer the question concerning procedural differences. Presumably, findings similar to the original studies would be obtained. Replication of a study is another reason why studies are sometimes undertaken even when contradictory findings are not a problem. In this case it may be that the initial results appear implausible or that the experiment was executed in a faulty manner. Finally, research is undertaken because information is not available on the question the scientist is asking. The question asked by the researcher may be of interest only to him or her or it may be of general interest. Obviously answers to all questions cannot be provided nor should they be. Clearly some questions are too trivial and meaningless to bother answering.

5.4 BASIC TERMS

When researchers are manipulating an environmental condition to determine its effect on behavior, they use terms that help describe these activities, such as independent and dependent variable. A **variable** is any condition that can vary or change in quantity or quality. The **independent variable** or treatment is under the control of and administered by the experimeter. The behavior that is affected by the treatment and which we measure is called the **dependent variable.** The dependent variable is always a measure of behavior that we record after first manipulating the independent variable. It is referred to as "dependent" because changes in it *depend* upon the effects of the independent variable. If a systematic relationship is found between the independent and dependent variables then we have established an empirical or causal relationship. It is also sometimes called a **functional relationship** since changes in the dependent variable are a *function* of values (different amounts) of the independent variable. From these lawful or functional relationships theories can be constructed and predictions concerning future behavior can be made.

VARIABLE   a condition that can vary or change in quantity or quality.

INDEPENDENT VARIABLE   a variable under the control of and administered by the experimenter.

DEPENDENT VARIABLE   a measure of behavior that is recorded after the independent variable is introduced.

FUNCTIONAL RELATIONSHIP   a relationship in which the value of one variable varies with changes in the values of a second variable.

Establishing lawful relationships is not an easy task and much of this text is devoted to the difficulties that confront the researcher in his or her quest.

Table 5.1
Examples of qualitative and quantitative independent variables found in psychological research. A quantitative variable involves a single continuum in which different treatment levels or amounts may be administered to subject. Qualitative variables differ in kind rather than in quantity.

Qualitative variables	Quantitative variables
Teaching methods (logic vs. rote)	Drug (e.g., dosage level administered)
Psychotherapeutic methods (e.g., psycho-analytic therapy, behavior therapy, etc.)	Deprivation (e.g., time since last feeding)
	Distance (e.g., the effect of distance from
Success vs. failure (e.g., some problems that can be solved vs. some that cannot)	object on visual acuity)
	Punishment (e.g., amount of painful
Evaluation of others (e.g., favorable vs. unfavorable)	stimulation)
	Reinforcement (e.g., amount of positive
Informed vs. misinformed (e.g., subject told or not told real purpose of study)	or negative reinforcer)

The independent variable may be either qualitative or quantitative. A **qualitative variable** (nominal scale) is one that differs in kind rather than in amount. There are many different kinds of psychotherapy, two different genders, and we may receive feedback or fail to receive feedback when learning a psychomotor task. In contrast, a **quantitative variable** (ordinal, interval, or ratio scale) differs in amount—the amount of punishment or positive reinforcement, the dosage level of a drug, the number of practice trials that involve the use of quantitative dimensions or continua as independent variables. Table 5.1 lists some qualitative and quantitative variables that are used as independent variables in psychological research. Two very basic considerations are choosing an independent variable and selecting dependent variables sufficiently sensitive to detect the treatment effects.

QUALITATIVE VARIABLE   one that differs in kind rather than in amount.
QUANTITATIVE VARIABLE   one that differs in quantity or amounts.

While we do not dwell on theoretical considerations in this chapter, we should note that the selection of both independent and dependent variables is often guided by theory. Further, if the theory is stated in sufficiently precise language, specific values of the independent variable may also be suggested. When theories are not available, the experimenter's curiosity and his or her general information may dictate the selection of dependent and independent variables. In this case, the experimenter might ask, "I wonder what would happen if. . . . ?" Some have described questions of the latter type as "empirical fishing expeditions." They, too, have played a prominent role in the development of science.

5.5 SELECTING VALUES OF AN INDEPENDENT VARIABLE

When we explore completely new areas, little information is available to serve as guidelines in selecting the independent variable. When dealing with quantitative independent variables, we are faced with the additional problem of selecting appropriate values of the variable. For example, when testing a new drug, how many milligrams per pound of body weight should be used as the dosage level? This decision is important since too low a dosage may be insufficient to produce an effect, whereas too much may be harmful or even lethal. When we explore new areas, little information is available to guide our decisions. We must rely on our judgment based upon experience, conversations with our colleagues concerning potential problems, and the information that experts in related areas may provide. In most instances however, our research builds upon previously published research. A rich data base is often available to assist in the selection of the appropriate values. In fact, most researchers choose what they consider proper values of a treatment condition based upon their own experiments and the published experiments of others.

Some obvious guidelines should be considered when choosing values of an independent variable. As we shall see, a minimum of two groups is necessary (experimental and control group) to determine whether the independent variable has an effect. Beyond that, when trying to ascertain if graduations of the independent variable systematically influence behavior, the choice of values of the variable can create problems. Let's direct our attention to the first of these problems: determining whether an experimental variable has an effect. When the values of the experimental treatments are too similar, what risk do we run? In short, the treatment may not affect behavior differentially and your efforts to establish a relationship may fail. To counter this, the first thought that often comes to mind is to select extreme values of the independent variable. The logic is straightforward and simple: The greater the difference in value between the experimental conditions, the greater the probability of showing that the independent variable has an effect. Therefore, choose two points along the continuum that are extreme values. Under certain circumstances the logic is good and would lead to an efficient way of determining whether the independent variable is powerful and worthy of additional investigation. Unfortunately, this simple logic could seduce us into error given certain relationships between the independent and dependent variable.

The reason for the problem is that a variety of relationships may exist. Some of these are depicted in Figure 5.1. When the relationship between the dependent and independent variable is monotonic, the curve is either continuously rising throughout (A and B in Figure 5.1) or continuously falling throughout (D and E in Figure 5.1). When the relationship is nonmonotonic (see Box 5.1), the curve rises at certain points then falls at other points (C and F in Figure 5.1). As you might expect, monotonic functions generally do not create difficulties for experiments that use the extreme group approach.

BOX 5.1　A NONMONOTONIC FUNCTION—YERKES-DODSON LAW

An interesting idea that relates effectiveness of performance to level of motivation and task difficulty has come to be called the Yerkes-Dodson Law (Yerkes and Dodson, 1908). The notion described by this "law" is that the optimal level of motivation depends upon task difficulty. The more difficult or complex the task, the lower will be the optimal level of motivation needed. According to the law, performance is poor with little motivation but, as motivation increases, performance also increases—but only to a point. Beyond that point, depending upon the task difficulty, further increases in motivation lead to a deterioration in performance. The relationship resembles an inverted U when performance is plotted (X axis) against motivation (Y axis). The so-called Yerkes-Dodson Law has not yet received convincing support but the idea is intuitively reasonable and some supportive data are available. From this view, optimal performance does not require the highest levels of motivation. In fact, as specified by the "law," too much motivation can result in inferior performance. Examples of this might be the athlete (golfer, tennis player, baseball player, etc.) who "chokes up" in an important game; the student who "chokes up" on an statistics exam and makes silly computational errors, or the student who draws an complete blank on an essay question. An inverse U function might also be found with different degrees of anxiety, arousal, expectations, the intensity of stimuli, pain, deprivation, etc. Experimenters must be alert to these possibilities.

With monotonic functions any two separated values on the horizontal axis could result in finding a difference between groups. Therefore, when the relationship is monotonic, the major limitation of the "extreme group" approach is that the shape of the relationship or function cannot be established with two groups. Obviously the effects of intermediate values cannot be determined with only two values of an independent variable.

However, if the relationship between the independent and dependent variable is nonmonotonic (C and F in Figure 5.1), simply using two groups at extreme points could lead to grossly inaccurate conclusions. For example, if the relationship between the independent and dependent variable is as depicted in C and F, a study using only two groups could easily conclude that the independent variable has no effect on behavior. If values 1 and 4 on the horizontal axis are selected, then both groups would perform in the same manner and no differences would be detected. The same would be the case with values 2 and 3. Finding no differences, the investigator might well conclude that the independent variable is not effective. Some promising research might wind up in the circular file when, in fact, it should be pursued.

The safest way to avoid the problem is to test at least three values of the independent variable. While selecting three points will not necessarily reveal the shape of the relationship, it will help you to avoid coming to incorrect conclusions in the event that a nonmonotonic relationship exists. The choice

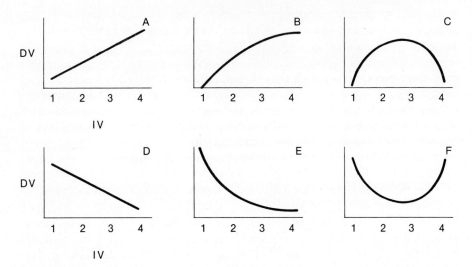

Fig. 5.1 Illustration of various types of relationships between the Independent Variable (IV) and the Dependent Variable (DV). Curves A, B, D, and E depict monotonic relationships; C and F show nonmonotonic relationships. The horizontal axis (IV) is referred to as the abscissa, while the vertical axis (DV) is referred to as the ordinate in graphing relationships.

between using two values or more than two values often depends upon the information available, the importance of the problem, and the cost of doing research.

5.6 CHOOSING A DEPENDENT VARIABLE

The selection of a dependent variable is not in the least a casual matter. Indeed, it is immensely important. It reflects our underlying assumption that the study of behavior is the doorway toward measuring psychological states. Moreover, it is the measure we use to ascertain whether the independent variable has an effect.

Generally, we choose a dependent measure because we judge that it will reveal unobservable but inferable processes that affect it and other behavioral measures. We often assume that our dependent variable reflects some underlying psychological state. For example, emotional processes are often inferred from changes in heart rate, respiration, or sweat gland activity. We might infer stress from ulceration or from adrenal activity. The process of learning is inferred from the elimination of errors, correct anticipation of words, and conditioned responses.

There must be no ambiguity concerning the identification of the dependent variable. Its occurrence or nonoccurrence must be ascertainable according to clearly defined criteria. For example, the dependent measure in an operant conditioning apparatus is any response that closes the microswitch and permits its delivery of reinforcement. Such measures as speed of responding, latency, time to complete a task, eye blinks, errors, heart rate, weight gain, lever press, or key peck may be unambiguously defined and readily recorded. This is not always the case, however. What about such measures as self-mutilating behavior in the autistic child, risk taking, aggression, and frustration? Are all lesions of the stomach or of the duodenum ulcers? Does a 200-ohm change in resistance constitute a galvanic skin response? High agreement among observers must be achieved before the experiment begins. (See Chapter 6.)

We should also note that automated responses such as a pigeon key peck or a rat lever press may be unambiguous in terms of a switch closure but ambiguous in what produced the closure. There may be many ways to produce a switch closure; for example, a rat may lever press with the left paw, the right paw, chin, tail, shoulder, or rump. The experimenter may be interested in the entire class of responses referred to as "lever presses" or he or she may be interested only in "paw presses."

5.6.1   Characteristics of a Good Dependent Variable

A good dependent variable must be accurately recorded and measured. This is another way of saying it must be *objective* and *quantifiable*. In addition, it must be sufficiently sensitive to detect small changes in the independent variable yet not be so sensitive that it is affected by the slightest uncontrolled factors in the environment.

Further, a good measure should have a "low floor" and a "high ceiling." In other words, the dependent variable should permit a wide range of values or change. Imagine a task so difficult that few individuals are capable of achieving it. For example, in a test of the effectiveness of vitamin supplements on physical strength, the experimenter sets a criterion of bench pressing 250 pounds or more. In this situation, very few subjects would reach criterion even if the *supplement actually increased physical strength.* The "floor" was simply set too high. In contrast, if the task had been to bench press 10 pounds, the "ceiling" would have been so low that virtually all subjects would achieve criterion whether or not the experimental variable affected physical strength.

Floor and ceiling effects occur sometimes when giving examinations to students. If an exam is so easy that all students correctly answered each test item (i.e., all received 100 percent correct), then the exam did not discriminate those knowing the material from those not knowing. In this case, the "ceiling" was too low. Students "topped out" and could not go higher. On the other hand, if the exam was so difficult that all students answered the test items incorrectly (i.e., all received 0 percent correct), then again, the exam did not discriminate those knowing the material from those not knowing. In this case, the "floor" was too high and everyone "bottomed out" and could not go lower. The sensitivity of the measuring instrument is always reduced when either "floor" or "ceiling" effects are prominent. In the event of too high a floor or too low a ceiling, the range of possible values of the dependent variable is so truncated that it loses its capacity to discriminate among various treatment conditions.

When we observe behavior, human or nonhuman, we find that many different forms of it occur—it appears continuous but changing. Even when we observe an organism for a short time we see different *frequencies* of behavior, e.g., walking, talking, writing, grooming, etc. Physiological and psychophysiological changes also occur at the same time. The responses that we observe occur for different *durations* and with greater *intensity*. Deciding what particular response to measure can be a difficult task. As we noted, selecting an insensitive dependent variable or one unresponsive to the independent variable may cause us to fail in our efforts.

There are several reliable and sensitive measures that you should keep in mind when planning your research. These measures are used frequently by researchers because of their sensitivity, reliability, and ease of measuring. They are: (1) *frequency* of responding, (2) *latency* (or speed) of responding, (3) *duration* of responding, and (4) *intensity* of responding. All four of these measures are sometimes taken within a given experiment. Frequency of responding may refer to the number of times a behavior occurs—also, a rate of responding measure can be derived if responses per unit of time are recorded. Latency usually refers to the time it takes to initiate a response following the onset of a signal. This measure can be converted to a speed measure if the reciprocal of latency is calculated. Intensity of responding is sometimes referred to as amplitude or magnitude of responding and relates to the vigor of the response. Finally, duration or time measures reflect how long a response continues, e.g., how long to consume the food, to solve the puzzle, to calculate the solution, or how much time was spent in one condition over the others.

5.5.2 Multiple Dependent Variables

Most experiments record only one dependent variable. One reason for this relates to interpreting what the different measures mean. Does each behavior recorded measure the same thing (that is, does each measure reflect the same inferred or assumed underlying processes?)? For example, is kicking a vending machine that fails to deliver a candy bar the same inferred underlying measure of frustration as other measures such as cussing at the machine, repeatedly pushing the selector button, etc.? A second reason is that when more than one measure is recorded, traditional statistics require a separate statistical analysis for each measure. The latter in turn made it difficult to interpret the true p value for a significant outcome. However, there are now excellent statistical techniques for assessing multiple dependent variables. Their use is increasing.

Two, three, or more dependent variables are recorded and analyzed in a single procedure referred to as a *multivariate analysis*. Multiple measures may vary together (i.e., they are correlated) thus suggesting a common underlying process for all measures. When they vary in an uncorrelated way, different processes are suggested. Both theoretical and practical considerations determine the number of measures used. A discussion of statistical procedures for analyzing concurrently several dependent measures is too advanced for a first course in research methods. Suffice it to say there are advantages to this type of analysis. Aside from statistical advantages, however, there are other reasons for recording two or more dependent variables. It may be that under the conditions of your experiment a single dependent measure may not show any systematic relationship to your independent variable. Your measure may be too insensitive or too variable. Had you recorded other different measures your chances of finding a systematic relationship may be increased. In addition, recording more than a single dependent variable will allow you to evaluate the relationship among them. You have little to lose and much to gain by recording more than a single dependent variable unless doing so is inconvenient, time consuming, or expensive. For those who are creative or resourceful, or for those who have a flair for originality and inventiveness, it may be possible to create or discover new dependent measures that possess the necessary attributes. In this case, a combination of traditional and novel dependent measures could be evaluated. Social scientists are always on the lookout for new and better ways to measure behavior.

The number of dependent measures recorded by researchers is determined by both theoretical and practical considerations. It is not uncommon for researchers to record different classes of responses within the same experiment. Behavioral, physiological, self-report, and other measures may be recorded.

5.7 RESPONSE CLASSES OF DEPENDENT VARIABLES

There are four response classes that are generally used by investigators studying behavior, whether in a laboratory or an applied setting. Whatever measure is used, great care must be taken when measuring and recording the response. These four classes of responses are motor responses, psychophysiological measures, physiological measures, and self-report measures. Each has special problems associated with its use. In this section, we will describe these measures and indicate some of these problems.

5.7.1 Motor Responses

Motor responses involve the skeletal muscle system in some way and the response system may vary in terms of frequency, latency, duration, or intensity. Some examples of these responses are walking, talking, drinking, eating, crying, fighting, running, smiling, studying, smoking, gambling, freezing, jumping, bar pressing, playing, key pecking, choosing, etc.

When motor responses are automatically recorded—mechanically or electronically—little difficulty is encountered concerning the reliability of the measure. Under these conditions, errors due to the human observer are virtually eliminated. However, only some motor responses can be automated and the recording of the other responses must be done by observers. Relying on observers to note and record our dependent variables is a serious problem for a considerable amount of research being done in psychology today. The problem is that human observers are not perfectly reliable at the task and, as such, represent an imperfect measuring instrument. This unreliability must be minimized. To do this requires that we carefully define the response (dependent variable) in which we are interested. We must establish clear criteria for its occurrence or nonoccurrence, carefully train our observers for what constitutes occurrence or nonoccurrence, monitor the accuracy of our observers, assess inter-observer reliability, and occasionally retrain them. (See Chapter 6.) When observers are used we must also be concerned with observer bias (systematic errors or errors biased in one direction as opposed to random error, i.e., errors distributed equally in each direction).

5.7.2 Psychophysiological Measures

These measures usually involve the autonomic nervous system. Those most frequently recorded are the electroencephalogram (EEG),* galvanic skin response (GSR), heart rate (HR), blood pressure (BP), pulse transit time (PTT), electromyogram (EMG), blood vessel constriction and dilation, and skin temperature.

Psychophysiological measures generally require expensive equipment and a degree of technical expertise. Also, unless computer facilities are available and an automated scoring system developed, hand scoring is required and it is both slow and tedious. The reliability of scoring records varies with the response measure chosen and inter-scorer reliability is crucial. When using psychophysiological measures the investigator must be familiar with the equipment, electrode application, proper recording sites, the reactivity of different measures, and a host of other important considerations. There is now a considerable amount of literature devoted to methodological considerations related to psychophysiological response systems. Researchers in this area are extremely active, so much so that a journal entitled *Psychophysiology* has been established which is devoted to publishing research with these measures. The journal frequently includes articles on methodological problems to alert researchers of artifacts that may affect their findings. Marked individual differences are found with psychophysiological response systems. Large changes in heart rate may occur to environmental stimulation for some subjects but

---

*EEG recordings are considered to be central nervous system activity.

little change in blood pressure. Others may respond markedly in terms of blood pressure but not so with heart rate. For others, GSR measures may be the most reactive. This lack of consistency among individuals can be troublesome.

5.7.3   Self-Report Measures

These are response measures that the subjects verbalize concerning how they are reacting to the treatment (independent variable) or control conditions. Subjects verbalize whether they are anxious, concerned, aroused, depressed, happy, etc. Exposure to different conditions presumably has an effect on how the subjects are reacting, and they are asked to self-monitor their reactions and then to report them to the investigator. Sometimes the task is structured rather than open-ended by a checklist of adjectives that might describe the subjects' reactions. A scale from 1 to 5 or 1 to 7 may also be used so that subjects can rate the intensity of their reaction. It is obvious that self-report measures are susceptible to distortion on part of the participant. Also, if the task of monitoring their reaction under certain conditions is difficult for the individuals, the reliability of verbal report measures may not be very high. Some researchers feel that the very task of asking subjects to monitor and verbalize their reactions may alter the measure, and instead of reacting to the independent variable they may be reacting to instructions. It has been argued that self-report measures, more so than other measures, may be more responsive to expectancy effects and demand characteristics along with false reporting. (See Chapter 8.) Because of this, some researchers are reluctant to use self-report measures alone; they therefore attempt to correlate self-report measures with psychophysiological responses (an autonomic response measure). Since autonomic responses are generally not under voluntary control, they would presumably be less susceptible to the criticism directed toward self-report measures.

5.7.4   Physiological Measures

Individuals recording these measures are often interested in how psychological variables, such as stress, pain, or conflict, may affect the physiology of the organism. Do physiological measures such as ulceration, blood sugar level, corticosterone, or weight of the adrenal glands vary systematically as a function of psychological variables? When researchers assess physiological dependent measures the same independent variables may be manipulated as when they assess behavioral measures.

These measures usually, but not always, involve penetrating the skin of the subject. Once this is done, biochemical changes may be assessed or electrophysiological recordings may be taken. Some investigators may be interested in the electrical activity of neural cells. Others may be interested in analyzing changes in neurotransmitters such as epinephrine and nor-epinephrine. Hormone changes resulting from endocrine gland activity may be evaluated. In some instances, "blood clotting time" or "wound healing time" is measured as a function of psychological variables. Quite often, physiological measures are derived from body fluids such as blood, urine, saliva, or sweat. These fluids are taken from the subject and then analyzed using biochemical techniques. To use these measures it is usually necessary to develop certain skills and to acquire knowledge of various laboratory procedures. In addition, considerable laboratory equipment is needed. It is unlikely that these measures would be used by the novice researcher. Although for some physiological assays commercial laboratories will perform the analysis for a fee.

As we have suggested several times, researchers generally measure several dependent variables in their research. These measures may be within the same class or across classes. It may be especially important to record several dependent measures when your knowledge of the independent variable is limited, when the effects are difficult to predict, or when you are interested in a possible relationship among several dependent variables.

In closing this sectiion we want to emphasize that whether using human or nonhuman subjects, experimenters should strive to record dependent measures that are not distressing to their subjects. In choosing both dependent and independent variables careful consideration of ethical principles should be kept foremost in mind. (See Chapter 1.)

CHAPTER SIX

OBSERVATIONAL PROCEDURES AND INTER-OBSERVER AGREEMENT

6.1 NOT ALL OBSERVATIONS MAY BE AUTOMATED

The following is an excerpt from a study involving face-to-face interaction between infant and mother and its relation to later infant-mother attachment.

> *The infants were visited at home at three-week intervals, from three to fifty-four weeks of age, each visit lasting approximately four hours. The mother was encouraged to maintain a typical daily routine while the visitor-observer took detailed notes of the infant's behavior and of his interactions with the mother and with other persons present. The notes were subsequently transcribed into narrative records. Four persons, two men and two women, served as visitor-observers, each following his assigned families throughout the babies' first year (Blehar, Lieberman, and Ainsworth, 1977).*

As in the above-cited study, there are numerous occasions when the data consist of the personal observations of investigators and/or their assistants. These studies are not restricted to natural settings nor are they necessarily applied.

Since the observations often cannot be automated, they require that humans make judgments about the occurrence of the behavior, its frequency, its duration, or its latency. These measures are the basic data used to describe naturally occurring behavior or to assess the effects of our independent variable. Therefore they must be gathered with care.

Behavior measures based upon response categories such as play, aggression, and self-assertion are more complex than specific responses such as talking, walking, or attending. These, in turn, are very different from the lever press, the key peck, heart rate, or eye blink responses. The latter are usually automated and there is little doubt about the criteria used for their occurrence or nonoccurrence. They do not require the judgment of human observers.

Data derived from human observers are playing an increasingly important and influential role in research, particularly in applied settings. They also play an important role in some laboratory settings. As you know, the interests of psychologists are extremely varied. Indeed, wherever there is behavior of any kind, that behavior is a valid target for psychological inquiry. This broad scope of interest has resulted in studying behavior under a wider variety of conditions than in the past. Some involve making unobtrusive observations of animals behaving in their natural settings, including primates and animals lower on the phylogenetic scale. Experimental psychologists often record laboratory observations over and above the behavior that is automatically recorded. These are often interesting behaviors in their own right. Applied psychologists sometimes encounter special problems. For example, behavior modifiers must be adept at recognizing when a given behavior achieves criterion (e.g., when the sound made by a mute autistic child is sufficiently close to "mama" to warrant rewarding the child).

Moreover, observers must be able to make fine distinctions between closer and more distant approximations to the criterion. Similarly, those studying the effects of "psychologically active" drugs and medicine must attend to a wide variety of both specific responses and broader classes of behavior. Reliable observations are essential in assessing the treatment effects.

In many instances, the primary and often the only data are derived from the direct observation by the investigators. It is essential that these primary data be accurate, objective, and reliable. In this chapter we will discuss some problems associated with using human observers and some factors that decrease the accuracy and reliability of observations. We will also discuss briefly some ways of assessing inter-observer reliability.

6.2   SOME RULES OF OBSERVATION

There are two broad classes of observing behavior: **participant observing** and **nonparticipant observing.** The excerpt with which we began the chapter involved participant observing. The investigators interacted with the infants at the same time they served as observers. In nonparticipant observation, the general rule is for the investigator to remain as unobtrusive as possible while making the observations. This is particularly the case where the potentials for reactivity to the observer is high and the investigator wishes to minimize the possibility that the observer may influence the behavior under observation. The following excerpt describes the habituating techniques used by one investigator who devoted years to the study of the mountain gorilla in its natural habitat:

> *My technique of habituating the gorillas was simple but essential, for I could only obtain unbiased data on their behavior if they remained relatively unaffected by my presence. I usually attempted to approach the group undetected to within about 150 feet before climbing slowly and in full view of the animals onto a stump or the low branch of a tree where I settled myself as comfortably as possible without paying obvious attention to them. By choosing a prominent observation post not only was I able to see the gorillas over the screen of herbs, but, reciprocally, they could inspect me clearly, which was the most important single factor in habituating the animals. Under such circumstances they usually remained in the vicinity to watch me, and even approached me to within 5 feet. I found it remarkably easy to establish rapport with the gorillas. This process was greatly facilitated by the placid temperament of the animals, and by certain conditions which I imposed on myself; (a) I carried no firearms which might imbue my actions with unconscious aggressiveness; (b) I moved slowly, and used binoculars and cameras sparingly at the beginning to eliminate gestures which could be interpreted as threat; (c) I nearly always approached them alone, leaving any companions behind and out of sight at the point where the animals were first noted; (d) I wore the*

same drab olive-green clothes every day; and (e) I almost never tracked the gorillas after they had voluntarily moved out of range. This last point was, I believe, of special value, for at no time were they subjected to pursuit, an action which could easily frighten them as well as increase the chance of attacks. By adhering to my conditions I not only habituated six groups to my presence quite well but also was never attacked, even though I inadvertently stumbled into the middle of a group or nearly collided with animals several times (Schaller, 1963, pp. 22–23).

PARTICIPANT OBSERVING   the investigators interact with the subjects while they are observing.

NONPARTICIPANT OBSERVING   the investigators do not interact with the subjects while they are observing.

Notice that when behavior is not continuously observed but is being time sampled, it is necessary to enter the observation area while behavior is ongoing. When this is the case, try to avoid disrupting the behavior of those being observed when you enter and when you leave. Do not begin making systematic observations until those being observed are accustomed to you. The time it takes may be a matter of a few minutes or it may take several days or even weeks. While the latter is unusual, there are instances where the researcher has had to return repeatedly before his or her presence was accepted and behavior of those observed returned to normal.

Careful consideration should be given to the location where you will be making observations. Choose an area from which you can observe and record easily and where movement on your part will not draw attention to you. You should also choose an area that can occasionally accommodate another observer in addition to yourself. The latter is essential when assessing inter-rater agreement (reliability). Recording devices, if used, should be quiet and unobtrusive. For counting, quiet wrist counters with several channels can be worn. Counts can be taken without any apparent movement on your part.

6.3   SCHEDULING OBSERVATIONS

Decisions must be made concerning frequency, duration, and the time of day for scheduling observations. These decisions depend upon the purposes served by the observations. Researchers may only be interested in a restricted, narrow time period or they may be interested in a broad, representative time period. If you are interested in a representative description of naturally occurring behavior it is necessary to observe over many different time periods and across several days. Jane Goodall's description of primate behavior under natural conditions is an excellent example of the latter. On the other hand, laboratory studies often follow a rigid schedule in that the experiment takes place at the same time each day for an hour or more. In this case, the observation period is confined to the laboratory session time. An applied program would follow a different approach. A behavioral modification program dealing with disruptive and unruly behavior in social settings would require that observations be made in each setting where the disruptions occur. Whatever the purposes served by the observations, individual observation sessions should be sufficiently long to provide an adequate sample of the response of interest. Behavior occurring with a low frequency may require longer observation periods relative to high frequency behavior. For some purposes it may be necessary to sample behavior at different times during the day to determine the range and variability. For most studies, however, observations are made at the same time each day so that observations are made under similar conditions from day to day. The procedure becomes routine for those being observed.

It is important to undertake a periodic check of the accuracy of your recorded observations by having another observer *independently* record his or her observations for the *same time periods*. These **independent observations** must not be influenced by the original observer's opinions or behavior. To accomplish this objective, it may be necessary to shield the two observers from each other. Even subtle recording movements on the part of one observer may be sufficient to bias the other observer. Having assured ourselves that the observations are independent, a check for inter-rater inter-observer reliability may be necessary.

INDEPENDENT OBSERVATION   when the observations of one observer do not influence the observations of another observer.

If the occurrence or nonoccurrence of complex behavior is being judged, the criteria for establishing the presence of this behavior must be established. Before the behavior is recorded as present, these criteria must be satisfied. To minimize the observer drifting away from the originally used criteria, a periodic review should be scheduled during the course of observing. Although **observer drift** has been a problem in some studies, it is usually correctable.

OBSERVER DRIFT   a gradual shift in the observational criteria during the course of the research.

6.4   DEFINING THE BEHAVIOR TO BE OBSERVED

As we have noted, our concern is to make observations that are both objective and reliable. We want to maximize "pure" observations and minimize the degree to which our observations are affected by our own interpretations and inferences. To accomplish this we attempt to define the dependent variable (behavior) in terms of specific observable responses and by clearly specifying the criteria for judging when the behavior has occurred. This is an important step if we are to ensure that different observers make similar observations. A good response measure will have relatively high inter-observer agreement. The more precise we are in specifying our definition of a response or of the behavioral criteria, the higher is the inter-observer agreement. For example, if we are interested in self-mutilating behavior of an autistic child, it would be unsatisfactory to instruct the observers to record every instance of self-mutilating behavior. The term is too broad, too abstract, and undefined to be useful or to assure agreement among observers. However, if we operationally defined self-mutilating behavior as "head banging," "biting one's body," or "beating oneself with fists," we could more easily and reliably measure this class of behavior.

6.5   RECORDING BEHAVIOR OR OBSERVATIONS

Consider the following. A research team is interested in observing the self-mutilating behavior of children diagnosed as autistic. Having decided on a satisfactory operational definition of the target behavior, the team must now decide on the observational technique to use. Three choices are commonly available: (1) to count the number of occurrences of self-mutilating behavior during an observational session (frequency method); (2) to record the period of time during which the target behavior lasts (duration method); or (3) to break the observational sessions into equal time intervals and record the occurrence of self-mutilating behavior within each interval (interval method). Let's take a closer look at each technique.

6.5.1   Frequency Method

The *frequency method* is simple, straightforward, and easily understood. The observer simply counts the number of occurrences of the behavior of interest in a given interval of time. The interval of time is arbitrary and may be as little as a few minutes or as much as several hours. Further, it may be based on one observation session or it may run across many sessions taken over several days. Often, interest is only in the frequency of the observations in a given session and not in changes that may occur during that session. However, when the interest centers on assessing change or obtaining inter-observer agreement within a session, the session may be divided into smaller equal time intervals. For example, a sixty-minute session may be divided into ten six-minute intervals and changes in frequency can be observed across this entire interval. Usually observation periods are the same duration from day to day. If not, then comparing frequencies based on fifteen minutes with those based on thirty minutes would not be appropriate. However, if different durations are used, it is necessary to convert to response rate. This measure can easily be derived by dividing the frequency of the response by the unit of time, e.g., responses per minute. The frequency method of recording observational data is most appropriate with discrete responses that take a relatively constant period of time to complete; for example, number of cigarettes smoked, number of words spoken, or number of head-banging incidents.

Responses occurring over long periods of time would not be appropriate for the frequency method. Responses such as time spent talking, sleeping, eating, or observing would be inappropriate. Counting these latter observations would be wasteful of information and counting their frequencies might not be a sensitive way to assess a treatment effect. For these responses, the duration method is more appropriate.

Frequency measures, particularly rate measures, are popular among psychologists interested in the experimental analysis of behavior. In applied settings attempts are often made to modify both excesses (e.g., fighting) and deficits of behavior, (e.g., not talking). In these settings, monitoring frequency is obviously important. Moreover, frequency and rate measures have been shown to be sensitive to the contingencies of reinforcement.

6.5.2   Duration Method

As we noted, in those instances where response duration is long and/or the occasions of its occurrence relatively infrequent, it is usually inappropriate to record frequency, e.g., sleep, inactivity. In cases like this, counting frequencies may not be the most sensitive way to assess treatments. Rather, it is necessary to measure the duration of the response. For example, our interest might be in the duration of time spent either in solitary or in social activity. Using a stop watch or an event recorder, the observer activates the instrument when the behavior begins and terminates the time recording when the behavior ends. Even though response frequency is not of primary interest, a frequency measure is possible to obtain by simply counting the number of times the recording instrument was activated. Judging when a response is initiated or terminated can often be difficult. For example, imagine you are studying the talking of an autistic child. There may be many pauses of varying durations, brief interruptions, or changes in the intensity of the behavior that requires a judgment as to whether a different response occurred.

Both perceptual and judgmental abilities of the observer are often taxed since it is difficult to specify in advance the precise criteria for deciding whether these pauses, brief interruptions, or changes in intensity represent the same or different responses. It must be kept in mind that another observer (inter-observer agreement) must also be able to make similar observations. Consequently, the decisions must be made as objective as possible.

6.5.3   Interval Method

The interval method is the most flexible and widely used recording method. This method permits the recording of any behavior, whether discrete (head banging) or continuous (sleeping). With this method, the observation period is broken into equal intervals, the size of which varies with the particular observations of interest. Behavior is recorded as occurring (yes) or nonoccurring (no) in each interval. The interval size may be as short as a few seconds or it may be as long as a few minutes, depending on the behavior under observation. A desirable length of time interval is one short enough to accommodate a single response but not long enough to accommodate more than one response. Our research interest is focused on the number of intervals during which the response occurs. For high rate, short duration responses, the interval should be short so that no more than one response per interval will occur. If more than a single discrete response can occur per interval, then counting the intervals may underestimate the frequency of the observed behavior. In contrast, if the intervals are so short that a single response might fall into two or more intervals, counting the intervals in which a response occurs may overestimate the frequency of behavior. Obviously the criterion for occurrence or nonoccurrence of behavior must be clear so that its occurrence can be quickly and reliably determined. The problem is more difficult than it at first appears since only a portion of the behavior may occur in a given interval. It becomes even more difficult if the observer is recording several different responses concurrently. When this happens, a decision rule is sometimes adopted; if a response fills one-half or more of the interval, it is scored as occurring in that interval. For continuous responses (e.g., talking), each interval in which talking occurred would be scored as an occurrence. Therefore, the interval scoring method allows the investigator to derive both frequency (discrete responses) and duration (continuous responses) data.

6.6   RECORDING MORE THAN ONE RESPONSE

With the interval method, it is common to score several different responses that occur concurrently in an interval. When this is done, it is essential to reserve time at the end of each interval for recording whether the different behaviors occurred. We will first give an example of scoring one response across different subjects, then we will give an example of scoring multiple responses.

Let us assume that our observational period will be daily thirty-minute sessions and we are interested in the occurrence or nonoccurrence of a single behavior. We decide that an interval size of thirty seconds is appropriate for our response. Therefore, we would divide the thirty-minute session into sixty thirty-second intervals. For each of these thirty-second intervals we would record whether or not the behavior occurred. Our interval scoring sheet would look like Table 6.1 if we are observing one subject, and like Table 6.2 if we are observing three subjects. Please note the documentation required for each

Table 6.1
Interval scoring sheet for scoring a single response with one subject.

Experiment _____ Researcher _____ Observer _____
Subject _____ Location _____ Date _____
Time _____ Behavior _____ Codes _____

Intervals

	1	2	3	4	5	6	7		60
Subject	+ −	+ −	+ −	+ −	+ −	+ −	+ −	----------	+ −

Table 6.2
Interval scoring sheet for single response with three subjects.

Experiment _____ Researcher _____ Observer _____
Subjects _____ Location _____ Date _____
Time _____ Behavior _____ Codes _____

Intervals

	1	2	3	4	5	6	7		60
Subject 1	+ −	+ −	+ −	+ −	+ −	+ −	+ −	----------	+ −
Subject 2	+ −	+ −	+ −	+ −	+ −	+ −	+ −	----------	+ −
Subject 3	+ −	+ −	+ −	+ −	+ −	+ −	+ −	----------	+ −

scoring sheet. This is important information that can easily be forgotten if not recorded in permanent form.

Since we are recording only one response or one kind of behavior whenever it occurs during the interval, we can circle the + as soon as it is observed. If, by chance, the response again occurred in that same interval, we would simply ignore it. Finally, we would circle the minus sign if the behavior did not occur during the interval.

When several subjects are observed during each session, only a single subject is observed at any given time. Thus, if there were thirty intervals, each subject would be observed independently thirty times. You could start with Interval 1, Subject 1, go to Interval 1, Subject 2, then to Interval 1, Subject 3. Then you could begin the sequence again with Interval 2.

When more than one behavior is being observed and recorded, it may be necessary to reserve a part of the interval for scoring purposes. Otherwise the time it takes to record the occurrence or nonoccurrence of several responses may interfere with the task of observing. As a result, some responses may be missed. It is not difficult to reserve time for recording purposes. With our thirty-second interval, we could designate the first twenty-five seconds for observing and the last five seconds for recording. If we were observing smiling

Table 6.3
Interval scoring sheet for a single subject and four different responses.

Experiment _____ Researcher _____ Observer _____
Subject _____ Location _____ Date _____
Time _____ Behavior smiling, frowning, hitting, biting

Codes S, F, H, B

Intervals

	1	2	3		30
Subject	S F (H)(B)	S (F) H (B)	S (F)(H) B	--------------	S F (H)(B)

(S), frowning (F), hitting (H), and biting (B), our data sheet might look like Table 6.3. If any of the behaviors occur during the twenty-five-second observation period, we would record it during the five-second recording period simply by circling the proper code.

We should note that when short intervals are used, it may be necessary to use a signaling device to identify the beginning and end of each interval. A cassette recorder with an ear piece can fill the bill admirably. The precise time intervals can be recorded prior to making observations and the playing of the tape can pace the observers through the session, telling them exactly when to observe and when to record. With time intervals of thirty seconds, the tape could be arranged to signal the beginning of the observation interval by pre-recording "Time Interval 1, Begin" and twenty-five seconds later "Time Interval 1, Record." Then the tape would identify "Time Interval 2, Begin" and so on. This procedure could be used when there is more than one observer. By coupling the recorder with two or more earpieces, we would have an excellent means of assuring ourselves that the investigators are observing and recording the same time periods. This achievement is particularly important when checking on inter-observer agreement.

Once the experiment is completed, the interval observations can be converted into percentages. This is done by taking the number of intervals in which the response occurred and dividing it by the total number of intervals and then multiplying by 100. Thus, if a response was observed during six out of thirty observational periods, the percentage would be: $6/30 \times 100 = 20\%$. Additional information concerning observational techniques, especially in applied settings, can be found in a book by Gelfand and Hartmann (1975).

6.7 INTER-OBSERVER AGREEMENT

We have noted several times that, when different raters, judges, or observers are used to record data, it is important to determine whether the observations are objective and reliable. We try to assure this objectivity by carefully defining the behavior of interest and clearly specifying criteria for the occurrence or nonoccurrence of the behavior. Only when the behavior meets the criteria would it be counted as an observation. However, this procedure is not sufficient in itself. We must have evidence that our observations are objective and reliable, and that we have avoided observer bias, subjectivity, and observer drift. We simply cannot determine the goodness of our data based upon the observations of a single observer. Therefore, a careful researcher will periodically use two or more observers simultaneously. Following this, a statistical measure is calculated to determine the degree of inter-observer agreement. There are several ways of calculating inter-observer agreement, which we will describe in the next section.

High inter-observer agreement suggests that the behavior being observed is sufficiently well defined that we can generalize the results recorded by one observer to a population of observers. This then makes the behavioral phenomenon more meaningful to the individual investigator and to other investigators as well. Low inter-observer reliability can cause problems. It could reduce the likelihood of finding an empirical relationship between the independent and the dependent variable. This would be unfortunate and wasteful of time and energy if, in fact, a relationship did exist. On the other hand, if an empirical relationship was found, low inter-observer reliability would most likely diminish the confidence that one has in the firmness of the relationship. If we cannot obtain high inter-observer agreement in spite of strong efforts to do so, then little confidence should be placed in the phenomenon since it may be impossible to detect systematic behavior of any kind or to assess the effects of any treatment. Reliability checks are expensive and time-consuming, but essential. Evaluation of inter-observer agreement should be undertaken before the experiment begins and periodically thereafter. If agreement is either low or variable, then additional work is needed on definitions, establishing criteria, and the training of observers. When agreement is low, a discussion should take place immediately after the inter-observer agreement check to develop new rules and techniques that might improve reliability.

Let's briefly summarize the steps for maintaining observer reliability.

1. Establish objective criteria for determining whether the behavior did or did not occur. Specify observation decision rules.

2. Determine whether inter-observer agreement occurs with the criteria established prior to beginning your research. Discussion should follow immediately concerning criteria.

3. If agreement is low or variable, additional work is needed. Reevaluate definitions or criteria. Behavior may not be well defined. Consider a training program for observers. Videotape can be very helpful.

4. If agreement is high, begin your study but periodic checks on observer reliability should be made, i.e., about once a week.

5. Periodic retraining may be necessary to avoid observer drift, i.e., drifting away from established criteria or definition. Inter-observer agreement should continue to be periodically assessed.

6. If possible, use observers "blind" to the purposes of the study to prevent bias. If this is not possible attempt to use a "blind" second observer when assessing inter-observer agreement.

6.8   MEASURING THE RELIABILITY OF OBSERVATIONAL DATA

As we have seen, the researcher commonly has one of three different recording procedures from which to select: frequency of occurrence of a target behavior, duration of the occurrence of that behavior, and the occurrence versus the nonoccurrence of a behavioral event within a time interval. We shall now consider some of the methods that are available to assess the reliability of observational data. More specifically, we shall look at measures involving percentage agreement among observers and correlational procedures modeled on the classical psychometric approach to reliability.

6.8.1   Percentage Agreement among Observers

Let's suppose we were observing self-mutilating behavior among autistic children, and that we agreed upon its definition. Using the occurrence-nonoccurrence procedures, we obtained the data shown in Table 6.4. Note that two different observers have independently recorded the presence or absence of self-mutilating behavior over four different observational intervals and five different sessions.

There are two methods of calculating the percentage agreement reliability for these data. One that is direct and easily understood simply involves dividing the session total of the observer with the smaller value by the correspond-

Table 6.4
Occurrence or nonoccurrence data involving two independent observers,
four observational intervals, and five sessions.

Session	Observational interval, Observer A					Session	Observational interval, Observer B				
	1	2	3	4	Total		1	2	3	4	Total
1	0	1	1	0	2	1	1	1	1	1	4
2	1	1	1	1	4	2	1	1	0	1	3
3	0	1	0	1	2	3	0	0	0	1	1
4	0	0	0	0	0	4	1	0	0	0	1
5	1	1	0	1	3	5	0	1	1	1	3

ing session total of the observer with the larger value. Multiplying the resulting proportion by 100 yields a percentage agreement. To illustrate, on Session 1 Observer A's total was 2 and B's total was 4. Dividing 2 by 4 and multiplying by 100 yields a percentage agreement of 50 percent. Similarly, the percentages for sessions 2, 3, 4, and 5 are, respectively, $3/4 \times 100 = 75$ percent, $1/2 \times 100 = 50$ percent, $0/1 \times 100 = 0$ percent, $3/3 \times 100 = 100$ percent. The main limitation of this measure is that it is highly dependent on the rate at which the behavior is occurring during a given session. If the rate is either high or low, so that the target behavior either occurs or fails to occur during most or all observational intervals, the percentage of agreement will be correspondingly high (Mitchell, 1979; Hartmann, 1977). Under these circumstances, it is also difficult to specify what constitutes chance levels of agreement.

A second percentage agreement statistic focuses on the percentage of session scores for which there is complete agreement between the two observers. Referring back to the total columns in Table 6.4, we see that the two observers have complete agreement only during session 5. Since there are five sessions, this percentage of agreement is $1/5 \times 100 = 20$ percent. Since this percentage measure of reliability imposes a strict criterion of agreement (both totals must be identical) and does not utilize much of the data, it is not often used as a measure of inter-observer reliability.

6.8.2 The Reliability Coefficient

The use of a measure of correlation—usually the Pearson Product Moment Coefficient (r)—finds its origin in the psychometric tradition. The reliability of a test is expressed in terms of the size of the correlation coefficient. Although the Pearson r may vary between -1.00 through $+1.00$, it is rare that a negative reliability coefficient is found. For all practical purposes, we can assume that reliability coefficients vary between 0.00 and 1.00, in which $r = 0.00$ means an absence of reliability and 1.00 means perfect reliability.

When using correlation to establish the reliability of observers, we regard the session total as a score. If two observers are in complete agreement, their totals for each observational session should be identical. Table 6.5 illustrates three different degrees of relationship between two observers in which N (the number of sessions) is 5. This is shown only for illustrative purposes, since N is not sufficiently large to establish the reliability with any given degree of confidence.

As we indicated, when observers are in complete agreement on their session totals, the correlation is 1.00. Generally, it is reasonable to assume that a high correlation means that both observers made the same or highly similar observations. On occasion, this may not be the case. It is possible to obtain a high or even a perfect correlation and still have observations that are not in agreement. This occurs because the correlation reflects only the relative position of paired observations and not the absolute values of these observations.

Table 6.5
Three degrees of correlation between the session totals of two observers. A negative correlation should rarely be found; if obtained, a serious review of observational procedures and recording techniques would be warranted.

Session	Observer A	B	Observer A	B	Observer A	B
1	2	4	2	3	2	3
2	4	3	4	4	4	1
3	2	1	2	1	2	1
4	0	1	0	1	0	4
5	3	3	3	3	3	3
	$r = 0.58$		$r = 0.83$		$r = 0.68$	

Table 6.6
Hypothetical data showing independent ratings by two observers of five subjects on self-assertiveness.

Subject	Observer A Rating	Rank	Observer B Rating	Rank
1	18	3	22	3
2	16	4	20	4
3	20	2	24	2
4	24	1	28	1
5	14	5	18	5

Imagine, for example, that two observers were simultaneously but independently rating a number of individuals on a scale of self-assertiveness. They obtain the results shown in Table 6.6.

Note that the ranks of the ratings are in perfect agreement. The individual judged as highest in self-assertiveness by Observer A was also rated highest by Observer B. However, the ratings of Observer B were systematically four units higher than those of Observer A. As noted in Chapter 3, it is important to realize that reliability estimates deal with the relative position (rank order) of individual scores. Inter-rater reliability may be very high in making observations yet it is very possible for one rater to be consistently higher or lower in the total number of observations that are made. For this reason, measures of central tendency should accompany reliability ratings. If this difference were to go uncorrected and each observer was subsequently assigned to different experimental conditions, this difference between observers would be mixed (confounded) with the independent variable. It would not be possible to separate the mixed effects of the independent variable from those of the observer. To eliminate this possibility of confounding, each observer should be required to observe an equal number of times under each experimental condition. However, while correcting confounding, the inter-observer differences would add to the variability of the dependent measure. Consequently, the ability to detect differences among experimental conditions would be reduced. What this all means is that utmost care must be taken to assure inter-observer reliability during all phases of the study.

CHAPTER SEVEN

ISOLATING THE EFFECTS OF THE INDEPENDENT VARIABLE

7.1 SYSTEMATIC VARIANCE

It is very difficult to do "good" research free from methodological problems. There are often many subtle sources of difficulty that are common to both human and nonhuman investigations. However, the greatest difficulty is encountered when using human subjects.

An experiment can be evaluated in terms of how well it answers the questions that are asked. If they can be answered unambiguously, without either qualifying comments or the availability of alternative explanations, the experiment may be considered unusually good.

When conducting experiments, we try to hold constant all factors but the one we are manipulating, i.e., our *independent variable.* If we are successful then we can say that any changes in behavior, i.e., *dependent variables,* are due to the effects of our manipulation. The change in behavior resulting from our independent variable is called the **treatment effect.** The treatment effect is also referred to as *systematic variance* or *between group variance.* Researchers try both to isolate and to enhance the effect of the experimental treatment while holding unwanted sources of variation to a minimum.

> **TREATMENT EFFECT** (systematic variance or between group variance) observed changes in the dependent variable resulting from the manipulation of the independent variable.

Unfortunately, more often than we would like, factors other than the independent variable contribute to systematic variance. When this occurs, we cannot determine whether the observed changes in behavior are due to our experimental treatment or to the unwanted extraneous factors. We are then faced with a dilemma. Was the change in behavior due to our treatment factor, to the extraneous factor, or to both? Although these extraneous factors are at times minor and their effects trivial, there are other times when their effects are sufficiently strong to be a major source of systematic error. The result is an uninterpretable experiment. **Confounding** is the technical term used to describe this mixing of the effects of unwanted variables with the possible effects of the independent variable. As we shall see, confounding can occur in many ways.

> **CONFOUNDING** intermixing of effects of extraneous variables with possible effects of the independent variable.

Confounding is also referred to as **systematic error** because the unwanted extraneous variables exert their effect primarily on a particular group or condition rather than on all conditions equally. In contrast, when the extraneous variables exert their effects equally on the subjects in all conditions, we refer to this as **random error.** Random error decreases the precision of our estimates of the treatment effects but it does not affect the interpretation of relationships that may be observed.

RANDOM ERROR   the operation of extraneous variables in a chance manner.
SYSTEMATIC ERROR   error due to confounding.

7.1.1   Internal Validity—More than One Factor Varies

Confounding is undesirable. Whenever it occurs, we compromise the **internal validity** of the experiment. We cannot be sure that the observed relationship is between our independent and dependent variable, since other factors also varied concurrently with the independent variable. The relationship obtained could be due to these confounding variables. When confounding occurs, the relationship that we observe is open to alternative interpretations. It is important to note that the mere suspicion of confounding is sufficient to compromise internal validity. The burden of ruling out the possibility of extraneous factors rests with the experimenter. The greater the number of plausible alternative explanations available to account for an observed finding, the poorer the experiment. Conversely, the fewer the number of plausible alternative explanations available, the better the experiment. As we shall see, true experiments properly executed rule out the greatest number of alternative hypotheses.

INTERNAL VALIDITY   when the independent variable is responsible for observed variations in the dependent variable.

7.1.2   External Validity—Generalizing Our Results

There is another form of validity with which you should be familiar. It is referred to as **external validity** and deals with generalizing our findings. We want to design our research so that our findings may generalize from a small sample of subjects to a population, from a specific experimental setting to a much broader setting, from our specific values of an independent variable to a wider range of values, and finally, from a specific behavioral measure to other behavioral measures. The greater the generality of our findings, the greater the external validity, but the issues are complex and beyond the scope of this text. Several excellent sources deal with this topic (Campbell and Stanley, 1963; Cook and Campbell, 1979) and with the related topics of statistical and construct validity (Cook and Campbell, 1979).

EXTERNAL VALIDITY   when the findings may generalize from a small sample to a population, from a specific setting to a broader setting, from specific values of the independent variable to a broader range of values, and from one behavioral measure to another.

7.2   RESEARCH STRATEGIES

The discussion dealing with confounding and internal validity suggests that the most important fundamental principle of doing research is to design and conduct the experiment so that the effects of the independent variable can be unambiguously determined. The task is not an easy one, and if it cannot be done properly, perhaps it should not be done at all.

In the following pages we will describe random assignment, the use of control groups, and careful experimental techniques as means of avoiding confounding. In brief, we will look at how research should be done. We'll also describe the various possible sources of threats to internal validity (confounding), in sufficient depth to enable you to avoid them. Keep this principle in mind: The time to avoid confounding is during the design phase. Possible sources of confounding should be anticipated and eliminated prior to gathering data. After the data are gathered it is too late to eliminate any confounding that may exist.

7.2.1   Designs

As noted earlier, some research procedures do not permit us to rule out very many alternative explanations of our findings. This is true especially with procedures that neither randomly assign subjects nor manipulate the independent variable, e.g., ex post facto research. Other research procedures do not permit the random assignment of subjects but do permit manipulation of the independent variable and the use of a comparison group (quasi-experimental procedure). The addition of manipulation and a comparison group greatly improves our research. They help to isolate the effects of the independent variable by reducing the number of plausible alternative interpretations of the observed relationship. Quasi-experimental procedures can be effective in isolating the effects of the independent variable but true experiments are even more effective. True experiments allow subjects to be assigned randomly to the treatment and comparison conditions and the independent variable to be fully manipulated. When we say fully manipulated, we mean that we have control over when it is introduced or withdrawn, where this will be done, and to whom we will administer it. Having the capacity to randomly assign, to manipulate, and to use control groups rules out more alternative explanations of an obtained relationship than any other procedure.

7.2.2   Primitive Research Designs

Attempts to rule out alternative explanations and possible source of confounding gave rise to the concept of a control or comparison group. Without proper control conditions, results are generally uninterpretable and the research is often useless. With a primitive design it is virtually impossible to determine whether the relationship is between the dependent and independent variables or between the dependent variable and some unwanted variable. With this type design it would not matter how carefully the observations were made; the data would remain uninterpretable.

Two primitive designs that are still occasionally used are the *One Group Post-Test Design* (Design 1) and the *One Group Pre- and Post-Test Design* (Design 2). Design 1 is depicted below.

Design 1:   Single Group--------Treatment-------Post-Test

With Design 1, a single group of subjects is selected, a treatment is given, and the behavioral effects of the treatment are measured (Post-Test). For example, let us say that we are interested in whether a course on human sexuality affects the attitudes of women toward "the Pill" as a form of birth control. We select from the college population a group of one-hundred women in their senior year to enroll in a specially constructed course on human sexuality. At the completion of the course, we give the participants a carefully constructed questionnaire to complete anonymously concerning their attitude toward different birth control techniques. We then carefully analyze each questionnaire. Unfortunately, no matter how complete our questionnaire or how carefully we assess the data, there is little that we can say about the relationship between the course and attitudes toward the Pill. The relationship could be strong, weak, or nonexistent. We are restricted to descriptive statements concerning the results. For example, we can report the proportion of women in the sample who preferred various birth control options. Beyond this, we won't go. There are too many unknowns and too many other alternative accounts that we cannot evaluate. For example, we do not know what the attitudes of the participants were prior to the course. Therefore we can't assess change in attitudes. Furthermore, other events took place during the same period of time that the course was attended. New knowledge concerning either the beneficial or hazardous effects may have made the news services. Other important *historical* factors could have occurred, in addition to the course, which we cannot assess with Design 1. There are various other problems with this design that we will not dwell on. Suffice it to say that it is primitive, lacking many features of better designs.

Design 2:   Single Group----Pre-Test----Treatment----Post-Test

Design 2 is an improvement over Design 1 but not much. It is an improvement because it permits us to say at least some things. In this case we ask the participants in the human sexuality course to complete our questionnaire prior to taking the course (pre-test) and again at the end of the course (post-test). In contrast to Design 1, we now have a standard (pre-test) against which to compare any changes in attitude that occur on the post-test. Let's imagine that we find a marked change in attitude between the pre- and post-test scores. Can we attribute the change to our independent variable, i.e., our course on human sexuality? Or are alternative accounts also possible? You would be correct if you concluded that Design 2 does not rule out alternative accounts.

Other factors could have occurred during the period that the sexuality course ran that were fully or partially responsible for the change in attitudes. However, their effects are confounded with the effects of the course. Again, as noted previously, news accounts publicizing either the beneficial or harmful effects of different techniques of birth control could have appeared during the same time the course was taken and could have had a powerful effect on attitudes. Older published accounts of these effects may have been encountered through reading or discussions with friends. Publicity efforts by different "lobby" groups may also have influenced attitudes apart from the course. It is also possible that the participants themselves changed during the period between pre- and post-test. As college seniors, they are continuing to mature psychologically, having new experiences, taking other courses, entering new relationships, considering graduation, marriage, jobs, etc.

Design 2 does not provide a way to assess such *historical* or *maturational* factors. Indeed, the effects of testing in itself may be a factor and should be considered as a possible basis for any change in attitude that is observed. Students taking the same or similar tests the second time often score differently. The pre-test may *sensitize* them to the kinds of issues involved and they may pursue information on their own, independent of the human sexuality course. Questions on the pre-test may make the participants more aware that issues exist. After taking the pre-test they may decide that certain answers are more socially desirable on the post-test. Further, participants may become more cooperative and trustful regarding the questionnaire only after experiencing the pre-test. Whether or not these things actually happened is not at issue. The point is that the possibility exists. Consequently, we are unable to untangle the effects of the independent variable from the "spaghetti" of possible alternative explanations.

In some instances our examples of alternative accounts may be weak and debatable. We do not want you to focus on this point. The important issue is that we cannot assess separately the possible effects of the human sexuality course and the possible effects of these other factors. We will not describe other problems associated with Design 2. These will become more apparent later, but they relate to factors such as regression toward the mean, demand characteristics, subject expectancies, experimenter bias, etc.

A point should be made that some of the criticisms of this design are not valid when the experiment is very short term and takes place under laboratory conditions in which the subject is relatively isolated. In short-term laboratory studies few events are likely to occur between pre- and post-testing nor are major changes in the subject likely to occur. However, **test sensitization** and the other factors noted above continue to play an important role.

PRE-TEST SENSITIZATION   changes in the subject's performance as a result of exposure to a pre-test.

7.2.3   Importance of Control Groups

A simple addition to Designs 1 and 2 would improve the research method considerably. This simple addition would rule out a number of the alternative interpretations that we noted were possible for Designs 1 and 2. Adding a control or comparison group that did not take the course on human sexuality would provide valuable additional information. The comparison group would have to be similar to the treatment group (experimental group) and treated in an identical manner on the pre-test, post-test. The only difference is that they would not take the course. Under these circumstances we could better isolate the effects of our independent variable. Given that the groups are *assigned randomly* and *treated properly,* we could eliminate most of the alternative accounts noted for Designs 1 and 2.

The use of control groups is important in both laboratory and applied settings. This is particularly the case when new techniques of therapy are being evaluated. Often a new medical or psychological therapy is introduced to a group of patients and they show a remarkable recovery. It is tempting to conclude that the improvement is due to the treatment. However, this conclusion cannot be supported without a control group. Recovery from the disorder *may not* be due to the treatment, i.e., medical therapy or psychotherapy, but it may arise from other factors. Some individuals may have *recovered spontaneously.* We are reminded of the frequent observation about the common cold. With the finest of medical treatment, it will be "cured" in a week. Otherwise, the patient will require seven days to recover. It is also possible that the simple act of showing concern and giving attention *(placebo effect)* for the well being of the individual may be the important factor. Subjects may expect to get better since experts are attending to them, technology is being used, and gadgets are on display, i.e., more placebo effects. Alternatively, **experimenter expectancies** may operate to the extent that the experimenter sees improvement when there is none. Control groups combined with a *blind* or *double-blind* procedure would be essential in the situation described. Boxes 7.1 and 7.2 illustrate examples of some difficulties encountered when proper control groups are not used, and ways of correcting these difficulties are suggested.

Sometimes data derived from studies without proper control groups (e.g., Design 2) are very compelling even though alternative accounts are plausible. These data do not have to be dismissed. They should serve as a basis for properly designing a study. The illustration in Box 7.2 dealing with blood dialysis with schizophrenics is an example. The initial findings were derived from a Design 2 study. Later, a more elaborate, properly designed study was undertaken. (See solution in Box. 7.3.)

EXPERIMENTER EXPECTANCIES   when the expectations of the experimenter lead to biased observations.

BOX 7.1   ELECTROSLEEP I: DESIGN 2

Electrosleep, or cerebral electrical stimulation, is a technique characterized by the passage of a low-amplitude, pulsating direct electrical current around and through the cranium. It is painless and similar to a mild vibration. Electrosleep is said to be effective for cases of anxiety and for insomnia. Some have used it for depression. Thousands of reports have been published in the European literature and many electrosleep clinics have been established in Europe. No serious side effects have been reported with the technique. It is believed that the direct action of the current itself is the important healing force during treatment whether or not the individual falls asleep. Treatment is usually for thirty minutes and runs consecutively over ten days. Currently (1980) the efficacy of the treatment is at issue with different results being reported in Europe and in the United States.

A recent study done at the University of Texas Medical School evaluated electrosleep treatment. A group of twelve outpatients with chronic symptoms were selected for study because they were unresponsive to anti-anxiety and antidepressive medication. The patients received a daily half-hour treatment successively for ten days. They reclined on a couch with a light mask covering their eyes to hold the electrodes in place. Two electrodes were placed over the eyes and two behind the mastoid. All patients felt a slight tingling sensation over the eyes or behind the mastoid—none felt discomfort. A number of measures were used for evaluation purposes both *before* and *after* treatment. The same researcher was involved with each patient. Of the twelve outpatients, nine had a relatively total remission of symptoms; one showed partial improvement, and two showed no improvement. Ratings on anxiety, sleep disturbances, and depression all fell considerably. What would you conclude from these results?

ELECTROSLEEP—CRITIQUE

Either a Design 3 or 4 would be more appropriate than the Design 2 that was used. Design 3 with the pre-test would be the most appropriate one. A control group is needed to assess expectancy, suggestions, or the effects of relaxation. Any one of these factors, as well as others, could be an alternative account of the findings. These patients had been seen for fifteen to thirty minutes once a month and then they were suddenly exposed to daily visits, many questions, and a new electrical treatment. A marked placebo effect could have occurred. A blind procedure is also essential but a double-blind procedure would be even better.

If the possibility exists that the technician operating the electrosleep apparatus could pass on cues to the patients regarding the condition they were in, then a triple-blind procedure may be necessary: The patient, therapist, and machine operator should all be ignorant of the conditions to which the patients have been assigned. Often it is not possible to do this because the equipment does not permit it. If feasible, a triple-blind procedure should be used in the dialysis experiment. (This is in a later Box.) A cross-over design (see text), if feasible, should be used in the present study. We should note that the control condition should be as identical to the experimental condition as possible except for the actual treatment. This means that the electrode placement for the control condition should be the same and that a "tingling" sensation at the electrode site should occur.

BOX 7.2   SCHIZOPHRENIA AND DIALYSIS: DESIGN 2

Researchers know very little concerning the basis for schizophrenia. One prominent view is that the disorder is linked to a chemical imbalance in the brain. A controversial study was recently reported that relates to the biochemical view. A University of Florida professor of medicine reviewed the evidence on schizophrenia and felt that a strong case could be made that it was an inherited disorder. He then assumed that it had an organic basis and that it might possibly be related to the individual's blood supply. If this was so, then it may be possible that the material circulating in the blood could be removed by dialysis. Dialysis is a process used to remove waste material from the blood of patients with kidney disorders. The researcher decided to try this "blood cleansing" process on schizophrenics. He selected sixteen patients diagnosed as schizophrenic and treated them with dialysis. The dialysis treatment he used was the traditional well-established one (the particulars are unnecessary) and the patients were fully informed of the what and why of the treatment. His results were remarkable. Hallucinations and depression disappeared in fourteen of the sixteen patients. These same patients also showed a considerably improved ability to adapt to normal social situations—often a difficult ordeal for schizophrenics. Could it be that our investigator has discovered a cure for schizophrenia?

SCHIZOPHRENIA AND DIALYSIS: CRITIQUE

Results may have been favorable because patients wanted to believe in the treatment and in a therapeutic/caring environment their expectations may be very high. Also, the therapist (researcher) evaluating the subsequent behavior of the schizophrenics was aware that they had undergone dialysis treatment. In this case, the experimenter's expectancies, if any, could be biasing the outcome. The question could also be raised concerning how the patients were treated by others during this period of receiving dialysis. If they were treated in a different way, then this is another form of treatment different from dialysis. The results were very dramatic and certainly suggested that follow-up research on the new technique be undertaken with a much better design.

BOX 7.3   DESIGN 3—SCHIZOPHRENIA AND DIALYSIS—CONTROL GROUP
CROSS-OVER DESIGN

To rule out expectancy effects, experimenter bias, other forms of inadvertent treatment, and other possibly important factors, a control group design using random assignment is needed. In contrast to Design 2, this design rules out a large number of alternative interpretations.

All schizophrenic patients would first be evaluated ("pre-tested") by a group of independent therapists not involved with the research. The patients would be *randomly* assigned to the *placebo control* condition (control for expectancy plus other factors) and to the experimental condition. The patients would be "blind" in the sense that they would not know what condition they were in. Those in the control group would go through a "dummy dialysis" procedure in that blood would be drawn but not treated. In other words, all patients would be treated exactly alike except for the actual dialysis given the experimental group. Only an attending physician would know who received the treatment. This procedure would assure that the therapists evaluating the subsequent behavior of schizophrenics was also "blind," thus avoiding therapist (experimenter) bias. Since both patients and experimenters would be blind, the study is described as a *double-blind* one. To avoid changes in our "instrumentation" the same therapist would evaluate the patients pre- and post-treatment. At the end of the first phase, all patients would be evaluated and the second *cross-over* phase begun. In the second phase, the experimental and control subjects would have the conditions reversed. Those that were in the experimental treatment would have it withdrawn and those in the control condition would have the treatment introduced, i.e., the groups would *cross-over* to the other condition. No information would be given at this time and subjects would be unaware that a change had taken place. It goes without saying that prior to the beginning of the experiment, all participants would be informed of the two conditions of the experiment and asked to consent to participate.*

*At least one study has been completed recently using a double-blind procedure and dialysis: Schulz, van Kammen, Balow, Flye, and Bunney (1981) studied eight chronic schizophrenic patients. None of the patients improved with dialysis; four patients got worse.

7.2.4   Designs with Control Groups

The importance of control groups cannot be exaggerated. When properly used, they allow us to isolate the effects of the independent variable. In doing so, we can distinguish the effects of the independent variable from the effects of other variables that might produce systematic effects. The proper control groups allow us to conclude that the observed relationship is between our independent and dependent variables.

As we noted, Designs 1 and 2 lack control groups and thus the data they provide, while suggestive, are uninterpretable. We will now describe two experimental designs that make use of random assignment and control groups.

These are powerful designs for isolating the effects of the independent variable. However, as noted in Chapter 4, on occasion it is not possible to randomly assign subjects to groups. This weakens the design somewhat in that it is not possible to rule out as many alternative interpretations. Recall that when subjects are not assigned to conditions at random, the design is referred to as quasi-experimental. It is a very useful design and should be considered when randomization is not possible. Another example of a quasi-experimental design is given in Box 7.4.

Designs 3 and 4   Designs 3 and 4 are true experimental designs that use randomization to assign subjects to the experimental treatment conditions and to the no-treatment control condition. The only difference between the two designs is that Design 4 uses only a post-test measure while Design 3 uses both pre-test and post-test measures.

Design 3—Randomization with Pre-test
Group 1----Pre-Test----Treatment----Post-Test (Experimental Group)
Group 2----Pre-Test----No-Treatment----Post-Test (Control Group)

BOX 7.4   QUASI-EXPERIMENTAL DESIGN WITH A CONTROL GROUP— NONRANDOM ASSIGNMENT

In this hypothetical study, researchers were interested in evaluating a study method, referred to as SQ3R (Study, Question, Read, Recite, Review), on school performance. To make the task manageable and to avoid discontent between experimental and control subjects in a given school, they decided to use schools in separate sections of the city. Two high schools were chosen, each having approximately the same number of students. One was chosen to use the SQ3R method (Experimental Group), the other remained with the traditional method (Control Group). A standardized pre-test was given to all students in both schools prior to the beginning of the school term. The experimental group received weekly instruction on the SQ3R method during the entire school term. The curriculum, textbooks, etc., were essentially the same for both schools. At the end of the year, a post-test was given to all students and evaluation of the study was completed. The school using the SQ3R method performed better than the school using the traditional method. Our question is: "Did the students perform better because of the SQ3R method or are there alternative interpretations that can be given?"

ANSWER TO QUASI-EXPERIMENTAL DESIGN—NONRANDOM ASSIGNMENT

The answer is "yes," alternative interpretations can be given. But first we should note that the use of a control group, even in this quasi-experimental design, results in most of the benefits derived from a true experiment using a control group and random assignment. This design is far better than Designs 1 and 2 but not as good as Designs 3 and 4, which use random assignment. Random assignment allows us to rule out more alternative accounts of an observed relationship. Two important ones we discuss later are subject selection bias and regression to the mean. In the study discussed here, random assignment was not used, but a pre-test was. The more similar the two groups on the pre-test, the more confident we would be that the difference between the two groups on the post-test measure was not due to differences in the capabilities of the subjects. We could also rule out regression to the mean as an explanation. We might note that differences in the pre-test measure between the two schools could have been found. This would complicate things a little. Also, students in the two schools may have scored the same on the pre-test measure but they may not be equivalent in other ways. These differences may affect their development, which may interact with other factors, so that the superior performance may not be a pure SQ3R effect. Had random assignment been possible, we could have assumed equivalence on all factors between the two conditions.

Design 4—Randomization
Group 1----Treatment----Post-Test (Experimental Group)
Group 2----No Treatment----Post-Test (Control Group)

The simplest instance of a control group procedure can be seen in these two designs. The treatment and no-treatment group are treated exactly alike except that one receives the independent variable, and the other doesn't. A comparison "baseline" condition is provided by the no-treatment control group to judge the effects of the treatment condition in the experimental group. We should add that the term *no treatment* should not always be taken literally. It simply means that the experimental treatment was not given to this group. At times some form of treatment different from the experimental treatment is given. On other occasions several groups are used, each receiving lesser amounts of the independent variable. The latter are *parametric designs,* i.e., systematic variations in the amount of a given independent variable, and will be discussed in Chapter 12.

Designs 3 and 4 are powerful. The addition of a control group combined with random assignment greatly increases our understanding of what is occurring in our experiment. If a relationship is found, these designs allow us to rule out many competing interpretations. Therefore, with these designs, we can separate the effects of our independent variable from such factors as individual histories, maturation, subject selection, testing, subject expectancies, regression effects, and various other possibilities that we will discuss shortly.

Since random assignment is used in these designs, it is likely that the two groups are about equal and that any differences observed on the post-test measure between the two groups are due to the independent variable and not to subject bias. In this regard, the pre-test in Design 3 has both positive and negative facets. Researchers sometimes use a pre-test measure to assure themselves that the random assignment procedure did, in fact, result in equivalent groups prior to the treatment. This assurance is not usually necessary and most researchers feel that random assignment in itself is sufficient.

Pre-tests can be useful. A pre-test measure makes it easier to assess whether any loss of subjects (attrition) during the course of the experiment results in a bias for one group (inequality between groups in terms of subject attributes). Determining whether attrition has biased one of the groups can be done easily with pre-test scores by assessing the scores of those remaining in the experiment in the two groups or by comparing those lost from the experiment for the two groups. Pre-tests permit more powerful statistical tests to be used such as analysis of co-variance, given that the assumptions for its use are met. A co-variance analysis is a finely tuned statistical instrument that permits the detection of small treatment effects. Pre-tests are also useful, sometimes necessary, if you want to assess how effective a treatment is for a specific individual; for example, determining the level of anxiety prior to therapy and again after therapy.

At times a pre-test measure may not be available or you may be concerned with the potential problem created by such. Pre-test measures require more time, effort, and expense. Moreover, they are often inconvenient for both subject and experimenter. Recall that they may also sensitize the subjects, causing some to form hypotheses concerning the purposes of the experiment (**demand characteristics**). If the purpose of a pre-test is to determine whether random assignment has resulted in equal groups, it can be dispensed with. Design 4 would be as effective. However, if subjects cannot be assigned randomly, such as in quasi-experimental designs, pre-test measures are essential. Without these measures, researchers would have little idea about the equivalence or nonequivalence of their groups.

DEMAND CHARACTERISTICS a change in the subject's performance as a result of his or her perception of the purposes of the experiment.

Obviously, Designs 3 and 4 have advantages and disadvantages depending upon the needs of the experimenter. These relate to the pre-test and whether or not it serves some essential function other than assessing the equivalence of groups.

7.3 ADMINISTERING THE TREATMENT—RANDOM ASSIGNMENT IN A NEW CONTEXT

We have emphasized the role of random assignment of subjects as a means of isolating the effects of our independent variable on our behavioral measure (dependent variable). Meticulous attention to all aspects of our experiment must be pursued right down to the administration of the treatments to the subjects. For example, it might be convenient for you to give the treatment to all subjects in the experimental group at the same time (all at once) in one session, and to subjects in the control group (all at once) in a different session. This is not an acceptable procedure. Under these conditions, the individual scores may not be independent. It is possible that any extraneous or unwanted event occurring during that session could have a marked effect on the performance of the entire group, and thereby affect their scores.

Whenever groups of subjects that are to receive different treatment conditions can be assembled at one time, and it is possible to administer the treatment to the group as a whole, experimenters are tempted to do so. The major attraction of this procedure is that it is a tremendous savings in time for the experimenter. If all subjects could be assembled in one session, if rooms could be arranged for the different conditions, and if a colleague or two could be enlisted to help, all our data could be gathered in one sitting (session). Our study could be completed in a fraction of the time that it would take to run individual subjects. We could, for example, collect data on one-hundred subjects in a group in one hour versus one-hundred hours of running individual subjects. However, the price paid for such convenience can be high in terms of risking a faulty interpretation.

The problems described in this section and some of those described in the preceding section apply whenever subjects in intact groups are run. In essence, we risk confounding the "time and setting" of administering the treatment with the treatment itself. The following are some examples: an uncooperative or unruly subject in one group and not in the other; a hot, noisy room versus a cold, damp room; a knowledgeable, helpful experimenter versus one less knowledgeable and helpful; some subjects may complete the task quickly in one condition and create "panic" among others in the group who perform more slowly; or the groups may interact differently and ask different questions concerning the task, instructions, etc., thus resulting in groups very different from what the experimenter envisioned. In short, many things may happen which affect all subjects in a particular condition. The scores of individual subjects would no longer be independent. Obviously, careful thought must be given when choosing between a procedure that administers treatments individually and one using intact groups.

Given that we decide to run subjects one at a time rather than in intact groups, then other considerations arise. Let us be more concrete. To start with, good experiments have, at a minimum, an experimental and control group to which subjects are randomly assigned and then run individually (one at a time). There is a proper procedure that should be followed when running subjects one at a time. On any given day an equal number of subjects from each condition (experimental and control group) should be run so that each treatment is represented daily. In an experiment with two conditions, at least two subjects (or multiples of two) should be run on any given day, one from each condition; in an experiment with three conditions, at least three subjects (or multiples of three) should be run on any given day, one from each condition, etc. *It is not* a proper procedure to administer the treatment to all subjects individually in one treatment condition first and then to all subjects in another treatment condition and so on. If the latter procedure were used, systematic changes that occur in the separate experimental sessions, or between the time when the first treatment was presented (Time 1) and when the second treatment was presented (Time 2), would be mixed with the effects of the independent variable, i.e., confounding. Surely as experimenters become more experienced in dealing with subjects, apparatus, instructions, and data recording, they change in some ways. If, in an experiment with two treatment groups, one group was run first and the other run second, the experimenter may be naive for the first group but knowledgeable and sophisticated for the second group. Further, the experimenter may be in a different psychological state (bored) or physical state (ill) for one group. These changes between Time 1 and Time 2 could result in the experimenter treating the two groups differently.

Other events capable of exerting a systematic effect could occur between Time 1, when the first group was treated, and Time 2, when the second group was treated. Some subjects in one group may be getting the treatment during mid-term or finals; the other group at a different time. Measuring instruments may become less reliable; clocks and other equipment may become biased; observers may change their scoring criteria. The important point of all of this is that the procedure of running one group or treatment condition first, either all at one time or individually, is a faulty one and should be avoided.

The following principle should be kept in mind when planning your experiment: *If any extraneous variable having the potential of exerting a systematic effect cannot be eliminated, then it must be held constant for each treatment group, i.e., its effects must be distributed to each treatment group as equally as possible.* Balancing subjects so that each condition is equally represented each day automatically takes into consideration possible variables such as time of year, seasons, and time of school term (mid-term, finals), etc. When more than one subject is run each day, balancing for the time of day that they are run is also necessary. We should note, also, that if more than one experimenter is involved in collecting data, then each should run an equal number of subjects under each condition. Balancing can be achieved using either random assignment or counterbalancing procedures. We want to emphasize that neither procedure eliminates the effects of the unwanted variable, instead they tend to distribute the effects evenly to each treatment group. A few words should be said about randomization when small numbers are involved. We assume that randomization, in the long run, leads to an even balance of the factors about which we are concerned. In the short run, however, there is no assurance of achieving balance. Imbalances can occur on the basis of chance, and the smaller the number of cases randomized, the higher the likelihood of an imbalance occurring. When balancing for factors such as order of presentation (first, second, third), time of presentation, etc., involves a small number of subjects, then counterbalancing is considered an attractive alternative to randomization. Counterbalancing is discussed in more detail when we describe some special problems that occur in those experiments where the same subject receives two or more treatment conditions. These problems are referred to as *practice* effects, *transient* effects, or *sensitization* effects. We deal extensively with these effects in Chapter 13.

7.3.1 Unit of Analysis

Some of the material in the previous section (i.e., intact Groups) relates to this section. When assessing whether a treatment condition leads to a reliable behavioral effect, researchers sometimes err in selecting the measuring unit (score) to use when performing the statistical analysis. This type of error is not common but it occurs sufficiently often to warrant a brief description. Suppose we plan to evaluate two different teaching styles—one a traditional lecture format, the other a discussion-recitation format. We decide to use two introductory psychology classes, each with forty students taught by the same instructor using the same book, assignments, exams, etc. The students are assigned randomly to the two classes at the beginning of the term. At the end of the term they are given a common comprehensive final exam. Can we treat the forty subjects in each class as though they each represent forty independent scores? We cannot. The crux of the issue is whether the scores are independent. They must be so if our statistical analysis is to yield a valid probability estimate. However, it takes only one disruptive student in a class to exert an effect on the others that might possibly lower these scores. Also, classes are different. In some classes, students interact in ways that facilitate learning, in others the interactions interfere with learning. It seems unlikely that students are responding independently to classroom instruction. As we have noted, this problem arises whenever subjects are given a treatment condition as an *intact group*. In our example, the proper unit of analysis would be the mean performance of the class. In other words, each class would constitute an N of 1. To obtain an N of 40, you would need forty classrooms (mean performance of all students in each) instead of forty students. Unlike students, the classes would be independent. Many researchers are unaware of the problem. Others are aware of it but tend to ignore it. The reason for ignoring it is not difficult to see. To deal with forty classrooms rather than forty students in one classroom is not an attractive alternative from the points of view of the logistics and economics of research.

7.3.2 Intentional Confounding

We have stressed the problems associated with confounding. Commonly it occurs without the awareness of the investigator. Confounding in this sense is undesirable and our position is firm on this score. However, there may be occasions when we intentionally confound, i.e., we vary several factors concurrently. Commonly, intentional confounding occurs when the treatment condition is a system or a method composed of several components, each of which could serve as an independent variable. The researcher's interest may be in the system as a whole and not the separate components. If, after showing that the system as a whole (independent variable) is effective as a treatment, interest may then shift to individual components as independent variables. In the latter case, the individual components would be assessed separately. For example, the Personalized System of Instruction (PSI) is characterized by a number of features: many small units of study, clear statements of instructional objectives for each unit, frequent testing, immediate feedback, the requirement that material be monitored, the freedom of students to proceed at their own pace, and other less important characteristics. The PSI system is therefore composed of many different components (potential independent variables). Initial research on PSI contrasted this method with the traditional lecture method, and usually PSI was found to be superior. Subsequent analysis has focused on separate individual components. Complex treatment conditions such as we have described are frequently encountered in applied settings, e.g., evaluation of different psychotherapeutic techniques or ascertaining the most effective displays of meters, switches, and valves in industrial settings.

There are yet other occasions when an experienced researcher has concluded that certain variables are trivial, i.e., they do not influence the dependent variable in the research setting. Under these circumstances, no special safeguards are taken to prevent confounding these variables with the independent variable. However, it is incumbent on the investigator to provide the reader with sound reasoning for accepting the confounding.

7.4   YOKED CONTROL PROCEDURE

The **yoked control** procedure allows the researcher to isolate the important effects of the response-outcome relationship while holding other possible factors constant. This control procedure allows us to separate the importance of the outcome (reward, punishment, aversive event, etc.) itself when it is independent of behavior (subject has no control) compared to that outcome when it is dependent on behavior (subject has control). For example, painful shocks or aversive events can be presented to subjects and subsequently terminated either by the subject (contingent—subject has control over shock) or terminated by the experimenter (noncontingent—subject has no control over shock). When these painful shocks are presented to subjects under these conditions (control versus no control), are the physiological stress responses such as ulceration, weight loss and debilitation the same? That is, is the debilitation due to the shock or is it due to psychological processes involved with having control?

YOKED CONTROL   a procedure in which two subjects are simultaneously exposed to the same condition but the behavior of only one subject can affect the outcome.

To answer the question we would have to be absolutely sure that the shock intensity, shock pattern, time intervals, and shock duration were exactly the same under the two conditions. The procedure or experimental design best suited to answering this question is the yoked control. With this procedure the subjects whose behavior affects the outcome (has control) is referred to as the experimental subject and the subject without control over the outcome is referred to as the yoked control subject. The control subject is bound (yoked) to the experimental subject in that events presented to control subjects are determined by the performance of the experimental subjects. If the experimental subject received a long shock for performing inefficiently, the yoked control subject would receive the same intensity, duration, and temporal distribution of shock. Both experimental and yoked subjects thus receive the same number of shocks, the same duration of shocks, and the same temporal distribution of shocks within each experimental session. The only difference between the subjects is that for one the response-outcome relationship is dependent (contingent---subject has control) and for the other the relationship is independent (noncontingent—subject has no control).

An experiment by Weiss (1968) illustrates the yoked control design. Weiss was curious whether differences in physical measures of stress would occur if painful shocks were delivered to animals when they had control over shock and when they did not have control. To assure that differences in his measures of stress were not due to differences in the characteristics of the shock received, Weiss employed the yoked control design. To further increase his control over the experimental conditions, Weiss used triplets of subjects rather than pairs (i.e., experimental subjects, yoked control subjects, and no-shock control subjects). Subjects in each triplet were also matched on the basis of present body weight and weight gained over a specified time period. Subjects were then randomly assigned to the experimental, yoked, or control conditions. Experimental subjects could avoid or escape electric shock by performing a specific response. Yoked subjects had no control over shock and they received the same duration and intensity of shock whenever experimental subjects received shock, i.e., shock was independent of their behavior. The no-shock control subjects received the same conditions except that they were never shocked. The results of this study showed that yoked subjects experienced far greater stress than did experimental subjects. The yoked control procedure is a very valuable one since yoked control subjects can be exposed to identical conditions in terms of environmental stimulus events and the time of their occurrence. The only difference between experimental subjects and yoked control subjects is the contingent relationship between responses made by experimental subjects and the environmental stimulus events.

As we noted earlier, it is critical that subjects be assigned randomly to the experimental and yoked conditions. When this is not done, serious problems in interpretation of results can occur. An example of problems resulting from nonrandom assignment in an otherwise elegant experimental design is seen in a study reported by Brady (1958). This study is still frequently cited in leading introductory and other texts; nevertheless, its interpretation may be incorrect. The results of this study are exactly opposite to those reported by Weiss (1971a, b, c), yet both studies dealt with similar phenomenon. Perhaps you recall reading about the "executive" (experimental) monkeys and the "employee" (control) monkeys described in Brady's study. Brady used a yoked control design, and experimental and control monkeys were placed in identical restraining apparatus where shock was periodically delivered. The only difference was that the experimental "executive" monkeys could avoid shock by responding properly. They learned the task quickly but not perfectly and, on some occasions, they received shock. Whenever the "executive" monkey received shock the "employee" monkey, yoked to the executive, also received shock. The executive monkeys, who could control whether or not shock was avoided, all developed serious ulcers but the employee monkeys did not. Brady concluded that ulceration was a function of the "executive" role forced upon the monkeys. This conclusion is intuitively satisfying to many people and belief in the debilitating effects of the executive role is widespread. Yet subsequent studies, such as those of Weiss, report opposite findings. Why the conflict in findings?

A look at Brady's assignment procedure suggests one reason why this may have occurred. Only four pairs of monkeys were used and they were assigned to experimental and yoked control conditions on the basis of pre-test avoidance scores. The monkeys assigned to the executive condition were those that had the highest rate of avoidance responding. The other four monkeys became the yoked control subjects. Unfortunately, rate of avoidance responding and ulceration are positively related. Therefore those assigned to the executive condition were probably more prone to ulceration than were the controls. Because of this, it is difficult to conclude that having control over aversive environmental events (executives) leads to greater physiological debilitation than not having control (employees). Indeed, the research of Weiss, where random assignment and the yoked control procedure were used, supports the opposite conclusion.

Several investigators have been critical of aspects of the yoked control procedure (Black, 1967; Church, 1964). Their comments relate to individual differences in response levels, learning rates, variations in individual sensitivity to stimulus events, and sample size. Some of their criticisms have been addressed by Kimmel and Terrant (1968). Students wanting to become more knowledgeable about the yoked control procedure will find the articles by Black, Church, and Kimmel and Terrant informative.

7.5 SINGLE- AND DOUBLE-BLIND STUDIES

Single- and double-blind procedures are used to control for the effects of expectations and also to prevent observer biases from affecting the results of experimental studies. The latter is of special concern when the principal data are based on the experimenter's observations.

It is sometimes appropriate to deal with subject bias or expectations in studies evaluating a drug or therapy by using a placebo control group and a single-blind procedure. In this case, control subjects would be treated in exactly the same manner as experimental subjects, except that they would not receive the independent variable, i.e., real drug or therapy. They would instead receive a placebo treatment, but they would not be aware that this is the case. When the subject is unaware of the condition he or she is in, this is referred to as a **single-blind study.** If both the experimenter and the subject are unaware of the conditions in effect, then we refer to this as a **double-blind study.** On occasion the subject may be aware of the condition, but the experimenter is not. When this is the case, the procedure is referred to as an *experimenter blind* one.

SINGLE-BLIND STUDY   when only the subject is unaware of the condition to which he or she is being exposed.

DOUBLE-BIND STUDY   when neither the subject nor experimenter is aware of the conditions in effect.

7.6 PLACEBOS AND PLACEBO CONTROL PROCEDURES

We will elaborate on the concept of the placebo. The word *placebo* comes from the Latin verb meaning "to please." The evolution of the term from both a research and therapeutic perspective is interesting. An in-depth discussion of the term can be found in the work of Shapiro and Morris (1978).

Medical historians have noted that almost any kind of treatment used in the early days of medicine seemed to have therapeutic properties. Even though these therapeutic treatments had no obvious direct relationship to the problem being treated, they did, in fact, alleviate distress. Remedies such as lizard blood, bat blood, crocodile dung, frog sperm, putrid meat, hoof of ass, and others were used (Shapiro and Morris, 1978). Often, complex rituals were used and the ingredients that were given caused bodily discomfort. These rituals and the administration of the "therapy" had the effect of arousing faith and also the expectation that the "therapy" would be effective. Rituals of a different kind are still used by physicians, therapists, and researchers.

Today, physicians and therapists are well aware of the placebo effect and often use it to their advantage. The phenomenon is well documented in medicine and psychotherapy. Interest in understanding more about the placebo is very high and prominent medical and physiological investigators are giving serious attention to studying it. There is now considerable evidence indicating that the placebo can act like medication and can result in marked physiological changes. Placebos have been shown to actually alter the body chemistry and to mobilize the defenses of the body. There is also evidence showing that administering a placebo has an effect on the neurochemistry of the brain. In studies dealing with the experience of pain, placebos have been shown to significantly reduce pain. These studies showed that placebos did this by triggering the brain to release internal opiates (endorphins), which are known to have a marked effect on the experience of pain. Why and how placebos do this is still a mystery.

7.6.1   Placebos and Research

The placebo effect is similar to *demand characteristics,* which we will describe in more detail later, in that cues or treatment in the situation give rise to expectations on the part of the subject. However, demand characteristics are more idiosyncratic and vary among individual participants, whereas the placebo effect tends to be specifically and directly tied to the treatment condition. The placebo effect in research settings is generally seen in outcome studies where different drug treatments or therapies are being compared. Outcome studies of treatments are different from experimental studies where other kinds of interests are evaluated. In outcome studies comparing either different therapies or drugs, a placebo control group is necessary simply to assess the therapeutic effects of believing that one has received a curative treatment.

We can illustrate the need for this type of control. For example, if we are interested in evaluating the effectiveness of a therapeutic drug, we would have to untangle the actual effects of the drug from the expectation that the drug has a therapeutic effect. Simply believing that a drug or a therapeutic treatment has an effect can lead to a consistent and marked change in behavior. In our experiment we would have two groups. One group would be responding to the drug *and* to whatever placebo effect it might have; the other group would respond to the placebo effect alone. In the latter case the placebo would be an inert substance or sugar pill appearing exactly like the drug itself. If differences in behavior follow, then we would attribute these differences to the effects of the drug since we have controlled for the placebo effect by allowing it to occur in both groups. The placebo is used to insure that subjects in both groups have the same expectations and beliefs. As noted, for the placebo to be effective, it must be indistinguishable in appearance from the actual drug. In some cases it may be necessary to provide side effects similar to those experienced with the actual drug. When using a placebo control procedure the expectation of subjects are distributed equally among the groups used in the experiments.

7.6.2   Placebo Control and Ethics

The "placebo control group" method for evaluating the effects of the independent variable is a powerful technique but, under some circumstances, its use presents real problems. These usually arise when evaluating the effectiveness of clinical-therapeutic procedures, e.g., psychological or medical treatment. Both ethical and practical problems can occur under the latter circumstances. When evaluating a therapeutic technique the placebo control method requires that a sample of individuals suffering from an illness or disorder be divided into at least two groups—one that receives the treatment therapy and one that receives the placebo condition, i.e., attention, etc. For example, in the case of a drug therapy the evaluation requires that the drug be given to the treatment group and be withheld from the placebo group, a drug that may in fact help them. What do you do under these circumstances when part way through the study the drug appears to be effective for the treatment group? This becomes an ethical issue. How do you maintain patients for the placebo control condition once information becomes available suggesting that a treatment is effective? This poses a practical problem. There are some available alternatives to the placebo control method in addition to the cross-over design. One is to use an **active control** procedure. With this procedure half the patients receive an established treatment where the degree of effectiveness is known. The other half receive the new treatment. Another method is the **historical control** procedure. In this case the new therapy is compared with clinical records of past patients who were untreated or who received other therapy. In still other instances if a drug or treatment clearly reduces pain, or lowers blood pressure, or prevents suicide, or *dramatically* reduces any important physical or behavioral problem *consistently,* then a placebo control study may not be necessary. There are also instances when all participants in a research study receive the treatment but in varying amounts of doses. Sometimes therapies have been adopted on the basis of the therapists' observations rather than controlled studies. Although controlled studies are far better for evaluating a therapy, it is sometimes difficult to argue with the observation that "people used to die without a drug or treatment but now live with it."

ACTIVE CONTROL   a procedure in which the control subjects receive an established treatment with a known degree of effectiveness.

HISTORICAL CONTROL   procedure in which the effects of a new treatment are compared to the past records of patients who were either untreated or received a different treatment.

7.7 CONVERGING OPERATIONS

Even though an experiment may be designed elegantly, executed meticulously, and analyzed fully, seldom is a single study sufficiently persuasive to establish a firm empirical relationship or to provide adequate confirmation for a theory. Additional converging evidence is needed. We describe below why this is the case.

Researchers sometimes disagree sharply on the validity of theories offered to explain empirical relationships; they sometimes also disagree on the validity of the empirical relationship itself. It is not unusual to find challenges leveled at theories and relationships, nor is it unusual for considerable controversy to emerge. The resolution of such controversy is often exciting to witness as a dialectic of thesis, antithesis, and synthesis evolves. While controversy over empirical relationships is relatively easy to resolve, controversy over theoretical issues is not. Seldom can a single study provide convincing support for one theoretical view over another. There are too many considerations that must be evaluated for a single study to be effective. Inevitably there are alternative considerations, questions concerning the proper controls, issues of logic, problems of analysis, subtle or blatant forms of confounding, ambiguity of results, etc. Yet, in spite of these manifold problems, science progresses. How? The answer that has slowly emerged over the last twenty years or so is the notion of *converging operations*. Converging operations mean simply that many experiments are conducted concerning either empirical relationships or prominent theories. When evidence from these different studies using different methods, designs, apparatus, etc., converge (report similar findings), we then have converging evidence for a theory or relationship.

CHAPTER EIGHT

CATEGORIES OF CONFOUNDING

8.1 STRATEGY OF RESEARCH

In planning any future strategy—be it a hand of bridge, a set of tennis, or a military campaign—effective strategists frequently employ a checklist of questions they ask themselves prior to making a commitment to a course of action. Some of the questions asked by each of these strategists are shown below:

- Declarer at Bridge: How many tricks have I contracted for? How many quick tricks can I count? How many additional tricks must I develop to make the contract? Which techniques are available? A finesse? A squeeze? A cross trump? An end play?

- Tennis Player: What do I know about my opponent? Left handed or right handed? Type of serve? Hard? Top spin? Deep in service court? Wide? Mostly to your backhand? What about my opponent's speed on the court? Quick? Slow to react? Vulnerable to a drop shot? Does my opponent tend to stay in the back court or come to the net at every opportunity?

- Military Strategist: How many troops are against us? What types of troops? Infantry? Armored? How are they deployed? Are we vulnerable to a flank attack? How about the enemy? What support is available to both sides? Number and type of artillery? Attack planes? Ground-to-ground missiles? Air-to-ground missiles?

Except for the questions asked, the process is not much different when planning research strategy. Since confounding is the most serious threat to internal validity, much of the researcher's preparation time should be spent in reviewing possible sources of confounding. This task is simplified somewhat by the work and thought of others who described and identified eleven different possible categories of confounding. Much of our discussion is drawn from the classic publications on the subject (Campbell and Stanley, 1963).

Determining whether the threat of confounding exists in any given experiment takes a bit of detective work. When evaluating your research or that of others, each possible source of confounding should be carefully and systematically considered to determine whether or not it can be ruled out as an alternative hypothesis. For each category of confounding, it is appropriate to ask, "Could this be an alternative interpretation for our results?"

When reading the following list of categories, keep in mind that identifying a possible source of confounding is much more important than labeling or categorizing it. The label itself is unimportant. Indeed, different individuals may place a possible source of confounding in different categories. The following is a checklist of categories of confounding and some of the questions experimenters should ask themselves during the planning stage of a research project.

8.2 CATEGORIES OF CONFOUNDING

- Task: Is the task well defined and the same for subjects in all experimental groups?

- History: Has some historical event occurred that accompanied one or more of the experimental treatments?

- Maturation: Have some developmental processes paralleled the treatment effects?

- Testing: If a pre-test is used, is it possible that changes have resulted from the pre-test?

- Instrumentation: Have changes in the instrument—human or physical—accompanied variations in the experimental conditions?

- Regression: Have the subjects been preselected so as to represent the extremes on the behavioral dimension of interest?

- Subject: How have subjects been selected for participation in the study and how were they assigned to experimental conditions?

- Attrition: When subjects have dropped out during the course of the study, was the attrition balanced over the various conditions or confined to selected treatment groups?

- Experimenter: Is it possible that the experimenter's theoretical bias led to unintentional recording errors? Or caused the experimenter to unintentionally communicate his or her expectations to the subject?

- Demand Characteristics: Is it possible that some aspects of the experimental setting provide clues that permit subjects to speculate about what is demanded of them in the study?

- Evaluation Apprehension: Does the experiment elicit undue concern among the subjects concerning the adequacy of their performance?

Some special problems of confounding that relate to longitudinal and cross-sectional studies are described in Chapter 15.

8.2.1 Confounding by Task

By the word *task* we mean "what the subjects have to do so that we can measure our dependent variable." If we are interested in reaction time as a dependent variable, do the subjects press a telegraph key, release it, or do we measure it in some other way? If we are interested in reading rate, what material does the subject read? How is it read? Subvocally? Aloud? In an experimental study, it is essential that participants in all groups perform *identical tasks*. If we knowingly or unknowingly vary both the independent variable and the task, any observed differences between groups could be due to the independent variable *or* to the different tasks they performed.

Sometimes task confounding is so obvious that we have no difficulty recognizing it. For example, we would not compare gasoline consumption of two different makes of automobiles of the same size, power, etc., by calculating the miles-per-gallon of one car on a testing track and the other one in real traffic. Similarly, if we were interested in comparing the ability of individuals to track a moving target while experiencing two types of distraction, we would want the target being tracked to move at the same speed for both types. The only thing that should vary is the type of distraction. In these latter two instances task confounding can be easily seen. However, on some occasions, task confounding is so subtle that it is difficult to recognize. To illustrate, researchers were interested in the effects certain colors have on learning words. A list of ten five-lettered words was prepared. Five of the ten words were printed in bold red and five were printed in subdued yellow. Twenty students were randomly selected from the college population and given the list of words to learn. All subjects learned the same list. The criterion for learning was two perfect recitals of the ten word list. The results showed that words printed in bold red were learned more rapidly than those printed in subdued yellow. On the surface, it appears that the speed of learning was a function of the color of the printed words. Before drawing this conclusion, however, we should ask, "Was the *task* the same for the different colored words?" A few moments' reflection should produce a negative reply. Why? Since different words appeared in the red as opposed to the yellow condition, the tasks were different. This suggests a possible alternative interpretation of the findings; namely, that the five words printed in bold red were easier words to learn, independent of the color used. This problem could have been avoided by using a different procedure. Instead of all subjects having the same five words printed in red and the other five words printed in yellow, a different set of words could have been *randomly* chosen *for each subject* of which five were printed in red and five in yellow. Box 8.1 describes a case of task confounding so subtle that many experts would miss it.

BOX 8.1   TASK CONFOUNDING

FREQUENCY OF TESTING

Folklore has it that the more frequently you test students, the more they learn. Imagine that instructors of introductory psychology courses are interested in improving learning in various sections of the course. One obvious possibility is to increase the frequency of testing. Before doing so, however, they must assure themselves that the folklore is correct. Consequently, they design a study to test the "frequency of testing" hypothesis.

Many classes of forty students each are available for research. Students and instructors are randomly assigned to courses that are to be tested different numbers of times. The researchers decide to give some students nine tests, others six tests, and still others, three tests. Only introductory sections are used, with an equal number assigned to each test frequency. The same book and chapter assignments are used. Further, all instructors select test questions from the same source book. All tests contained fifty multiple choice items. Grades on each exam are based on percentages: more than 90 percent correct, an A; 80 percent, a B; 70 percent, a C; 60 percent, a D. The results are clear and statistically significant. The more frequent the tests, the better the performance. Are there alternative interpretations to the frequency of testing hypothesis?

If each test contained 50 items, the number of items differed from condition to condition. Thus, the nine-test condition received 450 items during the semester; the six-test condition contained 300 items; and the three-test condition contained 150 items. In other words, each condition varied in terms of the number of items received during a semester as well as in the number of tests. The treatment condition was therefore confounded with task differences. To avoid this problem, the researchers could have limited the number of questions to 180 and then given nine tests each with 20 questions; six tests with 30 questions, and three tests with 60 questions. This way, the total number of items would be constant while allowing frequency of testing to vary. But a problem still remains. If the researchers allow an entire hour for each test, then the nine-test groups receiving only 20 questions could spend as much as three minutes per item, the six-test groups about two minutes, and the three-test groups, about one minute (given a sixty-minute class.) The investigators could give everyone only one minute per test question, then the nine-, six-, and three-test frequency groups would finish the exam in twenty, thirty, or sixty minutes. This is somewhat better but task confounding is still present if fatigue is a factor or warm-up time is necessary. The problems encountered here are excellent examples of the difficulties involved in doing well-controlled research.

8.2.2   Instructions and Task Confounding

When human subjects are used, instruction in some form is necessary to inform the subjects about what their tasks are. If they are to perform the task in the way that the experimenter wants them to, then the instructions must be clear. If unclear, instructions may result in greater variability in performance among subjects, or worse, they may result in subjects performing different tasks. The latter would vary depending on the level of understanding of the instructions. It is essential when using complex instructions to evaluate their adequacy before beginning the experiment. It is not unusual for instructions to go through several modifications before they are "etched in stone." Even then, the post-experimental interview might reveal that portions of the instructions were unclear for some subjects.

8.2.3   History

We have dealt with this source of confounding previously and pointed out the importance of control groups in eliminating it. Whenever more than one measure is taken in the course of an experiment, i.e., pre- and post-test measures, variables related to history may play a role. Specific events occurring between the first and second measures may affect the dependent variable. The longer the time period between the measurement periods and the less control over the participants (degree of isolation) during this period, the greater the likelihood that these factors will affect the participants.

Let's look at an example. During the latter part of 1979, the popularity of President Carter was very low in most opinion polls that were taken ("pre-test"). A concerted effort was made by his staff to enhance his popularity. Other opinion polls taken in early 1980 ("post-test") found that the President's popularity nearly doubled. Was this increase in popularity due to the efforts of President Carter's staff? Probably not. During this period, a number of important world events occurred, creating a "crisis-like" atmosphere in the United States. American hostages were seized in Iran and Russia invaded Afganistan. The effect was to unite the entire country in support of the President's efforts to deal with these world problems.

An experimental and control group procedure is usually an effective way to avoid factors related to history. This is the case, even when subjects cannot be randomly assigned, e.g., quasi-experimental procedure.

8.2.4 Maturation

With history, specific events occur that are often external to the subjects and are largely accidental. Similar to history are maturational events. However, these represent processes within the individual that result from maturation and development. Included under maturational events are such factors as growth, fatigue, boredom, and aging. Indeed, almost all biological or psychological processes that vary as a function of time and are independent of specific events may be considered maturational factors. On occasion, it is difficult to determine whether to classify an observation in one category or another. As we noted, this is not a matter of concern. The important thing is to recognize that other factors besides the independent variable may be considered as a rival explanation for behavioral change. The most effective way of controlling maturational factors is by using an experimental and control group procedure. Both groups should be similarly affected by maturational factors, but only the experimental group would also receive the treatment.

8.2.5 Testing

Researchers sometimes find it necessary to give a pre-test and a post-test. The pre-test is given before and the post-test after the experimental treatment. Presumably, any differences that occur between the pre- and post-tests are due to the treatment itself. However, a possible rival explanation is that the pre-test accounts for the results. There is a substantial body of evidence showing that individuals frequently improve their performance the second time they take a test. On occasion, the opposite may be found. The test may be a comparable test, an alternate form of the same test, or actually the same test. Since these changes in performance occur without any experimental treatment, it is important to assess them and to use the proper controls. Many researchers have expressed concern that the process of measuring apparently changes that which is measured. We are not yet sufficiently knowledgeable to know the reasons why this may be so. Pre-tests may sensitize subjects to selectively attend to certain aspects of the experiment simply by the nature of the questions asked. Therefore, changes observed on post-tests may be largely due to pre-tests alerting or "guiding" the subject. One way to control for the effects of testing is to use four groups—two control groups and two experimental groups with subjects randomly assigned. The design would look like the following:

Group 1	Pre-test	Treatment	Post-test
Group 2	Pre-test		Post-test
Group 3		Treatment	Post-test
Group 4			Post-test

Comparing Groups 2 and 4 on the post-test would provide information about a pre-test effect, since neither group received the treatment and the only thing that varied was the pre-test for Group 2. If there is a pre-test effect, Group 2 should perform differently. Comparing Groups 1 and 3 on the post-test would provide similar information, except that the treatment is present for both groups. The treatment effect would be evaluated by comparing Groups 1 and 2 or Groups 3 and 4. Other more technical analyses are also permitted by this procedure, i.e., interaction of treatment with testing.

A closely related problem involves the way individuals react to forms of measurement other than testing. Their reactivity to an experimental situation depends upon a number of factors. (See Demand Characteristics and Evaluation Apprehension.) Here again, we must be careful since the act of observing may change that which is observed independent of any treatment conditions.

8.2.6 Instrumentation

This class of extraneous variables is larger than the term implies. It not only includes physical instrumentation (electrical, mechanical, etc.) but also human observers, raters, or scorers. In much research, repeated observations are necessary. Any changes in performance between the first and all following observations may be due to changes in your measuring instrument—physical or human. Raters or observers may become more skillful in identifying certain behaviors but they may also become fatigued or bored. (See Chapter 6 for a fuller discussion.)

As an experimenter, you may be "nervous" at the beginning of the experiment and very relaxed once you become accustomed to your subjects and procedure. When handling animals, you may be initially timid, tentative, and somewhat uneasy. With experience and familiarity, your handling techniques improve. Grading essay exams poses a problem for instructors at times. The criteria for evaluation may change in a gradual and systematic fashion between the start and completion of the task. Papers read earlier may have either an advantage or disadvantage, depending on the direction that the criteria changed. Since psychologists must frequently rely on raters or observers, the problem of accurate reliable measuring techniques is important. To minimize changes in these measurments, careful training of observers is called for. Some investigators use more than one rater or observer and then calculate, periodically, the extent to which: (1) different observers or recorders agree with one another (inter-observer or inter-recorder reliability); or (2) the same observers or recorders agree with themselves at different times (intra-observer or intra-recorder reliability). Since some shifts are almost inevitable, it is wise to randomly assign the experimental treatment to the available experimental sessions. For example, if all subjects in one condition are seen first, and those in another condition are seen second, the treatment effects are completely confounded with possible systematic changes in instrumentation.

8.2.7 Regression to the Mean

Let us imagine that you have developed a procedure you feel will alleviate chronic depressive disorders. You administer a Depression Scale to large numbers of people. As your treatment group, you select a group drawn from those who obtained the highest depression scores. Subsequently, you administer the experimental treatment and find a significant improvement in their scores on the Depression Scale. Can you conclude that the treatment was effective?

This study is typical of many pilot research programs that report "exciting" initial results that are not substantiated by later, better-designed studies. It suffers from vulnerability to the regression phenomenon: Whenever we select a sample of subjects because of their *extreme* scores on a scale of interest, and test them again at a later date, the mean of the sample on these post-test scores typically moves closer to the population mean. This occurs whether or not the extremes are drawn from the low or high end of the scale. This movement of the extremes toward the center of the distribution is known as **regression to the mean.** There is nothing mysterious about this phenomenon. Whenever performance is exceptional, there are a number of factors that combine to produce this unusual outcome. Many of these factors are temporary and fleeting. They are what statisticians refer to as *chance variables*. If these variables combine in such a way as to lower performance at a given time, it is unlikely that they will repeat themselves the next time. Thus, the individual will appear to improve. On the other hand, an exceptionally good performance has enjoyed the confluence of many favorable chance factors. It is unlikely that these will repeat themselves on the next occasion. Thus, the individual will appear to get worse.

REGRESSION TO THE MEAN   individuals high or low on one testing are found to be closer (regress toward) to the mean on a subsequent testing.

In a word, regression to the mean is a function of using extreme scores and imperfect measuring instruments. The more extreme the scores and the lower the reliability of the instrument, the greater the degree of regression. Consider the following: In the 1980 Masters Golf Tournament, Tom Weiskopf made a 13 on a wind-swept hole of the Augusta National Golf Course. He plopped a ball into the lake on three consecutive strokes. What's the likelihood that he "improved" on the next round?

Any outstanding athletic achievement is a combination of both skill and "luck" (chance factors). When an athlete sets a world mark, he or she must be athletically gifted *and* benefit from excellent conditions surrounding the event. For a long-distance track star, the track must be "fast," the breezes minimal, and the competition challenging, to name but a few.

Regression is a statistical phenomena and is *not* due to any experimental treatment. Therefore, if we select subjects extremely low on a pre-test and then give these subjects a post-test (same test) without introducing a treatment of any kind, subjects would be expected to perform higher on the post-test. The reverse of this is true for extreme high scores, i.e., subjects should perform lower on the post-test. When a treatment condition is added between the pre- and post-testing period, investigators have often confused regression to the mean with the treatment effect and wrongly concluded that the treatment was effective.

Regression to the mean is illustrated in Figure 8.1 in two ways to emphasize that it is a statistical phenomena dependent upon extreme scores and errors of measurement. Figure 8.1.A illustrates what is expected on post-test if a sample of extreme scores is selected from a population of pre-test scores. Figure 8.1.B illustrates what is expected on a pre-test if a sample of extreme scores is selected from a population of post-test scores and traced backward to the pre-test scores. No treatment is imposed between the pre- and post-test tests.

The more extreme the score, the larger the error of measurement that it is likely to contain. Thus, when our measurement is not perfectly reliable, as is usually the case, the extreme scores most likely contain measurement errors that make them more extreme than they should be, based upon the subject's capability. For example, extreme low scores could reflect, in part, the subject's capability. However, they are likely to contain considerable error due to such possible factors as nervousness, illness, confusion, distraction, fatigue, irritability, etc. Because of these factors, extremely low scores do not necessarily reflect the individual's true capability. On the next occasion of testing individuals scoring at the bottom of the distribution, the only way is up. On the

*Selection of Extreme Pre-Test Scores
(High and Low)*

Regression to the mean going *from pre-test* to post-test sample means. Regression effect gives the impression that a treatment was given and that it improved performance on the post-test for those scoring low, but hindered those scoring high.

*Selection of Extreme Post-Test Scores
(High and Low)*

Regression to the mean going *from post-test* to pre-test sample means. Regression effect gives the impression that a treatment was given and that it hindered performance for those scoring low, i.e., students performed better on pre-test, and improved performance for those scoring high, i.e., students performed better on the post-test.

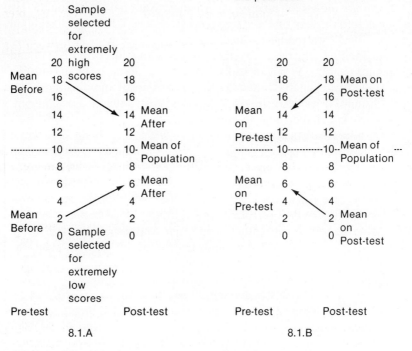

Fig. 8.1   Selection of extreme pre-test and post-test scores

post-test, these factors are less likely to occur and performance should improve slightly because of their absence. A similar process occurs for extremely high scores, except that the factors in this case tend to improve performance. Again, these factors would be unlikely to operate on the next testing occasion. Thus, performance should decrease slightly. (For individuals scoring at the top of a distribution, the only way is down.) In the middle range of scores, pre-test and post-test regression also occur, but within this range, an equal number of pre-test scores are increased as are decreased.

Regression effects in applied settings are not uncommon, yet they often go unrecognized. Individuals enter into psychotherapy when they are feeling their worst. After a period of time, a post-test reveals improvement. The problem is to isolate the effects of therapy from that of regression. Box 8.2 contains additional examples of regression.

When subjects are chosen for their extreme scores, it would be wise to consider the effects of regression to the mean as an explanatory hypothesis that rivals the treatment effect. To isolate the effect of the treatment from regression effects when using extreme groups, an experimental and control group with random assignment is necessary. A matching procedure without random assignment will not do. It is virtually impossible to match on all important variables—even if you know what they are. On the other hand, matching followed by random assignment is an effective technique. (See Chapter 10.) With random assignment, regression for both experimental and control subjects should be the same. Any differences that are observed between the two conditions should be due to the treatment effect.

BOX 8.2   TYPICAL EXAMPLES OF REGRESSION TO THE MEAN

MIDTERM AND FINAL EXAMS

I have just completed grading my midterm exam in my Research Methods course. The results were very disappointing and I now have to improve the performance of at least some of the students. I am especially concerned with those doing very poorly. During the remainder of the term, I introduce a number of new teaching procedures, carefully keeping a record of each. The final exam is given and I immediately compare the midterm and final exam scores of those who were doing very poorly. I find that the mean score of this group has increased. My satisfaction is enormous. This new teaching technique and its accomplishments should be shared with my academic colleagues. Question: Is this enthusiasm justified?

Probably not. As the instructor, I might be very unhappy and disappointed if I were to compare the midterm and final grades of those doing extremely well in the course. I would probably find that my most "brilliant" students did not perform as well on the final as they did on the midterm. Again, regression to the mean rather than the new teaching method is responsible.

BASEBALL BATTING AVERAGES

For any given year, we select fifty active baseball players with the poorest hitting record and calculate their mean batting average. In this group of fifty ballplayers, we will have some who are not very good hitters and they will always remain in this category of "poorest hitters." However, there are also those who are much better hitters than the current year batting averages reflect. They will no doubt improve their hitting the next year. The batting average of these better players may be reduced because of injury, illness, changing batting stance, dissatisfaction with play, unhappiness with teammates, playing a new position, etc. These factors lead to error variance, i.e., they result in an imperfect correlation between their batting record in one year and in the subsequent year. It is the latter group of players who will move the mean batting average upward to the mean. The two essentials are present for regression to the mean: extreme scores and imperfect correlation between pre- and post-measures due to error factors.

Improvements in the overall batting average (regression to the mean) *may* also be aided by those players who deserve to be in the "poorest hitter" category. If you *assume* that their average is so low that it cannot go lower (floor effect), then the only way they can change at this extreme is to improve.

PILOT TRAINING: THE PARADOXICAL EFFECTS OF REINFORCEMENT

Instructors at a flight school for pilots were concerned about their training procedures. They found that for certain important maneuvers their trainees attained a high skill level, but on occasion, performance deteriorated and errors were made. They wanted to eliminate these errors and therefore consulted with a human factors psychologist. The psychologist studied the problem and noted that performance was not perfectly reliable. He then recommended that reinforcement in the form of praise be used but only for the highest level of performance. He stated that intrinsic enjoyment of performing well on the task was sufficient to eliminate most errors, but not all. Reinforcement, used judiciously, would solve the instructors' problems. The instructors instituted the reinforcement contingency immediately but they were chagrined at the outcome. They found, contrary to psychological doctrine, that praise for excellent execution of the complex maneuver typically resulted in a decrement in performance on the next try.

This example was considerably elaborated here, but the basic illustration came from Kahneman and Tversky (1973). Their interesting comments follow: "Regression is inevitable in flight maneuvers because performance is not perfectly reliable and progress between successive maneuvers, if made, is slow. Hence, pilots who did exceptionally well on one trial are likely to deteriorate on the next, regardless of the instructor's reaction to success."

8.2.8   Subject Attrition (Loss)

In Chapter 1, we pointed out that human subjects must be permitted to withdraw from an experiment at any time. Some will exercise this option. Some may withdraw for reasons of illness, others because they do not find the research to their liking. In animal studies, some subjects may die while others become ill. Some attrition, in and of itself, is not serious. However, confounding may occur when the loss of subjects in the various comparison groups is different, thus resulting in the groups having different characteristics. This is referred to as *differential subject attrition* when it occurs. For example, in a study involving noxious stimulation, more subjects of a particular kind may drop out of the study from one of the treatments. Thus, groups that were initially comparable may end up with serious bias in their final comparison of subjects.

Let's look at an additional example. Imagine a research team is interested in comparing the traditional lecture approach to instruction with the Personalized System of Instruction (Keller Method). They randomly assign students to both the PSI and the Lecture Method sections. The students assigned to the lecture method will serve as a comparison group for students assigned to the PSI method. A pre-test on abilities at the beginning of the school term shows that the characteristics of students in the two instructional conditions is comparable. As is true in all classes, students drop courses for a variety of reasons as the term goes on. At the end of the school term a common final exam is given to all students in the lecture and PSI sections. It is found that "PSI students" do much better than do the "lecture students." However, the research team kept careful records of those who dropped out of the different instructional sections. It was found that more students of low ability dropped from the PSI than from the Lecture Method. Consequently, the comparison between the Lecture Method and the PSI Method was confounded. Not only did the method of instruction differ, but because of differential attrition, the abilities of students also differed. Because of this confounding, the actual differences obtained could be due to differences in instructional methods *or* to differences between high ability students in PSI and lower ability students in the Lecture Method. We should note that the research findings with PSI reveal it to be superior on final exam performance when attrition has not been a factor.

Particularly vulnerable to the effects of attrition are developmental and follow-up studies. The loss of subjects in itself, while unfortunate, does not lead to differential bias or confounding. Confounding occurs when subjects with certain kinds of characeristics tend to be lost in one group but not another. To avoid drawing a faulty conclusion, careful record-keeping is necessary. It must be possible to document and assess the loss of subjects.

8.2.9 Experimenter Bias

One of the great myths about scientists is that they are aloof, objective, unbiased, and disinterested in the outcomes of their research. They are interested in one thing and one thing only—scientific truth. Although objectivity is a goal toward which to strive, in actual fact many if not most scientists fall considerably short of the mark. Indeed, they have made a considerable personal investment in their research and theoretical reflections. They passionately want their theories confirmed in the crucible of laboratory or field research. The very intensity of their desires and expectations make their research vulnerable to the effects of experimenter bias. Two major classes of experimenter bias have been described: (1) errors in recording or computation, and (2) experimenter expectancies that are unintentionally communicated to the experimental subjects (Rosenthal, 1966).

Recording and computational errors do not affect the subject's behavior. Generally unintentional, they may occur at any phase of the experiment, such as when making observations, transcribing data, or analyzing results. If the errors are random, then no problem exists. It is when the errors are systematic that real problems develop. A simple example may be helpful. There is a form of ESP called psychokinesis. It is said to occur when a "mental" event controls a physical event. One experiment involved throwing a set of dice. An individual being tested was told by the experimenter to concentrate on throwing a particular number, e.g., "throw sixes." The subject then threw the dice hundreds of times and the experimenter recorded how often the dice were thrown and how frequently sixes appeared. Since we know the chance probability that sixes will occur, we can compare the obtained value (number of times sixes in fact occurred) with the theoretical chance value.

If the obtained value is significantly higher than the theoretical value, this could be taken as evidence for psychokinesis. When the experiment was run in the way described, evidence for psychokinesis was found, i.e., obtained frequencies were greater than the theoretical frequencies. However, when the study was modified slightly to include a "single-blind" technique (the experimenter was not told the number the subject was trying to throw), the results were quite different. No significant differences were found between the obtained and theoretical frequencies. Why did the first study find evidence of psychokinesis while the second did not? It was concluded that unintentional experimenter bias caused the differences. Since the experimenter in the first study knew that sixes were being attempted each time the dice were thrown, he or she would verbalize something similar to, "Sixes are being attempted, a five was thrown." When recording the results on paper, even though a five was thrown, verbalizing the word "sixes" and "five" often resulted in the experimenter writing "six" instead of the correct number.

In contrast to the above example, the second class of experimenter effects *do* affect the subject's performance. These are often referred to as *experimenter expectancies:* The behavior desired by the experimenter is unintentionally communicated to the subject. Perhaps one of the most interesting illustrations of experimenter expectancy is the story of Clever Hans. Clever Hans was a horse owned by a school teacher named von Osten during the 1800s. Clever Hans developed a reputation for solving various mathematical problems. If Clever Hans was asked the product of 3×3, he would stomp with one of his hoofs nine times. Similar feats were routinely performed. Interestingly, von Osten believed that Hans actually possessed advanced mathematical ability and invited scientific inquiry into the abilities of the horse. Detailed and painstaking research revealed that Hans was able to perform as billed but only under specific conditions.

The individual posing the problem had to be visibly present while the answer was being given and he or she had to know the answer. For example, if the questioner thought that the square root of 9 was 4, Hans would answer

"four." You may have guessed that the experimenter (questioner) unintentionally communicated the desirable behavior (correct answer) to the subject
(Clever Hans). It was later determined that Clever Hans was a very ordinary
horse, but one that had developed an uncanny ability to respond to slight cues.
It seems that when a question was asked, the questioner tilted his head forward
to look at Hans' leg and hoof. When the correct number of stomps occurred,
the questioner then looked up. This was a cue to Hans to stop "counting."
How the horse learned this difficult discrimination probably relates to operant
conditioning and reinforcement principles.

How expectancies may affect behavior in an experimental setting is illustrated in a study by Rosenthal and Jacobson (1968). We first must note that
the conclusions of this study have been seriously questioned by some (Elashoff
and Snow, 1971; Baker and Crist, 1971). Others have also been critical of aspects of Rosenthal's works (Barber and Silver, 1968a, 1968b). While these critics question Rosenthal's methods, they do not argue against the hypothesis of
expectancy effects. Now let's return to the Rosenthal and Jacobson study.

Rosenthal and Jacobson gave an intelligence test to students in grammar
school. They then told the instructors that some of the students were "late
bloomers" and that these children would show considerable improvement over
the year. In fact, the children described as "late bloomers" were chosen randomly and were no different from the others. The effects of these labels apparently were dramatic. When those identified as "late bloomers" were later retested, their mean score was much higher than other children who were not
labeled "late bloomers." We can speculate how instructors might treat children labeled as "bright" or "slow." Those carrying the bright label might be
given more attention, more encouragement, and greater responsibilities. In
short, the instructors' expectations probably affect the way they interact with
the student. The quality of this interaction may help or hinder the student, depending on the instructors' expectations. This is one reason why some educators are opposed to systems of education that segregate students on the basis
of tests of ability. With such systems, educators would have different expectations of students, thereby affecting the way the students are treated and what is
expected of them. These expectations might, in turn, affect the students' performance. Some have called this process "self-fulfilling prophecies."

To sum up, in each of these examples, internal validity was jeopardized.
The observed effects represented a confounding of experimenter expectancy
and experimental treatment.

There are several ways of minimizing the effects due to the experimenter.
Perhaps the most obvious one is to eliminate, wherever possible, the experimenter's interaction with the subject. This can be done by automating the experiment. Instructions can be placed on audio or videotape, sequencing of
events can be electronically programmed, etc. In some cases, it is possible to
eliminate entirely the experimenter's contact with the subject. In other cases,
this contact can be minimized substantially. However, we must always give top

priority to the safety and well-being of the subjects, while keeping in mind that they are humans and not "things."

Another way of dealing with experimenter effects is to use a "blind study" approach, in which the experimenters do not know which subjects are experimental or control, nor do they know the experimental hypotheses. There is little chance, under these circumstances, that they will communicate experimenter expectations.

8.2.10   Demand Characteristics

Different situations "demand" different behavior patterns. The behavior of people in church is very different from their behavior at a football game, or when they are at their place of employment. Similarly, behavior of students in classroom situations is typically different from their nonclassroom behavior. These patterns may vary with the size, type of class, and characteristics of the instructor. Frequently, situations tend to "call out" or "demand" expected behavior patterns. Experimental settings are similar. It is possible that the implicit and explicit cues found in research settings may be responsible for the observed behavior rather than the independent variable. If this is the case, we have compromised internal validity. We must remain aware that the very act of measuring behavior may change the behavior measured.

The investigator most responsible for calling our attention to the importance of demand characteristics in research settings is Martin Orne (1962). Since his initial observations, we have become very much aware of their influence on the outcome of experiments in many different areas. The implicit and explicit cues surrounding the experiment, referred to as *demand characteristics,* may consist of the instructions given, the questions asked, the apparatus used, the procedures, the behavior of the researcher, and an almost endless variety of other cues. Cues from these various sources allow subjects to speculate about the purpose of the experiment and the kind of behavior that is expected of them.

Demand characteristics can have different effects. They may lead the subjects to form hypotheses—either correct or incorrect—about the nature of the experiment. Some subjects may react in a compliant way "to help" the experimenter's efforts, whereas others may react in a defiant way "to hinder" the experimenter's efforts. And still other subjects may simply perform in a way they think is expected of them. Whatever the case, demand characteristics can effect the internal validity of the experiment. For example, some recent research on marijuana effects suggests that the "high" experienced from a "joint" is partly due to expectation (Penner, 1978). Subjects experienced with marijuana were given real joints and also joints that smelled and tasted like "grass" but without the psychoactive component. They then rated the quality of the marijuana smoked on a scale from 0 to 100. Interestingly, they rated both types of "joints" high on the scale.

Some of the early research on sensory deprivation effects (Orne and Schiebe, 1964) also reveals the effects of demand characteristics. These investigators treated two groups of subjects exactly alike except one group was told that they would participate in a sensory deprivation study and the other group was told that they were to serve as a control group for a sensory deprivation study. None of the subjects, in fact, experienced sensory deprivation. Even though there were no "treatment" differences between the experimental and control conditions, the subjects performed differently. Those who thought they were experiencing sensory deprivation conditions behaved as if they were undergoing sensory deprivation; control subjects did not.

Before describing how demand characteristics can be detected and their effects minimized, we should note that subjects are generally concientious when participating in research (Weber and Cook, 1972). There is little evidence that most subjects are either compliant (giving "right" data) or defiant (giving "wrong" data).

Although we cannot ignore demand characteristics, we should not become unduly concerned about them to the point of pessimism concerning research. *Debriefing* is one common method used to assess demand characteristics. Debriefing usually includes a post-experimental questionnaire aimed at how subjects interpreted the situation, their perceptions, beliefs, and thoughts of what the experiment was about. This information can reveal whether demand characteristics were operating. The researcher must be careful that the questions do not guide the subject. Otherwise, the answers to the questionnaire are themselves subject to demand characteristics. To obtain useful information, the investigator should use open-ended questions followed up by probing questions. Orne (1962) suggests yet another method for assessing demand characteristics. He suggests that the experiment be simulated and that subjects be asked to play the role of a subject in the experiment.

In the long run, the most valid way of ascertaining whether demand characteristics posed a problem is to evaluate the extent to which the results generalize. If the results generalize to other situations, laboratory or nonlaboratory, then demand characteristics that restrict our conclusions to a specific experimental setting were not operating.

8.2.11   Evaluation Apprehension

Subjects entering the laboratory bring with them a variety of concerns and motivations. The laboratory setting, as we have seen, leads to demand characteristics but it also leads to concern and apprehension about being evaluated. Many become particularly concerned about doing well or making a good impression. Under these circumstances, they may become sensitive and eagerly seek out cues from the experimenter. After the experimental session is over, the floodgates are open for a flow of questions. "How did I do, Doc?" "Did I pass?" "I didn't make a fool of myself, did I?"

The investigator most responsible for assessing concern of subjects about evaluation, Milton Rosenberg, (1969), has labeled the phenomenon "evaluation apprehension." His systematic work on this topic has shown that subjects' behavior in the laboratory is different when they sign up for an experiment entitled "Personality Assessment Project" as contrasted with a less threatening project title, such as "Mathematical Psychology Project."

The subjects' fear of being judged leads to several problems. One we have noted already: Subjects tend to be especially eager for cues from the experimenter. It is also possible that one treatment, in an experiment having several, may give rise to greater apprehension or concern about being judged than the others. If this happens, we then have the problem of confounding (internal validity) to cope with. By differentially arousing suspicion among subjects in an experiment, we have, in fact, created different conditions over and above the treatment condition. Anything in an experiment that arouses suspicion that a subject is being judged can create these difficulties.

CHAPTER NINE

SAMPLING

9.1 PREVIEW OF TOPICS

In this chapter we discuss several different sampling procedures and other related material. It has been our experience when discussing these matters that students sometimes confuse the purposes of random sampling and random assignment. Therefore, we begin the chapter by describing the different purposes served by the two procedures and this is followed by definitions of some key terms. Confusion sometimes also arises in distinguishing a sample from a population. This confusion is not restricted to students; experienced researchers sometimes confuse the two. After describing the difference between a sample and a population, we highlight a true incident to illustrate some problems that follow when the terms *sample* and *population* are confused. This material is followed by a detailed description of the various steps involved when using simple or stratified random sampling. We then contrast simple random sampling with convenience sampling. Contrary to the impression of many students, most laboratory research in psychology uses convenience sampling rather than random sampling. It is important to grasp fully what random sampling requires if you are to understand the limitation and potential problems associated with convenience sampling. The latter portion of the chapter deals with quota sampling, polling, sample size, and other related matters.

9.2 DISTINGUISHING RANDOM SAMPLING FROM RANDOM ASSIGNMENT

Random assignment and random sampling serve different purposes. **Random assignment** relates directly to internal validity and is concerned with the way in which we assign subjects to experimental conditions. It is an essential characteristic of experimentation. The purpose of random assignment is to avoid bias in the composition of the different groups. We want to create groups that are essentially equal so that any differences we subsequently find can be attributed, with some confidence, to the effects of the treatments themselves. We want to be reasonably sure that the independent variable gave rise to the obtained differences and not the method of assigning subjects to groups. Random assignment is the best way of doing this. Moreover, random assignment of subjects to experimental conditions is a basic assumption of many statistical techniques that we use to make inferences from samples to populations. Satisfaction of this assumption is essential for using these statistical procedures.

RANDOM ASSIGNMENT   assigning subjects to each experimental condition in such a way that any given subject is as likely to be assigned to one condition as another.

Random sampling, on the other hand, is concerned mainly with external validity and is designed to ensure that the sample is representative of the population of interest. Random sampling is the most effective way of assuring that the sample is composed of subjects similar to the population on all variables. It is important to establish this representativeness if we are to generalize the results from our sample to the general population of interest. Obviously, random selection of subjects without random assignment to the different experimental conditions can result in a representative sample but with biased treatment groups. For example, even though subjects are randomly selected from the population of interest they may be assigned to treatment conditions on a first come first served basis. Consequently, those coming to the experiment first may differ from those coming later. In fact, there is some evidence that shows subjects volunteering for experiments early in the school term are different from those volunteering late in the school term.

RANDOM SAMPLING   selecting samples in such a way that each sample of a given size has the same probability of being selected (each element in the population has an equal chance of being selected).

It must be emphasized that random sampling does not guarantee representativeness will be achieved, nor does random assignment guarantee comparability of groups. However, they are the best methods we know to achieve these characteristics. But since they are based on probability, random sampling may occasionally result in an unrepresentative sample and random assignment in noncomparable groups. The smaller the sample, the more likely the latter will occur.

9.3 DISTINGUISHING BETWEEN A SAMPLE AND A POPULATION—SOME KEY TERMS

It is necessary to define a few key terms before describing sampling procedures further. The word **population** means *all* members that meet a set of specifications or a specified criterion. For example, the population of the United States is defined as all people residing in the United States. The population of New Orleans means all people living within the city's limits or boundary. A population of inanimate objects can also exist, such as all automobiles manufactured in Michigan in the year 1982. The concept of population includes all members, animate or inanimate, that meet certain specifications. A *single* member of any given population is referred to as an **element.** When only some elements are selected from a population, we refer to that as a **sample,** and when all elements are included we call it a **census.**

POPULATION   all members that meet a specified criterion; all measurements meeting a set of specifications.

ELEMENT   a single member of a population.

SAMPLE   a subset of a population.

CENSUS   when all elements in a population are included in the study.

BOX 9.1 SAMPLE, POPULATION, AND STATISTICS

Two research psychologists were concerned about the different kinds of training that students in clinical psychology were receiving. They knew that different programs emphasized different things but they did not know which clinical orientations were most popular. Therefore they prepared a list of *all* doctoral programs in clinical psychology (in the United States) and sent each of them a questionnaire regarding aspects of their program. The response to the survey was excellent in that nearly 95 percent of the Directors of these programs returned the completed questionnaire. The researchers then began analyzing their data and also classifying schools into different clinical orientations, i.e., psychoanalytic, behavioristic, humanistic, Rogerian, etc. When the task was complete, they reported the percentage of schools having these different orientations and described the orientations that were most popular, which was next, etc. They also described other aspects of their data. The study was written up and submitted for publication to one of the professional journals dealing with matters of clinical psychology. The editor of the journal read their report and then returned it with a letter rejecting the manuscript for publication. In part, the letter noted that the manuscript was unpublishable at this time because the proper statistical analyses had not been performed. The editor wanted to know whether the differences in orientation found among the different schools were significant or if they were due to chance.

The researchers were unhappy and rightly so. They wrote back to the editor and informed him that they had surveyed *all* training programs (i.e., the population). In other words, they had obtained a census rather than a sample. Therefore their data were exhaustive—they included all programs and described what existed in the real world. It was not an estimate based upon a sample. They also pointed out that the editor would be correct only if they had sampled some schools and had wanted to generalize to all schools. The point is that the researchers were not asking whether a sample represented the population—they were dealing with the population.

A comparable example would be to count *all students* (i.e., the population) enrolled in a particular university and then report the number of male and female students. If we found that 60 percent of the students were female, and 40 percent male, it would be improper and irrelevant to ask whether this difference in percentage is significantly different from chance. The fact is that the percentages that exists in the school population is the parameter. They are not estimates derived from a sample. Had we taken a small sample of students and found this 60/40 split, it would then be appropriate to ask whether differences this large could have occurred by chance alone.

Data derived from the sample are treated *statistically* and various statistics are calculated, such as the mean and standard deviation. These are our sample statistics and they summarize aspects of the sample data. These data, when treated with other statistical procedures, allow us to make certain inferences. From the sample statistics we make corresponding estimates of the population. Thus, from the sample mean we estimate the population mean, from the sample standard deviation we estimate the population standard deviation, etc. (See Chapter 11.) Box 9.1 illustrates a problem that can occur when the terms *population* and *sample* are confused. The accuracy of our estimates depends on the extent to which the sample is representative of the population to which we wish to generalize.

9.4 PROBABILITY AND NONPROBABILITY SAMPLING

There are two major sampling techniques that are used: probability sampling and nonprobability sampling. With **probability sampling,** a researcher can specify the probability of an element (subject) being included in the sample. With **nonprobability sampling** there is no way of estimating the probability of an element being included in a sample. If the researcher's interest is in generalizing the findings derived from the sample to the general population, then probability sampling is far more useful and precise. Unfortunately, it is also much more difficult and expensive than nonprobability sampling.

PROBABILITY SAMPLING a researcher can specify the probability that an element will be included in the sample.

NONPROBABILITY SAMPLING there is no way of estimating the probability that an element will be included in the sample.

Probability sampling is also referred to as random sampling or representative sampling. The word *random* describes the procedure used to select elements (subjects, cars, test-items, people, etc.) of a population. When random sampling is used, each element in the population has an equal chance of being selected (simple random sampling) or a known probability of being selected (stratified random sampling). The sample is also referred to as representative since the characteristics of a properly drawn sample represent the parent population in all ways. We will now begin our description of simple random sampling.

9.4.1 Step 1: Simple Random Sampling—Defining the Population

Before a sample is taken, we must first define the population to which we want to generalize our results. The population of interest may differ for each study we undertake. It could be the population of professional football players in the United States, or all retired adults living in the state of Florida, or all women living in Ohio, or the registered voters in Bowling Green, Ohio. It could also be all college students in a given state, or college students at a given university, or all sophomores at the institutions. It could be female students, or introductory psychology students, or ten-year-old children, or senior citizens. The point should be clear—the sample that is drawn should be drawn from the population to which you want to generalize, i.e., the population in which you are interested. It is unfortunate that many researchers fail to make explicit their population of interest. Many investigators use only college students in their samples, yet their interest is in the adult population of the United States. To a large extent, the generalizability of sample data depends on what is being studied and the inferences that are being made. For example, imagine a study that sampled college juniors at a specific university. Its finding was that a specific chemical compound produced pupil dilation. We would not have serious misgivings about generalizing this finding to all college students, even tentatively to all adults, or perhaps even to some infra-human organisms. The reason for this is that physiological systems are quite similar from one person to another, and often from one species to another. However, if we find that controlled exposure to unfamiliar political philosophies lead to radicalization of the experimental subjects, we would be far more reluctant to extend this conclusion to the general population.

9.4.2   Step 2: Simple Random Sampling—Constructing a List

Before a sample can be chosen randomly, it is necessary to have a complete list of the population from which to select. In some cases the logistics and expense of constructing a list comprising the entire population is simply too great and an alternative procedure is forced upon the investigator. We could avoid this problem by restricting our population of interest—defining it narrowly. However, doing so might increase the difficulty of finding or constructing a list from which to make our random selection. For example, you would have no difficulty identifying female students at any given university and then constructing a list of their names from which to draw a random sample. It would be more difficult to identify female students coming from a three-child family, and even greater difficulty would be experienced if you narrowed your interest to first born females in a three-child family. Moreover, defining a population narrowly also means generalizing results narrowly.

Caution must be exercised in compiling a list or in using one already made up. The population list from which you intend to sample must be both recent and exhaustive. If not, problems can occur. (See Box 9.2.) By an **exhaustive list,** we mean that *all* members of the population must appear on the list. Voter registration lists, telephone directories, homeowner lists, and school directories are sometimes used but they may have limitations. They must be *up to date and complete* if the samples chosen from these sources are to be truly representative of the population. In addition, the directories may provide very biased samples for some research questions we ask. For example, a list of homeowners would not be representative of all individuals in a given geographical region since it would exclude transients and renters. On the other hand, the quality of the ready-made lists is often better and less expensive to obtain than it would be to construct a new list.

EXHAUSTIVE LIST   all members of the population appear on the list.

Some lists are available from a variety of different sources. Population and household lists can be obtained for cities with populations of 50,000 to 800,000 people. Many of these directories are published by R. L. Polk and Company and may be found in public libraries, chamber of commerce offices, or for sale by Polk (Sudman, 1976). Professional organizations such as the American Psychological Association, American Medical Association, American Dental Association, etc., have directory listings with mailing addresses of members. Keep in mind that these lists do not represent all psychologists, physicians, or dentists. Many individuals do not become members in their professional organizations. In universities and colleges, complete lists of students can be obtained from the Registrar.

BOX 9.2   POLITICAL POLLS

Information derived from sampling procedures often is used to predict election outcomes. Individuals in the sample are asked their preferences of political candidates prior to the election and then projections are made regarding the likely winner. More often than not, the polls predict with considerable accuracy the outcome. However, there are notable exceptions, such as the *Literary Digest Magazine* poll, which predicted "Landon by a Landslide" over Roosevelt, and the U.S. presidential election of 1948, which predicted Dewey would defeat Truman. (See Section 4.8.3.)

We have discussed the systematic error of the *Literary Digest* poll. Different reasons resulted in the wrong prediction in the 1948 presidential election between Dewey and Truman. Polls taken in 1948 revealed a large undecided vote. Based partly on this and early returns on the night of the election, the editors of the *Chicago Tribune* printed and distributed their newspaper before the election results were all in. The headline in bold letters indicated that Dewey defeated Truman. Unfortunately for them, they were wrong. Truman won and the newspaper became a collector's item.

One analysis of why the polls predicted the wrong outcome emphasized the consolidation of opinion for many undecided voters. It was this undecided group that proved the prediction wrong. Pollsters did not anticipate that those who were undecided would vote in large numbers for Truman. There are other factors that generally operate to reduce the accuracy of political polls. One is that individuals do not always vote the way they say they are going to. Others may intend to do so but may change their mind in the voting booth. Also the proportion of voters casting their ballot differs depending upon the political party and often upon the candidates who are running. Some political analysts feel (along with politicians) that even the position of the candidate's name on the ballot can affect the outcome.

We will describe the mechanics of random sampling shortly but we want to again note that in some cases random sampling procedures simply are not possible. This is the case for very large populations. Since random sampling requires a listing of all members of a population, the larger the population the more difficult it becomes. With very large populations other techniques are necessary. Descriptions of these techniques are found in texts devoted to sampling procedures (Sudman, 1976).

9.4.3   Step 3: Simple Random Sampling—Drawing the Sample

Once a list of population members is constructed, various random sampling options are available. Some common ones involve dice tossing, coin flipping, spinning wheels, playing cards, drawing names out of a rotating drum, and using a table of random numbers. Except for the table of random numbers, most of the techniques are slow and cumbersome. Tables of random numbers are easy to use, accessible, and truly random. A table with a million random digits generated electronically and checked for randomness (Table B.5) has been published by the Rand Corporation.

Let's look at the procedures for using the table. The first step is to assign a number to each individual on the list. If there were 1,000 people in the population, you would number them 0 to 999 and then enter the table of random numbers. Let us assume your sample size will be 100. Starting anywhere in the table, move in any direction you choose—preferably up and down. Since there are 1,000 people on your list (0 through 999) you must give each an equal chance of being selected. To do this, you use three columns of digits from the tables. If the first three-digit number in the table were 218, subject number 218 on the population list would be chosen for the sample. If the next digit were numbered 007, the subject assigned number 007 (or 7) would be selected. You would continue until you had selected all 100 subjects for the sample. If the same number should come up more than once, it is simply discarded.

In the preceding fictional population list, the first digit (9) in the total population of 1,000 (i.e., 0–999) was large. Sometimes the first digit in the population list is small, e.g., 200 or 2,000. When this happens, many of the random numbers encountered in the table will not be usable and therefore must be passed up. This is very common and does not constitute a sampling problem. Also, tables of random numbers come in different column groupings. Some come in columns of two digits, some three, some four, etc. These differences have no bearing on randomness. Finally, it is imperative that you not violate the random selection procedure. Once the list is compiled and the process of selection begun, the table of random numbers dictates who will be selected. The experimenter should not alter this procedure.

9.4.4.   Step 4: Simple Random Sampling—Contacting Members of a Sample

Researchers using random sampling procedures must be prepared to encounter difficulties at several points. As we noted, the starting point is an accurate statement identifying the population to which we want to generalize. Given this, we then must obtain a listing of the population, accurate and up-to-date, from which to draw our sample. Further, we must decide on the random selection procedure that we wish to use. Finally, we must contact each of those selected for our sample and obtain the information needed. Failing to contact all individuals in the sample can be a problem and the representativeness of the sample can be "botched" at this point.

To illustrate what we mean, assume that we are interested in the attitudes of college students at Bowling Green State University. We have a comprehensive list of students and randomly select one hundred of them for our sample. We begin our survey but find that after making an exhaustive effort we are able to obtain information on only eighty of the one hundred subjects in our sample; the other twenty could not be located no matter how intense our effort. We are faced with a dilemma. Is the sample of eighty students who participated representative? Since 20 percent of our sample was not located, does our sample underrepresent some views? Does it overrepresent other views? In short, can we generalize from our sample to the college population? Ideally all individuals in a sample should be contacted. As the number contacted decreases, so does the risk of bias and unrepresentativeness.

Thus, in our illustration, to generalize to the college population would be to invite risk. Yet we do have data on 80 percent of our sample. Is it of any value? Other than simply dropping the project or starting a new one, we can consider an alternative that other researchers have used. In preparing our report we would first clearly acknowledge that not all members of the sample participated and therefore the sample may not be random, i.e., representative of the population. Then we would make available to the reader or listener of our report the number of subjects initially selected and the final number contacted, the number of subjects cooperating, and the number not cooperating. An effort would be made to assess the reason or reasons subjects could not be contacted and whether differences existed between those for which there were data and those for which there were no data. If no obvious differences were found, we could feel a little better about the sample being representative. However, if any pattern of differences emerged, such as sex, education, religious beliefs, etc., a judgment would have to be made regarding how seriously the differences could have affected the representativeness of the sample.

Differences between those that participated and those that did not on any characteristic should not automatically suggest that the information they might give would also differ. Individuals can share many common values and beliefs, even though they may differ in sex, education, etc. The important thing when encountering situations requiring judgments, such as those noted, is for the researcher to describe the strengths and weaknesses of the study along with what might be expected as a result of them. Alert the reader or listener to be cautious in interpreting the data and provide them with the information necessary to make an informed judgment.

The problem just described may be especially troublesome when surveys or questionnaires are used that deal with matters of a personal nature. Individuals are usually reluctant to provide information on matters of a personal nature, such as sexual practices, religious beliefs, political philosophy, etc. The more personal the question, the fewer the number of people responding. Surveys or questionnaires of this nature may have a large number of individuals refusing to cooperate or refusing to provide certain information. Some of these surveys have had return rates as low as 20 percent. If you are wondering what value publishing such data has when derived from such a low return rate, you are in agreement with us. We, too, wonder why such data are published. Even if we knew the population from which the sample was drawn and if the sample was randomly selected, a return rate as low as 20 percent is virtually useless in terms of generalizing our findings from the sample to the population. Those individuals responding to a survey (20 percent of the sample) could be radically different from the majority of individuals not responding (80 percent of the sample).

BOX 9.3   SAMPLE BIAS

Both the reluctance of individuals to provide information on matters of a personal nature and the strong biasing effect that this reluctance may produce can be seen in survey research pertaining to sexual matters. In early 1970, the Playboy Foundation commissioned a large-scale sex survey to be conducted by a professional research organization called the Research Guild. This organization chose twenty-four cities in the United States, randomly chose names from their telephone books, and called individuals about participating anonymously in a discussion on sexual behavior. Only 20 percent of those contacted participated. The results of the study were presented in *Playboy* magazine and later in a book by Morton Hunt entitled *Sexual Behavior in the 1970s*. Can you generalize the results of this sample to that of the population? Only with great risk. It is extremely unlikely that the results of this survey with only 20 percent of the sample participating can be considered representative of the population. Also, selecting names from a telephone directory serves to introduce other sources of bias.

   Two large-scale sex surveys were conducted by *Psychology Today* (1969) and *Redbook* (1974) magazines. In both cases, readers were asked to fill out questionnaires that were included in that month's issue. More than 20,000 responses were returned to *Psychology Today* (mixed readership) and more than 100,000 responses were returned to *Redbook* (primarily women). While these are very large sample sizes, they are also likely to be very biased ones. It is likely that only people who feel relatively comfortable about giving out information about sexual practices responded to the surveys. In addition, it has been shown that those responding to the surveys were younger, better educated, and with higher incomes. Other biases were also present. It is obvious that the results of these surveys can be generalized to the population but only with considerable risk.

9.5 STRATIFIED RANDOM SAMPLING

This sampling procedure is also a form of probability sampling. Before describing some aspects of this procedure, we want to caution you: If you intend to use a sampling procedure other than simple random selection, you should consult a text on sampling.

To stratify means to classify or to separate people into groups according to some characteristics, such as position, rank, income, education, sex, or ethnic background. These separate groupings are referred to as *subsets* or *subgroups*. With a **stratified random sample** the population is divided into groups or strata. Unlike quota sampling, a random sample is selected from each stratum based upon the percentage that each subgroup represents in the population. Stratified random samples are generally more accurate in representing the population than are simple random samples. They also require more effort and there is a practical limit on the number of strata used. Since subjects are to be chosen randomly from each strata, a complete list of the population and each strata used must be constructed. Stratified sampling is generally used in two different ways. In one, primary interest is in the representativeness of the sample for purposes of commenting on the population. In the other, the focus of interest is comparison between and among the strata. Let's look at an example in which the population is of primary interest.

STRATIFIED RANDOM SAMPLE   random samples are selected from different strata or subgroups of the population.

Suppose we are interested in the attitudes and opinions of university faculty in a certain state toward faculty unionization. Historically, this issue has been a very controversial one evoking strong emotions on both sides. Assume that there are eight universities in the state, each with a different faculty size (faculty size = 500, 800, 900, 1,000, 1,400, 1,600, 1,800, 2,000 = total 10,000). We could simply take a simple random sample of all 10,000 faculty and send those in the sample a carefully constructed attitude survey concerning unionization. After considering this strategy, we decide against it. Our thoughts are that different-sized universities may have marked differences in their attitudes and we want to be sure that each university will be represented in the sample in proportion to their representation in the total university population. We know that, on occasion, a simple random sample will not do this. For example, if unionization is a particularly "hot" issue on one campus, we may obtain a disproportionate number of replies from that faculty. Therefore, we would construct a list of the entire faculty for each university and then sample randomly within each university in proportion to their representation in the total faculty of 10,000. Assuming a total sample size of 1,000, the university with 500 faculty members would represent 5 percent of our sample; therefore, 50 faculty would be randomly selected. The university with 2,000 faculty would represent 20 percent of our sample; thus, 200 of their faculty would be randomly selected. We would continue until our sample was complete. It would be possible but more costly and time consuming to include other strata of interest, e.g., full, associate, and assistant professors. In each case, the faculty in each strata would be randomly selected.

As previously noted, stratified samples are sometimes used to optimize group comparisons. In this case we are not concerned about representing the total population. Instead, our focus is on comparisons involving two or more strata. If the groups involved in our comparisons are equally represented in the population, a single random sample could be used. When this is not the case, a different procedure is necessary. For example, if we were interested in making comparisons between whites and blacks, a simple random sample with the size of one hundred might result in about ten to fifteen blacks and about eighty-five to ninety whites—hardly a satisfactory sample for making comparisons. With a stratified random sample, we could randomly choose fifty whites and fifty blacks and thus optimize our comparison. Whenever strata rather than the population is our primary interest, we can sample in different proportions from each strata.

9.6 CONVENIENCE SAMPLES—NONPROBABILITY SAMPLING

Convenience samples are used because they are quick, inexpensive, and convenient. They are useful for certain purposes and very little planning is necessary when using them. Researchers simply use subjects that are available at the moment. The procedure is casual and easy, relative to random sampling. Contrast using any subjects that are available with random sampling where you must have: (1) a well-defined population, (2) constructed a list of members of the population if one is not available, (3) sampled randomly from the list, and (4) then contacted and used as many individuals from the list as possible. Convenience sampling requires far less effort. However, there are potential problems for such convenience, which we will describe. Convenience samples are nonprobability samples, therefore it is not possible to specify the probability of any element of the population being selected for the sample. Indeed, it is not possible to specify the population from which the sample was drawn.

A number of examples of convenience sampling can be given. In shopping malls or air terminals, individuals are selected as they pass a certain location and interviewed over issues, candidates, etc. Phone surveys may be based on anyone answering the phone from the hours 9 A.M. to 5 P.M. Politicians use convenience sampling to decide the attitude of their constituents when they report on the number of letters voluntarily sent to them by their constituents. Statements such as the following are quite common: "My mail is running about 4 to 1 in favor of House Bill 865A. I guess I know how my constituents feel about the issue.'' Unfortunately, many of these samples are virtually without merit. We do not know what population (whom) they represent.

Some additional examples will further illustrate the point. Observations at air terminals may overrepresent high income groups, while observations taken at bus terminals may overrepresent low income groups. Surveys taken at a concert involving rock music would likely be different from those taken at a concert involving classical music. In the case of political attitudes, we do know that many special interest groups make it a matter of policy to write letters to their political representatives. One thousand people vitally concerned about an issue may write more letters than a million people who are indifferent. The point we are making is: Since the population from which the sample came is unknown, it is unclear to whom the data can be generalized. We can generalize to known populations but only with some risk. More is said about this below.

The examples used here are severe and the problems are obvious but there are instances where these problems are not as severe or as apparent. In these instances some researchers believe that convenience sampling is a good alternative to random sampling. As noted earlier, most laboratory research in psychology, human and nonhuman, uses a convenience sampling procedure. We will now discuss this and some problems that can result.

9.6.1 Convenience Sampling and the Introductory Psychology Subject Pool

Some universities require that students taking the introductory psychology course serve as subjects in research projects of their choosing. In this section we will describe potential problems associated with this procedure. When subjects are required to participate in research and are allowed to choose certain experiments over others, then, for any given experiment, it is simply impossible to specify the population to which the sample data can be generalized. In other words, to what individuals, other than those of the sample, are the data relevant?

Requiring students to participate in research serves several purposes. It assures that each student has an opportunity to learn firsthand about scientific research. In this regard, an attempt is made to make participation in research a worthwhile educational experience. It also assures that subjects are generally available for research, thus serving the purposes of the researcher and that of psychology as a science. The system requiring subjects to participate in research of their choosing operates in the following manner: Research projects to be undertaken are listed on a bulletin board with a brief description of the project and a sign-up sheet indicating the time, place, and experimenter. If our earlier description was clear, you will recognize this as a convenience sampling procedure. Although the students are required to participate in research, the particular project is chosen by them. If a subject is available at a given time, and the particular experiment appeals to them, they simply sign their name on the sign-up sheet.

Frequently the description on the sign-up sheet is neutral but often it is not. The titles alone are often threatening to some individuals. For example, "Reaction-Time to Electric Shock," "Problem Solving and Cognitive Skills," or "Personality Assessment." Obviously these are not neutral topics and you can anticipate what may occur. Subjects concerned about the words "Electric Shock" will avoid that particular experiment. Those concerned about their "Problem Solving" ability might think they are to be evaluated and thus avoid that particular experiment. And so it goes. Although all students may participate in research, certain experiments may attract students with certain characteristics. In principle, students with different characteristics represent different populations. Even experiments with titles and descriptions that appear neutral may attract certain kinds of subjects over other kinds. We will restate the point we stated earlier. Subjects participating in these experiments may be thought of as a sample of students from a population of students with certain characteristics—but a population that we cannot identify. Again, we ask: "To what individuals, other than those in the sample, are the data relevant or generalizable?" More concretely, conclusions drawn from the data of students who signed up for a study using electric shock could be very different from data of students who avoided the experiment. It would be improper to generalize the findings to all students.

Some researchers using convenience samples are not concerned about the population to which they can properly generalize because their interest is in assessing the relationship between the independent and dependent variables. Their concern is more focused on internal validity (minimizing confounding) rather than on external validity (generalizing their findings). Others, however, interested in generalizing from the sample to the population represented by it, argue that there is no good reason for assuming that students making up convenience samples are different from the general population of college students. Therefore, they would be willing to generalize their findings to all college students.

A similar argument is made by researchers using convenience samples of nonhuman subjects such as rats, cats, dogs, etc. In this case, sample findings are generalized to all rats, cats, dogs, etc., of a given strain. The argument that the sample results are generalizable to all college students or to all animals of a given species and strain may be right, but the argument is not based on firm theoretical grounds, nor can it seek support from statistical sampling theory. The argument is based more on an act of faith and intuition rather than on objective argument derived from sampling theory. To what populations can convenience samples be generalized? The population to which it is permissible to generalize is that from which the sample was drawn. Strictly speaking, the population from which the sample was drawn is unknown. The sample was not drawn randomly from a list of some well-defined population, thus the population to which the sample findings can be generalized cannot be identified. A real dilemma exists. We have a sample in search of a population. We want to generalize our results beyond the sample, but to whom? This dilemma is inevitable when convenience sampling is used. Under these circumstances, statements concerning generality should be cautious, conservative, and appropriately qualified.

Had a listing of all introductory psychology students at a given university been available, and an adequate number of subjects selected *randomly* from the list for any given experiment, we would not face the dilemma of generalizing our results. If we randomly drew names from this list, our sample would represent the population of introductory psychology students at the university. However, generalizing from our sample to introductory students at other universities would entail some risk. Our sample may not be representative of the population of introductory psychology students at other universities.

9.7 QUOTA SAMPLING

In many large-scale applications of sampling procedures, it is not always possible or desirable to list all members of the population and randomly select elements from that list. The reasons for using any alternative procedures include cost, timeliness, and convenience. One alternative procedure is **quota sampling.**

QUOTA SAMPLING   when lists are not available, interviewers are assigned a starting point, a specified direction, and a goal of meeting quotas of various subsets of the population.

This technique is often used by market researchers and those taking political polls. Usually, when this technique is used, the population of interest is large and there are no ready-made lists of names available from which to sample randomly. The Gallup Poll is one of the best known and well conducted polls to use quota sampling. This poll frequently reports on major public issues and on presidential elections. The results of the poll are syndicated for a fee which supports it. With this quota sampling procedure, localities are selected and interviewers are assigned a starting point, a specified direction, and a goal of trying to meet quotas for subsets (ethnic origins, political affiliations, etc.) selected from the population. In all, 1,500 adults are selected from 320 localities. Although some notable exceptions have occurred, predictions of national elections over the last few years have been relatively accurate—certainly, much more so than guesswork.

With the quota sampling procedure, we first decide which subjects of the population interest us. This, in turn, is dictated by the nature of the problem being investigated (the question being asked). For issues of national interest (e.g., abortions, drug use, or political preference), frequently used subsets are age, race, sex, socioeconomic level, and religion. The intent is to select a sample whose frequency distribution of characteristics reflects that of the population of interest. Obviously it is necessary to know the percentage of individuals making up each subset of the population if we are to match these percentages in the sample. For example, if you were interested in ethnic groups such as Italians, Jews, Germans, Russians, etc., and knew their population percentages, you would select your sample so as to obtain these percentages.

Within each subset, subjects *are not* chosen randomly. This is simply because there are usually no ready-made lists from which the researcher can select randomly. Often individuals are selected in the sample on a catch-as catch-can basis. For this reason quota sampling is less expensive. It would not be so if lists of the population of interest had to be constructed. However, if exhaustive ready-made lists were conveniently available for the population of interest, then choosing subjects randomly would be possible and preferable. In the absence of such lists, it is much more convenient to select quotas by knocking on doors, telephoning numbers, or sending mailings until the sample percentages for subsets match those of the population. Obviously, even though the quotas may be achieved and the sample may match the population percentages in terms of subsets, the sample may still not represent (reflect) the population to which we wish to generalize.

Often interviewers, for sampling purposes, concentrate on areas where large numbers of people are likely to be. This could bias the findings. As we noted earlier, samples taken in air terminals may overrepresent high income groups while those at a bus or rail depots may overrepresent low income groups, and samples at either place may underrepresent those who seldom travel. Also, people who are home during the day, and are therefore available for house-to-house interviews or telephone calls, may be quite different in important ways from those who are not home. In this respect, quota sampling and convenience sampling are similar. In spite of these difficulties, the quota system is widely used and will unquestionably continue to be so for economic and logistic reasons.

9.8   SAMPLE SIZE

We are always confronted with the question of how large a sample should be drawn. The size of the sample depends on various considerations. Some of these relate to population variability, statistical issues, economic factors, availability of subjects, and the importance of the problem. In inferential statistics it depends upon how big a difference between two groups that you consider important to detect. With large sample sizes, small differences can be detected. If the sample size is sufficiently large, virtually any population difference will result in statistical significance. On the other hand, the smaller the sample size, the larger must be the population differences to achieve statistical significance. Stated another way, other things equal, the greater the sample size, the less is the probability of drawing a conclusion that is in error. In carefully conducted survey research, the sample size determines how closely the sample values approximate the population values. Assuming valid sampling procedures, the larger the sample, the more closely (on the average) will the sample values approximate the population values. However, the relationship between sample size and sensitivity is a curve of diminishing returns. Beyond a certain point, the cost and effort required to achieve greater sensitivity becomes disproportionately large.

There is generally a trade-off between the accuracy of the sample in representing population values and the size of the sample. The larger the sample, the more confident we can be that it accurately reflects what exists in the population, but large samples can be extremely expensive and time consuming. On the other hand, a small sample is less expensive and time consuming, but it is not as accurate. Therefore, for those instances where small error and accurate prediction of population values are necessary, large samples will be required. In other cases where more error can be tolerated, small samples will do. It is not unusual to use relatively small samples to generalize to millions of individuals. (See Box 9.4.)

If an entire population were surveyed then we could specify the make-up of that population, e.g., number of Democrats, Republicans, Independents, income, sex, etc. However, to do this for the entire population of the United States would cost hundreds of millions of dollars. Once every ten years the U.S. Census is taken. The cost of the last census (1980) has been estimated to be over a billion dollars. For different purposes, far more limited than the U.S. Census, we could obtain a very good idea of some U.S. population characteristics from a relatively small representative sample of 2,000 to 3,000 people. That is, with a sample of this size we could generalize our results to the entire population. In fact, some have argued that sample surveys can produce more accurate results regarding a given population than can a census. A census requires skilled interviewers in greater numbers than available. It also requires that *all* members of a population be reached. This does not always happen and considerable unhappiness resulted in both the 1970 and 1980 U.S. censuses because of what many viewed as an undercount of segments of the population. Some cities were especially unhappy with the undercount because important funding decisions were tied to the census. A good sampling procedure may have been both less expensive and more accurate.

Researchers usually decide before selecting a sample the amount of "error" they are willing to tolerate and the confidence they have in stating so. This "error" is expressed in terms of the margin of error and **confidence intervals.** (For example, 95 percent of the time the sample will correctly reflect the population values with a margin of error plus or minus 4 percentage points.) Several factors determine what is considered an adequate sample size. Some of these are: the diversity of the population concerning the factors of interest and the number of factors. The greater the diversity among individuals and the greater the number of factors present, the larger the sample that is required to achieve representativeness.

CONFIDENCE INTERVAL   an interval which, with repeated sampling, will include the parameter of interest between its boundaries a specified percentage of the time, e.g., the 95-percent confidence interval.

BOX 9.4   SAMPLE SIZES: CARCINOGENS AND TV VIEWING

One of the most intense and closely researched controversies of our time deals with whether saccharin, an artificial diet sweetener, causes cancer. The controversy first appeared in 1977 when researchers from Canada reported that rats that were fed large amounts of the artificial sweetener developed bladder cancer. The size of the sample in animal studies such as this often are less than 200. Since so many people in the United States and elsewhere use the sweetener for diet and health reasons, there was great concern about how serious was the risk. A number of studies have been published since 1977. Obviously the issue is extremely important, involving hundreds of millions of humans.

In 1980, a report was published by two researchers of the Harvard School of Public Health. They compared the dietary habits of 600 cancer patients (bladder or urinary) with nearly as many people without cancer. Two other researchers from the American Health Foundation in New York questioned 367 patients and an equal number of healthy individuals. They also compared the level of use of saccharin between patients and nonpatients. Contrary to some previous findings, neither study found a significant relationship between saccharin and cancer. There was no consistent evidence that the sweetener was carcinogenic. An earlier study by the National Cancer Institute assessed 3,000 bladder-cancer patients. Their conclusion was that saccharin was a weak carcinogen for individuals who consumed large quantities of the substance. The issue is still not resolved. However, the important point is the relatively small sample sizes that are used to generalize to a massive population.

Another instance of a dramatic difference in size between the sample and the population to which the results are generalized is found in the Nielsen ratings. The television viewing habits of about 1,500 Americans are surveyed each week by the Nielsen organization. From this survey, estimates are made concerning the viewing habits of around *200 million* individuals watching television in the United States. This amounts to sampling about 1 in every 650,000 or more viewers. Even so, apparently the Nielsen estimates are sufficiently accurate to satisfy the competitive TV networks. This survey again illustrates that useful estimates of population values can be made using a small number of observations. The key factor in this case is the representativeness of the sample.

9.9   VARIABILITY AND SAMPLE SIZE

Members of any population vary among themselves in many ways. In some instances this variability may be small and in other instances it may be quite large. Variability of the population on the characteristic of interest is a factor that determines the size of sample that is needed to be representative. This can be seen in the following illustration. Say that we are interested in selecting a representative sample of height for individuals of any given population. If everyone in the given population were identically tall, e.g., six feet tall, then a sample with an N of 1 would be representative of the population. Even if our population varied slightly, say from five feet eleven inches to six feet one inch, a very small sample could be taken whose average would be representative of the population average. In fact, a sample with an N of 1, in this case, would not seriously misrepresent the population value. However, if the height of individuals in the population varied from four feet to seven feet, our sample would have to be relatively large to obtain an average that was representative of the population average. In this instance a small sample could seriously misrepresent the population average.

9.10 SAMPLING ERROR

Error that occurs in sampling can be either *systematic* or *random*. Systematic error is the fault of the investigation, but random error is not. When errors are systematic, they bias the sample in one direction. Under these circumstances, the sample does not truly represent the population of interest. Systematic error occurs when the sample is not drawn properly, such as in the poll conducted by the *Literary Digest Magazine.* It can also occur if names are dropped from the sample list because some individuals were difficult to locate, noncooperative, etc. Individuals dropped from the sample could be different from those retained. Those remaining could quite possibly produce a biased sample. Political polls often have special problems that make prediction difficult.

Sampling error, as contrasted to systematic error, is often referred to as *chance error.* This is due to the fact that, by chance, samples drawn from the same population will rarely provide identical estimates of the population parameter of interest. They will vary from sample to sample. For example, if you were to flip 100 unbiased coins, you would not be surprised if, on one trial, you obtained fifty-five heads, forty-nine on another, fifty-two on a third, etc. Thus, some samples will, by chance, provide better estimates of the parameter than others. Thus, some attributes of interest may be overrepresented and some underrepresented. However, this type of error is random. Moreover, it is possible to describe this error statistically and take it into account when drawing inferences. Thus, in sampling voters prior to an election, we can make such claims as, "The interval from 43 to 47 percent has a 95-percent probability of including the parameter in which we are interested, e.g., the proportion of voters who will cast their ballot for Candidate A."

Sampling error can affect inferences based on sampling in two important situations. In one situation we may wish to generalize from the sample to a particular population. With a small sampling error we can feel more confident that our sample is representative of the population. Thus we can feel reasonably comfortable about generalizing from the sample to the population. Survey research is most concerned about this kind of sampling error. The second situation in which sampling error plays a role is when we wish to determine whether two or more samples were drawn from the same or different populations. In this case we are asking if two or more samples are sufficiently different to rule out factors due to chance. An example of this is found when we ask the question: "Did the experimental group really differ from the control group other than on the basis of chance?"

CHAPTER TEN

CONTROLLING AND ANALYZING VARIABILITY

10.1 CENTRAL TENDENCY AND VARIABILITY

In the course of doing research we are called upon to summarize our observations, to estimate their reliability, to make comparisons, and to draw inferences. **Measures of central tendency** such as the mean, median, and mode summarize the performance level of a group of scores, while **measures of variability** describe the spread of scores among subjects. Both are important. One provides information on the level of performance and the other reveals the consistency of that performance.

MEASURE OF CENTRAL TENDENCY a measure that describes some aspect of the central region of a distribution of scores.

MEASURE OF VARIABILITY a measure that describes the extent of the dispersion of scores.

Let's illustrate the two key concepts of central tendency and variability by looking at a scenario that is repeated many times, with variations, every weekend in the fall and early winter in the high school, college, and professional ranks of our nation. It is the crucial moment in the football game. Your team is losing by four points. Time is running out, it is fourth and two, and you must obtain a first down to keep from losing possession of the ball. The quarterback must make a decision: run for two or pass. He calls a time out to confer with the offensive coach, who has kept a record of the outcome of each offensive play in the ball game. His report is summarized in Table 10.1

To make the comparison more visual, the statistician had prepared a chart of these data (Figure 10.1).

What we have are two frequency distributions of yards-per-play. A frequency distribution shows the number of times each score (in this case, the number of yards) is obtained. We can tell at a glance that these two distributions are markedly different. A pass play is a study of contrasts—it leads to extremely variable outcomes. Indeed, throwing a pass is somewhat like playing Russian roulette. Large gains, big losses, and incomplete passes (0 gain) are

Table 10.1
Yards gained (or lost) on twenty pass and twenty running plays, ordered from largest gain to smallest gain or largest loss.

Pass play				Running play			
31	9	0	−1	10	5	3	2
29	8	0	−5	10	4	3	1
20	5	0	−10	8	4	3	1
15	1	0	−15	8	3	3	1
10	0	0	−17	6	3	2	0

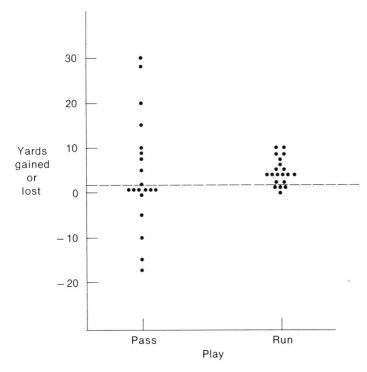

Fig 10.1 Yards gained or lost by passing and running plays. The dashed horizontal line indicates the two yards required for a first down. The mean gain per play is identical: +4 yards, for both running and passing plays.

intermingled. A pass doubtless carries with it considerable excitement and apprehension. You never really know what to expect. On the other hand, a running play is a model of consistency. If it is not exciting, it is at least dependable. In no case did a run gain more than ten yards but neither were there any losses. These two distributions exhibit extremes of variability. In this example, the coach and quarterback would probably pay little attention to measures of central tendency. As we shall see, the fact that the mean gain per pass and per run is the same would be of little relevance. What is relevant is the fact that the variability of running plays is less. It is a more dependable play in a short yardage situation. Seventeen of twenty running plays netted two yards or more. In contrast, only eight of twenty passing plays gained as much as two yards. Had the situation been different, of course, the decision about what play to call might also have been different. If it were the last play in the ball game and fifteen yards were needed for a touchdown, the pass would be the play of choice. Four times out of twenty a pass gained fifteen yards or more whereas a run never came close. Thus, in the strategy of football, variability is a fundamental consideration. This is, of course, true of many life situations.

Some investors looking for a chance of a big gain will engage in specula-
tive ventures where the risk is large but so too is the potential payoff. Others
pursue a strategy of investments in blue chip stocks, where the proceeds do not
fluctuate like a yo-yo. Many other real-life decisions are based on the considerations of extremes. A bridge is designed to handle a maximum rather than an
average load; transportation systems and public utilities (such as gas, electric,
water) must be prepared to meet peak rather than average demand in order to
avoid shortages and outages.

Researchers are also concerned about variability. By and large, from a researcher's point of view, variability is undesirable. It is like static on an AM
radio. It frequently obscures the very signal we are trying to detect. Often the
"signal" of interest in psychological research is a measure of central tendency,
such as the mean or median.

10.2   MEASURES OF CENTRAL TENDENCY

Two of the most frequently used and most valuable measures of central tendency in psychological research are the mean and the median. Both tell us
something about the central values or typical measure in a distribution of
scores. However, since they are defined differently, these measures will often
take on different values. The **mean,** commonly known as the *arithmetic average,* consists of the sum of all scores divided by their number. Symbolically
this is shown as: $\overline{X} = \Sigma X/N$ in which $\overline{X}$ is the mean; the sign Σ directs us to
sum the values of the variable X. Returning to Table 10.1, we find that the sum
of all yards gained (or lost) by pass plays is 80. Dividing this sum by N (i.e., 20)
yields the mean, 4.00. Since the sum of yards gained on the ground is also 80
and N is 20, the mean yards gained per carry is four. If we had only information about the mean, our choice between a pass or a run would have been up
for grabs. But note how much knowledge of variability adds to the decision-
making process. When considering the pass play, where the variability is high,
the mean is hardly a precise indicator of the "typical" gain (or loss). The signal (the mean) is lost in a welter of static (the variability). Not so the running
play. Here, where variability is low, we see that more of the individual
measures are near the mean. With this distribution, then, the mean is a better
indicator of the typical gain. It should be noted that each score contributes to
the determination of the mean. Extreme values draw the mean in their direction. Thus, if we had one running play that gained 88 yards, the sum of gains
would be 160, N would equal 21, and the mean would be 8. In other words, the
mean was doubled by the addition of one very large gain.

MEAN a measure of central tendency obtained by summing all the scores and
dividing by the number of scores.

The **median** does not use the value of each score in its determination. To find the median, you arrange the values of the variable in order—either ascending or descending. Count down $(N + 1)/2$ scores. This score is the median. If N is an even number, the median is half-way between the two middle scores. Returning to Table 10.1, we find the median gain on a pass play by counting down to the 10.5^{th} case (i.e., $(20 + 1)/2 = 10.5$). This is half-way between the tenth and eleventh scores. Since both are zero, the median gain is 0. Similarly, the median gain on a running play is 3. The median is a particularly useful measure of central tendency when there are extreme scores at one end of a distribution. Such distributions are said to be skewed in the direction of the extreme scores. The median, unlike the mean, is unaffected by these scores; thus, it is more likely than the mean to be representative of central tendency in a skewed distribution. Variables that have restrictions at one end of a distribution but not at the other are prime candidates for the median as a measure of central tendency. A few examples are time scores (zero is the theoretical lower limit and there is no limit at the upper end), income (no one earns less than zero but some earn in the millions), and number of children in a family (many have zero but only one is known to have achieved the record of 69 by a single mother).

MEDIAN   the middle score in a distribution of scores.

10.3   MEASURES OF VARIABILITY

We have already seen that a measure of central tendency by itself provides only a limited amount of information about a distribution. To complete the description, it is necessary to have some idea of how the scores are distributed about the central value. If they are widely dispersed, as with the pass plays, we say that variability is high. If compactly distributed about the central value, as with the running plays, we refer to the variability as low. But high and low are descriptive words without precise quantitative meaning. Just as we needed a quantitative measure of centrality, so also do we require a quantitative index of variability.

10.3.1   The Range

One simple measure of variability is the **range,** defined as the difference between the highest and lowest scores in a distribution. Thus, referring to Table 10.1, we see that the range for pass plays is $31 - (-17) = 48$; for a run, it is $10 - 0 = 10$. As you can see, the range provides a quick estimate of the variability of the two distributions. However, the range is determined by only the two most extreme scores. At times this may convey misleading impressions of total variability, particularly if one or both of these extreme scores are rare or unusual occurrences. For this and other reasons, the range finds limited use as a measure of variability.

> **RANGE** a measure of variability defined as the difference between the highest and lowest scores in a distribution.

10.3.2   The Variance and Standard Deviation

Two closely related measures of variability overcome these disadvantages of the range: **variance** and **standard deviation.** Unlike the range, they both make use of all the scores in their computation. Indeed, both are based on the squared deviations of the scores in the distribution subtracted from the mean of the distribution. Table 10.2 illustrates the fact that the squared deviations from the mean reflect the variability of the scores.

> **VARIANCE** a measure of variability based on the squared deviations of scores from the mean.
> **STANDARD DEVIATION**   the square root of the variance.

Note that the sum of the squared deviations mirror the variability of the samples. Now if we were to divide these sums by N—the sample size—we obtain the variance (s^2) of each sample. Thus,

$$s_1{}^2 = \frac{\Sigma(X - \overline{X})^2}{N} \qquad\qquad s_2{}^2 = \frac{\Sigma(X - \overline{X})^2}{N}$$

$$s_1{}^2 = \frac{10}{5} = 2 \qquad\qquad s_2{}^2 = \frac{90}{5} = 18.$$

If we next extract the square root of each variance, we obtain their respective standard deviations, i.e., $s = \sqrt{s^2}$. Therefore,

$$s_1 = \sqrt{2} \qquad\qquad s_2 = \sqrt{18}$$
$$= 1.41 \qquad\qquad\quad = 4.24.$$

Thus, both the standard deviation and variance reflect the variability of scores in a distribution. Beyond that, there are known proportions of area between the mean and various number of standard deviations from the mean. No matter what the form of the distribution, the minimum proportion of area lying within k standard deviations of the mean is $(1 - 1)/k^2$, where k is any positive number larger than 1. Let's illustrate this fundamental statistical fact, known as **Chebyshev's Theorem** by looking at distribution X_2. What is the minimum proportion of area between $\overline{X}_2$ and 2 standard deviations on either

Table 10.2
Two distributions of the same variable with identical means but differing in dispersion or variability. The values of sample X_1 are compactly distributed about the mean, whereas those of sample X_2 are widely distributed about the mean.

Variable X_1	$(X-\overline{X})$	$(X-\overline{X})^2$	Variable X_2	$(X-\overline{X})$	$(X-\overline{X})^2$
14	2	4	18	6	36
13	1	1	15	3	9
12	0	0	12	0	0
11	−1	1	9	−3	9
10	−2	4	6	−6	36
$\Sigma X = 60$		$\Sigma(X-\overline{X})^2 = 10$	$\Sigma X = 60$		$\Sigma(X-\overline{X})^2 = 90$

$$\overline{X} = \frac{60}{5} = 12 \qquad\qquad \overline{X} = \frac{60}{5} = 12$$

side of the mean? Substituting 2 for k within the formula, we obtain $(1 - 1)/4 = .75$. Thus, at least 75 percent of the area is between $\overline{X} \pm 2s$. Since $s = 4.24$, at least 75 percent of the area is between $\overline{X} \pm 2(4.24) = 12 \pm 8.48 = 3.76$ to 20.24. As you can see, 100 percent of the area actually falls between these two points. This is, of course, at least 75 percent.

> **CHEBYSHEV'S THEOREM**　a mathematical proof that specifies the minimum proportion of area between the mean and k standard deviations on either side of the mean for any form of distribution.

　　Now, if the variable is distributed in a bell-shaped fashion known as the *normal curve,* the relationships may be stated with far more precision. Specifically, between the mean and ± 1 standard deviation, approximately 68 percent of the area falls; between ± 2 standard deviation, we find approximately 95 percent of the area. Finally, 97.74 percent of the area lies between ± 3 standard deviation. These features of normally distributed variables are summarized in Figure 10.2.

　　Note that these areas under the normal curve may be translated into probability statements. The proportion of area found between any two points in Figure 10.2 represents the probability that a score, drawn at random from that population, will assume one of the values found between these two points. Thus, the probability of selecting a score that falls between 1 and 2 standard deviations above the mean is 13.59 percent. Expressed in a proportion, it is 0.1359. Similarly, the probability of selecting a score two or more standard deviations below the mean is 0.0215.

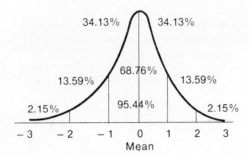

Fig 10.2 Areas between the mean and selected numbers of standard deviations above and below the mean for a normally distributed variable.

Many of the variables with which psychologists concern themselves are normally distributed, such as standardized test scores. What is perhaps of greater significance for the researcher is the fact that distributions of sample statistics tend toward normality as sample size increases. This is true even if the population distribution is not normal. Thus, if you were to select a large number of samples of fixed sample size, say $N = 30$, from a nonnormal distribution, you would find that separate plots of their means, medians, standard deviations, and variances would be approximately normal. We shall have more to say about this important point later in Chapter 13.

10.4   THE IMPORTANCE OF VARIABILITY

Why is variability such an important concept? In a word, in research it represents the noisy background out of which we are trying to fathom a coherent signal. Look again at Figure 10.1. Is it not clear that the mean is a more coherent representation of the typical results of a running play than is the mean of a pass play? When variability is large, it is simply more difficult to regard a measure of central tendency as a dependable guide to representative performance.

This also applies to detecting the effects of an experimental treatment. This task is very much like distinguishing two or more radio signals in the presence of static. In this analogy, the effects of the experimental variable represent the radio signals and the variability is the static. As we can see in Figure 10.3, if the radio signal is strong, relative to the static, it is easily detected; but if the radio signal is weak, relative to the static, the signal may be lost in a barrage of noise. (See Box 10.1.)

The experimental analogue is shown in Figure 10.4. In Cell A, where the variability is large relative to the effect of the experimental treatments (i.e., difference between means), we would be hard-pressed to perceive an experimental effect, even though the sample means are not the same. In view of the great variability in scores, it is quite possible that the mean difference simply

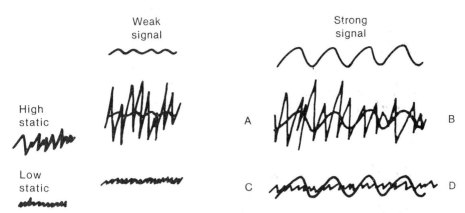

Fig. 10.3 Detection of a radio signal when the signal is either weak or strong and when the static is either low or high. Detection is most difficult when the signal is weak and the static is high (Cell A). Detection is most readily made when the signal is strong and the static is low (Cell D.)

represents sampling error. The difference between means in Cell C is somewhat more impressive, since the variability in scores is low. The large difference between means in Cell B is obscured by the variability of the scores in both conditions. The same mean differences in Cell D, when viewed against

---

BOX 10.1   DETECTING A SIGNAL UNDER QUIET AND NOISY CONDITIONS

As we noted in the text, our interest is in identifying systematic variance resulting from the effects of our treatment, i.e., our independent variable. To do this requires that systematic variance be greater than random variance, i.e., within treatment error variance. An analogy may be helpful in illustrating how systematic and error variance relate. Our analogy deals with detecting a signal against a background of noise. Imagine being in a room full of people, all of whom are talking, and we are told to react to a signal that will be presented from time to time. Our task is to identify the signal when it occurs. The signal (e.g., tone) would have to be very loud or strong for us to identify it when the background noise was loud. We would probably have many "misses" with few "hits." We could assure ourselves of detecting the signal by either making it very loud or by reducing the noise level, or by doing both. Noise could be reduced by identifying those individuals talking loud and removing them from the room. The more loud people removed from the room, the less the noise and the easier it becomes to detect the signal. Our signal to noise ratio (similar to F-ratio) would become large. With zero noise (random error variance), the probability of detecting the signal (systematic variance) would be very high. Doing research is similar to our analogy. The more noise removed from the experiment (random error variance), the more easily can we detect the effects of our independent variable (systematic variance).

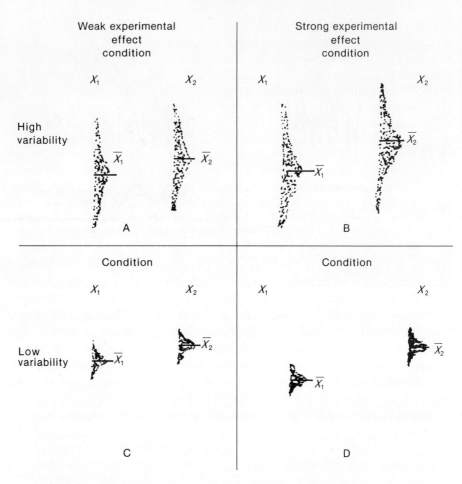

Fig. 10.4 Detection of differences between treatment effects (differences between means) when the size of the effect is either large or small and when the variability is either low or high. When the treatment effect is small and the variability high (Cell A), the difference between means is not sufficiently impressive for us to conclude that the means were probably drawn from different populations (Cell A), However, when the treatment effect is large, relative to the variability (Cell D), we are much more inclined to conclude that the means are representative of different populations, i.e., the treatment conditions produced differential effects.

the extremely low variability of scores, is quite impressive. We would not hesitate to ascribe this observed difference in means to the difference in experimental treatments.

In short, there are commonly two factors involved in assessing the effects of the experimental variable: a measure of centrality, such as the mean, median, or proportion, and a measure of variability, such as the standard deviation.

Broadly speaking, the investigator exercises little control over the measure of centrality.* If the effect of the treatment is large, the differences in measures of central tendency will generally be large. In contrast, considerable control over variability is possible. Indeed, much of the text focuses, directly or indirectly, on procedures for reducing variability. Recall the following in this respect: selecting a reliable dependent variable; providing uniform instructions and standardized experimental procedures; controlling obtrusive and extraneous experimental stimuli. We wish to limit the extent of this unsystematic variability for much the same reasons that a radio operator wishes to limit static or noise—to permit better detection of a treatment effect in the one case and a radio signal in the other. The lower the unsystematic variability, the more sensitive is our statistical test to treatment effects. (See Box 10.2.)

In later chapters we shall look at a number of different ways of assigning subjects to experimental conditions. This is in part what is commonly referred to as the *experimental design*. As we shall see, a properly designed experiment permits us to separate the variability due to systematic factors (such as the treatment conditions) from that due to unsystematic or random factors. Moreover, some designs permit us to tease out the effects of systematic factors that are usually considered to be components of unsystematic variation. Some of these designs are considered in Chapters 11 and 12.

BOX 10.2 PREDICTING THE TREATMENT CONDITION KNOWING THE MEAN AND RANGE

Another way of grasping the concept of error variance and its importance is to think about how variability could relate to predictability (postdiction in our example). If you were given a score of an individual subject who had participated in an experiment, could you identify the treatment condition the subject received knowing the mean and range of scores in the two treatment conditions? This sort of "prediction" is possible if the treatment had an effect and variability was low. With very little variability, very small treatment effects are identifiable. Let's return to our example of predicting the treatment experienced by a given subject. Assume that we have two treatment conditions, Treatment A and Treatment B with five subjects in each. The first example illustrates a treatment effect with zero variability for both treatments (we will use the range as a measure of variability). Knowing the mean and range of scores for both distributions allows us to say (postdict) precisely what treatment a given subject received by knowing his or her score. Since there is zero random variability, the scores in the two distributions do not overlap.

---

*We have already discussed one notable exception. In many applied research settings, the investigator will purposely confound different treatment variables in order to ascertain how large a difference can be produced by "loading the dice," so to speak, in favor of obtaining an experimental effect. See our prior discussion of Personalized Instruction.

Treatment A	Treatment B
$S_1 = 5$	$S_1 = 10$
$S_2 = 5$	$S_2 = 10$
$S_3 = 5$	$S_3 = 10$
$S_4 = 5$	$S_4 = 10$
$S_5 = 5$	$S_5 = 10$

Now we will begin introducing variability to the treatments. The distributions now show scores to range under Treatment A from 3 to 7 and from 8 to 12 for Treatment B.

Treatment A	Treatment B
$S_1 = 7$	$S_1 = 12$
$S_2 = 4$	$S_2 = 8$
$S_3 = 6$	$S_3 = 11$
$S_4 = 5$	$S_4 = 10$
$S_5 = 3$	$S_5 = 9$

Even with this amount of variability we could postdict with complete precision the condition each subject experienced if we knew the subject's score and the mean and range of the two distributions. Again, in this example, we can do this because the range of scores in the two distributions do not overlap. However, as variability increases and scores in the two distributions begin to overlap, we can no longer postdict with complete accuracy. In the example below the range of scores for Treatment A vary from 1 to 9 and for Treatment B they vary from 6 to 14. Scores of 6, 8, and 9 are common (overlap) to both treatment distributions.

Treatment A	Treatment B
$S_1 = 1$	$S_1 = 6$
$S_2 = 5$	$S_2 = 8$
$S_3 = 6$	$S_3 = 9$
$S_4 = 8$	$S_4 = 13$
$S_5 = 9$	$S_5 = 14$

The illustrations used here are intended to emphasize the importance of keeping error variance to a minimum.

10.5 ANALYZING VARIANCE

One technique for making comparisons between treatments requires that variance be analyzed. We refer to this technique as the *analysis of variance* (ANOVA). Different sources of variance are analyzed and decisions are made whether the observed differences are likely to have occurred either by chance

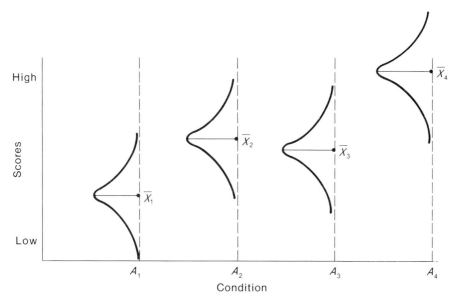

Fig. 10.5 Four treatment conditions with means $\overline{X}_1$, $\overline{X}_2$, $\overline{X}_3$, and $\overline{X}_4$. The between-group variance estimate is based on the dispersion (differences) among the sample means (•). The within-group variance estimates is based on the dispersion *within* each of the four treatment groups.

or as a result of the experimental treatment. To understand the procedure, it is necessary to be more familiar with the terms **between-group variance** and **within-group variance.** These measures are considered to be different and independent estimates of variance. The between-group variance is derived from the variability between treatment groups (differences between their means); the within-group variance is derived from the variability within each group, i.e., the variance discussed in Section 10.3. Figure 10.5 illustrates graphically the between-group and within-group variance estimates.

BETWEEN-GROUP VARIANCE   an estimate of variability derived from the variability among treatment groups.

WITHIN-GROUP VARIANCE   an estimate of variance derived from variability within each group; represents nonsystematic (random) error.

The between-group variance is generally a function of the strength of the independent variable, whereas the within-group variance is generally a function of individual differences and how carefully the experiment is conducted. Between-group variance is also referred to as *systematic variance* and within-group variance as *error variance* or *nonsystematic (random) error.*

Consider the following. Imagine the improbable situation in which you have two groups that are identical in every way. On a pre-test, all subjects receive precisely the same scores. Then Group A_2 receives an experimental treatment that raises each score by three points. The resulting two sets of scores are shown in Table 10.3. The between-group variance estimate would reflect the mean difference of three points between the groups.

Now let's be a bit more realistic. The subjects are not identical. They differ from one another in abilities, motivations, reactions to the experimental situation, mood, etc. To simulate reality, we go to a table of random numbers and select the first four single-digit numbers that we find. We alternately add and subtract these numbers from the scores of both groups. The numbers we found were 9, 4, 7, 8. The procedures are summarized in Table 10.4. What we have done, in effect, is to add "error" to our scores while preserving the difference between means. The difference between means is the basis for estimating the between-group variance. The variance between treatments contains systematic variance due to the effects (if any) of the treatment. In contrast, within-variance is due to factors other than treatments. It is what we have labeled error. As we shall see, it is the ratio between these two variance estimates that is important.

Given that the experiment is conducted properly, when the independent variable has a strong effect the between-group variance (systematic variance) will be large relative to the within-group variance (error variance). This difference would be reflected in the ratio of between-group variance to within group variance. We refer to this ratio of variances as the **F-ratio.**

$$F = \frac{\text{between-group variance}}{\text{within-group variance}}.$$

F-RATIO A ratio of two variance estimates. When testing the significance of difference among means, a large F-ratio means a large difference among means (the signal) relative to the experimental error (the noise).

The between-group variance contains both the effects of the experimental variable (if any) and error. The within-group variance consists of error. Thus, the F-ratio can also be thought of as follows:

$$F = \frac{\text{systematic variance} + \text{error}}{\text{error}}.$$

The F-ratio allows us to evaluate whether the difference between the means of two (or more) experimental conditions is due to our treatment or to random sources of error. To do this we first determine the extent of random sources of error by calculating the variation among subjects treated exactly alike, i.e., within-group variance. This variation is what we would expect be-

Table 10.3
A hypothetical situation in which two groups of identical subjects differ only by the effects of the experimental treatment.

	A_1	A_2
	9	12
	9	12
	9	12
	9	12
	$\overline{X}_1 = 9$	$\overline{X}_2 = 12$

Table 10.4
A hypothetical situation in which randomly selected members are alternately added and subtracted to the scores of two groups of subjects in which the mean difference between groups is 3. The effect is to add "within error" to the score of each group. Note that, before adding variability, the variances were zero, i.e., there was no variability. After adding variability, the variances were 7.18.*

A_1			A_2		
Original score	Add	New score	Original score	Add	New score
9	+9	18	12	+9	21
9	−4	5	12	−4	8
9	+7	16	12	+7	19
9	−8	1	12	−8	4
$\Sigma X = 36$		$\Sigma X_1 = 40 \overline{X} = 10$	$\Sigma X = 48$		$\Sigma X_2 = 52$
$\overline{X} = 9$		$s^2 = 7.18$	$\overline{X} = 12$		$\overline{X} = 13$
$s^2 = 0$			$s^2 = 0$		$s^2 = 7.18$

*The formula used for calculating variances was:

$$\frac{\Sigma(X - \overline{X})^2}{N}.$$

This describes a sample variance. Later, when we use sample variances to estimate population variances, the formula will be modified slightly, i.e.:

$$s^2 = \frac{\Sigma(X - \overline{X})^2}{N - 1}.$$

This formula has been shown to provide an unbiased estimate of the population variance.

tween two treatment conditions if our treatment had no effect. We conclude that our treatment had an effect only if the difference between our treatments (variance between treatments) is greater than what we could reasonably expect based upon random error (variance within a treatment).

Note that if there are no effects of the treatment variable, systematic variance is zero and the F-ratio is 1.00. If the independent variable has only a weak effect, then the between-group variance relative to the within-group variance will be only slightly larger, and the F-ratio derived from these estimates of variance will be small.

When this ratio is sufficiently large, we can conclude that the differences between treatment conditions (means) are significantly different from chance. It should be noted that in addition to increasing the sample size, i.e., N, the F-ratio can be increased either by increasing between-group variance (systematic variance) or decreasing within-group variance (error variance) or both.

10.6   REDUCING UNCONTROLLED VARIATION

Reducing **uncontrolled variation** has a direct effect on decreasing the within-group variance and thus reducing the denominator of the F-ratio. The effect is to increase our ability to detect true differences. There are four basic ways in which this can be done: (1) avoid random variation in treatment; (2) identify factors other than the independent variable, whose presence may contribute to systematic variation; (3) reduce individual differences in the subject population; and (4) use a statistical procedure known as analysis of co-variance. The first three ways of reducing within-group variance are experimental; the last is entirely statistical.

UNCONTROLLED VARIATION   variations due to variables not under experimental control.

10.6.1   Avoiding Random Variation

There is essentially one way of avoiding random variation in the treatment given to subjects and that is, apart from the independent variable, to treat all subjects as similarly as possible. If all conditions cannot be held constant, the experimental situation should be carefully assessed and perhaps constancy can be achieved by elimination of some extraneous variable.

It is often difficult to treat all subjects alike and, in some cases, doing so may introduce rigidity into the procedure when flexibility is needed. Unfortunately, a simple formula for "do" and "don't" cannot be substituted for thoughtful decision making. Common sense is often needed and this develops with research experience. While realizing that it is difficult, an attempt must be made to keep the experimental procedures, instructions, manner, mood, greetings, amenities, etc., as consistent across subjects as possible. The physical surroundings should also be controlled. Same or similar rooms should be used, with controls over seating arrangement, temperature, humidity, etc. Distractions such as hallway conversation, pedestrian traffic, noise, etc., should be eliminated. If alertness is required for the research, then time of day may be an important consideration, e.g., morning, afternoon, evening, before or after mealtime.

Treating subjects equally is especially difficult when more than one experimenter is involved. A special effort must be made to "train" the experimenters so that they perform in a similar fashion. As we noted earlier, it is also important that each experimenter run an equal number of subjects from each condition of the experiment. This is done primarily to prevent confounding experimenter effects with the experimental conditions.

10.6.2   Identifying Other Sources of Systematic Variation

Sometimes it is difficult to hold constant all conditions but we can identify the effects (or possible effects) of an **extraneous variable.** If so, we can make it an independent variable. Although this is done primarily for purposes of control, we may become interested in it in its own right, particularly if it exerts a potent influence. In any event, whenever we identify and quantify a source of variation, it is no longer an unknown component of random error. Consequently, its effect is removed from the error term, thereby decreasing the denominator of the *F*-ratio. The overall effect of identifying another source of systematic variation is determined by the potency of the variable. A hypothetical example illustrates this point.

EXTRANEOUS VARIABLES variables operating within the experimental setting (time of day, noise levels, etc.) or within the subjects (gender, motivational levels, etc.) that are randomly distributed over experimental conditions. Thus, they do not lead to confounding but they do increase variability (error).

Table 10.5
Hypothetical data of an experiment involving three degrees of induced stress and two different experimenters.

	Treatments		
	A1	A2	A3
E1	40	38	34
E2	36	34	32
E1	36	32	32
E2	34	30	28
E1	32	30	28
E2	32	28	26
E1	30	28	26
E2	28	26	24
M =	33.50	30.75	28.75
S.D. =	3.57	3.60	3.31

Let us assume that our experiment requires so much effort that two experimenters are required. There are three conditions in the experiment, referred to as Treatment A1, A2, A3. We assign randomly eight subjects to each condition. Our design and data are depicted in Table 10.5. We are interested in the reaction time, in milliseconds, of our subjects under three different levels of induced stress. Each experimenter will run four subjects from each treatment. The study is performed over many days and a mean score for each subject is computed.

If we were to analyze the difference between treatments A1, A2, A3 without any concern about the effects of the systematic variance possibly contributed by the experimenters, we would have the following:

| | *Means for Treatments* | | |
	A1	*A2*	*A3*
$\overline{M}$	33.50	30.75	28.75
S.D.	3.57	3.60	3.31

However, if we analyzed the variance due to the experimenter, we would then see the systematic contributions made by the two experimenters. By identifying and quantifying this source of systematic variation, we would reduce our error term and also identify an experimenter treatment effect. Our summary means would then look like this:

| | *Means for Treatments* | | | |
	A1	*A2*	*A3*	
Experimenter 1	34.5	32.0	30.0	$\overline{X} = 32.16$
Experimenter 2	32.5	29.5	27.5	$\overline{X} = 29.83$

10.6.3   Reducing Variation Due to Individual Differences

Another way to increase the precision (sensitivity) of the experiment for assessing the effects of treatments is by reducing the variability among subjects within each treatment, i.e., reducing within-subject variance. As noted, differences among individual subjects on our dependent variable determine the size of the denominator in the F-ratio. It is essential for the denominator to be small if we are to detect the effects of the independent variable. This notion can be seen by contrasting the data in Table 10.3 with that in Table 10.4. When variability within subjects is low, in this case absent (Table 10.3), the treatment effect is much more obvious than when within-subject variability is high (Table 10.4).

If cloning were feasible and its use ethical then we could have an effective way of increasing similarity of our subjects and thus the sensitivity of the experiment. Using clones of the same individual for subjects, combined with sound experimental methods, would keep variance among individuals at a minimum. If so, then we would be relatively assured of detecting even small effects of our independent variable. Obviously the use of clones is not an option available to us for reducing variation due to individual differences but other options are. There are two experimental ways and one statistical way of addressing the problem of variance due to individual differences. These are: (1) using the same subject for the different treatment conditions; (2) using homogeneous subjects by matching them on a variable related to the dependent measure; and (3) statistically, using an analysis of co-variance technique.

When the same subject is used under each treatment condition the method is often referred to as a *repeated measures procedure.* The term emphasizes that each subject is measured more than once. This procedure is discussed in later chapters. For now we will describe the other two methods for reducing individual differences. We shall begin with matching. However, it is important to emphasize that whether or not matching is used, subjects are assigned randomly to treatments.

Matching using a pre-test measure   This method involves matching the subjects on a variable that is correlated with the dependent variable. If there is no correlation, matching is of no value.* When there is a correlation between the variable on which subjects are matched and the dependent variable, then another source of systematic variation can be identified and removed from error variance. The higher this correlation, the greater the contribution of matching to the increase in precision of the experiment. The matching variable may be past records such as ACT, SAT, IQ test scores, or other pre-test measures that the researcher knows to be correlated with the experimental task. It is even possible at times to match subjects on the basis of performance on a task highly similar to the experimental task itself. For example, if the experimental task is reaction time, then reaction time under conditions different from the experiment can be used to match subjects. Care must be taken when using the latter matching strategy. The pre-test must in no way affect performance on the experimental task. It is sometimes difficult to detect the biasing effect of a pre-test task. (See Chapters 7 and 8.)

It may be helpful if we use a hypothetical example to describe one way of using the matching procedure. Assume that we are interested in determining whether the speed of learning a list of nonsense syllables (nonwords), referred to as CVCs (consonant-vowel-consonant), is related to the meaningfulness of the CVCs. The question is: "Are meaningful CVCs learned more quickly than nonmeaningful ones?" Lists of CVCs rated in terms of meaningfulness are available even though the CVCs themselves are not words. In this case meaningfulness is defined operationally in terms of the average number of associations given to each CVC by a large sample of subjects. The more associations, the more its meaningfulness.

---

*Indeed, for small N's in particular, matching may have an adverse effect since a larger F-ratio is required for significance.

We construct three lists of CVCs (ten in each list), each differing in meaningfulness, i.e., high, medium, or low. Past research revealed that marked individual differences in learning occur with such lists, therefore we decide to use a matching procedure. We decide to use reading speed as a matching variable because of its moderate to high correlation with learning CVCs. Since we have three lists of syllables we must have three groups of subjects divided into triplets (three subjects, one for each list) who are matched. That is, each triplet must be matched so that each triplet's reading scores, if not identical, are very similar. The latter point is important. If subjects in each triplet are not well matched, then little improvement in sensitivity can be expected of the experiment. With a matched group procedure the similarity of subjects in each triplet is more important than the similarity between triplets. The reason for this is that *each triplet provides information regarding the treatment effect.* It is the different effects of the treatment within a triplet that determines whether there is a treatment effect.

Let's get on with our description. To this point, we have reading scores on all potential subjects and we know that these scores correlate with our dependent variable. We next arrange subjects from high to low (or low to high) according to their reading scores, form our triplets of three matched subjects, and randomly assign each subject in the triplet to one of the three treatments. That is, we would select the three individuals with the highest scores (identical if possible) and assign them randomly to the three lists. The next three highest scores would then be selected for our second triplet and again subjects would be assigned randomly. We would continue doing this until we had assigned all subjects. In many cases subjects may not have identical scores. Under these circumstances it may be better to set up intervals. Instead of trying to match subjects on the score of 38, we might simply match them on an interval of 35–39, others on an interval of 30–34, and so on. This procedure would result in both similar means and variance on the matching variable.

Matching procedures are particularly feasible with relatively simple experiments involving few groups. However, as the complexity of the experiment increases, it becomes more difficult to achieve satisfactory matching. In such cases, other designs must receive careful consideration.

Analysis of co-variance   An **analysis of co-variance** technique is useful given that several important assumptions are met. Although the technique is far too technical for a full discussion at this level, we shall provide an example of its possible use to give you some idea of its potential. If you are interested in pursuing the topic in depth, you should consult any number of qualified statistical texts (listed in references).

ANALYSIS OF CO-VARIANCE a statistical procedure, based on regression, for accounting for and removing from error the variability contributed by extraneous sources of error.

Analysis of co-variance involves the analysis of variables that vary together. The research we have been describing to this point has dealt with the effects of an independent variable on a *single* dependent variable. Studies of this nature are referred to as *univariate analyses.* Analysis of co-variance allows another variable that correlates with the dependent variable to enter the analysis. It is a combination of regression analysis and analysis of variance. You will not need to be well acquainted with the latter two techniques to understand some of the logic of co-variance. Recall that, under most circumstances, individual differences account for the lion's share of error variance. If we can find some measure prior to the experiment that correlates with the dependent variable, we can use regression analysis to adjust the dependent measure in such a way as to "statistically remove" the effects of individual differences. The higher the correlation, the greater the effectiveness of the procedure. As noted, these measures should be based on measures obtained prior to the start of the experiment since the experimental treatment must in no way influence the magnitude of this variable. Prior measures used by some experimenters have included speed of learning, grade point average, and IQ scores.

Let us look at an example. Suppose we are interested in a long-term retention curve when only a fixed and limited amount of practice has been given. Our experiment looks like the following. All subjects receive ten trials to learn a fifteen-word list. Then subjects in Group 1 are tested for recall one minute later; Group 2 subjects are tested thirty minutes later; Group 3 subjects, sixty minutes later; and Group 4 subjects, ninety minutes later. Our dependent variable is the number of items retained from the fifteen-word list after these different intervals. Knowing that there is a well documented relationship between the extent of original learning and the amount of material retained, we use the degree of learning during the initial ten trials as a prior measure. Analysis of co-variance would then remove from the variability of scores on retention (the dependent variable) any variability predictable from the relationship between the initial measure and the dependent variable. The overall effect would be to reduce the denominator in the *F*-ratio and increase the probability of detecting differences. In this and other situations, co-variance analysis is a powerful tool for detecting the effects of experimental treatments when they exist.

CHAPTER ELEVEN

RESEARCH DESIGNS: RANDOMIZED GROUPS, RANDOMIZED BLOCKS, REPEATED MEASURES

11.1 MODELS OF EXPERIMENTAL DESIGNS

The score on a dependent variable may be considered the sum of both systematic and unsystematic factors. Symbolically:

$$Y = a + e$$

where:

Y = the observed value of the dependent variable
a = identifiable systematic factors in an experiment
e = unsystematic factors and unidentified systematic factors.

Thus, if a subject were participating in a study of the effects of a drug on reaction time, Y would represent the subject's reaction time. The effect of the drug is shown by a, and the contribution of unsystematic factors (variations in testing procedures, the presence of changing environmental stimulation, moment-to-moment variations on the subject, such as in attentiveness) as well as unidentified systematic factors (e.g., the subject's ability level) is represented by e.

In our analogy to the detection of a radio signal (Section 10.4), a represents the signal we are trying to detect (the treatment effect) and e the static (error). In a two-group design, in which subjects are assigned at random to experimental conditions, we are attempting to detect the *difference* in radio signals (difference in treatments). The two conditions, an experimental and a control, may be represented symbolically, as:

Experimental Condition	*Control Condition*
$Y = a_1 + e$	$Y = a_0 + e$
where a_1 identifies the experimental condition.	where a_0 identifies the control condition, usually the absence of the experimental treatment.

In this model, e is presumed to be the same for both groups. This will be the case if we have been successful in avoiding the confounding of systematic but unidentified components of e with the experimental conditions. For example, if the subjects in the experimental condition were at a higher ability level with respect to the dependent variable, the two e's would not be the same. Conclusions drawn with respect to the difference between a_1 and a_0 would, therefore, be unwarranted.

To complete the model, we must take into account the fact that, apart from treatment conditions and error components, there is a population value with respect to the dependent variable. For example, there is a population mean for the heights of males and females, their speed of running the hundred-meter dash, their scores on an achievement inventory, etc. Thus, the model for comparing the dependent measures in a two-group design with independent groups becomes

Experimental Condition	*Control Condition*
$Y = u + a_1 + e$	$Y = u + a_0 + e$

where u = the population mean on the dependent measure. Since the experimental subjects are assigned at random to the experimental conditions, their population means on the dependent measure are presumed to be equal. Thus, we assume that the two groups are equal in all respects except for the difference in experimental treatments (a_1 versus a_0).

11.2 ONE-WAY ANALYSIS OF VARIANCE, INDEPENDENT SAMPLES—RANDOMIZED GROUPS DESIGN

In a one-way analysis of variance, there is only one experimental or treatment variable. This variable may be either qualitative (e.g., methods of instructing math to third graders, types of psychotherapy, methods of dispersing welfare payments, or types of penal institution for handling prisoners convicted of violent crimes), or it may be quantitative (e.g., amount of drug administered to a group of psychiatric patients, amount of fertilizer applied to a given crop, or amount of positive reinforcement administered to subjects in a learning situation). Experimental designs such as this, using random assignment and independent groups, are also referred to as *randomized group designs* or *simple randomized designs*. Illustrations with ten subjects per cell are shown below:

	Drug		
A1	A2	A3	A4
$n = 10$	$n = 10$	$n = 10$	$n = 10$

Qualitative Variable

	Motivation	
High	Medium	Low
A1	A2	A3
$n = 10$	$n = 10$	$n = 10$

Quantitative Variable

While there is only one experimental variable in a one-way analysis of variance, there may be any number of subclasses or levels of treatment. For example, qualitative variables (nominal scale) might involve four methods of teaching math, eight types of psychotherapy, four methods of dispersing welfare payments, or five types of penal institutions for handling prisoners convicted of violent crimes. Quantitative variables (ordinal, interval, ratio scales) may involve four dosage levels or amounts of drug administered to patients, five different amounts of fertilizer applied to crops, or three different amounts of positive reinforcement administered to subjects in a learning situation.

11.2.1   Between-Group and Within-Group Variance Estimates

The one-way analysis of variance permits the researcher to collect data on several treatment groups simultaneously and evaluate the null hypothesis that the sample means were drawn from a common population of means. For example, in a five-group design, the null hypothesis is

H_0: $\mu_1 = \mu_2 = \mu_3 = \mu_4 = \mu_5$.

The alternative hypothesis (H_1) is that the samples were not all drawn from the same population of means. If H_0 is rejected, H_1 may be asserted—the researcher may feel confident that there is a treatment effect.

The test statistic (the F-ratio) is the ratio between two variance estimates, one based on the dispersion of scores within groups (within-group variance estimates), and the other based on the dispersion of means (between-group variance estimate). (See Section 10.5.) In the one-way analysis of variance, independent group design:

$$F = \frac{\text{between-group variance estimate}}{\text{within-group variance estimate}} = \frac{s_B^2}{s_W^2}.$$

If the between-group variance estimate is large (that is, the differences among means are large) relative to the within-group variance estimate (the differences among scores are relatively small), the F-ratio is large. In general, the larger the F-ratio, the greater the likelihood that H_0 will be rejected.

Another way of stating the null hypothesis is that the between-group variance estimates and the within-group variance estimates are both estimates of random error (σ_ϵ^2). When H_0 is true and there is no treatment effect, the between-group variance estimate will provide an estimate of σ_ϵ^2 (random error). The within-group variance, which contains no treatment effect, is also an estimate of random error (σ_ϵ^2). Thus, when H_0 is true, the F-ratio would consist of

$$F = \frac{\sigma_\epsilon^2}{\sigma_\epsilon^2}.$$

Allowing for random variations in error estimates from sample data, the expected value of F is 1.00 when H_0 is true.

When H_0 is false, however, the between-group sum of squares contains both treatment effects (σ_a^2) and random error (σ_ϵ^2). Thus, when H_0 is false, the F-ratio consists of

$$F = \frac{\sigma_\epsilon^2 + \sigma_a^2}{\sigma_\epsilon^2}.$$

The greater the treatment effect (σ_a^2) or the larger the between-group sum of squares, the greater the F-ratio becomes.

Appendix A presents a worked example of the statistical analysis of data in which a randomized group design was used.*

---

*The t-ratio may be used in those cases where there is one group (sample) and the question to be answered is: "Is it reasonable to hypothesize that the sample was drawn from a population with a mean of, say, 20, 80, 100?" The same t-ratio is usually used in the two-group case where one group receives a treatment (experimental group) and the other does not (control group). Worked examples of both cases are found in Appendix A. See Chapter 13 also.

11.2.2   Multicomparison Tests

Obtaining a statistically significant difference permits us to conclude that the treatment means were not drawn from a common population of means. However, when there are three or more treatment conditions, our research interest usually extends beyond the demonstration of an *overall* treatment effect. We often want to know where the *specific* differences lie, i.e., which of the means differ significantly from one another? To answer this question, a number of different tests have been developed. These are known as *multicomparison tests.*

Occasionally a researcher will plan, in advance of the conduct of the research, specific comparisons in which he or she has an interest. Such comparisons are referred to as **planned or a priori comparisons.** The overall F-ratio need not be significant in order to justify making these specific planned comparisons.

PLANNED OR A PRIORI COMPARISONS   comparisons among treatment groups that are specified in advance of data collection.

In contrast, many studies are designed in which the specific comparisons of interest are not noted in advance. Although the researcher expects there to be treatment effects, he or she is unable or unwilling to specify what these effects will be. Only if the F-ratio is statistically significant, is the researcher then free to investigate specific comparisons. Multicomparison tests administered after the fact are referred to as **unplanned comparisons, a posteriori comparisons, or post hoc tests.**

UNPLANNED, A POSTERIORI OR POST HOC TESTS   tests in which the comparisons of interest are not specified in advance of data collection.

To illustrate conceptually the use of Tukey's HSD (Honestly Significant Differences) test, imagine we had completed a study involving three conditions and a randomized group design. The sample means were $\overline{X}_1 = 3.57$, $\overline{X}_2 = 5.43$, and $\overline{X}_3 = 8.00$. The overall F-test is significant, meaning that the sample means were not drawn from a common population of means. The means are assigned in a matrix with the differences between paired means displayed in the appropriate cells. The matrix is shown in Table 11.1.

The multicomparison test yields a single value such that, if an obtained difference between means exceeds that value, the specific comparison between paired means is statistically significant at a given level. For example, if a dif-

Table 11.1
Matrix showing difference between pairs of means in a three condition randomized group design.

	$\overline{X}_1 = 3.57$	$\overline{X}_2 = 5.43$	$\overline{X}_3 = 8.00$
$\overline{X}_1 = 3.57$	—	1.86	4.43
$\overline{X}_2 = 5.43$	—	—	2.57
$\overline{X}_3 = 8.00$	—	—	—

ference of 3.61 were required for significance, only the difference between $\overline{X}_1$ and $\overline{X}_3$ (i.e., 4.43) would achieve statistical significance. (Appendix A presents a worked example involving the Tukey HSD test.)

11.3   Two-Way Analysis of Variance—Factorial Design

We have just seen that the one-way analysis applies to designs in which there are a number of subclasses or levels of a single experimental variable. However, there are many occasions when we wish to evaluate two or more variables at the same time. Often all interest is focused on the *interaction* of these variables, i.e., is the effect of one variable dependent upon the presence or the amount of a second variable? Multivariable designs also represent an efficient means of using research time and effort, since, in most cases, every observation provides information about each variable, interaction of variables, and error.

In a two-way analysis of variance, there are two experimental or treatment variables (independent variables). One or both of these variables may be either qualitative or quantitative. While there are only two experimental variables in a two-way analysis of variance, there may be any number of subclasses or levels of treatment of each variable. A given study might involve two levels of one variable and four levels of a second variable, or three levels of each variable, etc. The traditional way of designating a two-way analysis of variance is by citing the number of levels (or subclasses) of each variable. Some examples are: (a) A study with two levels of one variable and four levels of a second variable is referred to as having a 2 × 4 design. (b) A study with three levels of each variable is referred to as having a 3 × 3 design. (c) A study with three levels of one variable and four levels of a second variable is referred to as having a 3 × 4 design.

Conceptually, the statistical model of a **factorial design** is as follows:

$$Y = u + a + b + (a \times b) + e$$

when u = the population mean
               a = the effects of the a variable
               b = the effects of the b variable

$(a \times b)$ = the interaction of the a and b variables (See Section 11.3.1.)
      e = random error, including unsystematic error and unidenti-
        fiable systematic error.

FACTORIAL DESIGN   a design in which some level of each treatment variable is administered to each subject.

If there are no treatment effects or interactions between treatments, the score on the dependent variable consists of the population mean plus random error, i.e., $Y = u + e$ when $a = 0$, $b = 0$, and $a \times b = 0$.

11.3.1   The Concept of a Treatment Combination

In a factorial design, some level of each treatment variable is administered to each experimental subject. The particular combination of experimental conditions is referred to as a *treatment combination*. For example, if, in a 3×4 factorial design, a given subject is administered, the second level of variable A and the third level of variable B, the subject's treatment combination is A_2B_3.

Example a   *Treatment combinations in a 2 × 2 factorial design.*

	A_1		A_2	
	B_1	B_2	B_1	B_2
Treatment Combination	A_1B_1	A_1B_2	A_2B_1	A_2B_2

Example b   *Treatment combinations in a 2 × 3 factorial design.*

	A_1			A_2		
	B_1 B_2 B_3			B_1 B_2 B_3		
Treatment Combination	A_1B_1	A_1B_2	A_1B_3	A_2B_1	A_2B_2	A_2B_3

11.3.2   Possible Outcomes of a 2 × 2 Factorial Experiment

The total number of treatment combinations in any factorial design is equal to the product of the treatment levels of all factors or variables. Thus, in a 2×2 factorial design, there are four treatment combinations and there are six treatment combinations in a 2×3 factorial design. In more complex factorial designs, the same principle applies. In a $2 \times 3 \times 4$ factorial design, there are 24 treatment combinations.

    As noted, factorial designs introduce the concept of interaction. The concept is very important for the proper analysis and understanding of complex designs. Indeed, often the main interest of a study is focused on the interaction

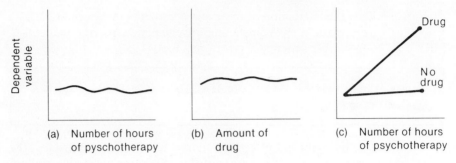

Fig. 11.1 Interaction of amount of drug and number of hours of psychotherapy.

of variables, i.e., is the effect of one variable dependent on either the presence or the amount of a second variable? For example, a psychoactive drug alone may have little effect on the treatment of disturbed patients. Psychotherapy alone may be equally ineffective. However, the combination of the two may produce the desired behavioral change. Without the two-variable design, this interaction might never be discovered.

Figure 11.1 illustrates a possible interaction of two variables—number of hours of psychotherapy and amount of a drug. Note that psychotherapy alone (a) and the drug alone (b) did not appear to bring about any improvements in the behavior of the patients, However, when both were combined (c), an improvement is noted.

Let's look at another exammple. Imagine you had conducted a study involving two levels of anxiety (A_1 = low, A_2 = high) and two levels of perceived difficulty of task (B_1 = easy, B_2 = difficult). The dependent measure is the time the individual continues to work at an unsolvable task. Figure 11.2 illustrates six different, although not exhaustive, possible outcomes of the experiment. Note that in (b), (c), and (d), the observed effect of one variable is found over both levels of a second variable. When this happens, we refer to the outcome as a **main effect**. A main effect of a given variable describes an effect of that variable over all levels of a second variable.

MAIN EFFECT   an effect of one variable found over all levels of a second variable.

Thus, in (b), high levels of perceived difficulty (B_2) is found to produce longer periods of task-related activities at both levels of induced anxiety. Similarly, in (c), the effect of low levels of anxiety is greater than high levels whether or not the task is perceived as easy (B_1) or difficult (B_2). Both of these are main effects. In contrast, (e) and (f) show interactions between the two variables. In (e), a task perceived as difficult (B_2) increases the time spent at the task only when induced anxiety is low (A_1). In (f), the interaction is complete. A high level of perceived difficulty produces a greater effect than a low

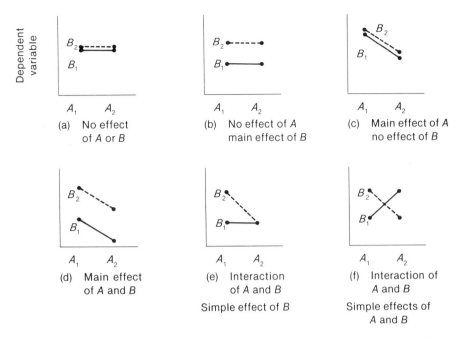

Fig. 11.2 Several possible outcomes of an experiment involving a 2×2 factorial design.

level only when induced anxiety is high (A_2). Here, a low level of perceived difficulty produces longer periods of task orientation only when induced anxiety (A_2) is high. Since the difference between low and high perceived difficulty is *not* found at both levels of induced anxiety, the effect is a **simple effect.**

SIMPLE EFFECT   an effect of one variable is not found over all levels of a second variable.

11.4 CORRELATED SAMPLES DESIGNS: IDENTIFYING SYSTEMATIC FACTORS CONTRIBUTING TO ERROR

In Section 11.2 we presented the following model for comparing the dependent measures in a two-group design employing independent groups:

Experimental Condition   *Control Condition*
$Y = \mu + a_1 + e$ $Y = \mu + a_0 + e$

Recall that μ represents the population mean on the dependent measure, a_1 the experimental treatment, a_0 the control condition, and e the unsystematic error and unidentified systematic error.

Table 11.2
**Examples of some unsystematic and systematic factors that contribute to error. By
identifying and quantifying one or more of the systematic factors, the error term may
be reduced.**

Error	
Unsystematic Factors	Systematic Factors
1. Momentary fluctuations in subject's responses (e.g., attention, motivation, mood, etc.)	1. Subject differences (ability, aptitude, gender, age, educational level, etc.)
2. Unintentional variations in experimental procedures	2. Repetitive aspects of the experimental setting (time of day, day of week, etc.)
3. Random changes in environmental stimulation (sudden noises, variations in illumination, etc.)	3. Experimenter and/or observer differences

Let's take a closer look at the error term. As we have seen, many factors
contribute to error. If we could identify and control all of them, it would be
theoretically possible to eliminate error. With *e* dropped from the equation,
the comparison between the experimental and control conditions would be
"pure," i.e., without the contamination of the "noise" or "static" caused by
these variables. As a matter of practical reality, the total elimination of error is
a forlorn hope. There are just too many factors, both within the subjects and
in the testing environment, that are elusive, momentary, and unpredictable. As
we have noted on several occasions there are also systematic factors that contribute to error. Identifying them would permit us to "remove" them from the
error term, thereby removing some of the "noise." This would allow a more
sensitive comparison among experimental conditions. (See Table 11.2.)

As we indicated earlier, one of the greatest contributors to "noise" or unwanted variability in the error term is individual differences. One subject may
be high in ability, or acuity level, or speed of reaction, or educational level,
while other subjects may be low on one or more of these factors. If these differences could be minimized and variability decreased, the error term would
also be reduced. The overall effect would be an increase in the sensitivity of the
experiment, i.e., our ability to detect smaller differences in treatment effects
would increase. With this in mind, researchers often try to identify important
sources of individual differences prior to beginning the research. Once
measures of individual differences are identified, the experimenter can then select subjects for study that are very similar. The primary consideration is that
the measure used to select (match) subjects must correlate substantially with
the dependent variable. The higher the correlation, the greater the reduction in
size of the error term. Some common measures that have been used for select-

ing homogeneous subjects are grade point average, years of education, motivational level, reading comprehension, anxiety level, vocabulary scores, ACT scores, IQ scores, male/female, etc.

Researchers can select a single group of highly homogeneous subjects to administer treatments to or they can select several levels of homogeneous subjects. Either procedure would reduce the size of the error term given that the correlation between the measure used to select subjects and the dependent variable was high. However, most researchers are not interested in selecting a single group of homogeneous subjects. The major reason is that the generalizability of the results would be considerably restricted to the narrow range of subjects used in the study. Therefore, instead of using a single homogeneous group of subjects, researchers more often use several levels or blocks of homogeneous subjects. For example, instead of using subjects highly similar on only one level of ability, several groups, each with different levels of ability, are selected. Designs such as this are generally referred to as a *treatment X levels design* or a *randomized block design*.

These designs are very similar to the matched group design presented in Chapter 10 except that in this case several different levels (blocks) are formed with subjects matched on each level. Again it is important to note that while subjects are grouped into homogeneous blocks or levels, within each level, subjects are assigned randomly to the different treatments. Since subjects are blocked on levels of some measure (e.g., ability) and then randomly assigned to different treatment conditions, the term *randomized block design* is particularly fitting.

You may have correctly noted the similarity between the randomized block design and the factorial design presented earlier. In this case they appear to be highly similar, and they are. However, they serve different purposes. Researchers use a randomized block design when one of their basic purposes is to reduce variability and thus the error term. They are not usually interested in "levels" as an independent variable. In contrast, with factorial designs, primary interest is in each treatment as an independent variable and in their interactions.

When successfully implemented, the randomized block design reduces the error term, i.e., the denominator in the *F*-ratio. It can do this in two ways. First, if our matching of subjects procedure is effective (i.e., the forming of levels that correlate with the dependent variable), then the subjects in each block are more homogeneous with respect to the dependent variable. This lessened variability thus results in a smaller error term. The second way that the design can reduce the error term is in identifying blocks (e.g., ability) as a source of systematic variance that can be removed from the error term.

One caution is necessary when considering the use of a randomized block design. As the number of blocks increases, degrees of freedom are lost. With fewer degrees of freedom, a larger *F*-ratio is required for statistical significance. For this reason, a randomized block design should be contemplated only when we are relatively certain that we have identified a matching variable. that correlates well with the dependent variable. Before going on to the next design, we will illustrate what a randomized block design looks like.

Treatments

	A_1	A_2	A_3
Level 1 ACT Scores (22–25)	$n = 10$	$n = 10$	$n = 10$
Level 2 ACT Scores (18–21)	$n = 10$	$n = 10$	$n = 10$

11.5 REPEATED MEASURES DESIGN

One way to be virtually sure that subjects are homogeneous under each treatment condition is to use a design where the same subject is tested under each treatment. When subjects are repeatedly tested in this manner the design is referred to as a *repeated measures design*. For example, let us say that we are interested in testing the effects of level of illumination (independent variable) on the speed of reading textbook material (dependent variable). We decide that neither the random groups nor the random blocks designs is sufficiently sensitive to detect the effects of our treatment on reading rate. We know that a random blocks design with subjects grouped into levels of different abilities is more sensitive than a random groups design where no effort is made to group or match subjects. However, we also know that using the same subjects across treatments could reduce our error term even more than a random blocks design. Therefore our preference is to use a repeated measure design and to measure the reading rate of the same individual across different levels of illumination. (Specific considerations and cautions concerning the use of the design discussed here are found in the following chapter.) We are not concerned about possible practice effects since we will be balancing for order of presentation concerning illumination; also, we have many passages of material all of equal difficulty.

Our study will include six subjects each of whom will read material of comparable difficulty under three different levels of illumination. The design is illustrated below.

Level of Illumination

	High	Medium	Low
S1			
S2			
S3			
↓			
S6			

Table 11.3
Counterbalancing order of treatment in a repeated measures design.

Block		Condition	Condition
	A₁	A₂	A₃
S1	1	2	3
S2	1	3	2
S3	2	1	3
S4	2	3	1
S5	3	2	1
S6	3	1	2

The order in which each level of illumination is presented to each subject could either be randomized or counterbalanced. Since there are only three treatment conditions, researchers would most likely use a counterbalancing procedure. The use of counterbalancing would balance the possible effects of order of treatment presentations. In our example using three treatment conditions, there are six possible orders: $A_1A_2A_3$, $A_1A_3A_2$, $A_2A_1A_3$, $A_2A_3A_1$, and $A_3A_1A_2$. We randomly assign the six different orders to our experimental subjects. The design is shown in Table 11.3.

The number in the cells of Table 11.3 indicate the ordinal position in which the treatments are administered. Thus, Subject 4 received the treatments in the following order: $A_2A_3A_1$, while Subject 3 received the following order: $A_2A_1A_3$, etc. Note that counterbalancing achieves the following: each treatment is administered 1st, 2nd, and 3rd an equal number of times. However, counterbalancing will not neutralize carryover effects. (See Chapter 12.) If carryover is a serious problem that cannot be dealt with properly, then it would be advisable to consider the use of a random blocks or a random groups design. Finally, in the preceding example, the order of administering treatments is completely confounded with the subject variable. Stated another way, we have no way of knowing if given subjects performed as they did because of the order in which conditions were presented or because of subject characteristics themselves. This does not pose a problem as long as our interest centers on removing the effects of these variables from error, rather than evaluating the effects of order of presentation. However if we wish to separately evaluate the ordering effect, we could replicate the orders of presentation. In the present example, replication would require that we increase our N in multiples of 6. The design with twelve subjects shown in Table 11.4 provides two independent assessments of each order of presentation. Thus, the order of presentation is no longer confounded with the subjects.

There are many additional experimental designs that researchers use other than those described here. The designs discussed in this chapter are three of the most basic ones. In some instances researchers combine one, two, or more dif-

Table 11.4
Counterbalanced order of presentation with replication, permitting the assessment of order effects.

Order of Presentation	Subject	Condition A_1	A_2	A_3
$A_1A_2A_3$	1			
	2			
$A_1A_3A_2$	3			
	4			
$A_2A_1A_3$	5			
	6			
$A_2A_3A_1$	7			
	8			
$A_3A_1A_2$	9			
	10			
$A_3A_2A_1$	11			
	12			

ferent designs into one grand one. For those of you interested in various designs that investigators use, several good sources are available (Keppel, 1973; Winer, 1971).

Before concluding this chapter we want to note that the designs that we have discussed have both strengths and weaknesses. It is important that the student be aware of them. We address these strengths and weaknesses in the next chapter.

CHAPTER TWELVE

DIFFERENT DESIGNS MAY LEAD TO DIFFERENT LAWS: RANDOMIZED GROUPS VERSUS REPEATED MEASURES DESIGNS

12.1   INTRODUCTION

One of the issues that we will discuss in this chapter deals with how our choices of research design may influence the kind of lawful relationships that we find. A growing body of evidence makes it clear that different relationships may be obtained between the independent and dependent variables when we use a repeated measures design as opposed to an independent group design. Thus, we should keep in mind that different research designs may give *different answers* to the *same question* when manipulating the *same variables*. This important discovery has generated much interest on the part of psychologists. There are available a number of studies in which the independent variable is the type of experimental design used.

Research directly comparing the results obtained when using repeated measures versus independent groups designs has been done in areas such as Pavlovian conditioning (e.g., Frey, 1970), verbal learning (e.g., Hopkins and Edwards, 1972), perception (e.g., Jones and Holding, 1975), and others. The problem addressed by these studies goes to the core of scientific methodology and dramatically illustrates the fact that selecting the proper research design is not an arbitrary affair.

As we noted earlier, repeated measures designs are often used because of their greater statistical precision. Since the same subject receives the different treatment conditions, individual differences are identified, quantified, and removed from error, thereby reducing the error term. The design is powerful since the reduced error variance results in greater sensitivity in detecting small differences in treatment effects. In contrast, the independent groups design uses different groups of subjects for each treatment condition. Since a considerable portion of error variance is due to individual differences, an independent groups design is less sensitive to small differences in treatment effects. If sensitivity to treatment effects were the only basis for choosing between the two designs, our choice would be an uncomplicated affair. But, as we have suggested, the problem is not that simple. Different designs have led to the discovery of different relationships. At the very least, these findings suggest the importance of considering the context in which the law or relationship was discovered.

12.2   ADVANTAGES OF REPEATED MEASURES DESIGNS

We have indicated that the greatest advantage of using a repeated measures design is the marked control over individual subject variation. Since each subject receives each treatment, subjects with identical characteristics necessarily receive each of the different treatment conditions. Given this, any differences in performance should result only from the treatment conditions. In fact, however, this does not happen. Even though the same subject is used across treatments, the subject may change in some systematic fashion. The subject may be less observant or attentive from one treatment to the other, motivational levels may increase or decrease, or perceptions may change. Further, inevitable variations in the experimental setting may affect performance. Therefore, since the subject and the environment may be somewhat different from treatment to treatment, there will still be some variability, but far less than if an independent groups design had been used.

Another advantage of the repeated measures design relates to the population of available subjects. If the availability of subjects is low, then a between-groups design may not be possible. This predicament arises on occasion and it is especially the case when the population of interest is very small, e.g., left-handed individuals with split-brain operations, identical twins separated at birth, etc. The independent groups designs require k times as many subjects than repeated measures designs (where k is the number of different treatments).

With fewer subjects comes greater efficiency and economy. In many cases, pretraining on a task may be needed one time only, and then a number of different treatments can be given. To illustrate, with four treatments and a task that requires a ten-minute pretraining period, a repeated measures design would save thirty minutes of training time over an independent groups design. Thus, considerable savings in time, effort, and expenses may be realized by having only one training period. A similar savings can occur with instructions. In experiments involving different treatment conditions, the same instructions or similar instructions are commonly used. These instructions can be long and tedious. A repeated measures design would reduce the time devoted to instructions, particularly when instructions are the same across treatments.

A final important advantage is that a repeated measures design may be the most appropriate for the study of certain phenomena. It is the design of choice for studying learning and transfer, or for assessing the effects of practice or repetition on performance. The independent variable is commonly the number of practice sessions given to individual subjects. In this case, we are interested in the effects that earlier treatments have on later performance. These effects are also referred to as **carryover effects.** Carryover effects, as we have seen, can be desirable or undesirable. Moreover, the concept of external validity enters into the choice of experimental design. The generalizability or representativeness of the research is related to the context in which it takes place. This is especially so when the results of the research are to be used in applied settings. The setting in which the research takes place should be similar to the setting to which the experimenter wishes to generalize his or her results. It may be the case that the researcher is interested in situations where each individual receives a number of conditions or receives extensive practice. If so, then a repeated measures design would have greater external validity. On the other hand, if the researcher is interested in performance under conditions which minimize practice, an independent groups design is necessary.

CARRYOVER EFFECTS   effects that earlier conditions have on later performance. Also called range effects.

12.3   PROBLEMS WITH REPEATED MEASURES DESIGNS

There are two classes of problems associated with a repeated measures design. One class of problems is related to methodological issues, the other class is related to statistical issues. We shall first consider the statistical issues.

12.3.1   Statistical Objections to Repeated Measures Designs

There are several considerations that relate to the use of repeated measures designs that center on statistical assumptions and are independent of carryover effects. Researchers using these designs should be familiar with these considerations.

Violation of assumptions when using repeated measures designs have more serious consequences than do similar violations when using independent measures designs. Two important assumptions should be met when using a repeated measures design: **homogeneity of variance** within treatments and homogeneity of co-variance between pairs of treatment levels. The first assumption specifies that there should be equal variability of scores in each of the treatment conditions. The second assumption specifies that subjects should maintain their relative standing in the different treatment conditions, e.g., if they are third highest in one treatment, they should be in the same ordinal position with respect to other treatments. That is, the relationship observed should be consistent in *any* pair of treatments and this consistency should be the same in *all* possible pairs of treatments. If this condition exists, then no treatment by subject interaction exists. A treatment by subject interaction would mean that subjects react in different ways to different treatments. The latter could be due to the treatment itself or to carryover effects. When these two assumptions are not satisfied, the significance level in the tables are not accurate. Generally, when we violate the assumptions, our statistical test is more lenient. Thus, we would conclude more often than we should that our independent variable is having an effect. That is, we would falsely reject the null hypothesis and make a Type 1 error. In effect, we would be using a test that is positively biased toward rejecting the null hypothesis.

HOMOGENEITY OF VARIANCE   equal variability in each treatment condition.

Violation of assumptions are often tolerated by researchers but efforts are made to minimize their effects. There are several techniques for dealing with them (Poor, 1973). These include adjustments in the degrees of freedom or the use of statistical tests that make different assumptions, e.g., multivariate analysis of variance.

12.3.2   Methodological Issues

A major methodological problem found with repeated measures designs is that they give rise to what some have called the "range effect" (Poulton, 1973) and others have called "carryover effects." Any treatment that changes the organism in such a way that it has a persistent effect on other treatments, we call carryover. We shall distinguish three categories of carryover effects: (1) transient effects, i.e., short-term effects that dissipate with time; (2) permanent effects, i.e., most often due to learning; and (3) sensitization effects, resulting from experiencing all treatments. These "carryover" effects pose a problem for us when they are unwanted and their occurrence is confounded with the effects of treatment. For a more complete treatment of some of these issues see Greenwald (1976).

12.3.3   Transient Effects

These short-term **transient effects** are often due to fatigue, boredom, or drugs. We give two examples below. The first deals with drug research, the second with fatigue or boredom.

> **TRANSIENT EFFECTS**   short-term effects of prior conditions, e.g., fatigue or boredom.

Let us say that we are interested in evaluating the effects of Drugs A and B against a placebo condition using a psychomotor task involving coordination. We decide to use a repeated measures design in which each subject will receive each drug, including the placebo, in some random order. A pursuit motor task is used in which the duration of contact with a moving target is recorded. Each subject is run once each day, but under a different condition. Imagine the following: On Day 1, one drug was evaluated and on Day 2, the second drug was tested. What would happen if the effects of the first drug had not worn off? Performance on Day 2 would be a function of the second drug plus the persistent effects of the first drug. In short, the effects of one drug treatment would still be present when testing the effects of the other drug. Obviously, this is undesirable and a case of blatant confounding, since we are not interested in the combined effects of the two drugs. This transient carryover effect may be easily corrected. Assuming that the changes in performance due to the drugs are not permanent, we could reduce this carryover by widely separating the treatments in time.

Another type of transient effect is that due to fatigue or boredom. Fatigue or boredom are especially likely to occur in nonchallenging studies requiring repetitive responding, or studies that take place over a long period of time. Therefore, when one treatment condition follows another, factors such as fatigue or boredom may contribute more so to one condition than to the other. The latter would be mixed with our independent variable thus making it impossible to evaluate. In short, we have confounding. An example of the fatigue or boredom effect may help. Let us say that we are interested in evaluating the speed of responding to an auditory signal versus a visual signal. For one treatment condition we use a five-second auditory signal and for the other a five-second visual signal. Our dependent variable is speed of responding (removing the index finger from a telegrapher key) to the two different signals. Subjects first receive 100 trials of practice without any signal to assure rapid responding will occur at the start of the experiment. All subjects then receive the auditory signal first for 500 trials followed immediately by the visual signal for another 500 trials. If we were to use the described procedure we could not adequately evaluate the effects of signal modality. The possibility exists that the subjects may experience either fatigue, boredom, or both during the second 500 trials with the visual signal. If so, then there could be a systematic decrease in reaction time due to fatigue and/or boredom, thus resulting in our underestimating reaction time to a visual signal.

One way to avoid the problem of fatigue or boredom contributing more to one condition than the other is to use a counterbalancing procedure. As we noted in Chapter 11, counterbalancing allows us to distribute transient effects evenly across the treatment conditions even though it does not eliminate them. It can be used easily with two treatments, less so with three, and only with difficulty with four or more treatments. Counterbalancing could be achieved in our reaction time experiment in several ways. The easiest way would be to have an equal number of subjects receive the treatments in an A-B order as in a B-A order. A and B would represent either the visual or the auditory signal. It is important to note that the use of such a procedure assumes that the transient effects of fatigue or boredom when going from Treatment A to Treatment B are the same as the transient effects when going from Treatment B to Treatment A. If, in our example, the second treatment was more fatiguing or boring than the first, then our assumption would be in error. Given the latter, counterbalancing would not distribute the transient effects evenly for the two conditions. The problem of equal treatment effects could be avoided and a within-subjects design still used by conducting the experiment over a two-day period. In this case, A and B would correspond to days 1 and 2.

We previously noted that counterbalancing gets more difficult as the number of treatments increase. With two treatments only 2 orders exist: A-B and B-A. With three treatments 6 orders exist: ABC, BCA, CAB, ACB, BAC, and CBA. However, with four treatments, we would have 24 orders, and with five treatments we would be overwhelmed with 120 orders. When the number of treatments is greater than three, a random assignment procedure is far easier to use.

12.3.4   Permanent Carryover Effects: Practice

There are special kinds of carryover effects often seen when repeated measures are taken on the same individual. These are referred to as *practice effects* or *learning effects* and they are considered to be relatively permanent.

In many instances, practice effects are the independent variable of primary interest, but in other instances we try to avoid them. Practice effects can confound our research in ways that make our results uninterpretable. As we have noted, when our interest is in an independent variable other than practice, then we must control practice effects so that they do not intrude on our results. In the preceding example where Drugs A and B were evaluated, we noted that the transient carryover effects of one drug on the other could be eliminated by widely spacing the time between tests. Knowing how long the drug remained active in the body would virtually assure us that we could eliminate transient effects. However, if for some unfortunate reason we did not randomize or counterbalance the presentation of drugs to each subject, a new problem would emerge. For example, if the effects of Drug A on the pursuit motor task were always tested first and the effects of Drug B were always tested second, then a marked practice effect (change in skill) could confound our results. Since trying to maintain contact with a moving target (pursuit motor task) is difficult, subjects would initially do poorly on the task but would subsequently improve. Therefore, always practicing the task under Drug A first may lead to better performance under Drug B. However, the improvement may have little to do with the drug. The individual may simply now be more skilled because of practice. If our results came out the reverse, we could propose a reasonable alternative explanation, namely, subjects became more fatigued by the time of the second treatment. However, this argument could be weakened by separating the time interval between treatments.

Two things could be done to avoid practice effects. One would be to give sufficient practice on the pursuit motor task prior to giving any treatment condition. Once improvement had stabilized or the limit of learning was attained, we could then introduce the treatments. This procedure would virtually assure that no increases in performance under the second treatment could occur as a result of practice. If our treatments were also widely separated in time, we could also rule out fatigue factors. But the solution to the problem may create a new one if our interest is directed toward evaluating improvement in performance. If, because of our extended practice, subjects are performing at their upper limits, further improvement in performance as a result of our treatment may not be possible. This "ceiling effect" would obscure any enhancing effect on the pursuit motor task that the drugs might have. We would only be able to determine if they detracted from performance.

We could also deal with order effects by randomly assigning the order of treatments to each subject or counterbalancing them as we described in the preceding section. When random assignment or counterbalancing are used, we

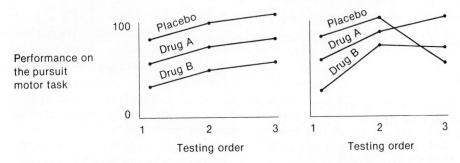

Fig. 12.1 Graphic illustration of the absence or the presence of confounding due to order of presentation of treatment conditions.

assume that the effects of practice due to the order of presenting the treatments are the same for each treatment. If the carryover effects of practice are different, we then have confounded practice (order of presenting treatments) with the treatment effects. Whether this type of confounding has occurred can be determined by plotting performance across the different testing orders. Figure 12.1 illustrates the absence and presence of confounding due to order of presentation.

If the results look like those on the left side of the figure then there is not a problem, since the practice effect is the same for each treatment whether it is given first, second, or third in the sequence. On the other hand, if the data look like those on the right side of the figure, then we have confounded practice (i.e., order) with the treatment effects. The right side of the figure shows an interaction between the treatment conditions and the order of testing. What this means is that the practice effect is different for each treatment and the effect on performance that we observed are not "pure" treatment effects. Clearly, the order of presenting the conditions has some effect. Our performance measure reflects the effects of the treatments plus the practice due to the preceding treatment. Results such as this suggest that an independent samples design would be more appropriate.

12.3.5   Sensitization

Our final category of carryover effects is referred to as sensitization. Experiencing the full range of treatments in an experiment may enhance the subject's ability to distinguish differences in treatments and the extent of these differences. This may, in turn, allow the subjects to contrast the various treatment conditions. Thus, their responses to a particular treatment may depend upon how they perceive that condition relative to the preceding one. Since subjects are exposed to the entire range of stimuli when a repeated measures design is used, the context in which the subject responds is very different from that of subjects receiving only one treatment. Moreover, the demand characteristics are likely to differ from one design to another. After subjects have received several treatments, they are more likely to form expectancies or hypotheses about the purpose of the experiment. If so, then these hypotheses may affect their performance over and above that of the treatments.

12.4 COMPARING REPEATED MEASURES DESIGNS WITH INDEPENDENT GROUPS DESIGNS

Since the context provided by exposure to all treatments is very different from the context provided by exposure to a single treatment, the subject's response to any given treatment may be, in part, a function of the research design. The most effective way to determine if different designs lead to different laws is to compare experiments using repeated measures designs with those using between-group designs. One researcher has argued "the day should come then when no reputable psychologist will use a (repeated measures) design, except for special purposes, without combining it with a separate group design." (Poulton, 1973). This position is extreme and some have taken issue with it (Greenwald, 1976; Rothstein, 1974). Determining the equivalence or non-equivalence of the two types of designs is important whenever different relationships are discovered and different designs are used to reveal them. The equivalence or nonequivalence of the two designs should then be determined. There are also other circumstances when this should be done that go beyond methodological considerations. For example, it may be important to do so for the construction of theories or for the application of findings to some practical problems. Doing so may also reduce the heated arguments and polemics that sometime result when one laboratory cannot replicate the findings of another.

12.5 ASSESSING WHETHER DESIGN TYPE AFFECTS THE OUTCOME OF A STUDY

The least appropriate way of attempting to deal with this issue is to collect data assessing the effects of an independent variable using both a repeated measures and a between-group design and then analyze the data separately. That is, once the data from both designs are in, separate statistical analyses of the data are undertaken. While this method allows the effects of the independent variable to be analyzed separately for the data derived from both designs, no direct statistical test of the interaction between the independent variable and the design type can be made. In substance, this approach is simply asking whether an effect of the independent variable will or will not be found with both designs. If an effect should be obtained in the same direction in both designs, there is no way to determine whether the obtained effect of the independent variable is significantly different (larger or smaller) with the two designs. Figure 12.2 indicates the kind of independent analysis we have described.

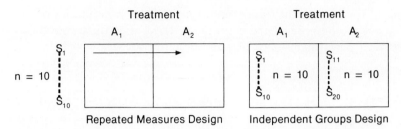

Fig. 12.2 Comparison of the effects of an independent variable when two different designs are used. Comparing the effects of the design is limited by the fact that separate analyses of data are performed, thereby ruling out the possibility of ascertaining the interaction between treatment and design.

Another approach is to make a direct statistical comparison between the two designs. To do this, we would again collect two sets of data, one with an independent groups design, the other with a repeated measures design. The procedure would be the same as in the preceding figure. However, in this case we would treat both sets of data as though they were independent groups data and of course, conduct an independent groups analysis. By so doing, we would, of course, be ignoring the fact that the scores derived from the repeated measures design were based on related measures. With this method, we could determine if the difference between Treatment A_1 and A_2 depended on which design was used. If the differences between Treatment A_1 and A_2 are not the same with the two designs, then an interaction will be evident. This would tell us that different designs give different results. (See Figure 12.3.)

While this procedure seems to be attractive, there are problems with it. For one, the scores in the repeated measures row are correlated while those in the independent samples row are uncorrelated. Although the procedure does allow a direct statistical analysis of the interaction and it has been performed by some investigators, it is not a statistically appropriate procedure. In the design shown in Figure 12.3, we treat the data as if they are based on observations of different individuals. Any initial differences that may have existed between the two groups would be magnified by the fact that the repeated

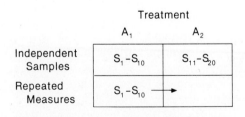

Fig. 12.3 Study combining independent samples and repeated measures designs but treating data as if forty independent subjects had been used.

Treatment

	A_1	A_2	A_3
Independent Samples	n = 10	n = 10	n = 10
Repeated Measures, Group 1	n = 10 X	———————→	
Repeated Measures, Group 2	n = 10 ———	——X——→	
Repeated Measures, Group 3	n = 10 ———		——→ X

Fig. 12.4 An experimental design permitting the assessment of the interaction of treatment with type of design. In evaluating the repeated measures condition, only the observations in cells marked by an X would be used.

measures group is more homogeneous than the independent samples group. Moreover, any interaction between treatments and subjects in the repeated measures condition would be lost when treating the observations as independent. Statistically inappropriate procedures often lead to bias in that they underestimate or overestimate the effects of the treatment conditions.

A more appropriate solution to the preceding problem involves elements of a within-group design and those of a between-group design. For the within-subjects design, however, additional groups would be run, depending upon the number of treatments. In fact, we would use the same number of groups as there are treatment conditions. Let's illustrate the procedure by using three treatment conditions. First, we would use three independent groups for our standard between-groups design. Each group would receive only one treatment. We would also use three groups for our repeated measures components. Further, the three repeated measures groups would each receive every treatment condition as is typical with this type of design. The distinguishing feature of this procedure is that the data for only *one treatment from each of the three groups* would be used for the statistical analysis even though all three treatments were received by each group. The design is conceptualized in Figure 12.4.

The figure depicts three separate independent sample groups (first row) composed of ten subjects, each receiving one of the three treatments A_1, A_2, or A_3. Also shown are the three repeated measures groups of subjects (last three rows), each composed of ten subjects but each receives each of the treatments A_1, A_2, or A_3. These treatments would be administered in either a random or **counterbalanced order** for each subject. As we noted, however, our analysis would use only the data from one treatment condition (marked with X) from each of the three repeated measures groups. Thus, each cell would have an independent group. Consequently, an independent group analysis would be appropriate. However, even though each cell would contain an independent group, subjects in the repeated measures comparison have been exposed to all the treatment conditions, whereas the subjects in the independent samples groups have been exposed to only one treatment. Therefore, if there is an

	A$_1$	A$_2$	A$_3$
Independent Samples Group	n = 10	n = 10	n = 10
"Independent Samples" Group (Drawn from Repeated Measures Group)	n = 10	n = 10	n = 10

Fig. 12.5 The matrix for analyzing the interaction of treatments and type of design based on Figure 12.4.

effect (knowing the range of the treatments, perceiving the context in which they occur, contrasting conditions one with another, or experiencing each treatment), this design should detect these effects. This is obviously important, since the use of one design over another may very well lead to very different conclusions.

> **COUNTERBALANCED ORDER** In repeated measures designs, ordering the treatments so that each treatment occurs at equal number of times at each ordinal position and each treatment precedes and follows each other treatment an equal number of times.

The design for purposes of computation would look like that in Figure 12.5.

Although we might be somewhat interested in the treatment conditions in themselves, our main interest would be in the interaction. That is, we would be interested in whether the *differences* found between treatments A$_1$, A$_2$, and A$_3$ with the independent samples groups condition are similar to or different from those found under the repeated measures condition. If they are different, we have an interaction. As noted earlier, we would then conclude that different research designs lead to different psychological laws. See Grice (1966) for a more extended treatment of this type analysis.

The procedure that we just described is a statistically acceptable way to analyze results but, if used only for tests of significance, it is somewhat wasteful of data. However, the data can be used for other purposes, such as plotting functions or estimating population parameters. For a discussion and computational example of another procedure for making comparisons between repeated measures and independent samples designs, see Erlebacher (1977).

CHAPTER THIRTEEN

THE RATIONALE OF STATISTICAL DECISION MAKING

13.1   FROM DESCRIPTIONS TO INFERENCES

In Chapter 10, we looked at several descriptive statistics that we use to make sense out of a mass of raw data. We briefly reviewed the calculation and interpretation of statistics that are used to describe both the central tendency of a distribution of scores or quantities (e.g., mean and median) and the dispersion of scores around central tendency (range, standard deviation, and variance). Our goal in descriptive statistics was to describe, with both accuracy and an economy of statement, aspects of samples selected from the population.

It should be clear that our primary focus is not on the sample statistics themselves. Their value lies primarily in the fact that they may shed light on characteristics of the population. Thus, we are not interested, as such, in the fact that the mean of the control group was higher or lower than the mean of an experimental group, nor that a sample of one-hundred voters revealed a higher proportion favoring Candidate A. Rather, our focus shifts from near to far vision, it shifts from the sample to the populations. We wish to know if we may justifiably conclude that the experimental variable has had an effect; or we wish to predict that Candidate A is likely to win the election. Our descriptive statistics provide that factual basis for the inductive leap from samples to populations.

In this chapter we shall take a conceptual tour of statistical decision making. The purpose is not to dwell on computational techniques but rather to explore the rationale underlying inferential statistics. Worked computations are shown in Appendix A.

13.2   THE ROLE OF PROBABILITY THEORY

Recall the distinction between deductive and inductive reasoning (Section 3.1). With deductive reasoning, the truth of the conclusion is implicit in the assumptions. Either we draw a valid conclusion from the premises or we do not. There is no in-between ground. This is not the case with inductive or scientific proof. Conclusions do not follow logically from a set of premises. Rather, they represent extensions of or generalizations based on empirical observations. Hence, in contrast to logical proof, scientific or inductive conclusions are not considered valid or invalid in any ultimate sense. Rather than being either right or wrong, we regard scientific propositions as having a given probability of being valid. If observation after observation confirm a proposition, we assign a high probability (approaching 1.00) to the validity of the proposition. If we have deep and abiding reservations about its validity, we may assign a probability that approaches zero. Note, however, we never establish scientific truth nor do we disprove its validity with absolute certainty.

Most commonly, probabilities are expressed either as a proportion or a percentage. As the probability of an event approaches 1.00 or 100 percent we say that the event is likely to occur. As it approaches 0.00 or 0 percent, we deem the event unlikely to occur. One way of expressing probability is in terms of the number of events favoring a given outcome relative to the total number of events possible. Thus,

$$P_A = \frac{\text{number of events favoring } A}{\text{number of events favoring } A + \text{number}} \text{ of events not favoring } A.$$

To illustrate, if a population of 100,000 individuals contains ten with phenylketonuria (PKU), what is the probability that one, selected at random, will have PKU?

$$P_{\text{pku}} = \frac{10}{10 + 99,990} = 0.0001 \text{ or } 0.01\%.$$

Thus, the probability is extremely low: one in ten thousand. This definition is perfectly satisfactory for dealing with discrete events (i.e., those that are counted). However, how do we define probability when the variables are continuous, e.g., weight, IQ score, reaction time? Here, probabilities can be expressed as a proportion of one area under a curve relative to the total area under a curve. Recall the normal distribution. The total area under the curve is 1.00. Also, between the mean and one standard deviation above the mean, the proportion of total area is 0.3413. If we selected a sample score from a normally distributed population, what is the probability that it would be between the mean and one standard deviation above the mean? Since about 34 percent of the total area is included between these points, $p = 0.34$. Similarly, $p = 0.34$ that a single randomly selected score would be between the mean and one standard deviation below the mean. Table B.1 (Appendix B), which shows areas under the standard normal curve, permits the expression of any value of a normally distributed variable in terms of probability.

Probability looms large on the scene of inferential statistics because it is the basis for accepting some hypotheses and rejecting others.

13.3   THE NULL AND ALTERNATIVE HYPOTHESES

Prior to the beginning of an experiment, the researcher sets up two mutually exclusive hypotheses. One is a statistical hypothesis that the experimenter expects to reject. It is referred to as the **null hypothesis** and is usually represented symbolically as H_0. The null hypothesis states some expectation concerning the value of one or more population parameters. Most commonly, it is an hypothesis of no difference. Let us look at a few examples:

1. If we were testing the honesty of a coin, the null hypothesis would read: H_0 the coin is unbiased. Stated more precisely, the probability of a head is equal to the probability of a tail: $P_h = P_t = 1/2$.

2. If we were evaluating the effect of a drug on reaction time, the null hypothesis might read: The drug has no effect on reaction time.

NULL HYPOTHESIS a statistical hypothesis the experimenter expects to reject; usually a hypothesis of no difference.

The important point to remember about the null hypothesis is that it always states some expectation concerning a *population parameter*—such as population mean, median, proportion, standard deviation, or variance. It is never stated in terms of expectations of a sample. For example, we would never state that the sample mean (or median, or proportion, etc.) of one group is equal to the sample mean of another. It is a fact of sampling behavior that sample statistics are rarely identical, even if selected from the same population. Thus, ten tosses of a single coin will not always yield five heads and five tails. The discipline of statistics sets down the rules for making an inductive leap from sample statistics to population parameters.

The **alternative hypothesis** (H_1) denies the null hypothesis. If the null hypothesis states that there is no difference in the population means from which two samples were drawn, the alternative hypothesis asserts that there is a difference. The alternative hypothesis usually states the investigator's expectations. Indeed, there really would be little sense embarking upon costly and time-consuming research unless we had some reason for expecting that the experimental variable will have an effect. Let's look at a few examples of alternative hypotheses:

1. In the study aimed at testing the honesty of a coin, the alternative hypothesis would read: $H_1: P_h \neq P_t \neq 1/2$; the probability of a head is not equal to the probability of a tail which is not equal to one-half.

2. In the effect of a drug on reaction time, the alternative hypothesis might read: The administration of a given dosage level of a drug affects reaction time.

ALTERNATIVE HYPOTHESIS an hypothesis denying the null hypothesis; usually expresses the experimenter's expectations.

13.4   THE SAMPLING DISTRIBUTION AND STATISTICAL DECISION MAKING

Now that we have stated our null and alternative hypothesis, where do we go from there? Recall that these hypotheses are mutually exclusive. They are also *exhaustive.* By this we mean that no other possibility exists. These two possible outcomes in our statistical decision making exhaust all possible outcomes. If the null hypothesis is true, then the alternative hypothesis must be false. Conversely, if the null hypothesis is false, then the alternative hypothesis must be true.

Considering these realities, our strategy would appear to be quite straight-forward—simply find out if the null hypothesis is true or false. Unfortunately, there is one further wrinkle. The null hypothesis can never be proved to be true. How would you go about proving that a drug has no effect, or that males and females are equally intelligent, or that a coin is honest? If you flipped it 1,000,000 times and obtained exactly 500,000 heads, wouldn't that be proof positive? No. It would merely indicate that, if a bias does exist, it must be exceptionally small. But we cannot rule out the possibility that a small bias does exist. Perhaps the next million, five million, or ten billion tosses will reveal this bias. So we have a dilemma. If we have no way of proving one of two mutually exclusive and exhaustive hypotheses, how can we establish which of these alternatives has the higher probability of being true?

Fortunately, there is a way out of this dilemma. If we cannot prove the null hypothesis, we can set up conditions that permit us to reject it. For exam-ple, if we had tossed the coin 1,000,000 times and obtained 950,000 heads, would anyone seriously doubt the bias of the coin? Clearly, we would reject the null hypothesis that the coin is honest. *The critical factor in this decision is our judgment that an outcome this rare is unlikely to have been the result of chance factors.* It happened for a reason and that reason is to be found in the characteristics of the coin or in the way it was tossed.

In this particular example, we did not engage in any formal statistical exercise in order to reject H_0. Our lifelong experience with coin-tossing experi-ments provided a frame of reference that permitted us to make the judgment. Since the obtained outcome is monumentally rare, we conclude that it did not occur by chance. However, in science, we often do not have frames of refer-ence, based on experience, that permit us to dispense with formal statistical analyses. Nor are we often afforded the luxury of a sample size equal to one million. The frame of reference for statistical decision making is provided by the **sampling distribution** of a statistic. A sampling distribution is a theoretical probability distribution of the possible values of some sample statistic that would occur if we were to draw all possible samples of a fixed size from a given population (Runyon and Haber, 1980, p. 194). There is a sampling distribu-tion for every statistic—mean, standard deviation, variance, proportion, median, etc.

SAMPLING DISTRIBUTION   A theoretical probability distribution of possible values of some sample statistic that would occur if we were to draw all possible samples of a fixed size from a given population.

To illustrate, imagine we had a population of six scores: 1, 2, 3, 3, 4, 5. Suppose we randomly select a single score from this population, return it, and

Table 13.1
Sample means resulting from selecting all possible samples of $N = 2$ from a population of six scores.

Second Selection	First Selection					
	1	2	3	3	4	5
1	1.0	1.5	2.0	2.0	2.5	3.0
2	1.5	2.0	2.5	2.5	3.0	3.5
3	2.0	2.5	3.0	3.0	3.5	4.0
3	2.0	2.5	3.0	3.0	3.5	4.0
4	2.5	3.0	3.5	3.5	4.0	4.5
5	3.0	3.5	4.0	4.0	4.5	5.0

Table 13.2
Frequency distribution and sampling distribution of means based on samples of $N = 2$ drawn at random from a population of six numbers. Note that the mean of the distribution of sample means is the same as the population mean.

	Sample Mean	Frequency	P
	1.0	1	.028
	1.5	2	.056
	2.0	5	.139
	2.5	6	.167
mean---->	3.0	8	.222
	3.5	6	.167
	4.0	5	.139
	4.5	2	.056
	5.0	1	.028
		36	1.002*

*The sum of the probabilities is 1.00. The slight disparity is due to rounding error.

randomly select a second score. We call these two scores a random sample of $N = 2$ and we calculate a mean. Now imagine that we selected all possible samples of $N = 2$ from that population and calculated mean for each. Table 13.1 shows all possible outcomes of this sampling experiment. Each cell shows the mean of the two scores that make up each sample. Thus, if the first selection is 1.0 and the second is 1.0, the mean of the sample is 1.0.

Now we may record the frequency with which each mean would be obtained. When we do so, we have constructed a frequency distribution of means of sample size $N = 2$. This is shown in Table 13.2.

Now if we divide the frequency with which a given mean was obtained by the total number of sample means (i.e., 36), we obtain the probability of selecting that mean. Thus, eight different samples of $N = 2$ would yield a mean equal to 3.0. The probability, then, is $8/36 = 0.222$. Note that, by chance, we would rarely select a mean of 1.0 ($p = 0.028$) or a mean of 5.0 ($p = 0.028$).

In this example, we used a very small population to illustrate a sampling distribution of a statistic. In real life, the populations are often extremely large or infinite. Let us imagine that we had a large population of scores and we selected a large number of samples of a given size (say, $N = 30$). We could construct a distribution of the sample means. We would find that the mean of this distribution equals the mean of the population and the form of the distribution would tend to be normal *even if the population distribution is not normal.* In fact, the larger the sample size, the closer the approximation of the distribution of sample means to a normal curve. (See Figure 13.1.) It is a fortunate fact of statistical life that distributions of sample statistics often take on the form of other distributions with known mathematical properties. This permits us to use this known distribution as a frame of reference against which to evaluate a given sample statistic. Thus, knowing that the distribution of sample means tends toward normality when the sample size exceeds 30 permits us to evaluate the relative frequency of a sample mean in terms of the normal distribution. We are then able to label certain events or outcomes as common, others as somewhat unusual, and still others as rare. For example, note that in Figure 13.1 a score of 130 is fairly common when $N = 1$, whereas a mean of

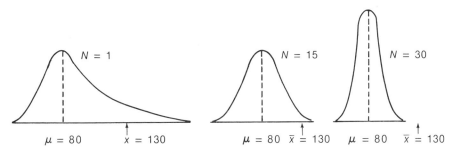

Fig. 13.1 Distribution of scores of a population ($N = 1$) and sampling distributions of means when samples are randomly selected from that population and the sample sizes are $N = 15$ and $N = 30$, respectively. Note that the parent distribution is markedly skewed. As we increase N, the distribution of sample means tends toward normality and the dispersion of sample means decreases. (The Greek letter mu (μ) represents a population mean.)

130 is unusual when $N = 15$, and rare when $N = 30$. Moreover, if we find that the occurrence of an event or the outcome of an experiment is rare, we conclude that nonchance factors (e.g., the experimental variable) are responsible for or have caused this rare or unusual outcome.

Table 13.3 shows the sampling distribution of a coin-tossing experiment when a single coin is tossed twelve times or when twelve coins are tossed once. It is the sampling distribution of a binomial or two-category variable when $N = 12$, and the probability of each elementary event (e.g., a head or a tail) is equal to $1/2$.

This sampling distribution provides the frame of reference for answering questions about possible outcomes of experiments. Is 12 out of 12 heads a rare outcome? Yes, exceedingly rare. It occurs, by chance, about twice out of every 10,000 repetitions of the experiment. Note that 0 out of 12 is equally rare. What about 7 heads out of 12? Not at all unusual. This outcome will occur about 19 times out of every 100 repetitions of the coin-tossing experiment. Can we define rare more precisely? Only by an agreement among fellow scientists. If the event in question or an event more unusual would have occurred 5 percent of the time or less, most psychological researchers are willing to make the judgment that the outcome is rare and ascribe it to nonchance factors. In other words, they reject H_0 and assert H_1. This cutoff point for inferring the opera-

Table 13.3
Sampling distribution of a binomial variable in which $P_h = P_t = 1/2$ and the number of trials equals 12.

Outcome expressed as number of heads	Probability
12	.0002
11	.0029
10	.0161
9	.0537
8	.1208
7	.1934
6	.2256
5	.1934
4	.1208
3	.0537
2	.0161
1	.0029
0	.0002
	$\Sigma P = .9998$*

*The sum of the probabilities should be 1.00. The disparity of .0002 represents rounding error.

tion of nonchance factors is referred to as the 0.05 *significance level*. When we reject the null hypothesis at the 0.05 level, it is conventional to refer to the outcome of the experiment as statistically significant at the 0.05 level.

Other scientists, more conservative about rejecting H_0, prefer to use the 0.01 significance level or the 1 percent significance level. When the observed event or one that is more deviant would occur 1 percent of the time or less, by chance, we assert that the results are due to nonchance factors.* It is conventional to refer to the results of the experiment as statistically significant at the 0.01 level.

The level of significance set by the investigator for rejecting H_0 is known as the **alpha (α) level**. When we employ the 0.01 significance level, $\alpha = 0.01$. When we use the 0.05 significance level, $\alpha = 0.05$.

ALPHA (α) LEVEL   level of significance set by the investigator for rejecting H_0; also the probability of falsely rejecting a true H_0.

Let us look at a few examples of this statistical decision-making process: Jeanette Brown has conducted a study in which she used $\alpha = 0.05$. Upon completing her statistical analysis, she found the probability of obtaining an outcome this rare or more rare was 0.02. Her decision? She rejects H_0 and asserts that the experimental variable had an effect on the dependent measure.

Roger Miller obtained a probability of 0.06, using $\alpha = 0.05$. Since his results failed to achieve the 0.05 cutoff point he does not reject the null hypothesis. Note that he cannot claim to have proved the null hypothesis, nor should he claim that "there is a trend toward significance." Once a significance level is set, its boundaries should be considered as quite rigid and fixed.

Table 13.4
The decision-making matrix in inferential statistics.

| | α-level | | |
	A	*B* 0.05	*C* 0.01
Probability of outcome	$P \leq 0.01$	reject H_0	reject H_0
	$0.05 \geq P > 0.01$	reject H_0	fail to reject H_0
	$P > 0.05$	fail to reject H_0	fail to reject H_0

The middle entry in Column A reads: if P is equal to or less than 0.05 and greater than 0.01, then. . . . Example: If $\alpha = 0.01$ and $P > 0.05$, look in column C, row 3. Here we see that we fail to reject H_0.

---

*Based on random sampling alone, results such as this would occur one time out of 100, therefore such a rare event is unlikely due to chance.

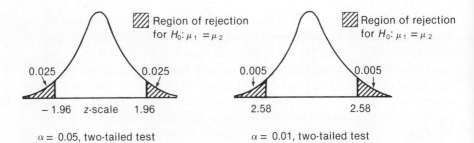

$\alpha = 0.05$, two-tailed test $\alpha = 0.01$, two-tailed test

Fig. 13.2 Region of rejection at $\alpha = 0.05$ and $\alpha = .01$ under the standard normal curve. If the obtained statistic is greater than 1.96 or less than -1.96 and $\alpha = 0.05$, we reject H_0. If $\alpha = 0.01$ and the test statistic exceeds the absolute value of 2.58, we reject H_0.

However, Miller's results are so close to the cutoff point, he would be wise to consider a repetition of the study and increasing the N, if still possible.

A research team set alpha at 0.01 and found the probability of their obtained outcome to be $p = 0.03$. They fail to reject H_0 since the probability of this outcome is greater than α. The statistical decision-making process is summarized in Table 13.4.

Many of the tables that are used by researchers and statisticians do not provide probability values for the sampling distributions to which they refer. Rather, they present **critical values** which define the **region of rejection** at various levels of α. The region of rejection is that portion of the area under a curve that includes those values of a test statistic that lead to the rejection of the null hypothesis.

CRITICAL VALUES   in some tables, critical values define the region of rejection of H_0 at various levels of α.

REGION OF REJECTION   portion of the area under a curve that includes values of a test statistic that lead to a rejection of H_0.

To illustrate, the two curves in Figure 13.2 show the regions for rejecting H_0 when the standard normal curve is used.

Let's look at a few examples:

If $\alpha = 0.05$ and the test statistic equals 1.43, we fail to reject H_0 since the test statistic does not achieve the critical value.

If $\alpha = 0.01$ and the test statistic equals 2.83, we reject H_0 since the test statistic is in the critical region.

If $\alpha = 0.05$ and the test statistic equals 2.19, we reject H_0 since the test statistic is in the critical region at $\alpha = 0.05$.

13.5 TESTS OF SIGNIFICANCE—*t* AND *F*

A statistical test that permits us to evaluate the status of the null hypothesis is known as a test of significance. Two of the most commonly used in psychology are the *t*-ratio and the *F*-ratio. Both employ sample statistics as a means of estimating population parameters, both assume that the dependent measures or scores are drawn from a normally distributed population, and both test for the significance of the difference between and/or among means.

The *t*-ratio may be used when there is either one (one-sample case) or two groups (two-sample case) involved in the study. As noted earlier, the *F*-ratio is used for more complex experimental designs as, for example, when there are more than two groups or more than one experimental variable. See Appendix A for a worked example.

13.5.1 One-Sample Case

Occasionally, a researcher will select a single sample from some population with unknown parameters and raise such questions as: "Is it reasonable to hypothesize that the sample was drawn from a population with a mean of, say, 20, 80, or 100?" The hypothesized value may be a known population parameter or a value based on a prediction from theory. What we do, in effect, is ascertain whether or not the sample mean might reasonably be considered representative of an actual or theoretical population.

Note that, in the **one-sample case**, there is no control condition against which to compare the mean of an experimental group. The null hypothesis usually states that the population mean from which the sample was drawn is some specific value.

ONE-SAMPLE CASE   a single sample statistic is tested against a known or hypothetical parameter.

For example, an automobile manufacturer may claim that odometers accurately reflect true mileage figures. A randomly selected set of odometers could be tested over a measured course of, say, ten miles. The sample statistic would be tested against the means specified under the null hypothesis, i.e., $\mu_0 = 10$.

An educator may claim that the mean IQ of children at a given school is 110. A random sample of IQ's would be obtained at random from the school population and the sample mean could be tested against $\mu_0 = 110$.

A worked example showing the calculation of the appropriate test statistic, *t*, in the one sample case, appears in Appendix A.

13.5.2   Two-sample Case, Independent Samples

When subjects or observations are drawn at random from a given population and are assigned at random to two groups, we speak of such a research design as the **two-sample case** with independent samples. Typically, one group (the experimental group) receives the experimental treatment and the other group (the control group) does not receive the experimental treatment. Scores are obtained on some criterion measure (e.g., performance on a psychomotor task, or change in a diagnosed medical condition); then the means of the two groups are calculated, and a test of significance is applied to determine if both groups might reasonably be considered representative of the same population.

TWO-SAMPLE CASE   when two sample statistics are compared to determine if they might reasonably have been drawn from the same population.

Appendix A shows a worked example of the test statistic appropriate to the two sample case when the population is assumed to be normally distributed.

13.6   TWO-SAMPLE CASE, CORRELATED SAMPLES

As we noted earlier, there are many factors that contribute to the variability of scores in behavioral research—variations in experimental techniques, differences in capabilities of subjects, and moment-to-moment fluctuations in such factors as the testing situation, attention and motivation of subjects, etc. All of these contribute to the variability of the error term. When these sources of variation are large, the error term is correspondingly large. It is also less sensitive in evaluating the significance of the difference between means. Research designs employing correlated samples frequently identify and quantify a large source of error and then "remove" this from the error term, to permit a more sensitive evaluation of the difference between and among means.

There are two main classes of correlated samples design—repeated measures and matched group designs. These are elaborated on in Chapter 12. Appendix A shows a worked example using correlated samples.

13.7   NONPARAMETRIC TESTS

Many data are collected in the behavioral sciences that either do not lend themselves to analysis in terms of the normal probability curve or fail to meet this basic assumption for its use. For example, many populations with which the researcher deals consist of two categories, e.g., yes-no, male-female, heads-tails, right-wrong, etc. Such populations are referred to as dichotomous or two-category populations. (We dealt with these earlier under the heading Nominal Scale.) Other data are best expressed in terms of ranks, i.e., ordinal scales. When comparing the attributes of objects, events, or people, we are often unable to specify precise quantitative differences. However, we are frequently able to state ordered relationships, e.g., event A ranks the highest with respect to the attribute in question, event B the second highest, etc. In addition to equivalence and nonequivalence, then, the mathematical relationships germane to such data are "greater than" ($>$) and "less than" ($<$). $a > b$ may mean: a is taller than b, of higher rank than b, more prestigious than b, prettier than b, etc. $a < b$ may mean a is less than b, of lower rank than b, less prestigious than b, etc.

Finally, many data collected by psychologists are truly quantitative. They may be meaningfully added, subtracted, multiplied, and divided. Moreover, equal differences in scale values are equal, i.e., interval or ratio scales. For example, in a timed task, a difference of one second is the same throughout the time scale. Most commonly, parametric tests of significance (e.g., the t-ratio, analysis of variance) are used with such variables. However, these tests always involve the assumption that the populations are normally distributed. There are occasions when the investigator has reason to doubt the validity of this assumption. At these times, he or she should consider as viable alternatives the many nonparametric tests of significance that are presently in the researcher's arsenal. This is particularly the case with small N's. With large N's, the sampling distributions of most statistics approach the normal curve even when the parent distributions deviate considerably from normality.

It is beyond the scope of this text to review the many nonparametric tests that are available. If you wish to read further, you may consult Runyon and Haber (1980), Runyon (1977), or Siegal (1956).

13.8   TYPE I, TYPE II ERRORS, AND STATISTICAL POWER

As we saw earlier in the chapter, there are two types of statistical decisions we can make: reject H_0 when the probability of the event of interest achieves an acceptable α-level (usually $p \leq 0.05$ or ≤ 0.01), or fail to reject H_0 when the probability of the event of interest is greater than α. With each of these decisions, there is an associated risk of error.

If we reject H_0 (i.e., conclude H_0 is false) when H_0 is true, we have made the error of falsely rejecting the null hypothesis. This type of error is called a Type α or **Type I error**.

TYPE I (TYPE α) ERROR   an error made when H_0 is true but is mistakenly rejected.

If we fail to reject H_0 (i.e., we do not assert the alternative hypothesis) when H_0 is false, we have made the error of falsely accepting H_0. This type of error is referred to as a Type β or **Type II error**.

TYPE II (Type β) ERROR   an error made when H_0 is actually false but is not rejected.

Let's look at a few examples.

1. H_0: $\mu_1 = \mu_2$, $\alpha = 0.05$. Obtained $p = 0.03$.
      Statistical decision: H_0 is false. Actual status of H_0: True.
   Error: Type I—rejecting a true H_0.

2. H_0: $\mu_1 = \mu_2$, $\alpha = 0.05$. Obtained $p = 0.04$.
      Statistical decision: H_0 is false. Actual status of H_0: False.
   Error: No error has been made. A correct conclusion was drawn since H_0
   is false and the statistical decision was that H_0 is false.

3. H_0: $\mu_1 = \mu_2$, $\alpha = 0.01$. Obtained $p = 0.10$.
      Statistical decision: fail to reject H_0. Actual status of H_0: False.
   Error: Type II—failing to reject a false H_0.

4. H_0: $\mu_1 = \mu_2$, $\alpha = 0.01$. Obtained $p = 0.006$.
      Statistical decision: Reject H_0. Actual status of H_0: False.
   Error: No error has been made since the statistical decision has been to
   reject H_0 when H_0 is actually false.

You should know that a Type I error can be made only when H_0 is true, since this type of error is defined as the *mistaken rejection* of a *true hypothesis*. The probability of a Type I error is given by α. Thus, if $\alpha = 0.05$, about five times out of one hundred we will falsely reject a true null hypothesis. In contrast, a Type II error can be made only when H_0 is false, since this type of error is defined as the mistaken acceptance of a false hypothesis, (i.e., H_0).

Table 13.5 summarizes the probabilities associated with acceptance or rejection of H_0 depending on the true status of this null hypothesis.

The probability of a Type II or β error must be obtained by calculation. It is beyond the scope of this book to delve into the calculation of β probabilities. Interested students may consult Runyon and Haber (1980, chapter 16) or Run-

Table 13.5
The type of error made as a function of the true status of H_0 and the statistical decision we have made. To illustrate, if H_0 is true (column 1) and we have rejected H_0 (row 2), we have made a Type I error. If H_0 is false (column 2) and we have rejected H_0, we have made a correct decision.

		true status of H_0	
		H_0 true	H_0 false
Decision	Accept H_0	correct $1 - \alpha$	Type II error β
	Reject H_0	Type I error α	correct $1 - \beta$

yon (1977, chapter 17). The concept of β error is important since, among other things, it relates to the economics of research. It would make little sense to expend large amounts of funds, tie up laboratory space and equipment, and devote hours of human effort in the conceptualization, conduct, and statistical analysis of research if, for example, the β probability were as high as 90 percent. This would mean that the probability of making a correct decision —rejecting the false null hypothesis—would be only 10 percent. It would hardly seem worth the effort. This latter probability—the probability of correctly rejecting the null hypothesis when it is false—is known as the **power** of this test. Power is defined as $1 - \beta$.

> **POWER**   the probability of correctly rejecting a false null hypothesis.

   There is a further risk when conducting research in which the power is low. A failure to find a significant difference may cause a researcher to prematurely abandon a promising line of experimentation. As a consequence, potentially important discoveries may never be made because the researcher relegated a seminal idea to the junk heap.

   Clearly, one of the goals of the careful researcher must be to reduce the probability of β error and, thereby, increase the power of the test. There are a number of factors that influence statistical power. Among them are sample size, α-level, and precision in estimating experimental error. Fortunately, all are under the control of the experimenter.

   Other things being equal, as you increase the sample size, you increase the power of your statistical test. In research in which the cost per subject is low, increasing the sample size may be an attractive way to boost power. However, the relationship between sample size and power is one of diminishing returns. Beyond a certain point, further increases in sample size lead to negligible increases in power.

   As the α level is decreased, we decrease the probability of a Type I error and increase the probability of a Type II error. Conversely, as the α level is increased, we increase the probability of a Type I error and decrease the probability of a Type II error.

   Since the power of the test is inversely related to the probability of a Type II error (i.e., power increases as the probability of a Type II error decreases), it follows that the power can be increased by setting a higher α level for rejecting H_0.

   Balanced against this is the fact that increasing the α level also increases the probability of falsely rejecting a true null hypothesis. The researcher must decide which of these risks is more acceptable. If the consequences of making a Type I error are serious (e.g., claiming a chemical compound cures a serious disease when it does not), it is desirable to set a low α level. However, the commission of a Type II error can also have serious consequences, as when failure to reject the null hypothesis is treated as if the null hypothesis has been proved.

Thus, a chemical compound "proved safe after exhaustive testing" could lead to the introduction of a lethal compound into the marketplace.

The third factor, control over the precision in estimating experimental error, is the one that should receive the most attention from a careful researcher. Any steps that lead to increased precision of our measurement of experimental error will also increase the power of the test. For example, in the two sample cases in which the t-ratio is appropriate, increased precision will reduce the standard error of the difference between means, which will in turn increase the magnitude of the t-ratio. There are numerous ways of increasing our precision in measuring experimental error, including: improving the reliability of our criterion measure, standardizing the experimental technique, and using correlated measures. In a matched pairs design, for example, the power of the test will increase as the correlation between paired measures increases. More about this important topic was said in earlier chapters where we noted that a feature of various research designs was the degree of precision in estimating both the effects of experimental treatments, and the error variance (Chapters 11 and 12).

13.9 PROBLEMS OF VERY SMALL OR VERY LARGE SAMPLES

On the surface it might seem that, barring economic and logistic considerations, the larger the sample size the better off we are as researchers. The advantages of a large sample are so obvious that, to question it, might seem like questioning the desirability of motherhood. As we shall see, however, a large sample is at times a mixed blessing.

Let us examine some of the advantages of a large sample. One we have already mentioned. In the event that the null hypothesis is false, the greater is the probability that we shall ascertain this fact when we have a large N. We referred to this increased ability to detect a difference as *statistical power*. However, not all research is directed primarily to testing null hypotheses in an experimental or laboratory setting. Much research conducted in the field has the primary objective of obtaining accurate estimates of one or more parameters. Take opinion polls as an example. If we are studying the presidential campaign, the bottom line of our polling procedures is to predict accurately the outcome of the frenzied electioneering that strikes our country late in the summer every fourth year and climaxes in the election in early November. As long as our sampling procedures are correct, the larger the sample size the more likely we are to obtain sample statistics that are representative of the population parameter of interest; namely, the proportion of registered voters who cast their ballots for each presidential candidate.

In a small sample, a small unrepresentative "run" of selections of a single candidate may greatly influence our estimate of the parameter. The same "run" with a large sample may have a negligible effect on the accuracy of our

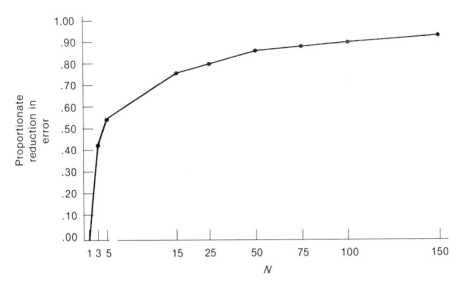

Fig. 13.3 The reduction of the error term as a function of N. Note that increasing N yields a curve of diminishing returns in terms of reduction in error. For Example, a threefold increase in N from 50 to 150 yields only about a 6-percent reduction in error whereas a threefold increase from 5 to 15 yields about a 32-percent reduction.

estimates. So the going rule in this sort of research is to obtain as large a sample as is consistent with economic and logistic realities. Obviously, not everyone can be polled because there would be insufficient funds for such an undertaking, nor would there be adequate supportive personnel (e.g., trained pollsters) and materials (e.g., computer terminals). Moreover, like power, the increased precision of estimating the parameter follows the law of diminishing returns as we increase N. (See Figure 13.3.) Relatively small increases in N when the initial sample size is small yield much larger returns than the same increases when the initial sample size is large. What this all means is that increasing sample size should not be looked at as a panacea, a sort of cure-all for the ills that often afflict ongoing research programs.

However, large sample size can provide a measure of comfort when the researcher seriously questions the extent to which he or she has met the basic assumptions of a given statistical test. The assumption of normality underlies the parametric test of significance. But what if we have serious doubts that the parent population is normally distributed? It is an interesting fact that, even when statistics, such as the mean, median, standard deviation, are drawn from nonnormal populations, the sampling distributions of these statistics approach normality with increasing sample size. Thus, departures from the assumption of normality of the population of scores are not as worrisome when the sample size is large. Indeed, as previously pointed out, the sampling distributions of

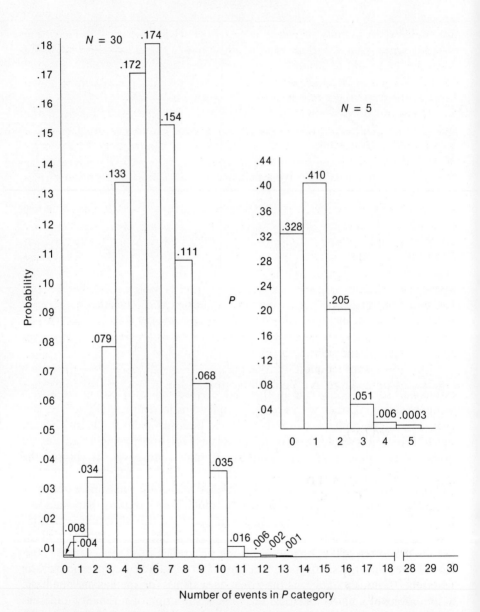

Fig. 13.4 Sampling distribution of the binomial when $P = .20$, $Q = .80$, and $N = 5$. Note the extreme asymmetry of the binomial when N = 5. When N = 30, the sampling distribution of the binomial becomes more symmetrical and begins to resemble the normal curve in form. Note that no bars are shown for events in the P category equal to or greater than 15. This is due to the fact that the area remaining is extremely small—the probability of an outcome 15 or greater is only about .00023.

nominally and ordinally scaled variables approach normality with increasing sample size. Figure 13.4 contrasts two sampling distributions of the binomial when $P = 0.20$ and $Q = 0.80$. Note the extreme asymmetry when N is small ($N = 5$). When N is larger ($N = 30$), the resemblance to the symmetry and form of the normal curve is already quite pronounced.

Up to this point, we have seen that most of the advantages line up on the side of large N's, particularly in research where the primary thrust is to obtain an accurate estimate of the parameter of interest. About the only factors seeming to favor small N's are economics and logistics. These are, of course, not inconsiderable and should receive a painstaking review at the inception of any research project.

In most experimental research, the main objective is to determine whether or not the experimental variable has an effect. This objective is achieved by putting the null hypothesis to the test. If rejected, we may justifiably claim an effect. What is the relationship between the sample size and our confidence that we have made a correct decision when we reject H_0? Let us look at a hypothetical case. Imagine that we conducted two studies, one with an N of 10 and the other with an N of 1,000. Imagine further that both studies yielded identical P values, which permitted us to reject H_0 at $\alpha = 0.05$. In which case is our rejection of H_0 more likely to be valid? Neither. The risk of making a Type I error is precisely the same in both instances. It is 0.05.

Let's raise another question. Which result impresses us more: the one with the small N or the larger N? Your answer should be, "The study with the small N." Why? Differences must be much larger to be significant with a small N than with a large N. This can best be understood in terms of another statistic, omega squared (ω^2).

13.10 OMEGA SQUARED—ESTIMATING DEGREE OF ASSOCIATION BETWEEN THE EXPERIMENTAL AND DEPENDENT VARIABLES

The finding of a statistically significant t-ratio means that some degree of association exists between the experimental and dependent variables. However, the fact of statistical significance does not automatically confer "importance" to a finding. Given a sufficiently large N, even a trivial difference may be found to be statistically significant.

One way of clarifying the importance of a statistically significant difference is to ascertain the extent to which variations in the experimental variable (the treatment administered) account for variations in the dependent measure, i.e., the strength of the association. In general, the higher the degree of relationship (the association), the greater the importance of the finding. When the strength of the association is strong, the independent variable can be thought of as powerful.

One measure of association is ω^2 (**omega squared**), which is estimated by

$$\text{est } \omega^{2*} = \frac{t^2 - 1}{t^2 + N_1 + N_2 - 1}.$$

> OMEGA SQUARED a measure of association that indicates the proportion of variation in the dependent variable accounted for by variations in the independent variable.

Let us imagine that we conducted a two group study and found $t = -4.634$ with $N_1 = N_2 = 10$. Our estimated omega squared would be:

$$\text{est } \omega^2 = \frac{21.47 - 1}{21.47 + 19}$$

$$= \frac{20.47}{40.47}$$

$$= 0.51.$$

This may be interpreted to mean that approximately 51 percent of the variance in the dependent measure is accounted for in terms of variations of the treatment variable, i.e., 51 percent of the variance is explained. This is a high degree of association.

Let us imagine that we had found the same t-ratio (-4.634) but with a vastly larger N; namely, $N_1 = N_2 = 1,000$, for a total N of 2,000. Now the estimated variance in the dependent variable accounted for by variations in the treatment variable would be:

$$\text{est. } \omega^2 = \frac{21.47 - 1}{21.47 + 1999}$$

$$= 0.01.$$

This is a negligible amount—about 1 percent of the total variance. Even though statistically significant, we would have to regard the finding as trivial. We should note that there are several techniques used for determining the degree of association between the independent and dependent variables. Omega squared (ω^2) is only one of them. Most modern statistical texts have a section devoted to the topic. We might add that there are instances where the strength of the calculated association is weak, yet the relationship between the indepen-

---

*If $|t|$ is less than 1.00, ω^2 will be negative. Since a negative ω^2 is meaningless, we arbitrarily set $\omega^2 = 0$ when $|t| \leq 1.00$.

dent and dependent variables is still considered important. The latter sometimes occurs when evaluating new theoretical views or when considering new
therapeutic treatments.

It is interesting to note that performance differences in males and females
on tasks of verbal ability, quantitative ability, and visual-spatial ability, when
statistically significant, are generally quite small. Male/female differences in
performance often account for no more than 1 to 5 percent of the population
variance.

CHAPTER FOURTEEN

SINGLE-SUBJECT RESEARCH

14.1 WHAT IS SINGLE-SUBJECT RESEARCH?

The single-subject approach is a method designed to study the behavior of individual organisms. As the method continues to evolve and improve, it also has become more popular for both scientific and therapeutic purposes. Its track record in both areas is impressive. The single-subject approach should not be confused with the case-study or case-history approach where a single individual is also studied exhaustively. The case-study approach is an uncontrolled inquiry into history (retrospective) and it may yield interesting information. However, the lack of control severely limits any conclusions that can be drawn. There are two serious problems with the case-study approach: (1) lack of experimental control, and (2) obtaining precise measures of behavior. Neither of these apply to the single-subject approach.

Using the single-subject approach does not mean that you must investigate only a single subject—although you can. More often than not, several subjects are studied very intensively—usually somewhere between three and five. However, *in each case interest is always in the careful analysis of the individual subject separately and not in the average performance of the group.* With the single-subject approach there is very little interest in averaging across subjects and great emphasis is placed on careful and rigorous experimental control. Unwanted environmental variables are either excluded from the study or they are held constant so that their effects are the same across subjects and conditions. As we shall see, important features of this procedure for determining the reliability of the findings are actual **replications** rather than inferential statistics. We shall describe two types of replication although there are others (Sidman, 1960). These are intra-subject replication (replications within an individual subject) and inter-subject replication (replications between individual subjects). As with other research methods, the single-subject approach has both strengths and limitations. We first discuss the strengths of the approach and later describe its limitations.

REPLICATION   an independent repetition of an experimental procedure under as similar conditions as the experimental materials permit.

Those who use the single-subject approach find it both a powerful and satisfying research method. One reason for this is that the method provides immediate feedback to the investigator about the effects of the treatment conditions. The experimenter knows immediately whether the treatment is "working" or "not working." Day-to-day changes can be observed first hand, immediately and in individual subjects. If changes are necessary on a day-to-day basis, they can be made. Seldom do scientists have available procedures that do this. In contrast to the single-subject approach, a large sample statistical approach may take weeks or months of running subjects, calculating means, then performing statistical analyses, etc., and unfortunately, often nothing may be known about the effects of the treatment conditions until the final statistical analysis is complete. Even then, as we have seen, the derived knowledge is limited to statements concerning group performance and not to the performance of specific individual subjects.

A complete treatment of the single-subject method cannot be given in one chapter but we will attempt to give you a representative view. For a fuller discussion dealing with application of the method to basic research, see the excellent book by Sidman (1960). For an excellent treatment of the single subject approach in applied research, see Hersen and Barlow (1976).

14.2   "TRUE EXPERIMENTS" AND THE SINGLE-SUBJECT APPROACH

In our previous chapters we stressed that the great strength and value of true experiments is in determining causal relations. We made the point repeatedly that true experiments rule out a greater number of rival or alternative interpretations of our findings than other research strategies, e.g., case studies, ex post facto research, quasi-experimental research. Recall that random assignment and manipulation of the independent variable are features that distinguish a true experiment from one that is not. A true experiment, of course, implies the use of proper control groups.

Random assignment to groups more than any other technique increases the likelihood that the groups composing the experiment are equal in all ways. Assuming that the experiment is properly designed and executed, this feature allows us to make comparisons among our different groups in terms of the effects of the independent variable. We introduce the term *true experiment* initially to contrast a large sample research procedure based on random assignment from other large sample research procedures in which random assignment was lacking. "True experiment" implies the potential use of all necessary controls. If done properly, such an experiment permits us to draw strong conclusions concerning the treatment conditions responsible for the differences found between groups.

The single-subject method also allows us to draw strong conclusions regarding the factors controlling the dependent variable, yet the method does not use random assignment. The method allows strong conclusions because investigators employing it use procedures that provide rigorous control over environmental-experimental conditions with great emphasis on obtaining stable behavior with each subject. To be an acceptable scientific work, the research must demonstrate for each subject that behavior is controlled by the treatment condition and he or she must also show both intra- and inter-subject replication. That is, control must be shown both within a single subject and also between the subjects. The method is relatively popular today but it hasn't always been. A brief description of some difficulties experienced by those using the single subject approach in earlier years is contained in Box 14.1.

BOX 14.1   EARLIER TIMES—SINGLE-SUBJECT RESEARCH

Research in psychology started out using small numbers of subjects, and investigators relied heavily on their ability to control conditions so that the conditions were reasonably constant among subjects. Rigorous methodology was only beginning to evolve. After the data were gathered, conclusions about effects of the independent variable were based on subjective visual inspection—referred to facetiously by some, as "the interocular test." Groups were not formed randomly and objective statistical aid for decision making were not yet available. Investigators realized the shortcomings of their method and made attempts to minimize subjectivity in their analyses.

The introduction of random assignment and statistical analyses were tremendous advances for research. Random assignment enhanced the likelihood that groups were initially equal on all variables. Statistical procedures permitted researchers to decide objectively whether the observed effect was more likely a chance occurrence or an outcome of the treatment condition. These powerful research tools were readily accepted by investigators and large sample statistical studies rapidly became popular. As interest in large sample methods increased, it became difficult to publish nonstatistical research or even studies based on a small number of subjects. Some researchers strongly preferred the single-subject approach refined by B. F. Skinner and elaborated by Sidman (1960). They continued using and refining it. Controversies and arguments frequently erupted between researchers using the single-subject approach and those using a statistical one. It is ironic that, even though psychology was defined as the study of individual behavior, investigators studying individual behavior could not easily get their research published in the established journals. This was the case even though strong behavioral control by the treatment condition was shown repeatedly in individual subjects. It was this difficulty in getting their research published that led to the formation of the Society for the Experimental Analysis of Behavior and the subsequent establishment of the journal entitled *Journal of the Experimental Analysis of Behavior.* The journal publishes basic research involving the study of individual subjects. Subsequently, a second journal devoted to the study of individual subjects was established focusing on applied research and entitled *Journal of Applied Behavior Analysis.*

With the passage of time, both the large sample and single-subject procedures have become better developed and their strengths and weaknesses more apparent. These methods continue to evolve, as do other research methods. Because of this, a greater variety of useful tools are becoming available to those interested in either basic or applied research.

14.3   WHY SOME RESEARCHERS USE THE SINGLE-SUBJECT METHOD

Investigators who use the single-subject method do so for different reasons. One of the main reasons is that their interest is in the behavior of individual subjects. The large sample group approach places emphasis on group averages rather than individual subjects. Unfortunately, the behavior reflected by the group average may not represent the individual subject. The following example illustrates how distant the overall results for the group may be from the performance of any given individual subject. Say that we are interested in learning as a function of practice. The particular form or shape of the curve is what we are trying to determine. We choose twenty subjects to participate in our study, choose a learning task that we want to evaluate, and then give practice trials to the subjects until the task is learned. After all the data are gathered, we plot a learning curve to determine its form or shape (see Figure 14.1), which in turn will reveal to us how quickly and smoothly subjects learned the task. The learning curve in Figure 14.1 is based on the performance of all twenty subjects. Each data point on the graph represents an average (five trials) of an average (twenty subjects).

A description of how these averages were computed may be helpful. First the performance of each subject on each block of five trials is averaged. Then the average for each average block of five trials is obtained for all twenty subjects. This average of averages produces a smooth, negatively accelerated learning curve. But does this group curve reflect the performance of a single individual? It is quite unlikely that any one individual in a group of twenty subjects would perform like the group curve. In other words, plots of each individual subject may be different from the group curve. Usually a statistical approach that relies on the analysis of group means masks the performance of each subject, whatever the problem being studied. A related point follows.

A group performance curve may not only mask the performance of an individual but may also be misleading. While the group average may indicate an increase in performance as a result of the treatment condition, not all subjects may have increased; some individuals comprising the group may, in fact, perform at a lower than "normal" level. The point is that individual reactions to the experimental conditions are not taken into account. Failure to address individual reactions may be especially unfortunate in more applied research, particularly if assessing different therapeutic techniques. If the therapy is harmful (or helpful) to certain individuals, this fact may be lost in the group mean. Others have made a similar argument in terms of the statistical analysis.

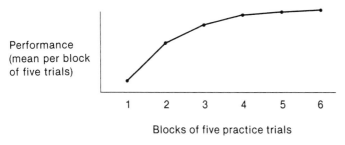

Fig. 14.1 Mean performance of twenty subjects on each of six blocks of five practice trials

Table 14.1
Comparison of single-subject and large sample approaches.

	Single Subject	Large Sample
Random Assignment	Not applicable	Yes
Control Groups	Not applicable	Yes
Manipulation	Yes	Yes
Determining Reliability	Replications	Statistically
Determining Generality	Replications	Sampling
Number of Subjects	Usually 1–5	Usually 10 per group
Flexibility of Procedure	High	Low
Measurement of Behavior	Continuous monitoring	Varies
Focus of Interest	Individual	Group
Time to Complete Experiment	Relatively long term	Relatively short term
Knowledge of Results	Moment to moment	After study is complete
Type 1 and 2 Errors	Not applicable	Yes
Statistical Assumption	Not applicable	Yes
Statistical Power	Not applicable	Yes
Laboratory Experiments	Yes	Yes
Field Experiments	Yes	Yes
Actuarial Experiments	No	Yes
Comparison Experiments	No	Yes

The analysis may reveal statistically significant differences between group comparisons but the differences may be due to only a few subjects. On the other hand, however, the analysis may not be statistically significant overall but some subjects may change markedly as a result of the treatment conditions.

The dependence on statistical evaluation of the data with large sample methods is also a source of unhappiness for some researchers. Have the assumptions underlying the statistical test been satisfied? Is the sample size sufficiently large to give the needed power? Is the sample size too large so that trivial differences between group comparisons will be significant? What about Type 1 and Type 2 errors? Some researchers are concerned that investigators are placing greater concern on statistical issues per se and placing less concern on rigorous methodology. Statistical analyses cannot salvage a poor experiment. Complete confounding of variables cannot be corrected by statistical analysis.

Other researchers favor the single-subject method because large numbers of subjects are simply not usually available. Consequently, a large sample procedure cannot be used. In applied research dealing with specific behavioral problems, the researcher-therapist might have to wait months or years before obtaining a sufficiently large sample. Applied psychologists are often interested only in a small number of individuals. They need a method sufficiently flexible to allow treatment of individual cases, one that can be altered quickly to adjust to the responsiveness of the individual. Large sample statistical procedures do not have this flexibility.

Table 14.1 compares characteristics of both the single-subject approach and the large sample statistical approach.

14.4   SINGLE-SUBJECT METHOD

As noted, when using the single-subject method the effects of the treatment must be shown in individual subjects. To accomplish this the experimenter must have considerable control over the experimental situation at all stages of the research. Moreover, he or she must use the proper methodology. As with other research methods, the dependent variable must be clearly defined. Where possible, it should be defined in terms of operations that objectively identify the occurrence or nonoccurrence of the response. (You may want to reread the section dealing with the characteristics of a good dependent variable, Chapter 5.) In single-subject research the dependent variable is often "rate of responding" and great emphasis is placed on steady state (stable) performance rather than behavior in transition, i.e., in the process of changing.

14.4.1   Establishing a Baseline

In many ways the single-subject approach is similar to a time series analysis (Campbell and Stanley, 1963) in that the stability and changes in behavior are studied across time or experimental sessions. When assessing steady-state behavior in a given condition the behavior is assessed relative to some comparison point. With the single-subject approach, the comparison point is the **baseline** condition. To establish a baseline, repeated observations of the natural frequency of the behavior of interest (dependent variable) are first made. In effect, you observe the frequency with which the behavior occurs before the treatment (independent variable) is introduced. This baseline serves as a sort of bench mark against which to ascertain whether the subsequent introduction of the treatment condition has an effect. The behavioral effect may be either an increase over baseline responding (**facilitation**) or a decrease under baseline responding (**suppression**).

BASELINE   comparison point established by repeated observations of the natural frequency of the behavior of interest.

FACILITATION   an increase of responding when compared to baseline.

SUPPRESSION   a decrease of responding when compared to baseline.

Since the baseline serves as a point from which the treatment effects are judged, it is important that a stable baseline be established. There is no set number of days or experimental sessions that define baseline stability. Instead, a criterion of stability is established such as "four experimental sessions in which the frequency of the target behavior does not vary by more than 5 percent." In other instances a less demanding criterion of 10 percent may be used. Some subjects may take only four days to meet the criterion, while others may take a week or more before the session-to-session variability is less than 5 or 10 percent. The choice between 5 percent or 10 percent is somewhat arbitrary but these values are often used. If baseline behavior is so variable that a 5 or 10 percent criterion of stability cannot be met, then the investigator should strive to acquire greater control over all variables related to the experimental situation. This can be a very difficult task. What is needed is a careful assessment of all aspects of the experiment for possible sources of unwanted variability. This would include the instructions, procedure, apparatus, independent variable, dependent variable, and any other possibilities. It is wiser to assume that the reason for the variability is extrinsic (environmentally induced) and then seek ways to reduce it, rather than to assume that the variability is intrinsic (inherent) and cannot be reduced. If all efforts to reduce variability fail, then the percentage criterion, e.g., 5 or 10 percent, may have to change upward. Some criterion is necessary to avoid arbitrary decision making.

14.4.2   Optimal Baseline

An **optimal baseline** requirement for any given response is that it be stable, i.e., little change in frequency from session to session under natural (baseline) conditions. In addition, if the treatment is expected to lead to increases in frequency of responding, then baseline responding should not be so high that further increases would be difficult to obtain ("ceiling effect"). On the other side of the coin, what if the treatment is expected to lead to decreases in frequency of responding? Now the opposite is true. Baseline responding should not be so low that further decreases would be difficult to achieve ("floor effects"). In some situations the experimenter may be interested in demonstrating both increases and decreases in responding but at different phases of the experiment. If this is the case, then a baseline level that permits both increases and decreases in responding would be necessary. Such a baseline level is shown in Figure 14.2.

> **OPTIMAL BASELINE**   when the baseline shows little change of frequency from session to session.

Once the treatment condition is introduced, departures from the baseline, either upward or downward, can be easily observed. If the frequency of responding neither increased nor decreased nor changed in terms of session-to-

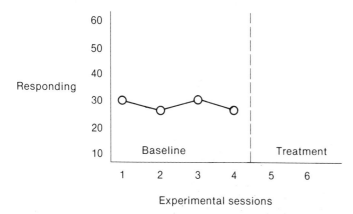

Fig. 14.2 Baseline when treatment is expected to lead to both increases and decreases in responding at different phases of the experiment

session variability, then our independent variable (treatment condition) obviously had no measurable effect.

Recall an earlier chapter in which we discussed the use of different degrees of an independent variable for purposes of identifying a function or trend. We saw that a minimum of three different points or values were needed. A similar requirement is necessary when establishing a baseline across sessions; never less than three sessions should be devoted to establishing a stable baseline since it is not possible to identify a stable pattern with less than three sessions. Reasons for this will become more apparent as we describe different possible baseline conditions.

14.4.3   Baselines to Avoid

There are several types of baselines that should be avoided simply because they evidence trends that make it difficult to interpret the effects of the treatment condition. For example, if you are evaluating the effects of praise on the amount of time spent studying, the baseline depicted in Figure 14.3 would not

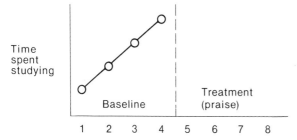

Fig. 14.3 An inappropriate baseline to use in a single subject design when evaluating a condition that is expected to lead to increases in the dependent variable

Fig. 14.4 An inappropriate baseline to use when evaluating a condition that is expected to lead to decreases in the dependent variable

be appropriate. It would be difficult to assess whether obtaining an increase in study time on the fifth session when praise was introduced was a result of the treatment (praise) or a result of continued increases in study time under the baseline condition.

Imposing a treatment on a steadily increasing baseline should be avoided where it is possible. Similarly, the effects of an independent variable may be difficult to interpret with a baseline that continues to decrease, and the effects of the treatment are also expected to lead to a decrease in performance. For example, if we were interested in assessing the effects of punishment on disruptive classroom behavior we would not want to use a baseline as shown in Figure 14.4. Further decreases at session 5 and beyond may be a result of the natural downward trend, a result of punishment, or both factors. In fact, with a baseline either increasing throughout or decreasing throughout, any change or no change in the pattern would be difficult to assess. The soundest procedure would be for the researcher to continue baseline measurement until it leveled off and reached a rigorous criterion of stability. If the measure fails to reach the stability criterion, then we should attempt to achieve greater control over the conditions or find a different measure. Additional options are available to experienced researchers (Sidman, 1960).

Finally, if marked variability in responding occurs from one experimental session to the next, it is difficult to interpret any effect that the treatment might have. Figure 14.5 depicts such a pattern. In basic laboratory research, a baseline pattern of this type is of little use. The investigator should make an effort to reduce the variability by eliminating sources of extrinsic (environmental) variability. If unsuccessful in doing so, a different response measure should be considered. At times, simply extending the period across more sessions results in a more stable baseline. However, most investigators would suggest that a careful, systematic assessment of the experimental situation be undertaken to identify sources of variability and then remove or alter them. Again, this means assessing the procedure, apparatus, task, instructions, experimenter, etc.

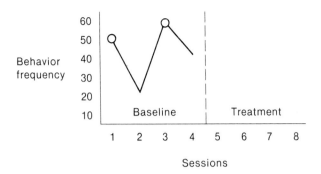

Fig. 14.5 An inappropriate baseline to use when evaluating conditions that are expected to lead to either increases or decreases in the dependent variable

In applied areas, such as evaluation of therapeutic techniques, efforts to obtain a stable baseline may be less successful and the investigator, after an exhaustive search for solutions, may have to impose a treatment condition over an unstable baseline. If the effects of the treatment are strong, then they may be seen in terms of both greater stability and a higher (or lower) frequency of responding.

We have not exhausted the different kinds of difficult baselines that are encountered when doing research but we have described the more bothersome ones. The issue of what constitutes an acceptable baseline is a complex one that we have tried to simplify. We will now discuss the treatment phase of research.

14.4.4   Analysis of Treatment Effects

The analysis of treatment effects will be more understandable to you if we give an overview of the design strategy. It is customary to refer to the baseline phase of an experiment as the "A" condition and the treatment phase as the "B" condition. If there are different kinds of treatment conditions, then the others are referred to as "C," "D," etc.

The most powerful design strategy (best method for assessing treatment effects) that we will discuss is the ABAB design. Later we will describe why this design strategy is more effective than the AB or the ABA designs. The ABAB design is a shorthand way for stating that we first determine a baseline (A), then we introduce the treatment for the first time (B). After the criterion of stability is achieved we then withdraw the treatment and reintroduce the baseline condition (A). Finally, after baseline stability is reestablished, we present the treatment condition (B) for the second time. This ABAB design, when used, is a very powerful design that allows the researcher to make strong conclusions concerning the treatment effects. With this design the researcher demonstrates the degree of control over behavior in two ways—first by *introducing* the treatment condition, then by *removing* it. Again, we will repeat the procedure. After the baseline is established (A), the treatment condition (B) is *introduced* and the extent to which the treatment influences behavior (the extent to which behavior departs from baseline) is assessed. Then, following stable performance, the treatment condition is removed (baseline condition (A) again presented). Performance should then return to the original baseline. The final phase requires that we again present the treatment condition (B) and end the experiment with it. We will now give an example of an ABAB design strategy.

Researchers are interested in whether subjects prefer predictable over unpredictable painful events. Experiments dealing with this question have been published. (See Badia, Harsh, and Abbott, 1979 for a review). Many used the single-subject method with an *N* of 3 or 4 subjects. It is interesting to note that the studies used very similar procedures even though different species were involved, e.g., fish, birds, rats, humans. The initial studies in this area used rats as subjects, electric shock as the painful stimulus, and a tone to signal if shock was to occur. Researchers first exposed the animals to predictable shock (a five-second tone signaled when shock occurred) and to unpredictable shock (unsignaled shock) to acquaint them with the conditions and to make sure that they had equal experience with both. (The number of predictable and unpredictable shocks was the same.)

During this initial exposure to the two conditions, subjects could not alter (change) the condition from one to the other. However, their responses on a response lever were recorded, even though responses on this lever had no effect at all. This period served as a baseline period (A) to measure how frequently they pressed the lever when there were no consequences. Responses on the lever occurred but were low in frequency during the baseline phase. After four days of being exposed to both signaled and unsignaled shock and with baseline responding stable, animals were given a choice between the signaled and unsignaled conditions. During this choice phase (treatment phase), the response lever was functional and responses now changed the conditions from one to the other. Animals at this time were placed in the unsignaled condition but if the lever was pressed the condition changed. A response on the lever changed the condition to the signaled one for a period of one minute. At the end of this one-minute period, the condition automatically changed back to the unsignaled condition and remained there unless another lever response was made. If the predictable (signaled) condition was reinforcing (preferred), response rate should increase over baseline; if it was punishing (not preferred), response rate should decrease. After choice behavior stabilized and preference was determined, the baseline condition was reinstated. This was followed by another treatment condition (preference testing). The results of the experiment were similar to those shown in Figure 14.6.

During the baseline conditions (A) subjects lever-pressed at a rate sufficient to remain in the predictable shock schedule (had the levers been effective) only about 20 percent of the time. When the treatment condition (B) was intro-

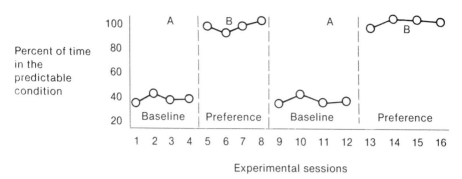

Fig. 14.6 Single subject ABAB design in which the subject could choose between predictable (signaled) or unpredictable (unsignaled) shock. The results would be similar whether percent of time or number of lever presses were used as the dependent variable.

duced, subjects changed from the unpredictable schedule at a rate sufficient to spend 90 percent of the time in the predictable condition. When the treatment condition was withdrawn and the baseline condition reinstated (session 9), responding again returned to a low level. This showed that withdrawing the treatment *reversed* performance from high to low responding. Finally, when the treatment condition was introduced for the second time (session 13), responding on the levers increased to a high level. Data such as this demonstrate convincingly, without the need for a statistical analysis, that the treatment condition is systematically controlling behavior.

14.4.5   Intra-Subject Replication

The preceding study exposed each subject twice to the baseline and treatment condition. When the conditions are repeated with the *same* subject, we are using **intra-subject replication.** This is an important part of the single subject method. As we have noted, the primary interest among psychologists is focused on the behavior of individual organisms. Intra-subject replication focuses on the individual subject and identifies the factors affecting the subject. By introducing and withdrawing the treatment condition, systematic behavioral changes can be observed in individual subjects. Intra-subject replication, then, demonstrates that our method is reliable, that the treatment effect is real, and that we have control over behavior.

INTRA-SUBJECT REPLICATION   replication within the same subject.

The decision on the number of intra-subject replications that are necessary is sometimes difficult and may vary from experiment to experiment. Often a single replication is enough, i.e., ABAB. The number of intra-subject replications decided upon may vary according to the size of the treatment effects, the stability of the behavior, whether inter-subject replication is obtained, whether inter-species replications exist, whether similar related findings exist, and how well the present findings fit in with established findings.

A word should be said about the size of the effect. Small but consistent treatment effects combined with stable individual baselines can be important. Such effects, even though small, indicate experimental control over behavior. Perhaps with more effort and exploration, the conditions leading to a larger effect will be discovered.

14.4.6   Inter-Subject Replication

We have seen that it is possible to demonstrate repeatedly consistent behavioral changes as a function of the treatment in an individual subject. It is also possible to demonstrate the same effect consistently in other subjects. This **inter-subject replication** establishes the generality of the findings. There are no hard and fast rules on the number of subjects for which inter-subject replication must be shown. Much of the published research involves three to five subjects per experiment. However, it is not unusual to find either fewer or more subjects in different experiments. In addition to demonstrating that your findings can be generalized to other subjects, inter-subject replication also demonstrates that the researcher has identified the controlling factors sufficiently to permit replication to other subjects. On occasion, however, inter-subject replication is unsuccessful. When this occurs, additional detective work is usually necessary. It may be that greater control over the experimental situation is necessary. It is also possible that, because of individual differences, some subjects react less to a given treatment. If the treatment were increased slightly (intensity, duration, frequency, etc.), inter-subject replication might be successful. This ability to treat individual subjects in a flexible manner is one of the great strengths of the single subject approach.

INTER-SUBJECT REPLICATION   replication with a different subject or subjects.

14.4.7   Reversible and Irreversible Behavior

When intra-subject replication is achieved, we have demonstrated that baseline responding under the nontreatment condition can be recovered again once the treatment condition is withdrawn. We refer to the *behavior* as being **reversible behavior.** Without this feature, intra-subject replication is not possible. In contrast, **irreversible behavior** refers to those occasions when the original baseline cannot be recovered after the treatment has been withdrawn. The baseline level of responding remains at the same level as it was under the treatment condition. Many critics of the single-subject approach argue that this is one of its weaknesses and that the method cannot be used when baseline responding is not recoverable. However, supporters argue that irreversible behavior may not be due to uncontrollable intrinsic factors (factors within the subject) but, instead, may be due to extrinsic controlling factors (experimental-environmental factors). They argue that a careful assessment of the situation and thoughtful changes based upon this assessment, more often than not, will produce reversible behavior. Often it is achieved only after a number of attempts. However, they do not argue that all behavior is reversible. For a fuller discussion, see Sidman (1960).

REVERSIBLE BEHAVIOR   when behavior returns to baseline after treatment is withdrawn.

IRREVERSIBLE BEHAVIOR   when behavior does not return to baseline after treatment is withdrawn.

There may be situations in which the behavior is not reversible. For example, drug research may encounter carry-over effects in which the effects of the drug last longer than anticipated and continue to affect behavior after the treatment (drug) is thought to be removed. The solution to this problem is to allow enough time for the drug to dissipate. A more difficult problem may arise when a single-subject design involves experimentally-induced brain lesions. If the tissue damage is permanent, the treatment cannot be withdrawn, thus precluding the ABAB design. To overcome this difficulty, researchers have used pharmacological agents that only temporarily affect brain functions instead of producing permanent impairment. There are yet other instances where behavior appears irreversible because of learning factors. For example, if a number of problems have the same solution and the solution is learned through a reinforcement procedure, you can withdraw the reinforcement but the solution to the problem will remain. Conceivably, then, researchers on occasion will encounter behavior that does not reverse (return to baseline levels) when the treatment condition is withdrawn. Given this state, the powerful ABAB design strategy cannot be used. For this reason, and others, there is an alternative procedure, referred to as the multiple baseline procedure. The latter procedure is also useful in therapeutic situations where withdrawing a therapeutic treatment for purposes of identifying the controlling factor may be undesirable or unethical.

14.4.8   Multiple Baseline Procedure

As we noted, the ABAB design is not appropriate when we are unable to recover our baseline level of performance or when the withdrawal of treatment poses an ethical dilemma. Under these circumstances, a different design strategy such as the **multiple baseline procedure** is necessary. Other techniques are also available (see Hersen and Barlow, 1976). In effect, the multiple base-line procedure allows the researcher to perform intra-subject replication with *different responses* rather than the same response.

> **MULTIPLE BASELINE PROCEDURE** intra-subject replication with different and independent (uncorrelated) responses.

The multiple baseline procedure *requires* that baselines be provided for several different responses and that these *responses be independent* of each

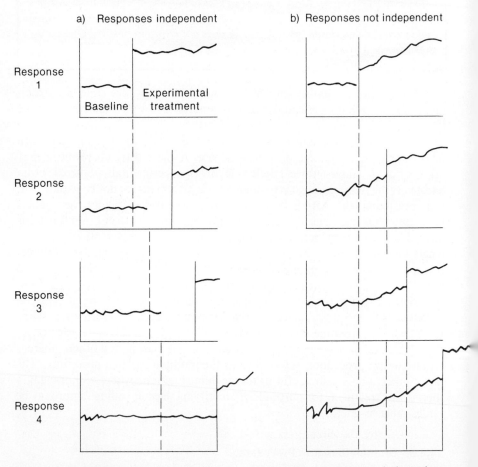

Fig. 14.7 Illustration of multiple baseline procedures when responses are independent (a) and not independent (b). Note that when experimental treatments are introduced in (a), the baselines of the remaining responses are unaffected. In (b), the introduction of each treatment produces a change in the baseline levels of the remaining responses (hypothetical data).

other. To say that the responses are independent means that increases or decreases in frequency of one response do not affect (lead to increases or decreases) in the frequency of other responses. (See Figure 14.7.) Usually, baselines for three or more different responses are needed when the multiple baseline procedure is used. Baseline responding is established in the same manner as described previously except that baselines for several responses are plotted at the same time. Then the different responses are treated one at a time.

To illustrate, after stable baseline levels are established, the treatment condition is applied to only one of the responses (target response). The other responses are not treated and remain under the baseline condition. Changes in the target response are recorded to assess the treatment effects but the other responses, those not receiving any treatment, continue to be monitored in the baseline condition. After the target response stabilizes to the treatment condition, the experimenter then applies the treatment to the second response until it stabilizes, then the third response is treated. Since a withdrawal phase is not used with this procedure, the treatment of each response following the establishment of the baseline is essentially an AB design. As with any of the single-subject designs, the effectiveness of the treatment condition is assessed by a change in behavior relative to the baseline level. In the case of the multiple baseline procedure, the treatment effects are assessed by comparing the response receiving the treatment with its no-treatment baseline and also with the baseline of the untreated responses. The latter would be meaningless if the responses were not independent. Although the multiple baseline procedure is not as effective as ABA or the ABAB design, it does demonstrate replication of the treatment condition *across responses.*

Examples of multiple baseline procedure   An example of a study using the multiple baseline procedure is cited by Leitenberg (1973). Two investigators used punishment to deal with a case of transvestism. A male patient reported becoming sexually excited by dressing as a woman and was apparently unhappy about his feelings. Although, at the age of twenty-one, the patient had never had girlfriends, he wanted to have a normal heterosexual relationship. Aversion therapy was used twice daily. It consisted of shocks to his arm or leg while he was either dressing as a woman (cross-dressing) or while thinking (fantasizing) about dressing as one. In the latter instance, the subject signaled the investigator when fantasies occurred. Shocks were withheld if the subject discarded the female garments. One response measure was sexual arousal, as determined by the circumference of the penis, to female pajamas, panties, slips, skirts, or a slide of a nude woman. Latency of the response was also recorded. After baseline responses to these garments were determined, the treatment of shock was introduced. The investigators found that, after the response of putting on panties was shocked a number of times, penile erection to this stimulus was suppressed. However, erections to the other garments continued to occur. Then responses of dressing up in the other garments were shocked until erections ceased to each. It was shown by the investigators that while erection no longer occurred to the female clothing, it continued to occur to the nude slide.

The multiple baseline procedure is also illustrated in an interesting study by Barton, Guess, Garcia, and Baer (1970). These investigators used punishment to successfully modify undesirable mealtime behavior among sixteen severely retarded males. The undesirable behavior included *stealing* food from others, *eating with fingers* rather than utensils, *pigging* (eating spilled food

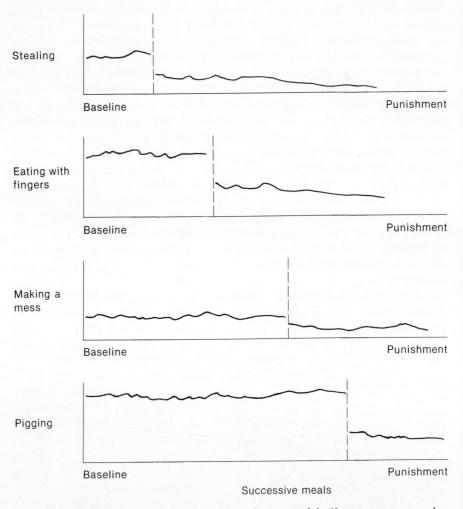

Fig. 14.8 An idealized graphic representation of a successful effort to suppress undesired behavior by the use of punishment using the multiple baseline procedure. Note that the treatment effects appear to be relatively independent and that all four undesirable responses were successfully suppressed.

from the floor or lapping food directly from the tray), and *making a mess,* such as spilling or dropping food. The study ran nearly four months. Punishment consisted of removal (time-out) from the dining area whenever the undesired behavior occurred. In some instances, removal was for the entire meal; in other instances, for a shorter period. The investigators started by recording baseline frequencies for each behavior (stealing, pigging, etc.). The first response had only a six-day baseline before the punishment (treatment time-out) was introduced, e.g., stealing. While punishment was being given for stealing behavior, baseline recording continued for the other responses. When stealing stabilized, then punishment was introduced for the second response while baseline recording continued for the remaining two responses. This procedure continued until all responses were under the punishment procedure. For the most part, but not entirely, independence among the responses was observed, i.e., punishing one response affected primarily only that response and not the others. The efforts of the researchers were successful: The undesirable mealtime behavior greatly improved as did the morale of the workers. An idealized depiction of the study appears in Fig. 14.8. The figure also clearly outlines the procedure.

We want to repeat, before leaving this topic, that the multiple baseline procedure is used either because the baseline level of responding cannot be recovered when the treatment condition is withdrawn, or withdrawal of the treatment may have an adverse effect on the participant, especially in a therapeutic setting. The multiple baseline procedure is not as powerful as the ABAB design where both intra- and inter-subject replication can be shown by both the introduction and withdrawal of the treatment. However, as we have shown, replication across responses within the same subject can be shown with this procedure.

14.4.9   AB, ABA, and ABAB Designs

So far, we have discussed only the ABAB design. However, there are two others that warrant attention. These are the AB and ABA designs. As noted, when discussing single-subject designs, the "A" condition refers to the baseline phase and the "B" condition to the treatment phase. In this section, we shall describe how the ABAB design is superior to both the AB and the ABA designs.

The weakest design in terms of drawing conclusions and ruling out alternative interpretations is the AB design. This design does not permit the systematic assessment of the treatment condition. There are problems with a single presentation of the baseline and treatment condition (i.e., AB). For example, what would be the natural course of the behavior across the same time period if the treatment had not been presented? It is similar to conducting an experiment without using a nontreatment control group. Without a control group, we cannot be sure that the behavior was altered by the treatment condition, rather than by some extraneous condition. The same is true of the AB design. It is possible that changes in behavior during the treatment phase result from some unknown environmental event not related to the treatment. The AB design does not permit ruling out this alternative hypothesis. It is sometimes tempting to accept the results of an AB design and conclude that the treatment had an effect when low levels of baseline behavior (A) are followed by sudden dramatic increases with the introduction of the treatment (B). But to do so would be inappropriate, since proper control procedures were not present. Nevertheless, results of this kind would certainly be very encouraging and should be pursued further, but with a more powerful design. One such design is the ABA procedure. The AB design should be used only under circumstances that do not permit a more adequate method. These instances are more common in applied settings. For a more comprehensive discussion of the AB design in an applied setting, see Hersen and Barlow (1976).

The ABA design is a far more powerful design than the AB design simply because the treatment condition is *introduced* for a period of time and then *withdrawn*. There are two opportunities to assess whether the treatment condition is effective—introducing it and withdrawing it. If behavior shows a systematic change, then your confidence is increased that the treatment, rather than some unknown environmental event, is the reason for the behavioral change. It is quite unlikely that natural conditions would increase and then decrease behavior as it did when the treatment was presented and then withdrawn. Showing the same or similar relationships in other subjects (inter-subject replication) would further strengthen your confidence that the treatment was responsible. As we indicated earlier, inter-subject replication reveals that your findings with the original subject are not unusual and that you have sufficient control to replicate your findings with other subjects.

The ABA design is generally criticized on two counts. One is that intra-subject replication is not shown. The importance of this type of replication was described earlier. The second problem relates to the applied setting where behavior modification is considered desirable. If the treatment (e.g., therapy) is effective in modifying behavior, then it is desirable to end the investigation on a treatment phase rather than a baseline phase.

14.5 LIMITATIONS AND PROBLEMS OF THE SINGLE-SUBJECT APPROACH

One obvious limitation of the single-subject approach is that the method is unsuitable for answering actuarial types of questions. Questions such as , "How many of the one-hundred people exposed to a particular treatment will respond favorably and how many will respond unfavorably?" A similar question relates to studies comparing two or more different treatments on the same behavioral measure. For example, which of the various treatments is the most effective? Ineffective? Debilitating? The method cannot be used if you are interested in treating an entire group of subjects, such as a classroom, in an identical way on a daily basis, i.e., when changes in procedures are made, they are made for everyone in the group at the same time and for the same period. A different method is also required if "after the fact" studies (ex post facto, correlational, passive observational) are of interest. Moreover, the single-subject approach makes heavy time demands. It may, on occasion, take several months to completely "run" a single subject. Often researchers are unwilling or unable to devote the required time. In addition to these limitations, there are also some recurring problems. Establishing a criterion and acquiring stable baselines for the response of interest are sometimes very difficult. Further, determining whether variability in behavior is intrinsic or extrinsic can be troublesome. Nonreversible (irreversible) behavior poses its own set of problems and it precludes the use of an ABAB design. Failure to obtain intra- and inter-subject replication for whatever reason creates problems for the single-subject approach. Sometimes decisions regarding the necessary number of both intra- and inter-subject replications are largely subjective. Nevertheless, in spite of the limitations and problems described here, the single-subject method does provide researchers with another powerful way to assess behavior.

CHAPTER FIFTEEN

PROGRAM EVALUATION

15.1 PURPOSES OF PROGRAM EVALUATION

In recent years, the word *accountability* has come into common use. Politicians are held accountable for their voting records and their appropriations of taxpayers' money; teachers are held accountable for their classroom effectiveness; industry is held accountable for reducing air and water pollution; workers are held accountable for their productivity levels and the quality of their workmanship. The same is true of research. The demand for evaluation research is increasing. Indeed, many programs funded by state and federal governments require a plan to evaluate the success or failure of the program before the research itself can be undertaken.

Program evaluation can be important and few would object to it in principle. Does the program work or doesn't it? Is it effective? Are changes in the program necessary? It is when the specifics of evaluation must be decided that disagreements often occur. Some evaluation plans are extremely elaborate —detailing the measures that will be taken, when, by whom, what the changes mean, etc. On the other hand, some evaluation plans amount to little more than testimonials solicited from participants in the program regarding their reactions. Programs obviously vary in their complexity and scope, with the degree of control exerted over the program by the investigator, with the availability of behavioral measures to assess change, with the reliability and validity of these measures, and with the duration of the program. All of these factors, plus others, affect the way in which a program is evaluated.

To an extent, what we include in this chapter is arbitrary. Clearly, all the factors previously discussed are relevant but other factors are also important. We shall discuss additional concepts, techniques, and concerns related to research and evaluation.

Program evaluation means different things to different people. Keep in mind that a program (broadly defined) is designed for a target population based on the needs of that population. Program goals compatible with the needs are specified and a method and procedure designed to achieve them are developed. At different points, evaluation is undertaken to assess whether the program is operating efficiently and whether the goals of the program and needs of the population are being achieved. Programs can be specific and narrow, such as a tutoring program for students doing poorly in a specific class, or initiating behavioral therapy for phobic individuals. It can also be as broad as Head Start or alcohol and drug rehabilitation. Other examples include political and advertisement campaigns, stop-smoking efforts, weight-reducing diets, senior citizen concerns, energy conservation programs, school busing, etc.

Evaluation concerns itself primarily with the extent to which a program achieves its goals. It may also determine whether negative consequences occur as a result of the program. Often, the behavioral measures (dependent variables) used to assess the success or failure of a program are obvious. They are frequently dictated by the nature of the problem addressed and the needs of the target population. Smoking clinics can be evaluated in terms of the percentages of people who stop or reduce smoking. The success or failure of a reading clinic can be evaluated in terms of changes in comprehension and speed of reading. For drug rehabilitation, we can assess the number of participants who "kick" the habit and for how long. Questionnaires, surveys, and attitude scales can be used to answer many questions. They may be administered on the basis of cross-sectional or longitudinal sampling procedures, or both.

However, complications sometimes arise. Standard measures are often unavailable for evaluating programs; the researcher may feel the need for other measures, or the program directors may not be sufficiently clear about the goals they are trying to achieve. Whatever the case, evaluating the successes and failures of a program often requires innovative and imaginative dependent behavioral measures, either direct or indirect. A number of indirect and inventive measures can be found in the book by Webb, Campbell, Schwartz, Sechrest, and Grove (1981) entitled *Nonreactive Measures in the Social Sciences.* Emphasis is placed on nonstandard measures. A valuable source for selecting a measuring instrument related to aptitude, creativity, attitudes, and abilities is the *Mental Measurement Yearbooks,* edited by Buros. These yearbooks list measuring instruments by category and provide reviews and references for potential users.

In brief review, evaluation includes the following:

1. Identification of the needs of the target population

2. Specification of the program, its goals, and a statement of how the needs, in whole or in part, of the target population expect to be met

3. Description of the evaluation plan, procedure, and the important behavioral measures to be recorded

4. Establishing a time frame for evaluation

5. Specifying what constitutes positive effects, negative effects, success, or failure.

We do not want to give the impression that evaluation is a simple process—it is not. It is extremely difficult to do well. Because of this, it is frequently not done at all. Consequently, some programs have become institutionalized without ever once being evaluated. This is unfortunate. There are questions with no simple answers or with answers that require value judgments that are beyond the pale of science. Indeed, decisions are seldom made on the basis of scientific considerations alone; more often political, economic, and philosophical considerations exert great influence. Moreover, with increased emphasis on accountability, issues dealing with a cost-benefit analysis are often raised. These are difficult to resolve and involve more than strictly scientific considerations.

15.2 STAGES OF PROGRAM EVALUATION

15.2.1 Formative Evaluation

The dictionary definition of *formative* is "giving form, helping to shape, or mold." This definition suggests the meaning of **formative evaluation.** It involves the continuing development, modification, and evaluation of a project or program while it's in progress in order to increase its chances of achieving the stated goals. Different procedures are examined and evaluated to ascertain if they are effective. Is the training period long enough? Should meetings be held more or less often? What is the optimal duration of a session? Are the instructions unambiguous? What size groups are best? Formative evaluation is *not* concerned with assessing the overall outcome of the program, it is concerned with getting there. As such, it focuses on the components and processes within the program in hopes of improving their effectiveness. In short, it is an evaluation that helps form, shape, and mold the components and processes of the program. It may include pilot research, feedback from participants, observations, etc.

FORMATIVE EVALUATION   continuing development, modification, and evaluation of research while it is in progress.

15.2.2 Summative Evaluation

When the program has run its course and the data are analyzed, we can begin asking questions. Did the program work? Was it successful? Were the goals achieved? To what extent? Were there any negative consequences? **Summative evaluation** attempts to provide the answers to these and many other questions. Many of the techniques used to evaluate the program were decided prior to initiating the program. Some additional measures may be suggested by the data obtained and by the process of evaluation. Now it is time to sum it up. If the program or study was done properly, then the summative evaluation should be straightforward. As previously noted, there will be political, philosophical, and economic considerations in addition to those that are purely scientific. Thus, we may be expected to answer such questions as: If the program achieved its goals, is it worthwhile implementing the program on a larger scale? What benefits will accrue to society? How costly will it be? How does it compare in cost effectiveness to alternative programs? These are often difficult questions to answer.

SUMMATIVE EVALUATION   evaluation of a research program after it has been completed.

15.3 DIFFICULTIES IN PROGRAM EVALUATION

The difficulty may be increased by the fact that the investigators (evaluators) may have little control over the program. Programs are usually introduced to deal with a problem. The goals of the program are to identify the magnitude of the problem and then reduce it. Reducing the extent of the problem usually has priority over evaluating the specifics of the program. Therefore, periodic assessment of how things are going (formative evaluation) may reveal that a substantial change should be made in the program if it is to be effective. This type of evaluation is important but the changes in the program that are suggested by it make other forms of evaluation more difficult. It is very difficult to evaluate the key components of a program that led to a final outcome (summative evaluation) when many things have changed during the course of the program. Isolating the important factors (independent variables) when a program is constantly changing is virtually impossible. Under these circumstances, formative evaluation, accompanied by some general statements dealing with the current state of affairs, may be all that can be done.

Program evaluation may be further complicated by the fact that those responsible for the program may have a vested interest in its success. They are committed to its effectiveness and may not be cooperative about an objective evaluation. They would be pleased, perhaps overjoyed, to receive confirmation of the program's success, but be unwilling to even consider the possibility of less. Obviously their personal involvement in the success of the program can create many problems.

Program evaluation is also difficult when the program spans a considerable time period. Turnover in personnel can be high with a resulting loss in information and in inefficient performance. Under these circumstances, evaluators or personnel new to the program must continue to "reinvent the wheel." For this and other reasons, good record-keeping is every bit as essential as with laboratory research. Full notes and full descriptions of events, conditions, incidents, etc., along with limited use of abbreviations and idiosyncratic acronyms are helpful in record-keeping. It is extremely difficult to retrieve the meaning of an abbreviation or the specifics of an incident, etc, after a period of time elapses. Similarly, full documentation regarding dates, places, and names, is essential.

Often compromises are made in evaluation research that would not be tolerated in laboratory research. It is not always possible to use random assignment to conditions or groups; for that matter, it is often not possible to use control groups at all. For example, when facing important social problems, it is difficult to maintain a control condition that requires the withholding of a potentially valuable treatment. Indeed, there may be times when proper evaluation of a program may not be possible. The program may be too broad-based or too vague; measures of change may be unavailable or of uncertain reliability; the experimental treatment may be too capricious, or poorly specified. Think for a moment of the difference involved in evaluating the effectiveness of the Peace Corp Program as contrasted with a "new math" program.

15.4 INFLUENCE OF NONEXPERIMENTAL FACTORS

Evaluative studies are commonly directed toward ascertaining differences in performance, attitudes, values, or beliefs of different populations. Frequently the populations of interest are different age groupings. The investigator may be interested in how behavior, attitudes, etc., change as a function of age. The questions may be disarmingly simple, but the answers are correspondingly difficult. Whenever age differences or age changes are involved, several different strategies vie for consideration. It is not sufficient to consider only *maturational age* (growing older). Individuals are members of *different generations* with whom they share some characteristics in common (**generational or cohort group**). Thus, if we study two different age groups, eighteen-year-olds and forty-year-olds, we may find that the older group generally expresses more patriotic attitudes than the younger group. Can we conclude that patriotic attitudes increase with maturation, or is it possible that generational differences (different life experiences with war, depression, prosperity, etc.) promoted differential patriotic feelings? Finally, we must consider historical and environmental factors operating at the *time of measurement*. Had patriotic attitudes been measured during the Afghanistan and Iranian hostage crises, the result might well have been different from surveys taken at other times.

COHORT OR GENERATIONAL GROUP   individuals in the same generational or age group.

Maturational age, cohort groups, and time of measurements relate to **cross-sectional, longitudinal, and time-lag research designs.** We will define each shortly. Before doing so, we want to emphasize, as we have previously, that the type of research design used may lead to fundamentally different conclusions.

CROSS-SECTIONAL DESIGN   individuals in different cohort groups are tested at the same point in time.

LONGITUDINAL DESIGN   the same individuals are tested at different points in time.

TIME-LAG DESIGN   the comparison of independent same-aged groups at different time periods.

Let's look at a recent example. The question of interest concerns changes in intelligence as a function of age. Does intelligence decline progressively with the advent of middle age and beyond? Surprisingly, the answer depends upon whether longitudinal or cross-sectional designs are used. For example, studies testing different individuals at the same time (cross-sectional designs) typically show a decline in measures of intelligence at about thirty years of age. The decline becomes progressively greater as the individuals pass through their forties, fifties, etc. These data suggest, as far as intellectual performance is concerned, that people reach their peak at thirty and it is all downhill from there on. In marked contrast, data from longitudinal studies (the same individuals tested at different times) reveal a different outcome. These data show little if any decline in performance on tests of intelligence as people pass thirty and into their forties, fifties, and sixties, except on some tests involving a speed requirement. Actual increases have been reported by some.

As we shall see, different factors are present for the cross-sectional and longitudinal designs. Cross-sectional data are most likely strongly affected by cohort factors (generational factors) while these factors play a small role in the longitudinal data. Before describing these designs further, let's take a closer look at the three classes of events that affect them: maturational age differences, cohort or generational differences, and time of measurement differences.

15.4.1 Maturational Age

This term refers to changes in performance as a function of the changes that take place in the aging individual from birth to death. These performance differences are presumably due to changes in the physiology of the individual as he or she matures. They are not due to environmental factors. This factor plays a role in both cross-sectional and longitudinal studies.

15.4.2 Generational or Cohort Groups

Differences in this factor impact on cross-sectional designs and the time-lag design. These differences refer to the unique environments that each generation develops or grows up in. Sixty-year-olds experienced a different environment from the environment experienced by today's ten-year-olds—some of these are: the quantity and quality of education; health care systems (diagnosis, treatment, prevention); religious beliefs; life-style; values and attitudes; economic conditions; world affairs; women's roles; technology (Xerox, computers, television, telecommunication), etc. These changes have had different impacts on different generations, resulting in many marked differences between older and younger people.

15.4.3 Time-of-Measurement

The time-of-measurement factor refers to cultural, experiential, and environmental changes that take place during the lifetime of the study, i.e., *changes that take place after the study was begun*. This class of events includes changes in the physical health of the participants, alterations in their education, the impact of world and domestic affairs (international crises, inflation, recession), experimenter effects, subject effects, etc. To illustrate, a subject effect could be a problem if tests are repeated two or more times on the same subject (longitudinal design). The subject is different the second time he or she is tested compared to the first testing. Experience with the task or test (practice) is greater and knowledge of what to expect is present. Changes unrelated to the study may also have occurred. For example, the marital status of some subjects may have changed, their employment may be different, their education may have advanced, etc.

15.5   DIFFERENT DESIGNS FOR PROGRAM EVALUATION

Imagine that, back in 1950, you were a member of a research team responsible for evaluating both the benefits and the possible hazards of a psychoactive drug. Figure 15.1 illustrates three possible evaluation strategies that were available to you. You could have administered the drug in equal-sized samples at six different age levels during the first year of the study. In the figure, this design is represented by the column at the year 1950. Since these results would provide data on a cross-section of various age groups, it is referred to as a cross-sectional design. Alternatively, you might have wanted to monitor the

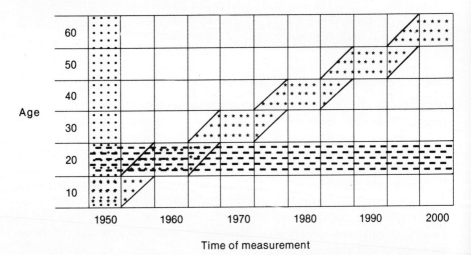

Fig. 15.1 Three possible research strategies for studying changes in the dependent variable as a function of age, cohort, or time of measurement. The vertical line at 1950 involves comparison among six different age groups at a single point in time (cross-sectional design); the diagonal line involves repeated measures of the same individuals at different points in time (longitudinal design); and the horizontal line involves the comparison of six independent same-aged groups at different time periods (time-lag design).

same individuals over a period of time. Since the study would be extended over time, it is referred to as a longitudinal design. It is shown in Figure 15.1 as a diagonal stretching from the lower left-hand corner to the upper right-hand corner. Finally, you might have wanted to study the effects of a drug on a single age group, but extended over time. This is shown as a time-lag design. The horizontal bar at age 20 would represent a time-lag design for this particular age group, i.e., twenty-year-olds at different time periods.

15.5.1   Cross-Sectional Design

This design is shown in Figure 15.2 and indicates that different individuals at different age levels are assessed at the same period of time. The intention is to assess maturational age on some behavioral measure such as sexual attitudes, political attitudes, performance on tests of all kinds, etc. With this design, all data are gathered in the same time period. When comparing individuals of different ages, inevitably we are also looking at generational (cohort) differences. Older individuals have grown up in a very different environment from younger individuals. The greater the differences in age, the greater will be the generational differences. Therefore, while the design focuses on maturational age, cohort differences also occur. This is the major problem with the cross-sectional design—it confounds maturational age with generational factors. Differences in results may be due to either or both factors. In some instances, sound judgment may allow you to argue in favor of one factor or the other, but a definitive statement of cause is not possible. Clear, meaningful descriptions of the data can be made, but unambiguous, causal statements cannot.

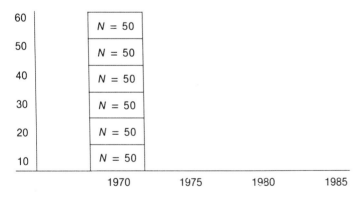

Fig. 15.2 Illustration of cross-sectional design. Six different age groups are tested at the same time. This design confounds maturational age with generational (cohort) differences.

There are several advantages to a cross-sectional design relative to either a longitudinal or a time-lag design. All the data are gathered at one time, thus providing useful information quickly. In addition, the researcher can randomly select subjects representative of each age level. Further, since the experiment is conducted over a short period of time, a general or differential loss of subjects (attrition) is not a problem.

15.5.2 Longitudinal Design

This design is shown in Figure 15.3. Performance of the same individuals (representing a single generation) is assessed across a span of time. That is, the same individuals at different ages are retested or reevaluated. Longitudinal designs focus on changes, differences, or stability within an individual as a function of changing age level. This design permits the intensive study of the same individuals across time. While identifying any changes that may occur across time is not difficult, ascertaining the cause of the changes poses a problem. This is due to the fact that longitudinal design confounds maturational age changes with time of measurement changes. As we already noted, the various conditions accompanying one measurement period can be very different from the conditions at another period. The subject may be "test wise" during later evaluations, more knowledgeable and better prepared; the experimenter is older, more experienced; technological changes may have occurred, and the "cultural environment" may be quite different. Consequently, a longitudinal design does not permit a definitive conclusion that observed changes are due to maturational factors. However, in spite of this limitation, there are

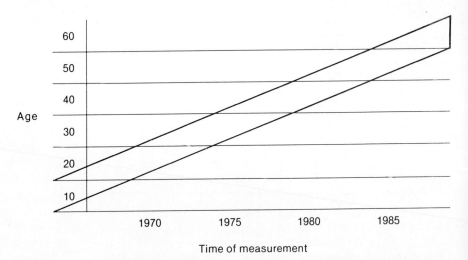

Fig. 15.3 Longitudinal design. The same individuals are studied over a period of time. This design confounds maturational age with time of measurement.

times when the investigator can reasonably rule out time of measurement factors. For example, if the study involves changes in the acuity of one of the senses as a function of age, and if the conditions of testing are comparable at different time periods, it would seem reasonable to ascribe changes in acuity to maturational factors.

There are some other problems associated with longitudinal designs. Since the subjects who are repeatedly retested are drawn from the same age group, there is also confounding of maturational factors with both cohort and time of measurement (Botwinick, 1978). Moreover, it is by far the most costly in terms of money, time, and record-keeping. There is also a problem with the loss of subjects, which may come at different points during the experiment. A random representative sample may be very unrepresentative at the end of the study. Other subjects may become ill, debilitated, or die. Still others will move and not be found later. Sometimes the loss of subjects affects all conditions equally (general **attrition**). If this occurs and the total loss of subjects is not too great, then no major problems should be presented. On the other hand, there are times when a greater number of subjects are lost from one condition. This systematic attrition can have a serious biasing effect. For example, if two forms of therapy are being evaluated on chronic juvenile offenders and the program is to run over a five-year period, systematically losing more subjects from one treatment condition poses a serious problem. Are they being lost because the therapy was successful or unsuccessful? Also, what may have started out as comparable groups as a result of random assignment, may no longer be equal because of attrition. Any differences emerging from the research could be due to some other factor present in those who remain. (See third variable problem in Chapter 4.)

ATTRITION loss of subjects.

15.5.3 Time-Lag Design

This design is shown in Figure 15.4. With this design, measurements are taken at different time periods. In this sense, it is similar to a longitudinal design. However, with the time-lag design, the same age level across each time period is assessed. In this regard, it is similar to the cross-sectional design in that different generations are involved, i.e., they may all be forty years old but some are forty in 1960 and some are forty in 1980. The intent of this design is to assess generational effects on behavior by separating cohort effects from age effects. Since age is held constant, differences found should be due to generational factors. However, a source of confounding is also present with the time-lag design. The major source of confounding is between cohort and time of measurement factors.

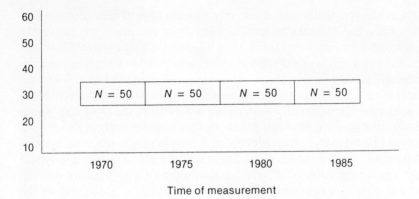

Fig. 15.4 Time-lag design. Same-aged individuals are studied over different time periods. This design confounds generational differences with the time of measurement factor.

BOX 15.1   SOME POSSIBLE REASONS FOR DECLINING SAT SCORES

1. Schools may be demanding less of their students. Teachers may be less well prepared and the level of instruction is lower. Teachers may be less involved.

2. Students may be less motivated to learn; they may also be less competitive. These changes may reflect cultural changes affecting more than the behavior of students. The "work ethic" may no longer be as respected in society in general.

3. Students read less today. The major "villain" could be television.

4. Lower test scores could be due to family size and the spacing of children. The larger the family and the closer the children, the poorer the performance on some standardized tests. If so, then the changing pattern in family size and spacing should result in an increase in SAT scores.

5. The measurement process itself may be the problem. Tests may be more difficult today. This hypothesis is unlikely, since each year some students are given both the old and the current SAT.

6. The changing student population may in some way be affecting SAT scores. There is a higher proportion of women and minorities attending college today.

Some researchers have been interested in time of measurement factors rather than cohort factors when using the time-lag design. For example, the ongoing evaluation of SAT scores is a time-lag design. Many high school juniors and seniors take this test annually. They have been the same age since the SAT's began. When scores are compared for students at different time periods, a falling trend has been discerned. Sometimes the drop is precipitous. It is no simple matter to account for the drop in scores. Many critics of education have wanted to lay the blame at the feet of the schools and teachers. However, it must be acknowledged that many other changes have taken place over the years, involving both time of measurement and generational factors. Again, we can point meaningfully to the data but we cannot provide an unambiguous interpretation. (See Box 15.1 for some possible reasons.) Time-lag designs have also been used in assessing political attitudes of people the same age but living in different times. Other, more complicated designs, dealing with the problems described here can be found in Botwinick (1978).

15.5.4 In Summary

As shown in Figure 15.2, the performance of different individuals at different age levels is assessed at the same time. The advantage of this cross-sectional design is that the data can be gathered quickly, the researcher can randomly select subjects representative of each age level, and specific attitudes, values, and characteristics can be described for the different generations contained in the sample; for example, religious beliefs, women in the working force or with college degrees, sexual attitudes, etc. The major problem is in interpreting the data, since both maturational age and cohort or generational differences are confounded.

Figure 15.3 illustrates a longitudinal design in which measurement of the *same* individuals at different times (ages) is undertaken. This design permits the intensive study of the same individual across time and the description of changes that take place. Major disadvantages are that the design confounds maturational age with time of measurement and generational differences. Also, it is subject to attrition which, if differential, can cause serious problems in interpretation.

Figure 15.4 illustrates a time-lag design in which measurements of different individuals at the same age level are obtained at different times. This time-lag design separates cultural change from maturational age changes. The major source of confounding is time of measurement with generational changes, since both vary together.

15.6 HAZARDS OF MATCHING IN EVALUATION RESEARCH—REGRESSION TOWARD THE MEAN

We have discussed the difficulties encountered in interpreting research findings when subjects are chosen because of their extreme scores and the correlation between pre- and post-test scores is less than perfect. You will recognize the phenomenon we speak of as regression to the mean. Unfortunately, regression to the mean can and has mislead some investigators in their program evaluation efforts. The problems encountered can be quite subtle as we describe below.

Imagine the following scenario. You were participating in a project aimed at upgrading the educational skills of disadvantaged children in their early elementary school years. Such tasks as reading, writing, and problem-solving were targeted for special attention. Substantial sums of money were made available for the project, permitting the recruitment of talented people to plan and run the program. Various local communities enrolled large numbers of disadvantaged students in the program.

In one major large-scale evaluation, children enrolled in the special program were after-the-fact matched on a pre-test with other children who were not in the program. However, you experienced one severe obstacle—it was extremely difficult to match the children who were in the program. This was due to the fact that children not in the program generally achieved higher scores on the pre-test than those who were in the program. In other words, two different populations were being sampled—lower scoring versus higher scoring disadvantaged children. These two populations are represented in Figure 15.5.

Note that, in order to match subjects in the program with those who are not, it is necessary to draw all subjects from the shaded area where both distributions overlap. In other words, neither the experimental or control samples may be considered representative of the populations from which they were drawn. The subjects in the program were generally drawn from those who scored *high* in the pre-test. Conversely, the sample of subjects not in the program was composed mainly of *low* scorers. What are the possible consequences of a matching procedure that results in a biased selection of subjects from two different populations? In a word, regression toward the mean.

Let us suppose that there were no effects of the treatments. What are you likely to find? Based on regression, most of the subjects in the program would be expected to regress toward the mean of their population. Since the mean is generally lower than their pre-test score, they would regress toward a lower

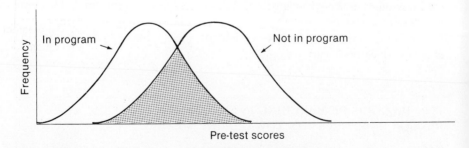

Fig. 15.5 Pre-test scores. Two hypothetical populations of disadvantaged school-aged children. Those in the program generally scored lower on the pre-test than those not in the program. In order to achieve matching on pre-test measures, all subjects had to be drawn from the shaded areas.

value and appear to have done poorly as a result of the special program. In contrast, the subjects not in the program would expect to regress toward a higher mean. Thus, with no experimental treatment whatsoever, they would appear to have improved. Indeed, even if the treatment had been effective for the children in the program, the effects might well have been masked by regression. The masking effect of regression to the mean is illustrated in Figure 15.6.

Up to this point, our scenario has dealt with a hypothetical program. As a matter of actual fact, a large-scale study similar to the preceding was actually undertaken. It involved students in the federally funded Head Start program. Students in the program were matched with those not in the program on the basis of a pre-test measure. After the program was in operation for a sufficient period of time, a post-test was given to compare the development of children in the program with those not enrolled. The results were shocking. The program not only failed to improve the skills of the disadvantaged, it in fact *appeared* to be harmful to them. No one had anticipated that the program could conceivably be harmful, but the data were clear on this point. The data were published in a reputable scientific journal and a storm of controversy ensued. Many alternative interpretations of the results were suggested. An insightful analysis of the results of this study by Campbell and Erlebacher (1975) proposed that regression toward the mean may well have been the culprit.

Even though the program was an applied socially oriented one, the problems illustrated here could have been avoided by using random assignment to conditions. The proper procedure would be to select a random sample of children from the disadvantaged population and then randomly assign them to an experimental (program) group and to a control (no-program) group. The no-program group could then be given some form of "treatment" that would not be expected to affect cognitive skills but would act as a control for attention, motivation, etc. Given random assignment, we would then be dealing with two

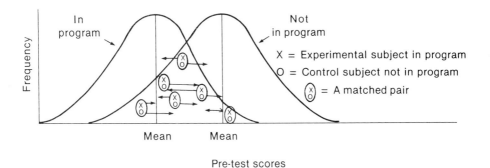

Pre-test scores

Fig. 15.6 Expected effect of regression toward mean when each matched pair is selected from a different population. Note that the majority of experimental subjects will be expected to regress toward a lower score. In contrast, the majority of control subjects will be expected to regress toward a higher score.

groups, equally able, representing a single population (one distribution). If matching were desired, the matched pairs could be selected from a common pool of subjects. One member of each pair would then be randomly assigned to each condition. Our example illustrates that matching after-the-fact is a hazardous procedure. It should be considered an improper procedure also.

It may not be possible to use a random assignment procedure in applied settings without making an effort to inform and educate the participants of why it is necessary. Even then considerable resistance may be encountered. Individuals do not want to be deprived of possible benefits and may become resentful. Ways of addressing this issue are discussed by Cook and Campbell (1979).

In this chapter we have dealt with several important issues related to program evaluation. Obviously there are others that we have not addressed. The knowledge that you have gained from this and other chapters in the text will allow you to bring an informed view both to claims and to criticisms of various social programs. It should also allow you to become a constructive critic concerning program evaluation in general.

CHAPTER SIXTEEN

ANATOMY OF A MANUSCRIPT

We will preface our description of the components of a manuscript with some important comments concerning scholarship. Then we will describe in detail the different sections found in scientific reports. There are additional sections dealing with writing style and with ways to avoid sexism in your writing in Appendix C. Other instructions and helpful suggestions for preparing a manuscript appear in the APA Publication Manual (1974), some of which can also be found in Appendix C. The manual is more extensive and more detailed than our comments below. Our comments deal with the most frequent problems undergraduates experience when beginning to write scientific reports. You will want to consult the APA manual for questions not treated here.

A good research report is a mixture of scholarship and craftsmanship in writing. Both characteristics require time to develop along with considerable practice and feedback from your instructors. In this section we will discuss aspects of scholarship and writing style.

16.1 SCHOLARSHIP

Whether one writes well or writes poorly reflects the person's developmental history in the acquisition of writing skills. Although good writing is an essential requirement for effective communication, it is not sufficient in itself. Good writing must be buttressed by good scholarship. The term *scholarship* implies such characteristics as accuracy, thoroughness, and objectivity. In addition, the writer must have the highest regard for presenting important aspects of a topic in a precise, unbiased, and fair manner. Special care must be taken to acknowledge and cite the ideas and works of other writers if their material is used in the report. Failure to do so, or to imply that their work is your own when it is not, is called *plagiarism*. It is unethical and can also be illegal. Keep in mind that the author of a written report is responsible for all aspects of its contents. From the inception of the research idea, through researching the literature, data acquisition, statistical analysis, and the final written report, great care must be taken to be honest, accurate, precise, and thorough.

16.1.1 Read Original Sources

One way to avoid error and to ensure the accuracy and thoroughness of a report is to read the *original* sources of the information about which you are writing. Relying on secondary sources can result in problems that range from minor inaccuracies to major misstatements of fact. When assertions are made by a writer concerning the work of another writer, it is your responsibility to verify their factual basis before citing them in your report. The only way to do this is to read the original sources they cite. There are many instances in science where a secondary source misstated or misinterpreted the primary source material. Other researchers, reading the secondary source, perpetuate the errors in their writing. When continued by third- and fourth-generation writers, the errors become so deeply ingrained in the literature that they take on the qualities of a myth. At this point, they become exceedingly difficult to refute.

16.1.2 *Ad Hominem* Arguments

Often controversial scientific issues result in heated arguments that sometimes stray from the scientific issues and become personal. In some cases, writers have attacked the personal characteristics of their opponents in an effort to win support for their side of an issue and lessen the appeal of their opponents. When dealing with scientific issues, writers should rely on reason rather than prejudices. They should debate the issues, not attack the opponent's personal characteristics. When discussing the issues pertaining to data or to theory, your opponent's sex, dress, manner, personal attributes, or temperament, are really quite irrelevant. Their political ties, geographic location, ethnic affiliation, or beliefs concerning religion do not matter. What does matter are the merits and quality of the argument. When you appeal to prejudices or to personal attributes you are using an ***ad hominem* argument.** We should make an effort to keep ad hominem arguments from entering the archival literature (recorded or published writings available to the public).

AD HOMINEM **ARGUMENTS**   arguments based on personal characteristics of those in conflict rather than on the issues.

16.2 TITLE

Most psychologists do not pick up a journal and read it cover to cover. They read what interests them. When they receive their scientific journal (or any magazine), they scan the table of contents for articles of interest. If the title of an article is uninformative or misleading, it may not attract readers to the research. Short and informative titles are preferred (limited to not more than fifteen words). Within these fifteen words you should state with clarity the dependent and independent variables or the theoretical issues with which the article deals. The title should be a statement of content so that it alone can be used by various information retrieval systems (e.g., *Psychological Abstracts*). Abbreviations should be avoided. If the title is adequate, it will be referenced appropriately and, thereby, improve the probability that it will gain the attention of its intended audience. Clever titles are permissible if they convey the necessary information and are understandable. Writers with established reputations sometimes use clever titles containing very little information but their works are read routinely because of past contributions to the literature. When working out a title, avoid redundant information. You do not have to include the words *investigation* or *experiment* in the title; that is already understood. Often authors first state the title in a long and fully descriptive way then begin to shorten it to the essentials. For example, the following title "An Investigation of the Choice Behavior of Subjects for Either Predictable or Unpredictable Events" could be reduced to "Choosing Between Predictable and Unpredictable Shock." The new title tells us as much as the old one in a more appealing and specific way and with fewer words (fourteen versus six).

16.3   AUTHORSHIP

When there is only one person responsible for the research project, authorship for the manuscript is not a problem. However, deciding the authorship of a manuscript when several people have been involved can be a delicate issue. Only individuals judged to have made a substantial contribution to the research should be authors. The first author of a manuscript is usually the individual who took the primary responsibility for initiating the research and supervising its completion. Subsequent authorship is assigned in terms of the amount of responsibility taken by each author. Usually, the first author also takes the major responsibility for writing the manuscript. When order of authorship cannot be resolved, some writers have relied on a coin toss for a decision. Whatever the order of authorship, the professional reputation and responsibility for the content of the manuscript are shared equally.

In addition to the authors, others may have made some contributions along the way (e.g., statistical analysis, review of a draft of the manuscript). It is appropriate to acknowledge their contribution in a footnote.

16.4   ABSTRACT

This, too, is an important part of the manuscript and considerable effort should be devoted to writing it. Like the title, it serves indexing and information retrieval systems. *Psychological Abstracts* is only one of many such systems. Moreover, if the title is sufficiently informative and interesting, the next step for the journal reader is to go to the abstract. Some readers whose major research interests are in other areas may go no further than the abstract. Clearly the abstract should inform them as fully as possible about the contents of the article so that an informed decision may be made. Other researchers, more directly interested in the topic will read the abstract both for its content and to determine if the manuscript warrants the commitment of the time necessary to reading and understanding it. Whatever the case, the abstract allows the reader to quickly survey the material.

Since the abstract is usually written after the entire manuscript is completed, the flow of the abstract follows that of the manuscript. You can look upon the abstract as a compressed version of the manuscript. It should contain in very brief form all of the important information, such as the statement of the problem, subject sample and characteristics, design, procedure, summary of results, statistical analyses, and conclusions. The abstract may vary in length between 100 and 175 words. No material or information should appear in the abstract that is not in the manuscript. Usually the first several drafts of the abstract are well beyond the 175-word limit. This forces the writer to make decisions concerning the relative importance of the information—then eliminating material considered less important. The number of words can also be reduced by carefully going over the structure of each sentence and saying things more concisely. Eliminating articles and prepositions also reduces the number of words. References are typically not included in the abstract.

16.5   INTRODUCTION SECTION

No heading is required since, in effect, the manuscript begins here. A difficult decision involves judging the level at which the manuscript should be written. Should you assume a highly sophisticated, knowledgeable audience or one that is naive? The answer is "neither." Instead, assume a generally informed individual who is not specifically familiar with your topic. How long should the introduction be? It should be long enough to provide sufficient information so that the reader may comprehend the content of your paper. Therefore, for some papers, only a few paragraphs are necessary. For others, the length may be considerably longer.

16.5.1   First Introductory Paragraph

Your first paragraph should prepare the reader for what is to come. It should broadly identify the problem or question that your research addresses. In fact, the very first sentence could be used to introduce the general topic of your paper, i.e., what the paper is about—the general thesis. The last sentence of the introductory paragraph could identify the hypothesis, problem, or question more specifically. Sentences between the first and last may be devoted to a *brief general* rationale leading to the question with which your research deals. You do *not* state specifically what your independent and dependent variables are, the logic leading to the question, the hypothesis, your expectations, or the procedure that you will use. The first paragraph simply sets up the reader for what will follow.

16.5.2   Intermediate Paragraphs

These paragraphs should relate to both the preceding paragraph and the paragraph to follow. They are tied together by transition sentences. Transition sentences allow the reader to go smoothly without unexpected changes from one paragraph to the next. A transition sentence may be the first sentence of a new paragraph or it may simply include a word or idea that ended the last paragraph. For example, after describing one approach to a problem, you then state either at the end of one paragraph or the beginning of the other, "Badia suggested a different approach to the problem." Words such as *therefore, nevertheless, however, of course,* are often used with transitions. An outline containing main ideas, literature survey, etc., may help you write a smoothly flowing introduction. Also, read carefully the section on writing style (Appendix C-1).

These intermediate paragraphs should be used to develop a logical argument and rationale for your research, the origin of the problem and a summary of the present state of knowledge. The directly relevant research is reviewed in these paragraphs. This background literature is not intended to be exhaustive. You simply summarize the *major* points of *directly* relevant literature. If exhaustive general reviews of the literature are available, you can refer them to the reader. In these paragraphs you acknowledge the work of others that relates to your research, and also any theoretical development that you wish to undertake. A critique of previous research may be given if it relates to the purposes of your study. Whatever your interest, it is important that you develop a rationale (a logical argument) for your research, i.e., how did your study evolve?

16.5.3   Final Introductory Paragraph

Here you summarize for the reader what you have been saying in preceding paragraphs. You restate your problem, summarize your arguments, and present your rationale or logic. You make it clear for the reader what the specific purpose of your research is and indicate how you intend to provide an answer. It is important that you be specific about your hypothesis, your expectations, or your predictions. Your rationale must follow logically. To be specific means that you will have to identify your dependent and independent variables and the general procedure used to test your hypothesis, and what you expect to find.

16.6   METHOD

The method must be appropriate for the problem or question under investigation. How did you go about answering the research question? This section must be sufficiently descriptive to allow a reader to evaluate how well this was done. It must be sufficiently complete to allow others to replicate your method. For some aspects of the study, considerable detail will be necessary; others will require less detail. You must make this decision. Too much detail concerning relatively unimportant information may be more confusing than helpful. Keep two things in mind when deciding on details: (1) are they important to the outcome of the study, and (2) are they necessary for understanding or for replicating the study? The method section is usually divided into subsections that include *subjects* or *participants, apparatus,* or *stimulus material, procedure,* and, in some cases, *design.* This division is for the reader's convenience when questions arise concerning specific information about the method. The method section should be written while you are running the experiment. Trying to reconstruct it at a later time may be difficult and some important details may be omitted.

16.6.1 Subjects

Here we include details concerning the participants of the study. Who were they? How many? Their sex? Age or age range? How were they selected? Were they paid? Volunteers? Was participation a class requirement? Geographic area? Did any subjects fail to complete the study? Why? Were the data from any subject discarded? Why? Were they informed of the hypothesis being tested?

Different details are necessary when animals are used. We must specify the genus, species, and strain. In addition, the vendor from whom the animals were purchased must be specified. It is also necessry to give their sex, age or age range, and weight. How were they housed and maintained? Was any special treatment given?

16.6.2 Apparatus

This section should not be confused with the following procedure section. It is sometimes difficult not to do so. Include in this section the apparatus and materials used in the experiment. In some cases, only testing material will be used. If so, important information concerning the tests must be given. Under this circumstance, the title of this section might be changed to Materials or Tests. When commercial laboratory equipment is used, identify the model number and the company. Custom-built equipment that was central to the research should be described in sufficient detail to allow others to build it. In the latter case, a drawing or photograph may also be helpful.

16.6.3 Procedure

Detail is necessary in this section. The questions that must be clearly answered are: "What did you do and how did you do it?" State precisely what treatment was given to each subject. If different groups received different treatments, be sure that your description identifies these differences. Independent, dependent, and control variables must be clearly identified for the reader. Identify experimental and control groups and indicate how they were formed. Time intervals, durations, and sequences of important events should be described. Instructions should be summarized or paraphrased. If instructions are studied themselves as an independent variable, then they should be presented verbatim. If counterbalancing or randomization is used, describe how this was accomplished.

16.6.4   Design

For some complex experiments a design section may be appropriate. If so, then this section would include the type of experimental design that was used (e.g., within subjects, between subjects, mixed design) along with the treatment conditions and a description of the statistical analyses or model. When a design section is used, some of the material in the procedure section would be placed in this section.

16.7   RESULTS

This section is used for describing the results of the research and for evaluating their reliability. It is sometimes difficult to present your results without also discussing them. In fact, on occasion, some writers do combine the Results and Discussion sections under one heading. However, more often than not, the two sections are kept separate. All data relevant to the purposes of your research should be presented, whether favorable or unfavorable to your views. Different formats, in addition to verbal description, can be used. Tables and figures are the most common method used to supplement and clarify the verbal description. They are intended only as supplements and should not serve as the only source of information concerning results. Avoid presenting the same data in several places. (If data appear in a table, they generally should not appear in a figure and vice versa.)

Different methods are used to determine whether the obtained results are reliable (significant). When group data are presented, the results are usually analyzed statistically and their reliability (significance level) reported in terms of a t, F, χ^2, or other statistics along with a given p (probability) value. When a single-subject approach is used, data from *individual subjects* are presented and their reliability is assessed by intra-subject and inter-subject replication.

A reasonably standard format is used when reporting tests of significance. First, a verbal description of the results (data) are given. This is followed by presenting the outcome of statistical analyses of these results. For example, after describing the data obtained with Groups A and B under two different conditions, you might then report the following: "The difference between Group A and B under the first condition was significant, $F(1,21) = 9.01$, $p < .01$, but it was not significant under the second condition, $F(1,21) = 1.55$, $p > .05$." Note the manner in which the statistical test is reported. First, the symbol of the statistic is given (italicized), followed by the degrees of freedom (parentheses), an equal sign followed by the value of the statistic, a comma, an underlined lower case p (probability), followed by a less than $<$ or greater than $>$ sign, and finally the level of significance. Again we state, it is important to first describe your data and only then give the outcome of tests of significance.

16.8 DISCUSSION

If the experiment is a simple one with few findings reported in the Results section, you can begin the discussion with a clear, unambiguous statement of the contribution that your study makes. If a question was raised or a hypothesis stated, you should make a direct statement concerning an answer to the question or whether the hypothesis was or was not supported. When the Results section consists of many findings, it is appropriate to open the discussion with a brief summary of your findings.

The important points brought out in the introduction should be addressed in your Discussion. Also the major findings of your study should be evaluated and interpreted. In this section you describe the relationship of your findings to those of others and identify existing similarities and differences. You may want to emphasize some of your findings while qualifying others. Indicate whether your procedure, subject population, or experimental manipulations restrict or limit the generalizations that can be drawn. Theoretical speculation closely related to your data is appropriate in this section. However, avoid rambling ideas and speculation distant from your data. The practical implications of your data, if any, should be noted here. If you feel that your study has some unusual strengths, then it is appropriate to note them. Also, weaknesses, if any, should be briefly identified with suggestions to correct them. You may want to conclude your discussion by pointing to future research. The insight derived from your study may suggest additional research or even a different direction that should be undertaken.

16.9 REFERENCE NOTES

Communication among scientists takes many forms in addition to published articles and books, e.g., personal communication occurs between scientists; written reports are circulated to a limited group; papers are given at scientific meetings, symposia are presented; technical reports may be available, unpublished manuscripts may be accessible. There are also other informal sources of information to which we may need to refer when writing a report. Material of this type is placed under Reference Notes rather than the Reference section.

The use of this type of material is usually restricted to that which is essential for the article. When cited in the text of a report, the format differs from a regular reference. In citing a regular reference in the text of a report we use the date, e.g., either Runyon (1980) or (Runyon, 1980). In citing reference note material, we replace the date with the word "Note," e.g., Defran (Note 1). If later in the text additional reference note material is cited, it becomes Note 2, e.g., Harsh (Note 2). When notes and references are used together, notes appear after the reference and in numerical order, separated by a semicolon, e.g., (Runyon, 1980; Defran, Note 1, Harsh, Note 2).

When including this type of information in the Reference Notes, give as much information as possible concerning author, title, date, availability of material. Notes are numbered in the order they appear in the text. An example follows:

Reference Notes

1. Penrod, S. *Jury Simulation Research: Defendant and Juror Characteristics.* Unpublished manuscript, Harvard University, 1976.

2. Harsh, J. Personal communication, November, 1982.

3. Abbott, B., and Badia, P. *Choosing Signaled Shock: Some Answers to Recent Criticisms.* Paper presented at the meeting of the Psychonomic Society, Washington, D.C., November, 1977.

4. Badia, P., and Harsh, J. *Theoretical Views of Predictability.* Manuscript submitted for publication, 1982.

16.10   REFERENCES

Only references cited in the report are included in the Reference section and these are ordered alphabetically by the first author's last name. The Reference format described here is simple and efficient but it differs from that used by some other professions. There are usually four components of each reference: author(s), title, publication, and date of publication. The format differs among journal articles, authored books, edited books, chapters appearing in edited books, and unpublished manuscripts. At the end of this text, you will find examples of the proper reference format to use. In addition, one example of each of the different types previously mentioned is given here:

Article in a Journal:
Badia, P., Harsh, J., and Abbott, B. Choosing between predictable and unpredictable shock conditions. Data and theory. *Psychology Bulletin,* 1979, *86,* 1107–1131.

Authored Book
Sidman, M. *Tactics of Scientific Research.* New York: Basic Books, 1960.

Edited Book
Brush, F. R. (Ed.). *Aversive conditioning and learning.* New York: Academic Press, 1971.

Chapter in a Book

Seligman, M. E. P., Maier, S. F., and Solomon, R. L. Unpredictable and uncontrollable aversive events. In F. R. Brush (Ed.), *Aversive conditioning and learning*. New York: Academic Press, 1971.

16.11   WRITING STYLE

Some very helpful guidelines concerning writing style are described in the *APA Publication Manual* (1974). As noted earlier, several pages from this manual can be found in Appendix C-1. In addition to working on improving your writing style, it is necessary to develop skill in using nonsexist language in your writing. To aid you in doing this, we have included an APA publication on the use of nonsexist language in Appendix C-2.

16.12   WRITING THE MANUSCRIPT

For many, the most difficult task of doing the research is writing the report. Writing is a solitary activity and it is not compatible with socializing. To write a concise, coherent report requires planning, persistence, skill, and concentration. It is easy to put off writing until the deadline is upon you. For many, simply getting started writing is a very difficult task. Other tasks are suddenly given higher priority or they become more urgent. One major reason for procrastinating is that the task of writing the report seems overwhelming. You are probably thinking of going from the beginning to the final copy—from "start" to "finish" in one marathon session. You are concerned about getting all the ideas in the report and expressing the ideas adequately.

Let's look at some procedures that should be helpful for writing your report. Perhaps the single most important consideration is to allow sufficient time to complete the report. Don't hobble yourself with added stress of fighting a course deadline. Consider the advantages and benefits that you will derive from finishing early. Set a realistic deadline earlier than the one set by the instructor. Perhaps you can use some self-control techniques, such as rewarding yourself for progress and punishing yourself for falling behind.

To make the task of writing the report more manageable, consider doing one section at a time. You do not have to start with the introduction and proceed through each section in their given order. There are no binding rules concerning which section should be written first. Begin with the section that is of greatest importance to you. Once this decision is made, then develop an outline that will organize what you want to say. If your notes and references are on cards (3 × 5 or 5 × 7), you can arrange them in the order you plan to write as an alternative to the outline.

Once the outline is arranged, then start to write. Let your ideas flow. Do not worry about revising and restructuring your sentences. Writing and revising are two different tasks requiring two different mental sets. Revising requires more intense effort and concentration on a single sentence. Writing requires that the ideas and thoughts simply be expressed. After the ideas are out, some reorganization can take place and sentences can be refined or restructured. Your first draft will be and should be "rough."

Upon completion of the first draft, begin the task of revising it. Is the organization reasonable? Correct errors in spelling, grammar, and logic. Look at your sentences and word structure. Are there any ambiguous expressions or awkward sentences? Again, do not attempt to compose a final "polished" report. After this second revision is complete, place the report aside for a few days. Placing the report aside is important for several reasons. It allows you to do other things that may be beginning to distract you. Setting the report aside also allows you to return to it with a different perspective. Errors become more glaring, cumbersome sentences stand out, needed revisions become more obvious. Also, new insights may occur during the period the report was set aside. During the period you may want to have a fellow student read the report simply for clarity. Often a fresh reader can detect unclear or confusing statements that you may have repeatedly missed.

In completing the final draft, do not be satisfied with anything less than your best efforts. You should also be your own severest critic. If you would like a standard with which to compare your writing, ask your instructor to name a few excellent writers whose published works you can read. It is sometimes helpful to observe their writing style when trying to improve your writing skills. You can develop your own distinctive style once you have mastered some of the basic skills. There are also some excellent books that can be very helpful (e.g., Baker, 1973; Tichy, 1966). We have included in Appendix D-1 and D-2 two student research reports to give you some idea as to what constitutes an excellent paper (i.e., grade of "A") and what constitutes an average paper (i.e., grade of "C").

16.13 ARRANGEMENT OF MANUSCRIPT

The *APA Publication Manual* specifies a precise arrangement of the manuscript. This arrangement is necessary when submitting a manuscript to a journal for publication. It differs in a number of ways from the appearance of the published article. Many instructors request that the report be submitted on a form similar to the published article. In particular, tables and figures might be placed in the Results section where the data are described. The arrangement below is suggested by the APA manual:

1. Cover page (separate page)—includes title, authors, affiliation

2. Abstract (starts on separate page)—the word "Abstract" centered at top of page. No title, author affiliation, or paragraph indentation.

3. Pages of text (starts on separate page)—title at top of page but no author or affiliation noted. Do not start a new page because of a heading (e.g., Method, Results, Discussion) until Reference Notes.

4. Reference Notes (starts on separate page).

5. Footnotes (starts on separate page).

6. Tables (each on a separate page).

7. Figure captions (starts on separate page)

8. Figures (each on a separate page).

16.13.1   Headings

There are three levels of headings usually found in written reports: main headings, side headings, and paragraph headings. Short papers may need only one or two levels of headings.

<u>Main Headings</u>

Main headings are the principal headings. They are centered on the page, the first letter of each main word is capitalized, all words are underlined, and no period is placed at the end.

<u>Side Headings</u>

The second level of headings is referred to as side headings. These headings are typed at the side of the page flush with the margin. Again, the first letter of each main word is capitalized; all words are underlined, and no period is placed at the end.

<u>Paragraph headings.</u>   The third level of headings is referred to as a paragraph heading. These headings are typed with the paragraph indentation as here. Only the first letter of the first word is capitalized. The heading is underlined, the last word is followed by a period, and two spaces later the text begins.

16.13.2   Tables

Tables are not intended to duplicate the text of a manuscript. They are used to supplement it and to display a large amount of data in a clear and compressed way. Whenever a table is used, it must be referred to in the text. However, it is not necessary to launch into a detailed description of all the data in the table. Only the most important data need be described. Tables are sometimes difficult to construct and they require both thought and trial and error. For helpful suggestions, the APA manual should be consulted. Tables are always referred to by number, e.g., Table 1, Table 2, etc., and they require a brief but explanatory heading. Often headings identify the dependent and independent variable. Tables may also have footnotes immediately below them that provide additional information to make them easier to understand.

16.13.3   Figures

Another way to present considerable data in a clear and compressed way is to use figures. As with tables, each figure must be referred to in the text along with a description of the important data they display. They, too, are used only to supplement the text. Figures are also referred to by number, e.g., Figure 1, Figure 2, etc. and they must be accompanied by a figure caption (title). The caption is usually descriptive and includes the dependent and independent variables that compose the figure. If additional information is needed to identify specific groups or conditions, then a legend is included (e.g., open circles = placebo group, closed circles = experimental group). The vertical and horizontal areas must be clearly labeled. Heavy dark lines should be used when drawing these axes. The dependent variable is plotted along the vertical axis while the independent variable is plotted along the horizontal axis. Usually no more than four curves should be plotted on any figure. Careful consideration should be given to the proper scale that is used along the ordinate. It is possible to distort the visual display of the findings by using different scale values. Decimal values, e.g., .1, .2, etc., may exaggerate the obtained differences while a scale value in units of 10, e.g., 10, 20, etc., might minimize the obtained differences.

16.14   THE HISTORY OF A MANUSCRIPT

Publishing a scientific article is an interesting process and one with which students are usually unfamiliar. There are estimated to be over one hundred journals in which psychologists publish their work. Not all of these are considered scientific journals; many are popularized. Contrary to common belief, authors who publish their work in scientific journals are not paid for their contribution. Nor are journals obligated in any way to accept for publication a manuscript submitted to the journal. Some journals receive hundreds of manuscripts each year and reject as many as 90 percent of them. In fact, the average rejection rate for manuscripts submitted to journals published by the APA for the year 1978 was 76 percent (Reported by the Council of Editors, 1978). As you can see, publishing the fruits of your scientific labors can either be exhilarating (manuscript accepted for publication) or depressing (manuscript rejected). Decisions concerning the acceptance or rejection of a manuscript are made by the journal editor after consulting with experts (usually two) who have read the manuscript carefully. An illustration of the publication process from initiation of the research to its publication is given below. Although the time periods depicted in the illustration are intended to approximate the real world of scientific research, *much longer* periods are not uncommon.

January 1, 1981. The research idea is discussed and a plan is laid out to undertake the research. Equipment is ordered, etc.

February 1, 1981. All material is available, research design is agreed upon, and the research is initiated. Project begins.

May 1, 1981. Data acquisition is completed and the results are ready for analysis.

June 1, 1981. Results are analyzed. Tables and figures are prepared. It is agreed upon which journal to submit the manuscript to. First draft begins.

June 15, 1981. First draft of the manuscript is completed and revising begins.

July 1, 1981. Second draft of the manuscript is prepared. It is decided that a third draft is necessary. The manuscript is left untouched for two weeks.

August 1, 1981. Third draft is completed and given to colleagues for their comments and criticism.

October 1, 1981. Final draft is prepared, taking into account the comments of our colleagues. This draft is submitted to journal editor for consideration. A short cover letter is enclosed along with two copies (varies with journal) of the manuscript. The cover letter indicates title, authors, institution, and general topic of the manuscript.

October 15, 1981. Editor of the journal acknowledges that the manuscript was received and sends it out to two consultants (reviewers) to determine the scientific worth, i.e., does the manuscript make a contribution to the scientific literature? The review and evaluation of the report is usually done anonymously by the reviewers. Editors and reviewers are very carefully selected. Usually, they are individuals who have achieved recognition for their own scientific contributions.

January 1, 1982. Editor returns the manuscript to the authors with a cover letter and the anonymous comments of the reviewers. The cover letter indicates the action or decision made by the editor. There are four types of decisions that the editor can make: (1) accept as is; (2) accept, but with some revisions; (3) reject with revisions; or (4) reject. When a manuscript is rejected with revisions, it means that it may be submitted again after revisions are made and treated as a new manuscript. In our fictitious illustration, the editor's decision was to accept with revision. Process of revising begins following several days of exhilaration. Several days of depression would have followed a rejection. If the manuscript is rejected, it is still possible to submit it to another journal.

March 1, 1982. Revisions suggested by the editor are made and the revised copy is returned to the editor. Editor evaluates whether the revisions are adequate. If so, the manuscript is sent to the managing editor at APA.

The manuscript is prepared in the format that the printer can follow, and then it is sent to the printer for typesetting.

April 1, 1982. Final acceptance regarding publication is received from the editor. Authors are informed that the publication lag (waiting time before report is published) is about eight months.

November 1, 1982. Authors receive galley proofs from the managing editor for proof-reading.

January 1, 1983. Article is published in the journal.

In general, the above example is a fair representation of what an author goes through whenever a manuscript is submitted for publication. Manuscripts submitted to one journal cannot be submitted to another at the same time. Nor can the same article be published in two or more journals, although it can be reprinted in a book. Perhaps we should note that the two-year period from start to finish is on the optimistic side. The entire process often takes longer.

16.15   REPRINTS OF ARTICLES

When a report is published in a journal, the author generally receives 50 free reprints and usually orders an additional 100 or 200 reprints of the article, at his or her own cost. These are simply exact copies of the article as they appear in the journal. Authors generally and happily send individual reprints to those who request them (as long as their supply lasts). A post card is usually sufficient to request a reprint. Be sure to identify the title, date of publication, journal, and include your own address.

APPENDICES

APPENDICES

STATISTICS: WORKED EXAMPLES

A.1 THE STUDENT t-RATIO, ONE-SAMPLE CASE

In the one-sample case, t is defined as follows:

$$t = \frac{\overline{X} - \mu_0}{s_{\overline{X}}}$$

in which

$\overline{X}$ = mean of sample,

μ_0 = population mean specified under H_0,

$s_{\overline{X}}$ = standard error of the mean.

In turn, the formula for calculating the standard error of the mean is:

$$s_{\overline{X}} = \sqrt{N\frac{SS}{(N-1)}}$$

in which

$$SS = \Sigma X^2 - \frac{(\Sigma X)^2}{N}.$$

There is a separate t-distribution for each value of N. Each sampling distribution is plotted in terms of degrees of freedom. In the one-sample case, $df = N - 1$. Table B.2 shows the critical values for rejecting H_0 at the 0.05 and 0.01 levels. Obtained t is significant if its absolute value (i.e., ignoring the minus sign when t is negative) equals or exceeds the tabled critical value. Let's take a look at an example.

Example Consumer groups have often accused automobile manufacturers of installing odometers that overestimate mileage traveled in order to make the miles-per-gallon figure look more attractive. (For example, if a car travels 100 miles on eight gallons of gas, the miles per gallon is 12.5. However, if the odometer reads, say, 109 miles, the automobile owner will erroneously conclude that his or her miles-per-gallon figure is 13.5) To test this hypothesis, twelve new cars were run over a measured course of 100 miles. The odometer readings were: 103, 97, 101, 100, 99, 104, 102, 103, 100, 102, 105, and 103. Test the null hypothesis, using $\alpha = 0.05$, one-tailed test.

1. *Null hypothesis* (H_0): The population mean from which the odometer samples were drawn is equal to 100; that is, $\mu_0 = 100$.

2. Alternative *hypothesis* (H_1): The population mean is not equal to 100; that is, $\mu_0 \neq 100$.

3. *Statistical test:* Since we are involved in a comparison of a sample mean with an hypothesized value, the Student *t*-ratio, one-sample case, is appropriate.

4. *Significance level:* $\alpha = 0.05$.

5. *Sampling distribution:* The sampling distribution is the Student *t*-distribution with df $= N - 1 = 12 - 1 = 11$.

6. *Critical region:* By referring to Table B.2, we find that the critical value for significance at 0.05 level when df $= 11$ is 2.201. If the absolute value of obtained *t* equals or exceeds 2.201, we shall reject H_0 and assert H_1.

Step 1.   Find ΣX, and divide by N to obtain $\overline{X}$.

$$\Sigma X = 1219,$$
$$\overline{X} = 101.58.$$

Step 2.   Find the sum of squares (SS) by squaring each score, summing, and subtracting $(\Sigma X)^2/N$:

$$SS = \Sigma X^2 - \frac{(\Sigma X)^2}{N}$$
$$= 123{,}887 - 123{,}830.08$$
$$= 56.92.$$

Step 3.   Find $s_{\overline{X}}$:

$$s_{\overline{X}} = \sqrt{\frac{SS}{N(N-1)}}$$
$$= \sqrt{\frac{56.92}{132}}$$
$$= 0.66.$$

Step 4.   Find t:

$$t = \frac{\overline{X} - \mu_0}{s_{\overline{X}}}$$
$$= \frac{101.58 - 100}{0.66}$$
$$= 2.39.$$

Since obtained $t = 2.39$ exceeds the critical value of 2.201, we reject H_0. It would appear that the odometers are from a population with a mean greater than 100. In other words, there is support for the hypothesis that odometers overestimate distance traveled.

A.2   THE STUDENT *t*-RATIO, TWO INDEPENDENT SAMPLES

Typically, we have drawn samples from a population or populations with unknown parameters, and must estimate the parameters from the sample statistics themselves. When parameters are unknown, the appropriate test statistic is the t-ratio:

$$t = \frac{\overline{X}_1 - \overline{X}_2 - (\mu_1 - \mu_2)}{s_{\overline{X}_1 - \overline{X}_2}},$$

in which

$\overline{X}_1 - \overline{X}_2$ is the difference in sample means,

$\mu_1 - \mu_2$ is the difference in the population means from which the samples were presumed to have been drawn,

$s_{\overline{X}_1 - \overline{X}_2}$ is the standard error of the difference between means when estimated from sample variances.

The most common null hypothesis is that the samples were selected from the same population or from populations with identical means. In other words, H_0 becomes $\mu_1 = \mu_2$, or alternatively, $\mu_1 - \mu_2 = 0$. To investigate the null hypothesis of no difference between population means, the *t*-statistic simplifies to

$$t = \frac{\overline{X}_1 - \overline{X}_2}{s_{\overline{X}_1 - \overline{X}_2}}.$$

When *N*'s are equal.   When the N in each group is the same, the convenient computational formula for $s_{\overline{X}_1 - \overline{X}_2}$ is:

$$s_{\overline{X}_1 - \overline{X}_2} = \sqrt{\frac{\text{SS}_1 + \text{SS}_2}{N(N-1)}}$$

in which SS_1 is the sum of squares of condition X_1 and is defined as

$$\text{SS}_1 = \Sigma X_1^2 - \frac{(\Sigma X_1)^2}{N_1}.$$

SS_2 is the sum of squares of condition S_2 and is defined as

$$\text{SS}_2 = \Sigma X_2^2 - \frac{(\Sigma X_2)^2}{N_2}.$$

Example Given $\Sigma X_1 = 451$, $\Sigma X_1^2 = 20969$, $N_1 = 10$, $N_2 = 10$, $\Sigma X_2 = 491$, $\Sigma X_2^2 = 24{,}953$; then

$$SS_1 = 20{,}969 - \frac{(451)^2}{10}$$
$$= 628.9;$$

$$SS_2 = 24{,}953 - \frac{(491)^2}{10}$$
$$= 844.9;$$

$$s_{\overline{X}_1 - \overline{X}_2} = \sqrt{\frac{628.9 + 844.9}{90}}$$
$$= 4.05.$$

When N's are unequal When the N in each group is not the same, a convenient formula for $s_{\overline{X}_1 - \overline{X}_2}$ is

$$s_{\overline{X}_1 - \overline{X}_2} = \sqrt{\left(\frac{SS_1 + SS_2}{N_1 + N_2 - 2}\right)\left(\frac{1}{N_1} + \frac{1}{N_2}\right)}.$$

Example Given: $\Sigma X_1 = 38$, $\Sigma X_1^2 = 228$, $N_1 = 11$, $\Sigma X_2 = 40$, $\Sigma X_2^2 = 222$, $N_2 = 9$; then

$$SS_1 = 228 - \frac{(38)^2}{11}$$
$$= 96.73;$$

$$SS_2 = 222 - \frac{(40)^2}{9}$$
$$= 44.22;$$

$$s_{\overline{X}_1 - \overline{X}_2} = \sqrt{\frac{96.73 + 44.22}{18}\left(\frac{1}{11} + \frac{1}{9}\right)}$$
$$= \sqrt{\frac{140.95}{18}(0.20)} = \sqrt{\frac{28.19}{18}}$$
$$= 1.25.$$

A.2.1 Testing the Null Hypothesis

The Student t-distributions are the appropriate sampling distributions for testing the null hypothesis of no difference between means when parameters are not known.

Example The manager of a school cafeteria believed that women (Group X_2) consume more coffee daily than men (Group X_1). He asked a total of twenty randomly selected students on randomly selected days how many cups of coffee they had consumed during the previous twenty-four-hour period. He obtained the following results:

$$\overline{X}_1 = 3.45, \qquad \Sigma X_1 = 38, \qquad \Sigma X_1^2 = 228, \qquad N_1 = 11,$$
$$\overline{X}_2 = 4.44, \qquad \Sigma X_2 = 40, \qquad \Sigma X_2^2 = 222, \qquad N_2 = 9.$$

Use $\alpha = 0.05$, two-tailed test.

Step 1. Specify the null hypothesis. In the present example, H_0 is that there is no difference in the population means of daily cups of coffee consumed by male and female students, i.e., $\mu_1 = \mu_2$.

Step 2. Specify the alternative hypothesis. The alternative hypothesis is that the population means from which samples were drawn are not the same, i.e., $\mu_1 \neq \mu_2$.

Step 3. Specify the statistical test. In the present example, the *t*-statistic is appropriate since the population standard deviations are not known.

Step 4. Specify the significance level. We shall use $\alpha = 0.05$.

Step 5. Specify the sampling distribution. In the present example, the sampling distribution is the Student *t*-distribution with df $= N_1 + N_2 - 2$ or $11 + 9 - 2 = 18$ (Table B.2).

Step 6. Specify the critical region. The critical region consists of all values of $t \geq 2.101$ and $t \leq -2.101$.

Step 7. Find t. In the present example;

$$t = \frac{3.45 - 4.44}{\sqrt{\dfrac{SS_1 + SS_2}{N_1 + N_2 - 2}\left(\dfrac{1}{N_1} + \dfrac{1}{N_2}\right)}}$$

and

$$SS_1 = 228 - \frac{(38)^2}{11}$$
$$= 96.73,$$

$$SS_2 = 222 - \frac{(40)^2}{9}$$
$$= 44.22.$$

Therefore:

$$s_{\bar{X}_1 - \bar{X}_2} = \sqrt{\frac{96.73 + 44.22}{18}\left(\frac{1}{11} + \frac{1}{9}\right)}$$
$$= 1.25,$$

and the t-ratio becomes

$$t = -\frac{0.99}{1.25}$$
$$= -0.792.$$

Since $t = -0.792$ is not within the critical region, we fail to reject H_0. The results of this study do not permit us to conclude that women students drink more coffee daily than men students.

A.3   THE STUDENT t-RATIO, CORRELATED SAMPLES

The test statistic employed with correlated samples is the Student t-ratio,

$$t = \frac{\bar{D} - \mu_D}{s_{\bar{D}}},$$

in which

$\bar{D}$ is the difference between the means of the two experimental groups,
$\mu_{\bar{D}}$ is the difference between means hypothesized under H_0,
$s_{\bar{D}}$ is the standard error of the mean difference.

Example   If $\bar{D} = 6.4$, $\mu_{\bar{D}} = 2$, and $s_{\bar{D}} = 4.3$, then

$$t = \frac{6.4 - 2}{4.3}$$
$$= \frac{4.4}{4.3}$$
$$= 1.02.$$

The most common null hypothesis is that $\mu_{\bar{D}} = 0$. In this event, the Student t-ratio becomes

$$t = \frac{\bar{D}}{s_{\bar{D}}}.$$

Example   Given H_0: $\mu_D = 0$, $\bar{D} = 8.42$, and $s_{\bar{D}} = 3.72$, then

$$t = \frac{8.42}{3.72}$$
$$= 2.263.$$

Table A.1

A worked example of the calculation of the *t*-ratio for correlated samples (before-after design).

	Median Systolic Blood Pressure			
Subject	Last 5 control sessions	Last 5 experimental sessions	Control minus conditioning (D)	D^2
1	139.6	136.1	3.5	12.25
2	213.3	179.5	33.8	1142.44
3	162.3	133.1	29.2	852.64
4	166.9	150.4	16.5	272.25
5	157.8	141.7	16.1	259.21
6	165.7	166.6	− 0.9	.81
7	149.0	131.7	17.3	299.29
			$\Sigma D = 115.5$	$\Sigma D^2 = 2838.89$

$$\bar{D} = \frac{\Sigma D}{N}$$

$$= \frac{115.5}{7} = 16.5$$

$$SS_D = \Sigma D^2 - \frac{(\Sigma D)^2}{N}$$

$$= 2838.89 - 1905.75$$

$$= 933.14$$

$$t = \frac{\bar{D}}{s_{MD}}$$

$$= \frac{16.5}{4.71}$$

$$= 3.503$$

$$s_{MD} = \sqrt{\frac{SS_D}{N(N-1)}}$$

$$= \sqrt{\frac{933.14}{42}}$$

$$= 4.71$$

Let us look at an actual example in which operant conditioning techniques were used in an effort to lower the systolic blood pressure of seven patients suffering essential hypertension (Benson, 1975). The median systolic pressure during the last five control and conditioning sessions are presented in Table A.1. By treating these medians as scores, we may use the *t*-ratio for correlated samples in order to evaluate the statistical significance of these results.

Stated in formal statistical terms:

1. *Null hypothesis (H_0):* The mean difference is zero.

2. *Alternative hypothesis (H_1):* The mean difference is not zero.

3. *Statistical test:* Since we are employing a before-after design, the Student *t*-ratio for correlated samples is appropriate.

4. *Significance level:* $\alpha = 0.05$.

5. *Sampling distribution:* The sampling distribution is the t-distribution with df = $N - 1$ or $7 - 1 = 6$.

6. *Critical region:* $t \geq (2.447)$. Any value equal to or greater than 2.447 or equal to or less than -2.447 will lead to the rejection of H_0 and the assertion of H_1.

Table A.1 summarizes the data, the calculation of t, and the statistical decision.

Since obtained t exceeds the critical value, we reject H_0. We may conclude that the conditioning procedures produced a significant reduction in systolic blood pressure.

A.4 RANDOMIZED GROUP DESIGN

Let us imagine that twenty-one students enrolled in an advanced class in matrix algebra were randomly assigned to three different instructional groups. Three different teaching techniques were used to instruct the students on a specific set of principles. Following the instruction, all students were administered a twenty-item test to determine their ability to apply the principles to various situations. The scores of the students in the three treatment groups are shown in Table A.2. We'll test H_0 that the sample means were drawn from a common population of means, using $\alpha = 0.05$.

Table A.2
Data for randomized group design.

		Condition			
A_1		A_2		A_3	
X_1	X_1^2	X_2	X_2^2	X_3	X_3^2
2	4	7	49	8	64
2	4	3	9	4	16
7	49	7	49	5	25
2	4	9	81	9	81
5	25	4	16	10	100
4	16	5	25	11	121
3	9	3	9	9	81
$\Sigma X_1 = 25$	$\Sigma X_1^2 = 111$	$\Sigma X_2 = 38$	$\Sigma X_2^2 = 238$	$\Sigma X_3 = 56$	$\Sigma X_3^2 = 488$

Step 1. Find SS_T.

$$SS_T = \Sigma X^2 - \frac{(\Sigma X_T)^2}{N_T}$$

$$= (2)^2 + (2)^2 + \ldots + (9)^2 - \frac{(\Sigma X_T)^2}{N_T}$$

$$= 837 - \frac{(119)^2}{21}$$

$$= 837 - 674.33$$

$$= 162.67$$

Step 2. Find df_T.

$$df_T = N_T - 1.$$

$$= 20$$

Step 3. Find the between-group sum of squares by squaring each ΣX, dividing by the N in the condition, and summing. Subtract $(\Sigma X_T)^2/N_T$ from this sum. In the present example,

$$SS_B = \frac{(\Sigma X_1)^2}{N_1} + \frac{(\Sigma X_2)^2}{N_2} + \frac{(\Sigma X_3)^2}{N_3} - 674.33$$

$$= \frac{(25)^2}{7} + \frac{(38)^2}{7} + \frac{(56)^2}{7} - 674.33.$$

Since the N's are equal, there will be less rounding error if we put all the quantities to be squared over the least common denominator (7). Thus,

$$SS_B = \frac{(25)^2 + (38)^2 + (56)^2}{7} - 674.33$$

$$= \frac{5205}{7} - 674.33$$

$$= 69.24.$$

Step 4. Find $df_B = k - 1$. In the present problem, the number of groups (k) is equal to 3. Thus $df = 3 - 1 = 2$.

Step 5. Find the within-group sum of squares. This may be obtained by subtracting, since

$$SS_W = SS_T - SS_B$$

$$= 162.67 - 69.24$$

$$= 93.43.$$

However, if you have made an error in calculating SS_T or SS_B, the error may go undetected. It is recommended that you obtain SS_W as a check of the accuracy of your calculations. The following formula is employed to obtain SS_W directly:

$$SS_W = \Sigma X_1^2 - \frac{(\Sigma X_1)^2}{N_1} + \Sigma X_2^2 - \frac{(\Sigma X_2)^2}{N_2} + \Sigma X_3^2 - \frac{(\Sigma X_3)^2}{N_3}$$

$$= 111 - \frac{(25)^2}{7} + 238 - \frac{(38)^2}{7} - 488 - \frac{(56)^2}{7}$$

$$= 21.714 + 31.714 + 40.000$$

$$= 93.43.$$

Step 6. Find $df_W = N - k$. In the present problem, the number of groups (k) is equal to 3. Thus, $df_W = 21 - 3 = 18$.

Step 7. Check to ascertain that $SS_T = SS_B + SS_W$, and $df_T = df_B + df_W$.

Step 8. Find the between-group variance estimate by dividing the between-group sum of squares by df_B. In the present problem,

$$s_B^2 = \frac{69.24}{2} = 34.62.$$

Place in the summary table shown in Step 13.

Step 9. Find the within-group variance estimate by dividing the within-group sum of squares by df_W:

$$s_W^2 = \frac{93.43}{18} = 5.19.$$

Step 10. Find the F-ratio by dividing the between-group variance estimate by the within-group variance estimate (error).

$$F = \frac{s_B^2}{s_W^2} = \frac{3462}{5.19} = 6.67, \text{ df } 2/18.$$

Step 11. Look up $F = 6.67$ in Table B.3, under 2 and 18 degrees of freedom. If obtained F equals or exceeds the tabled value at $\alpha = 0.05$, reject H_0 and assert that the experimental conditions cause differences in performance. Since obtained $F = 6.67$ is greater than the F required for significance at $\alpha = 0.05$ (i.e., $F = 4.38$), we reject H_0. We may assert that the different conditions of instruction produced differential learning scores.

A.5 THE TUKEY HSD (HONESTLY SIGNIFICANT DIFFERENCE) TEST NUMBER OF PAIRWISE COMPARISONS

The Tukey HSD test may be used to make pairwise comparisons between treatment means. The number of pairwise comparisons for k treatment conditions is given by

$$\frac{k(k-1)}{2}.$$

Examples If there are four treatment conditions, the number of pairwise comparisons is

$$\frac{4(3)}{2} = 6.$$

If there are eight treatment conditions, the number of pairwise comparisons is

$$\frac{8(7)}{2} = 28.$$

The difference between two means is significant at a given α level if it equals or exceeds HSD:

$$\text{HSD} = q_\alpha \sqrt{\frac{s_\epsilon^2}{N}}$$

in which

s_ϵ^2 = the error variance,
N = number of subjects in each condition,
q_α = tabled value for a given α-level found in Table B.4 for the error degrees of freedom (df) and the number of means (k).

We shall illustrate the use of the Tukey test by using the worked example appearing in Section A.4. We obtained an F-ratio of 6.67 which was significant at $\alpha = 0.05$. The means of the three conditions were as follows:

$$\overline{X}_1 = \frac{\Sigma X_1}{N_1} = \frac{27}{7} = 3.57,$$

$$\overline{X}_2 = \frac{\Sigma X_2}{N_2} = \frac{38}{7} = 5.43,$$

$$\overline{X}_3 = \frac{\Sigma X_3}{N_3} = \frac{56}{7} = 8.00.$$

We also found s_w^2 (i.e., s_ϵ^2) to be 5.19, with 18 df.

Step 1. Prepare a matrix showing the mean of each condition and the difference between pairs of means.

	$\overline{X}_1 = 3.57$	$\overline{X}_2 = 5.43$	$\overline{X}_3 = 8.00$
$\overline{X}_1 = 3.57$	—	1.86	4.43
$\overline{X}_2 = 5.43$	—	—	2.57
$\overline{X}_3 = 8.00$	—	—	—

Step 2. Referring to Table B.4 under error df = 18, $k = 3$, and $\alpha = 0.05$, we find $q_\alpha = 3.61$.

Step 3. Find HSD by multiplying $q_\alpha = 0.05$ by

$$\sqrt{\frac{s_W^2}{N}}.$$

In our present example, $s_W^2 = 5.19$, and N per condition is 7. Thus:

$$\text{HSD} = 3.61\sqrt{\frac{5.19}{7}}$$
$$= (3.61)(0.86)$$
$$= 3.10.$$

Step 4. Referring to the matrix in Step 1, we find that only one pairwise difference between means is significant. We conclude that the mean of condition X_3 is significantly greater than the mean of condition X_1.

A.6   RANDOMIZED BLOCK DESIGN

The total sum of squares (SS_T) may be partitioned into three components: the between-group sum of squares (SS_B), the blocks sum of squares (SS_{Bl}), and a residual sum of squares representing the interaction of blocks and the between-group (treatment) variable ($\text{SS}_{bl \times B}$).

		Treatment condition		
Block	X_1	X_2	X_3	Block sum
1	15	13	11	39
2	13	9	10	32
3	12	10	9	31
4	11	13	12	36
5	9	5	7	21
6	8	6	4	18
7	7	5	2	14
	$\Sigma X_1 = 75$	$\Sigma X_2 = 61$	$\Sigma X_3 = 55$	

The between-group sum of squares represents the treatment effects, the blocks sum of squares represents the blocking or matching variable, and the residual sum of squares represents random error. Given the following data in which there are three treatment conditions and twenty-one subjects formed into seven blocks, determine the significance of the treatment effects, employing $\alpha = 0.01$.

Step 1. Find ΣX for each condition. Add these together to find ΣX_T. In the present problem

$$\begin{aligned} \Sigma X_T &= \Sigma X_1 + \Sigma X_2 + \Sigma X_3 \\ &= 75 + 61 + 55 \\ &= 191. \end{aligned}$$

Step 2. Square ΣX_T and divide by N. With the present data,

$$\frac{(\Sigma X_T)^2}{N} = \frac{(191)^2}{21} = 1737.19.$$

Step 3. Square each score in each condition and sum to obtain ΣX^2 for each group. Add these together to obtain ΣX_T^2. In the present problem,

$$\begin{aligned} \Sigma X_T^2 &= \Sigma X_1^2 + \Sigma X_2^2 + \Sigma X_3^2 \\ &= 853 + 605 + 515 \\ &= 1973. \end{aligned}$$

Step 4. Find the total sum of squares by subtracting the value found in Step 2 from the sum found in Step 3:

$$\begin{aligned} SS_T &= \Sigma X_T^2 - \frac{(\Sigma X_T)^2}{N} \\ &= 1973 - 1737.19 \\ &= 235.81. \end{aligned}$$

Step 5. Find the total number of degrees of freedom:

$$\begin{aligned} df_T &= N - 1 \\ &= 21 - 1 \\ &= 20. \end{aligned}$$

Step 6. Find the between-group sum of squares by squaring each ΣX, dividing by the N in the condition, and summing. Subtract the value found in Step 2 from this sum. Since the N's are equal, there will be less rounding error if we put all the quantities to be squared over the least common denominator (7):

$$\begin{aligned} SS_B &= \frac{(75)^2 + (61)^2 + (55)^2}{7} - 1737.19 \\ &= 1767.29 - 1737.19 \\ &= 30.10. \end{aligned}$$

Step 7. Find $\mathrm{df}_B = k - 1$. In the present problem, the number of groups or treatment conditions (k) is 3. Thus $\mathrm{df}_B = 3 - 1 = 2$.

Step 8. Find the blocks sum of squares. This can be found by summing the scores in each block, squaring, dividing by the N in each block, and summing the squared values. Then

$$\frac{(\Sigma X_T)^2}{N}$$

is subtracted from this quantity:

$$SS_{Bl} = \frac{(\Sigma X_{Bl_1})^2}{N_{Bl_1}} + \frac{(\Sigma X_{Bl_2})^2}{N_{Bl_2}} + \ldots + \frac{\Sigma X_{Bl_k}}{N_{Bl_k}} - \frac{(\Sigma X_T)^2}{N},$$

in which ΣX_{Bl_k} is the sum of the last block and N_{Bl_k} is the N in this block.

However, since the N's are equal, it's preferable to employ the following raw score formula:

$$SS_{Bl} = \frac{(\Sigma X_{Bl_1})^2 + (\Sigma X_{Bl_2})^2 + \ldots + (\Sigma X_{Bl_k})^2}{N_{Bl}} - \frac{(\Sigma X_T)^2}{N},$$

in which N_{Bl} is the N in any block.

In the present problem,

$$SS_{Bl} = \frac{(39)^2 + (32)^2 + (31)^2 + (36)^2 + (18)^2 + (14)^2}{3}$$

$$- 1737.19$$

$$= \frac{5763}{3} - 1737.19$$

$$= 1921 - 1737.19$$

$$= 183.81.$$

Step 9. Find the number of degrees of freedom for blocks $\mathrm{df}_{Bl} = Bl - 1$, in which Bl is the number of blocks. In the present problem,

$$\mathrm{df} = Bl - 1$$
$$= 7 - 1$$
$$= 6.$$

Step 10. Find the residual (block $\times$ treatments interaction) sum of squares by subtraction:

$$SS_{Bl \times B} = SS_T - SS_B + SS_{Bl}$$
$$= 235.81 - (30.10 + 183.81)$$
$$= 21.90.$$

Step 11. Find the number of degrees of freedom for the residual term:

$$df_{Bl \times B} = (Bl - 1)(B - 1)$$
$$= (6)(2)$$
$$= 12.$$

Step 12. Prepare a summary table for representing the relevant statistics in a randomized block design:

Source of Variation	Sum of Squares	Degrees of Freedom	Variance Estimate	F
Between groups	30.10	2	15.05	
Between blocks	183.81	6	—	
Residual (error)	21.90	12	1.82	
Total	235.81	20		

Step 13. Check to ascertain that

$$SS_T = SS_B + SS_{Bl} + SS_{Bl \times B}$$

and

$$df_T = df_B + df_{Bl} + df_{Bl \times B}.$$

Step 14. Find the between-group variance estimate by dividing the between-group sum of squares by df_B. In the present problem

$$s_B^2 = \frac{30.10}{2} = 15.05.$$

Place in the summary table shown in Step 12.

Step 15. Find the residual variance (error) estimate by dividing the blocks × between-groups sum of squares by $df_{Bl \times B}$:

$$s_{Bl \times B}^2 = \frac{21.90}{12} = 1.82.$$

Place in the summary table shown in Step 12.

Step 16. Find the F-ratio by the following:

$$F = \frac{s_B^2}{s_{Bl \times B}^2} = \frac{15.05}{1.82}$$
$$= 8.27, \quad df\ 2/12.$$

Step 17. Look up $F = 8.27$ in Table B.3, under 2 and 12 df. If $F = 8.27$ equals or exceeds the tabled value at $\alpha = 0.01$ (boldface type), we reject H_0 and assert that the samples were not drawn from a common population of means. Since $F = 8.27 > 6.93$, we reject H_0. Apparently the experimental conditions have produced an effect. (Note: Since the overall F-ratio is statistically significant, you should use the Tukey HSD test (Section A.5) to evaluate pairwise differences among means. The residual variance estimate, $s^2_{Bl \times B}$, replaces s^2_e in the formula for HSD.)

A.7 FACTORIAL DESIGN

A.7.1 Partitioning the Sum of Squares

In this section, we shall look at the analysis of a 3×3 factorial design. However, the analysis may be readily generalized to any number of levels or subclasses of each of the two variables.

In a two-way analysis of variance, the total sum of squares is partitioned into two broad components—within-group sum of squares and treatment combinations sum of squares:

$$SS_T = SS_W + SS_{TC}.$$

The treatment combinations sum of squares is itself partitioned into three components—sum of squares for the A variable (SS_A), sum of squares for the B variable (SS_B), and sum of squares for the interaction of the A and B variables ($SS_{A \times B}$):

$$SS_{TC} = SS_A + SS_B + SS_{A \times B}.$$

When divided by the appropriate number of degrees of freedom, each of the treatment effects provides an independent estimate of the population variances:

$$\text{est } \sigma^2_A = \frac{SS_A}{df_A}, \quad df_A = A - 1,$$

in which A is the number of levels of A;

$$\text{est } \sigma^2_B = \frac{SS_B}{df_B}, \quad df_B = B - 1,$$

in which B is the number of levels of B;

$$\text{est } \sigma^2_{A \times B} = \frac{SS_{A \times B}}{df_{A \times B}}, \quad df_{A \times B} = df_A \times df_B.$$

When divided by the appropriate degrees of freedom, the within-group sum of squares provides an independent estimate of the population variance:

$$\text{est } \sigma^2_W(\text{error}) = \frac{SS_W}{df_N}, \quad df_N = N - TC,$$

in which TC is the number of treatment combinations.

A.7.2   A Worked Example Using a 3 × 3 Factorial Design

Determine if there is a significant effect of the A variable, the B variable, or an interaction between the two variables. Use $\alpha = 0.01$.

	A_1			A_2			A_3		
	B_1	B_2	B_3	B_1	B_2	B_3	B_1	B_2	B_3
	2	3	6	1	2	5	4	5	6
	4	5	7	3	5	8	5	8	10
	5	8	9	6	7	6	3	7	12
	7	11	12	7	9	11	7	9	11
Treatment	A_1B_1	A_1B_2	A_1B_3	A_2B_1	A_2B_2	A_2B_3	A_3B_1	A_3B_2	A_3B_3
Combination Σ	18	27	34	17	23	30	19	29	39
					$\Sigma X_T = 236$				

Step 1. Find SS_T. Square each score, sum all of the squared values, and subtract $(\Sigma X_T)^2/N$:

$$SS_T = \Sigma X_T^2 - \frac{(\Sigma X_T)^2}{N}.$$

In the present example,

$$SS_T = 2^2 + 4^2 + 5^2 + \ldots + 11^2 - \frac{(236)^2}{36}$$
$$= 1842 - 1547.11$$
$$= 294.89.$$

Step 2. Find df_T:

$$df_T = N - 1$$
$$= 36 - 1$$
$$= 35.$$

Step 3. Find the sum of squares for the treatment combinations. In the present problem,

$$SS_{TC} = \frac{(\Sigma A_1B_1)^2}{N_{A_1B_1}} + \frac{(\Sigma A_1B_2)^2}{N_{A_1B_2}} + \ldots + \frac{(\Sigma A_3B_3)^2}{N_{A_3B_3}} - \frac{(\Sigma X_T)^2}{N}$$
$$= \frac{(18)^2}{4} + \frac{(27)^2}{4} + \ldots + \frac{(39)^2}{4} - 1547.11.$$

Since N is the same for each treatment combination, there will be less rounding error if the squares of the treatment combination are summed and then divided by the n in each group:

$$SS_{TC} = \frac{(\Sigma A_1 B_1)^2 + (\Sigma A_1 B_2)^2 \ldots + (\Sigma A_3 B_3)^2}{N_{TC}} - \frac{(\Sigma X_T)^2}{N}$$

$$= \frac{(18)^2 + (27)^2 + (34)^2 + (17)^2 + (23)^2 + (30)^2 + (19)^2 + (29)^2 + (39)^2}{4}$$

$$- 1547.11$$

$$= \frac{6650}{4} - 1547.11$$

$$= 1662.50 - 1547.11$$

$$= 115.39.$$

Step 4. Find the number of degrees of freedom for the treatment combinations sum of squares:

$$df_{TC} = TC - 1,$$

in which TC is the number of treatment combinations. In the present example,

$$df_{TC} = 9 - 1 = 8.$$

Step 5. Begin the partitioning of the treatment combinations sum of squares by finding the sum of squares for the A variable. Since N is the same for each A condition, there will be less rounding error if the squares of each level of A are summed and then divided by the N in each A condition:

$$SS_A = \frac{(\Sigma X_{A_1})^2 + (\Sigma X_{A_2})^2 + (\Sigma X_{A_3})^2}{N_A} - \frac{(\Sigma X_T)^2}{N}$$

$$= \frac{(70)^2 + (70)^2 + (87)^2}{N_A} - 1547.11$$

$$= \frac{18710}{12} - 1547.11$$

$$= 1559.17 - 1547.11$$

$$= 12.06.$$

Step 6. Find the number of degrees of freedom for the A condition:

$$df_A = A - 1,$$

in which A is the number of levels of A. In the present example,

$$df_A = 3 - 1$$
$$= 2.$$

Step 7. Find the sum of squares of the B variable.

$$B = \frac{(\Sigma X_{B_1})^2}{N_{B_1}} + \frac{(\Sigma X_{B_2})^2}{N_{B_2}} + \frac{(\Sigma X_{B_3})^2}{N_{B_3}} + \frac{(\Sigma X_T)^2}{N}$$

$$= \frac{(54)^2}{12} + \frac{(79)^2}{12} + \frac{(103)^2}{12} - 1547.11.$$

Since N is the same for each B condition, there will be less rounding error if the squares of each level of B are summed and then divided by the N in each condition:

$$= \frac{(54)^2 + (79)^2 + (103)^2}{12} - 1547.11$$

$$= \frac{19{,}766}{12} - 1547.11$$

$$= 1647.17 - 1547.11$$

$$= 100.06.$$

Step 8. Find the number of degrees of freedom for the B condition:

$$\mathrm{df}_B = B - 1,$$

in which B is the number of levels of B. In the present example,

$$\mathrm{df}_B = 3 - 1$$
$$= 2.$$

Step 9. Find the interaction sum of squares by subtraction:

$$\mathrm{SS}_{A \times B} = \mathrm{SS}_{TC} - (\mathrm{SS}_A + \mathrm{SS}_B)$$
$$= 115.39 - (12.06 + 100.06)$$
$$= 3.27.$$

Step 10. Find the number of degrees of freedom for the interaction sum of squares:

$$\mathrm{df}_{A \times B} = (A - 1)(B - 1)$$
$$= (2)(2)$$
$$= 4.$$

Step 11. Find the within-group sum of squares. The within-group sum of squares may be obtained by subtraction:

$$\mathrm{SS}_W = \mathrm{SS}_T - \mathrm{SS}_{TC},$$
$$= 294.89 - 115.39$$
$$= 179.5.$$

Step 12. Find the within-group degrees of freedom:

$$df_W = N - TC$$
$$= 36 - 9$$
$$= 27.$$

Step 13. Prepare a summary table.

Source of Variation		Sum of Squares	Degrees of Freedom	Variance Estimate	F
Treatment Combinations		115.39	8		
A variable	12.06		2	6.03	0.91
B variable	100.06		2	50.03	7.52
$A \times B$	3.27		4	0.82	0.12
				6.65	
Within-group (error)		179.50	27		
Total		294.89	35		

Step 14. Check to ascertain that

$$SS_{TC} + SS_W = SS_T$$

and

$$SS_A + SS_B + SS_{A \times B} = SS_{TC}.$$

Step 15. Find the $A \times B$ interaction variance estimate by dividing the interaction sum of squares by $df_{A \times B}$:

$$s^2_{A \times B} = \frac{SS_{A \times B}}{df_{A \times B}}$$

$$= \frac{3.27}{4}$$

$$= 0.82.$$

Step 16. Find the B variable variance estimate by dividing the B variable sum of squares by df_B:

$$s^2_B = \frac{SS_B}{df_B}$$

$$= \frac{100.06}{2}$$

$$= 50.03.$$

Step 17. Find the A variable variance estimate by dividing the A variable sum of squares by df_A:

$$s_A^2 = \frac{SS_A}{df_A}$$
$$= \frac{12.06}{2}$$
$$= 6.03.$$

Step 18. Find the within-group variance estimate (error) by dividing the within-group sum of squares by df_W:

$$s_W^2 = \frac{SS_W}{df_W}$$
$$= \frac{179.50}{27}$$
$$= 6.65.$$

Step 19. Find the interaction F-ratio by dividing the interaction estimated variance by the within-group estimated variance:

$$F = \frac{s_{A \times B}^2}{s_W^2}$$
$$= \frac{0.82}{6.65} = 0.12, \ df = 4/27.$$

Step 20. Consult Table B.3 under 4 and 27 df to find the critical value of F required to reject H_0 at the $\alpha = 0.01$ level. Since $F_{0.01} \geq 4.11$, we fail to reject H_0.

Step 21. Find the B variable F-ratio by dividing the estimated B variance by the within-group estimated variance:

$$F = \frac{s_B^2}{s_W^2}$$
$$= \frac{50.03}{6.65}$$
$$= 7.52, \ df = 2/27.$$

Step 22. Consult Table B.3 under 2 and 27 df to find the critical value of F required to reject H_0 at the $\alpha = 0.01$ level. Since $F_{0.01} \geq 5.49$, the obtained ratio of 7.52 is in the critical region for rejecting H_0. There is a significant effect of the B variable.

Step 23. Find the A variable F-ratio by dividing the estimated A variance by the within-group estimated variance:

$$F = \frac{s_A^2}{s_W^2}$$

$$= \frac{6.03}{6.65}$$

$$= 0.91, \text{ df} = 2/27.$$

Step 24. Consult Table B.3 under 2 and 27 df to find the critical value required to reject H_0 at the $\alpha = 0.01$ level. Since $F_{0.01} \geq 5.49$, the obtained F of 0.91 is not within the critical region. We fail to reject H_0.

Conclusion   Of the three effects evaluated—A variable, B variable, and the interaction of A and B—only the B variable was found to be statistically significant. It is now appropriate to employ Tukey's HSD test in order to test pairwise differences among the B means.

NORMAL PROBABILITY

The use of Table B.1 requires that the raw score be transformed into a z-score and that the variable be normally distributed.

The values in Table B.1 represent the proportion of area in the standard normal curve, which has a mean of 0, a standard deviation of 1.00, and a total area also equal to 1.00.

Since the normal curve is symmetrical, it is sufficient to indicate only the areas corresponding to positive z-values. Negative z-values will have precisely the same proportions of area as their positive counterparts.

Column B represents the proportion of area between the mean and a given z. Column C represents the proportion of area beyond a given z.

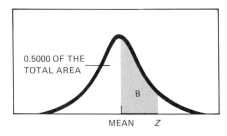

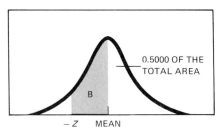

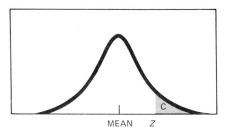

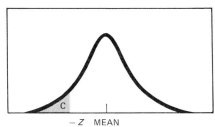

Table B.1
Proportions of area under the normal curve.

(A) z	(B) area between mean and z	(C) area beyond z	(A) z	(B) area between mean and z	(C) area beyond z	(A) z	(B) area between mean and z	(C) area beyond z
0.00	.0000	.5000	0.55	.2088	.2912	1.10	.3643	.1357
0.01	.0040	.4960	0.56	.2123	.2877	1.11	.3665	.1335
0.02	.0080	.4920	0.57	.2157	.2843	1.12	.3686	.1314
0.03	.0120	.4880	0.58	.2190	.2810	1.13	.3708	.1292
0.04	.0160	.4840	0.59	.2224	.2776	1.14	.3729	.1271
0.05	.0199	.4801	0.60	.2257	.2743	1.15	.3749	.1251
0.06	.0239	.4761	0.61	.2291	.2709	1.16	.3770	.1230
0.07	.0279	.4721	0.62	.2324	.2676	1.17	.3790	.1210
0.08	.0319	.4681	0.63	.2357	.2643	1.18	.3810	.1190
0.09	.0359	.4641	0.64	.2389	.2611	1.19	.3830	.1170
0.10	.0398	.4602	0.65	.2422	.2578	1.20	.3849	.1151
0.11	.0438	.4562	0.66	.2454	.2546	1.21	.3869	.1131
0.12	.0478	.4522	0.67	.2486	.2514	1.22	.3888	.1112
0.13	.0517	.4483	0.68	.2517	.2483	1.23	.3907	.1093
0.14	.0557	.4443	0.69	.2549	.2451	1.24	.3925	.1075
0.15	.0596	.4404	0.70	.2580	.2420	1.25	.3944	.1056
0.16	.0636	.4364	0.71	.2611	.2389	1.26	.3962	.1038
0.17	.0675	.4325	0.72	.2642	.2358	1.27	.3980	.1020
0.18	.0714	.4286	0.73	.2673	.2327	1.28	.3997	.1003
0.19	.0753	.4247	0.74	.2704	.2296	1.29	.4015	.0985
0.20	.0793	.4207	0.75	.2734	.2266	1.30	.4032	.0968
0.21	.0832	.4168	0.76	.2764	.2236	1.31	.4049	.0951
0.22	.0871	.4129	0.77	.2794	.2206	1.32	.4066	.0934
0.23	.0910	.4090	0.78	.2823	.2177	1.33	.4082	.0918
0.24	.0948	.4052	0.79	.2852	.2148	1.34	.4099	.0901
0.25	.0987	.4013	0.80	.2881	.2119	1.35	.4115	.0885
0.26	.1026	.3974	0.81	.2910	.2090	1.36	.4131	.0869
0.27	.1064	.3936	0.82	.2939	.2061	1.37	.4147	.0853
0.28	.1103	.3897	0.83	.2967	.2033	1.38	.4162	.0838
0.29	.1141	.3859	0.84	.2995	.2005	1.39	.4177	.0823
0.30	.1179	.3821	0.85	.3023	.1977	1.40	.4192	.0808
0.31	.1217	.3783	0.86	.3051	.1949	1.41	.4207	.0793
0.32	.1255	.3745	0.87	.3078	.1922	1.42	.4222	.0778
0.33	.1293	.3707	0.88	.3106	.1894	1.43	.4236	.0764
0.34	.1331	.3669	0.89	.3133	.1867	1.44	.4251	.0749
0.35	.1368	.3632	0.90	.3159	.1841	1.45	.4265	.0735
0.36	.1406	.3594	0.91	.3186	.1814	1.46	.4279	.0721
0.37	.1443	.3557	0.92	.3212	.1788	1.47	.4292	.0708
0.38	.1480	.3520	0.93	.3238	.1762	1.48	.4306	.0694
0.39	.1517	.3483	0.94	.3264	.1736	1.49	.4319	.0681
0.40	.1554	.3446	0.95	.3289	.1711	1.50	.4332	.0668
0.41	.1591	.3409	0.96	.3315	.1685	1.51	.4345	.0655
0.42	.1628	.3372	0.97	.3340	.1660	1.52	.4357	.0643
0.43	.1664	.3336	0.98	.3365	.1635	1.53	.4370	.0630
0.44	.1700	.3300	0.99	.3389	.1611	1.54	.4382	.0618
0.45	.1736	.3264	1.00	.3413	.1587	1.55	.4394	.0606
0.46	.1772	.3228	1.01	.3438	.1562	1.56	.4406	.0594
0.47	.1808	.3192	1.02	.3461	.1539	1.57	.4418	.0582
0.48	.1844	.3156	1.03	.3485	.1515	1.58	.4429	.0571
0.49	.1879	.3121	1.04	.3508	.1492	1.59	.4441	.0559
0.50	.1915	.3085	1.05	.3531	.1469	1.60	.4452	.0548
0.51	.1950	.3050	1.06	.3554	.1446	1.61	.4463	.0537
0.52	.1985	.3015	1.07	.3577	.1423	1.62	.4474	.0526
0.53	.2019	.2981	1.08	.3599	.1401	1.63	.4484	.0516
0.54	.2054	.2946	1.09	.3621	.1379	1.64	.4495	.0505

Table B.1
(continued)

(A)	(B)	(C)	(A)	(B)	(C)	(A)	(B)	(C)
z	area between mean and z	area beyond z	z	area between mean and z	area beyond z	z	area between mean and z	area beyond z
1.65	.4505	.0495	2.22	.4868	.0132	2.79	.4974	.0026
1.66	.4515	.0485	2.23	.4871	.0129	2.80	.4974	.0026
1.67	.4525	.0475	2.24	.4875	.0125	2.81	.4975	.0025
1.68	.4535	.0465	2.25	.4878	.0122	2.82	.4976	.0024
1.69	.4545	.0455	2.26	.4881	.0119	2.83	.4977	.0023
1.70	.4554	.0446	2.27	.4884	.0116	2.84	.4977	.0023
1.71	.4564	.0436	2.28	.4887	.0113	2.85	.4978	.0022
1.72	.4573	.0427	2.29	.4890	.0110	2.86	.4979	.0021
1.73	.4582	.0418	2.30	.4893	.0107	2.87	.4979	.0021
1.74	.4591	.0409	2.31	.4896	.0104	2.88	.4980	.0020
1.75	.4599	.0401	2.32	.4898	.0102	2.89	.4981	.0019
1.76	.4608	.0392	2.33	.4901	.0099	2.90	.4981	.0019
1.77	.4616	.0384	2.34	.4904	.0096	2.91	.4982	.0018
1.78	.4625	.0375	2.35	.4906	.0094	2.92	.4982	.0018
1.79	.4633	.0367	2.36	.4909	.0091	2.93	.4983	.0017
1.80	.4641	.0359	2.37	.4911	.0089	2.94	.4984	.0016
1.81	.4649	.0351	2.38	.4913	.0087	2.95	.4984	.0016
1.82	.4656	.0344	2.39	.4916	.0084	2.96	.4985	.0015
1.83	.4664	.0336	2.40	.4918	.0082	2.97	.4985	.0015
1.84	.4671	.0329	2.41	.4920	.0080	2.98	.4986	.0014
1.85	.4678	.0322	2.42	.4922	.0078	2.99	.4986	.0014
1.86	.4686	.0314	2.43	.4925	.0075	3.00	.4987	.0013
1.87	.4693	.0307	2.44	.4927	.0073	3.01	.4987	.0013
1.88	.4699	.0301	2.45	.4929	.0071	3.02	.4987	.0013
1.89	.4706	.0294	2.46	.4931	.0069	3.03	.4988	.0012
1.90	.4713	.0287	2.47	.4932	.0068	3.04	.4988	.0012
1.91	.4719	.0281	2.48	.4934	.0066	3.05	.4989	.0011
1.92	.4726	.0274	2.49	.4936	.0064	3.06	.4989	.0011
1.93	.4732	.0268	2.50	.4938	.0062	3.07	.4989	.0011
1.94	.4738	.0262	2.51	.4940	.0060	3.08	.4990	.0010
1.95	.4744	.0256	2.52	.4941	.0059	3.09	.4990	.0010
1.96	.4750	.0250	2.53	.4943	.0057	3.10	.4990	.0010
1.97	.4756	.0244	2.54	.4945	.0055	3.11	.4991	.0009
1.98	.4761	.0239	2.55	.4946	.0054	3.12	.4991	.0009
1.99	.4767	.0233	2.56	.4948	.0052	3.13	.4991	.0009
2.00	.4772	.0228	2.57	.4949	.0051	3.14	.4992	.0008
2.01	.4778	.0222	2.58	.4951	.0049	3.15	.4992	.0008
2.02	.4783	.0217	2.59	.4952	.0048	3.16	.4992	.0008
2.03	.4788	.0212	2.60	.4953	.0047	3.17	.4992	.0008
2.04	.4793	.0207	2.61	.4955	.0045	3.18	.4993	.0007
2.05	.4798	.0202	2.62	.4956	.0044	3.19	.4993	.0007
2.06	.4803	.0197	2.63	.4957	.0043	3.20	.4993	.0007
2.07	.4808	.0192	2.64	.4959	.0041	3.21	.4993	.0007
2.08	.4812	.0188	2.65	.4960	.0040	3.22	.4994	.0006
2.09	.4817	.0183	2.66	.4961	.0039	3.23	.4994	.0006
2.10	.4821	.0179	2.67	.4962	.0038	3.24	.4994	.0006
2.11	.4826	.0174	2.68	.4963	.0037	3.25	.4994	.0006
2.12	.4830	.0170	2.69	.4964	.0036	3.30	.4995	.0005
2.13	.4834	.0166	2.70	.4965	.0035	3.35	.4996	.0004
2.14	.4838	.0162	2.71	.4966	.0034	3.40	.4997	.0003
2.15	.4842	.0158	2.72	.4967	.0033	3.45	.4997	.0003
2.16	.4846	.0154	2.73	.4968	.0032	3.50	.4998	.0002
2.17	.4850	.0150	2.74	.4969	.0031	3.60	.4998	.0002
2.18	.4854	.0146	2.75	.4970	.0030	3.70	.4999	.0001
2.19	.4857	.0143	2.76	.4971	.0029	3.80	.4999	.0001
2.20	.4861	.0139	2.77	.4972	.0028	3.90	.49995	.00005
2.21	.4864	.0136	2.78	.4973	.0027	4.00	.49997	.00003

STUDENT *t*-RATIO

Table B.2

Critical values of *t*. For any given df, the table shows the values of *t* corresponding to various levels of probability. Obtained *t* is significant at a given level if it is equal to or *greater than* the value shown in the table.

df	Level of significance for one-tailed test					
	.10	.05	.025	.01	.005	.0005
	Level of significance for two-tailed test					
	.20	.10	.05	.02	.01	.001
1	3.078	6.314	12.706	31.821	63.657	636.619
2	1.886	2.920	4.303	6.965	9.925	31.598
3	1.638	2.353	3.182	4.541	5.841	12.941
4	1.533	2.132	2.776	3.747	4.604	8.610
5	1.476	2.015	2.571	3.365	4.032	6.859
6	1.440	1.943	2.447	3.143	3.707	5.959
7	1.415	1.895	2.365	2.998	3.499	5.405
8	1.397	1.860	2.306	2.896	3.355	5.041
9	1.383	1.833	2.262	2.821	3.250	4.781
10	1.372	1.812	2.228	2.764	3.169	4.587
11	1.363	1.796	2.201	2.718	3.106	4.437
12	1.356	1.782	2.179	2.681	3.055	4.318
13	1.350	1.771	2.160	2.650	3.012	4.221
14	1.345	1.761	2.145	2.624	2.977	4.140
15	1.341	1.753	2.131	2.602	2.947	4.073
16	1.337	1.746	2.120	2.583	2.921	4.015
17	1.333	1.740	2.110	2.567	2.898	3.965
18	1.330	1.734	2.101	2.552	2.878	3.922
19	1.328	1.729	2.093	2.539	2.861	3.883
20	1.325	1.725	2.086	2.528	2.845	3.850
21	1.323	1.721	2.080	2.518	2.831	3.819
22	1.321	1.717	2.074	2.508	2.819	3.792
23	1.319	1.714	2.069	2.500	2.807	3.767
24	1.318	1.711	2.064	2.492	2.797	3.745
25	1.316	1.708	2.060	2.485	2.787	3.725
26	1.315	1.706	2.056	2.479	2.779	3.707
27	1.314	1.703	2.052	2.473	2.771	3.690
28	1.313	1.701	2.048	2.467	2.763	3.674
29	1.311	1.699	2.045	2.462	2.756	3.659
30	1.310	1.697	2.042	2.457	2.750	3.646
40	1.303	1.684	2.021	2.423	2.704	3.551
60	1.296	1.671	2.000	2.390	2.660	3.460
120	1.289	1.658	1.980	2.358	2.617	3.373
∞	1.282	1.645	1.960	2.326	2.576	3.291

Table B.2 is taken from Table III (page 46) of Fisher and Yates: *Statistical Tables for Biological, Agricultural and Medical Research*, published by Longman Group Ltd., London (previously published by Oliver and Boyd, Edinburgh), and by permission of the authors and publishers.

TABLE OF F

Table B.3

Critical values of F. The obtained F is significant at a given level if it is equal to or *greater than* the value shown in the table 0.05 (light row) and 0.01 (dark row) points for the distribution of F. The values shown are the right tail of the distribution obtained by dividing the larger variance estimate by the smaller variance estimate. To find the complementary left or lower tail for a given df and α level, reverse the degrees of freedom and find the reciprocal of that value in the F-table. For example, the value cutting off the top 5% of the area for df 7 and 12 is 2.85. To find the cutoff point of the bottom 5% of the area, find the tabled value at the $\alpha = 0.05$ level for 12 and 7 df. This is found to be 3.57. The reciprocal is $1/3.57 = 0.28$. Thus 5% of the area falls *at or below* an $F = 0.28$.

Degrees of freedom for numerator

denom df	1	2	3	4	5	6	7	8	9	10	11	12	14	16	20	24	30	40	50	75	100	200	500	∞
1	161 / 4052	200 / 4999	216 / 5403	225 / 5625	230 / 5764	234 / 5859	237 / 5928	239 / 5981	241 / 6022	242 / 6056	243 / 6082	244 / 6106	245 / 6142	246 / 6169	248 / 6208	249 / 6234	250 / 6258	251 / 6286	252 / 6302	253 / 6323	253 / 6334	254 / 6352	254 / 6361	254 / 6366
2	18.51 / 98.49	19.00 / 99.01	19.16 / 99.17	19.25 / 99.25	19.30 / 99.30	19.33 / 99.33	19.36 / 99.34	19.37 / 99.36	19.38 / 99.38	19.39 / 99.40	19.40 / 99.41	19.41 / 99.42	19.42 / 99.43	19.43 / 99.44	19.44 / 99.45	19.45 / 99.46	19.46 / 99.47	19.47 / 99.48	19.47 / 99.48	19.48 / 99.49	19.49 / 99.49	19.49 / 99.49	19.50 / 99.50	19.50 / 99.50
3	10.13 / 34.12	9.55 / 30.81	9.28 / 29.46	9.12 / 28.71	9.01 / 28.24	8.94 / 27.91	8.88 / 27.67	8.84 / 27.49	8.81 / 27.34	8.78 / 27.23	8.76 / 27.13	8.74 / 27.05	8.71 / 26.92	8.69 / 26.83	8.66 / 26.69	8.64 / 26.60	8.62 / 26.50	8.60 / 26.41	8.58 / 26.30	8.57 / 26.27	8.56 / 26.23	8.54 / 26.18	8.54 / 26.14	8.53 / 26.12
4	7.71 / 21.20	6.94 / 18.00	6.59 / 16.69	6.39 / 15.98	6.26 / 15.52	6.16 / 15.21	6.09 / 14.98	6.04 / 14.80	6.00 / 14.66	5.96 / 14.54	5.93 / 14.45	5.91 / 14.37	5.87 / 14.24	5.84 / 14.15	5.80 / 14.02	5.77 / 13.93	5.74 / 13.83	5.71 / 13.74	5.70 / 13.69	5.68 / 13.61	5.66 / 13.57	5.65 / 13.52	5.64 / 13.48	5.63 / 13.46
5	6.61 / 16.26	5.79 / 13.27	5.41 / 12.06	5.19 / 11.39	5.05 / 10.97	4.95 / 10.67	4.88 / 10.45	4.82 / 10.27	4.78 / 10.15	4.74 / 10.05	4.70 / 9.96	4.68 / 9.89	4.64 / 9.77	4.60 / 9.68	4.56 / 9.55	4.53 / 9.47	4.50 / 9.38	4.46 / 9.29	4.44 / 9.24	4.42 / 9.17	4.40 / 9.13	4.38 / 9.07	4.37 / 9.04	4.36 / 9.02
6	5.99 / 13.74	5.14 / 10.92	4.76 / 9.78	4.53 / 9.15	4.39 / 8.75	4.28 / 8.47	4.21 / 8.26	4.15 / 8.10	4.10 / 7.98	4.06 / 7.87	4.03 / 7.79	4.00 / 7.72	3.96 / 7.60	3.92 / 7.52	3.87 / 7.39	3.84 / 7.31	3.81 / 7.23	3.77 / 7.14	3.75 / 7.09	3.72 / 7.02	3.71 / 6.99	3.69 / 6.94	3.68 / 6.90	3.67 / 6.88
7	5.59 / 12.25	4.74 / 9.55	4.35 / 8.45	4.12 / 7.85	3.97 / 7.46	3.87 / 7.19	3.79 / 7.00	3.73 / 6.84	3.68 / 6.71	3.63 / 6.62	3.60 / 6.54	3.57 / 6.47	3.52 / 6.35	3.49 / 6.27	3.44 / 6.15	3.41 / 6.07	3.38 / 5.98	3.34 / 5.90	3.32 / 5.85	3.29 / 5.78	3.28 / 5.75	3.25 / 5.70	3.24 / 5.67	3.23 / 5.65
8	5.32 / 11.26	4.46 / 8.65	4.07 / 7.59	3.84 / 7.01	3.69 / 6.63	3.58 / 6.37	3.50 / 6.19	3.44 / 6.03	3.39 / 5.91	3.34 / 5.82	3.31 / 5.74	3.28 / 5.67	3.23 / 5.56	3.20 / 5.48	3.15 / 5.36	3.12 / 5.28	3.08 / 5.20	3.05 / 5.11	3.03 / 5.06	3.00 / 5.00	2.98 / 4.96	2.96 / 4.91	2.94 / 4.88	2.93 / 4.86
9	5.12 / 10.56	4.26 / 8.02	3.86 / 6.99	3.63 / 6.42	3.48 / 6.06	3.37 / 5.80	3.29 / 5.62	3.23 / 5.47	3.18 / 5.35	3.13 / 5.26	3.10 / 5.18	3.07 / 5.11	3.02 / 5.00	2.98 / 4.92	2.93 / 4.80	2.90 / 4.73	2.86 / 4.64	2.82 / 4.56	2.80 / 4.51	2.77 / 4.45	2.76 / 4.41	2.73 / 4.36	2.72 / 4.33	2.71 / 4.31
10	4.96 / 10.04	4.10 / 7.56	3.71 / 6.55	3.48 / 5.99	3.33 / 5.64	3.22 / 5.39	3.14 / 5.21	3.07 / 5.06	3.02 / 4.95	2.97 / 4.85	2.94 / 4.78	2.91 / 4.71	2.86 / 4.60	2.82 / 4.52	2.77 / 4.41	2.74 / 4.33	2.70 / 4.25	2.67 / 4.17	2.64 / 4.12	2.61 / 4.05	2.59 / 4.01	2.56 / 3.96	2.55 / 3.93	2.54 / 3.91
11	4.84 / 9.65	3.98 / 7.20	3.59 / 6.22	3.36 / 5.67	3.20 / 5.32	3.09 / 5.07	3.01 / 4.88	2.95 / 4.74	2.90 / 4.63	2.86 / 4.54	2.82 / 4.46	2.79 / 4.40	2.74 / 4.29	2.70 / 4.21	2.65 / 4.10	2.61 / 4.02	2.57 / 3.94	2.53 / 3.86	2.50 / 3.80	2.47 / 3.74	2.45 / 3.70	2.42 / 3.66	2.41 / 3.62	2.40 / 3.60
12	4.75 / 9.33	3.88 / 6.93	3.49 / 5.95	3.26 / 5.41	3.11 / 5.06	3.00 / 4.82	2.92 / 4.65	2.85 / 4.50	2.80 / 4.39	2.76 / 4.30	2.72 / 4.22	2.69 / 4.16	2.64 / 4.05	2.60 / 3.98	2.54 / 3.86	2.50 / 3.78	2.46 / 3.70	2.42 / 3.61	2.40 / 3.56	2.36 / 3.49	2.35 / 3.46	2.32 / 3.41	2.31 / 3.38	2.30 / 3.36

Degrees of freedom for denominator

G. W. Snedecor and William G. Cochran, *Statistical Methods*, 7th ed. (Ames, Iowa: Iowa State University Press © 1980).

Table B.3 (continued)

Degrees of freedom for denominator																								
13	4.67	3.80	3.41	3.18	3.02	2.92	2.84	2.77	2.72	2.67	2.63	2.60	2.55	2.51	2.46	2.42	2.38	2.34	2.32	2.28	2.26	2.24	2.22	2.21
	9.07	6.70	5.74	5.20	4.86	4.62	4.44	4.30	4.19	4.10	4.02	3.96	3.85	3.78	3.67	3.59	3.51	3.42	3.37	3.30	3.27	3.21	3.18	3.16
14	4.60	3.74	3.34	3.11	2.96	2.85	2.77	2.70	2.65	2.60	2.56	2.53	2.48	2.44	2.39	2.35	2.31	2.27	2.24	2.21	2.19	2.16	2.14	2.13
	8.86	6.51	5.56	5.03	4.69	4.46	4.28	4.14	4.03	3.94	3.86	3.80	3.70	3.62	3.51	3.43	3.34	3.26	3.21	3.14	3.11	3.06	3.02	3.00
15	4.54	3.68	3.29	3.06	2.90	2.79	2.70	2.64	2.59	2.55	2.51	2.48	2.43	2.39	2.33	2.29	2.25	2.21	2.18	2.15	2.12	2.10	2.08	2.07
	8.68	6.36	5.42	4.89	4.56	4.32	4.14	4.00	3.89	3.80	3.73	3.67	3.56	3.48	3.36	3.29	3.20	3.12	3.07	3.00	2.97	2.92	2.89	2.87
16	4.49	3.63	3.24	3.01	2.85	2.74	2.66	2.59	2.54	2.49	2.45	2.42	2.37	2.33	2.28	2.24	2.20	2.16	2.13	2.09	2.07	2.04	2.02	2.01
	8.53	6.23	5.29	4.77	4.44	4.20	4.03	3.89	3.78	3.69	3.61	3.55	3.45	3.37	3.25	3.18	3.10	3.01	2.96	2.89	2.86	2.80	2.77	2.75
17	4.45	3.59	3.20	2.96	2.81	2.70	2.62	2.55	2.50	2.45	2.41	2.38	2.33	2.29	2.23	2.19	2.15	2.11	2.08	2.04	2.02	1.99	1.97	1.96
	8.40	6.11	5.18	4.67	4.34	4.10	3.93	3.79	3.68	3.59	3.52	3.45	3.35	3.27	3.16	3.08	3.00	2.92	2.86	2.79	2.76	2.70	2.67	2.65
18	4.41	3.55	3.16	2.93	2.77	2.66	2.58	2.51	2.46	2.41	2.37	2.34	2.29	2.25	2.19	2.15	2.11	2.07	2.04	2.00	1.98	1.95	1.93	1.92
	8.28	6.01	5.09	4.58	4.25	4.01	3.85	3.71	3.60	3.51	3.44	3.37	3.27	3.19	3.07	3.00	2.91	2.83	2.78	2.71	2.68	2.62	2.59	2.57
19	4.38	3.52	3.13	2.90	2.74	2.63	2.55	2.48	2.43	2.38	2.34	2.31	2.26	2.21	2.15	2.11	2.07	2.02	2.00	1.96	1.94	1.91	1.90	1.88
	8.18	5.93	5.01	4.50	4.17	3.94	3.77	3.63	3.52	3.43	3.36	3.30	3.19	3.12	3.00	2.92	2.84	2.76	2.70	2.63	2.60	2.54	2.51	2.49
20	4.35	3.49	3.10	2.87	2.71	2.60	2.52	2.45	2.40	2.35	2.31	2.28	2.23	2.18	2.12	2.08	2.04	1.99	1.96	1.92	1.90	1.87	1.85	1.84
	8.10	5.85	4.94	4.43	4.10	3.87	3.71	3.56	3.45	3.37	3.30	3.23	3.13	3.05	2.94	2.86	2.77	2.69	2.63	2.56	2.53	2.47	2.44	2.42
21	4.32	3.47	3.07	2.84	2.68	2.57	2.49	2.42	2.37	2.32	2.28	2.25	2.20	2.15	2.09	2.05	2.00	1.96	1.93	1.80	1.87	1.84	1.82	1.81
	8.02	5.78	4.87	4.37	4.04	3.81	3.65	3.51	3.40	3.31	3.24	3.17	3.07	2.99	2.88	2.80	2.72	2.63	2.58	2.51	2.47	2.42	2.38	2.36
22	4.30	3.44	3.05	2.82	2.66	2.55	2.47	2.40	2.35	2.30	2.26	2.23	2.18	2.13	2.07	2.03	1.98	1.93	1.91	1.87	1.84	1.81	1.80	1.78
	7.94	5.72	4.82	4.31	3.99	3.76	3.59	3.45	3.35	3.26	3.18	3.12	3.02	2.94	2.83	2.75	2.67	2.58	2.53	2.46	2.42	2.37	2.33	2.31
23	4.28	3.42	3.03	2.80	2.64	2.53	2.45	2.38	2.32	2.28	2.24	2.20	2.14	2.10	2.04	2.00	1.96	1.91	1.88	1.84	1.82	1.79	1.77	1.76
	7.88	5.66	4.76	4.26	3.94	3.71	3.54	3.41	3.30	3.21	3.14	3.07	2.97	2.89	2.78	2.70	2.62	2.53	2.48	2.41	2.37	2.32	2.28	2.26
24	4.26	3.40	3.01	2.78	2.62	2.51	2.43	2.36	2.30	2.26	2.22	2.18	2.13	2.09	2.02	1.98	1.94	1.89	1.86	1.82	1.80	1.76	1.74	1.73
	7.82	5.61	4.72	4.22	3.90	3.67	3.50	3.36	3.25	3.17	3.09	3.03	2.93	2.85	2.74	2.66	2.58	2.49	2.44	2.36	2.33	2.27	2.23	2.21
25	4.24	3.38	2.99	2.76	2.60	2.49	2.41	2.34	2.28	2.24	2.20	2.16	2.11	2.06	2.00	1.96	1.92	1.87	1.84	1.80	1.77	1.74	1.72	1.71
	7.77	5.57	4.68	4.18	3.86	3.63	3.46	3.32	3.21	3.13	3.05	2.99	2.89	2.81	2.70	2.62	2.54	2.45	2.40	2.32	2.29	2.23	2.19	2.17
26	4.22	3.37	2.89	2.74	2.59	2.47	2.39	2.32	2.27	2.22	2.18	2.15	2.10	2.05	1.99	1.95	1.90	1.85	1.82	1.78	1.76	1.72	1.70	1.69
	7.72	5.53	4.64	4.14	3.82	3.59	3.42	3.29	3.17	3.09	3.02	2.96	2.86	2.77	2.66	2.58	2.50	2.41	2.36	2.28	2.25	2.19	2.15	2.13
27	4.21	3.35	2.96	2.73	2.57	2.46	2.37	2.30	2.25	2.20	2.16	2.13	2.08	2.03	1.97	1.93	1.88	1.84	1.80	1.76	1.74	1.71	1.68	1.67
	7.68	5.49	4.60	4.11	3.79	3.56	3.39	3.26	3.14	3.06	2.98	2.93	2.83	2.74	2.63	2.55	2.47	2.38	2.33	2.25	2.21	2.16	2.12	2.10

Table B.3
(continued)

Degrees of freedom for numerator

df	1	2	3	4	5	6	7	8	9	10	11	12	14	16	20	24	30	40	50	75	100	200	500	∞
28	4.20	3.34	2.95	2.71	2.56	2.44	2.36	2.29	2.24	2.19	2.15	2.12	2.06	2.02	1.96	1.91	1.87	1.81	1.78	1.75	1.72	1.69	1.67	1.65
	7.64	5.45	4.57	4.07	3.76	3.53	3.36	3.23	3.11	3.03	2.95	2.90	2.80	2.71	2.60	2.52	2.44	2.35	2.30	2.22	2.18	2.13	2.09	2.06
29	4.18	3.33	2.93	2.70	2.54	2.43	2.35	2.28	2.22	2.18	2.14	2.10	2.05	2.00	1.94	1.90	1.85	1.80	1.77	1.73	1.71	1.68	1.65	1.64
	7.60	5.52	4.54	4.04	3.73	3.50	3.33	3.20	3.08	3.00	2.92	2.87	2.77	2.68	2.57	2.49	2.41	2.32	2.27	2.19	2.15	2.10	2.06	2.03
30	4.17	3.32	2.92	2.69	2.53	2.42	2.34	2.27	2.21	2.16	2.12	2.09	2.04	1.99	1.93	1.89	1.84	1.79	1.76	1.72	1.69	1.66	1.64	1.62
	7.56	5.39	4.51	4.02	3.70	3.47	3.30	3.17	3.06	2.98	2.90	2.84	2.74	2.66	2.55	2.47	2.38	2.29	2.24	2.16	2.13	2.07	2.03	2.01
32	4.15	3.30	2.90	2.67	2.51	2.40	2.32	2.25	2.19	2.14	2.10	2.07	2.02	1.97	1.91	1.86	1.82	1.76	1.74	1.69	1.67	1.64	1.61	1.59
	7.50	5.34	4.46	3.97	3.66	3.42	3.25	3.12	3.01	2.94	2.86	2.80	2.70	2.62	2.51	2.42	2.34	2.25	2.20	2.12	2.08	2.02	1.98	1.96
34	4.13	3.28	2.88	2.65	2.49	2.38	2.30	2.23	2.17	2.12	2.08	2.05	2.00	1.95	1.89	1.84	1.80	1.74	1.71	1.67	1.64	1.61	1.59	1.57
	7.44	5.29	4.42	3.93	3.61	3.38	3.21	3.08	2.97	2.89	2.82	2.76	2.66	2.58	2.47	2.38	2.30	2.21	2.15	2.08	2.04	1.98	1.94	1.91
36	4.11	3.26	2.86	2.63	2.48	2.36	2.28	2.21	2.15	2.10	2.06	2.03	1.98	1.93	1.87	1.82	1.78	1.72	1.69	1.65	1.62	1.59	1.56	1.55
	7.39	5.25	4.38	3.89	3.58	3.35	3.18	3.04	2.94	2.86	2.78	2.72	2.62	2.54	2.43	2.35	2.26	2.17	2.12	2.04	2.00	1.94	1.90	1.87
38	4.10	3.25	2.85	2.62	2.46	2.35	2.26	2.19	2.14	2.09	2.05	2.02	1.96	1.92	1.85	1.80	1.76	1.71	1.67	1.63	1.60	1.57	1.54	1.53
	7.35	5.21	4.34	3.86	3.54	3.32	3.15	3.02	2.91	2.82	2.75	2.69	2.59	2.51	2.40	2.32	2.22	2.14	2.08	2.00	1.97	1.90	1.86	1.84
40	4.08	3.23	2.84	2.61	2.45	2.34	2.25	2.18	2.14	2.07	2.04	2.00	1.95	1.90	1.84	1.79	1.74	1.69	1.66	1.61	1.59	1.55	1.53	1.51
	7.31	5.18	4.31	3.83	3.51	3.29	3.12	2.99	2.88	2.80	2.73	2.66	2.56	2.49	2.37	2.29	2.20	2.11	2.05	1.97	1.94	1.88	1.84	1.81
42	4.07	3.22	2.83	2.59	2.44	2.32	2.24	2.17	2.11	2.06	2.02	1.99	1.94	1.89	1.82	1.78	1.73	1.68	1.64	1.60	1.57	1.54	1.51	1.49
	7.27	5.15	4.29	3.80	3.49	3.26	3.10	2.96	2.86	2.77	2.70	2.64	2.54	2.46	2.35	2.26	2.17	2.08	2.02	1.94	1.91	1.85	1.80	1.78
44	4.06	3.21	2.82	2.58	2.43	2.31	2.23	2.16	2.10	2.05	2.01	1.98	1.92	1.88	1.81	1.76	1.72	1.66	1.63	1.58	1.56	1.52	1.50	1.48
	7.24	5.12	4.26	3.78	3.46	3.24	3.07	2.94	2.84	2.75	2.68	2.62	2.52	2.44	2.32	2.24	2.15	2.06	2.00	1.92	1.88	1.82	1.78	1.75
46	4.05	3.20	2.81	2.57	2.42	2.30	2.22	2.14	2.09	2.04	2.00	1.97	1.91	1.87	1.80	1.75	1.71	1.65	1.62	1.57	1.54	1.51	1.48	1.46
	7.21	5.10	4.24	3.76	3.44	3.22	3.05	2.92	2.82	2.73	2.66	2.60	2.50	2.42	2.30	2.22	2.13	2.04	1.98	1.90	1.86	1.80	1.76	1.72
48	4.04	3.19	2.80	2.56	2.41	2.30	2.21	2.14	2.08	2.03	1.99	1.96	1.90	1.86	1.79	1.74	1.70	1.64	1.61	1.56	1.53	1.50	1.47	1.45
	7.19	5.08	4.22	3.74	3.42	3.20	3.04	2.90	2.80	2.71	2.64	2.58	2.48	2.40	2.28	2.20	2.11	2.02	1.96	1.88	1.84	1.78	1.73	1.70
50	4.03	3.18	2.79	2.56	2.40	2.29	2.20	2.13	2.07	2.02	1.98	1.95	1.90	1.85	1.78	1.74	1.69	1.63	1.60	1.55	1.52	1.48	1.46	1.44
	7.17	5.06	4.20	3.72	3.41	3.18	3.02	2.88	2.78	2.70	2.62	2.56	2.46	2.39	2.26	2.18	2.10	2.00	1.94	1.86	1.82	1.76	1.71	1.68
55	4.02	3.17	2.78	2.54	2.38	2.27	2.18	2.11	2.05	2.00	1.97	1.93	1.88	1.83	1.76	1.72	1.67	1.61	1.58	1.52	1.50	1.46	1.43	1.41
	7.12	5.01	4.16	3.68	3.37	3.15	2.98	2.85	2.75	2.66	2.59	2.53	2.43	2.35	2.23	2.15	2.06	1.96	1.90	1.82	1.78	1.71	1.66	1.64
60	4.00	3.15	2.76	2.52	2.37	2.25	2.17	2.10	2.04	1.99	1.95	1.92	1.86	1.81	1.75	1.70	1.65	1.59	1.56	1.50	1.48	1.44	1.41	1.39
	7.08	4.98	4.13	3.65	3.34	3.12	2.95	2.82	2.72	2.63	2.56	2.50	2.40	2.32	2.20	2.12	2.03	1.93	1.87	1.79	1.74	1.68	1.63	1.60
65	3.99	3.14	2.75	2.51	2.36	2.24	2.15	2.08	2.02	1.98	1.94	1.90	1.85	1.80	1.73	1.68	1.63	1.57	1.54	1.49	1.46	1.42	1.39	1.37
	7.04	4.95	4.10	3.62	3.31	3.09	2.93	2.79	2.70	2.61	2.54	2.47	2.37	2.30	2.18	2.09	2.00	1.90	1.84	1.76	1.71	1.64	1.60	1.56

Degrees of freedom for denominator

Table B.3
(continued)

Degrees of freedom for numerator

Degrees of freedom for denominator	1	2	3	4	5	6	7	8	9	10	11	12	14	16	20	24	30	40	50	75	100	200	500	∞
70	3.98 / 7.01	3.13 / 4.92	2.74 / 4.08	2.50 / 3.60	2.35 / 3.29	2.32 / 3.07	2.14 / 2.91	2.07 / 2.77	2.01 / 2.67	1.97 / 2.59	1.93 / 2.51	1.89 / 2.45	1.84 / 2.35	1.79 / 2.28	1.72 / 2.15	1.67 / 2.07	1.62 / 1.98	1.56 / 1.88	1.53 / 1.82	1.47 / 1.74	1.45 / 1.69	1.40 / 1.62	1.37 / 1.56	1.35 / 1.53
80	3.96 / 6.96	3.11 / 4.88	2.72 / 4.04	2.48 / 3.56	2.33 / 3.25	2.21 / 3.04	2.12 / 2.87	2.05 / 2.74	1.99 / 2.64	1.95 / 2.55	1.91 / 2.48	1.88 / 2.41	1.82 / 2.32	1.77 / 2.24	1.70 / 2.11	1.65 / 2.03	1.60 / 1.94	1.54 / 1.84	1.51 / 1.78	1.45 / 1.70	1.42 / 1.65	1.38 / 1.57	1.35 / 1.52	1.32 / 1.49
100	3.94 / 6.90	3.09 / 4.82	2.70 / 3.98	2.46 / 3.51	2.30 / 3.20	2.19 / 2.99	2.10 / 2.82	2.03 / 2.69	1.97 / 2.59	1.92 / 2.51	1.88 / 2.43	1.85 / 2.36	1.79 / 2.26	1.75 / 2.19	1.68 / 2.06	1.63 / 1.98	1.57 / 1.89	1.51 / 1.79	1.48 / 1.73	1.42 / 1.64	1.39 / 1.59	1.34 / 1.51	1.30 / 1.46	1.28 / 1.43
125	3.92 / 6.84	3.07 / 4.78	2.68 / 3.94	2.44 / 3.47	2.29 / 3.17	2.17 / 2.95	2.08 / 2.79	2.01 / 2.65	1.95 / 2.56	1.90 / 2.47	1.86 / 2.40	1.83 / 2.33	1.77 / 2.23	1.72 / 2.15	1.65 / 2.03	1.60 / 1.94	1.55 / 1.85	1.49 / 1.75	1.45 / 1.68	1.39 / 1.59	1.36 / 1.54	1.31 / 1.46	1.27 / 1.40	1.25 / 1.37
150	3.91 / 6.81	3.06 / 4.75	2.67 / 3.91	2.43 / 3.44	2.27 / 3.13	2.16 / 2.92	2.07 / 2.76	2.00 / 2.62	1.94 / 2.53	1.89 / 2.44	1.85 / 2.37	1.82 / 2.30	1.76 / 2.20	1.71 / 2.12	1.64 / 2.00	1.59 / 1.91	1.54 / 1.83	1.47 / 1.72	1.44 / 1.66	1.37 / 1.56	1.34 / 1.51	1.29 / 1.43	1.25 / 1.37	1.22 / 1.33
200	3.89 / 6.76	3.04 / 4.71	2.65 / 3.88	2.41 / 3.41	2.26 / 3.11	2.14 / 2.90	2.05 / 2.73	1.98 / 2.60	1.92 / 2.50	1.87 / 2.41	1.83 / 2.34	1.80 / 2.28	1.74 / 2.17	1.69 / 2.09	1.62 / 1.97	1.57 / 1.88	1.52 / 1.79	1.45 / 1.69	1.42 / 1.62	1.35 / 1.53	1.32 / 1.48	1.26 / 1.39	1.22 / 1.33	1.19 / 1.28
400	3.86 / 6.70	3.02 / 4.66	2.62 / 3.83	2.39 / 3.36	2.23 / 3.06	2.12 / 2.85	2.03 / 2.69	1.96 / 2.55	1.90 / 2.46	1.85 / 2.37	1.81 / 2.29	1.78 / 2.23	1.72 / 2.12	1.67 / 2.04	1.60 / 1.92	1.54 / 1.84	1.49 / 1.74	1.42 / 1.64	1.38 / 1.57	1.32 / 1.47	1.28 / 1.42	1.22 / 1.32	1.16 / 1.24	1.13 / 1.19
1000	3.85 / 6.66	3.00 / 4.62	2.61 / 3.80	2.38 / 3.34	2.22 / 3.04	2.10 / 2.82	2.02 / 2.66	1.95 / 2.53	1.89 / 2.43	1.84 / 2.34	1.80 / 2.26	1.76 / 2.20	1.70 / 2.09	1.65 / 2.01	1.58 / 1.89	1.53 / 1.81	1.47 / 1.71	1.41 / 1.61	1.36 / 1.54	1.30 / 1.44	1.26 / 1.38	1.19 / 1.28	1.13 / 1.19	1.08 / 1.11
∞	3.84 / 6.64	2.99 / 4.60	2.60 / 3.78	2.37 / 3.32	2.21 / 3.02	2.09 / 2.80	2.01 / 2.64	1.94 / 2.51	1.88 / 2.41	1.83 / 2.32	1.79 / 2.24	1.75 / 2.18	1.69 / 2.07	1.64 / 1.99	1.57 / 1.87	1.52 / 1.79	1.46 / 1.69	1.40 / 1.59	1.35 / 1.52	1.28 / 1.41	1.24 / 1.36	1.17 / 1.25	1.11 / 1.15	1.00 / 1.00

TUKEY HSD

Table B.4
Percentage points of the Studentized range.

Error df	α	\multicolumn{10}{c}{k = number of means or number of steps between ordered means}									
		2	3	4	5	6	7	8	9	10	11
5	.05	3.64	4.60	5.22	5.67	6.03	6.33	6.58	6.80	6.99	7.17
	.01	5.70	6.98	7.80	8.42	8.91	9.32	9.67	9.97	10.24	10.48
6	.05	3.46	4.34	4.90	5.30	5.63	5.90	6.12	6.32	6.49	6.65
	.01	5.24	6.33	7.03	7.56	7.97	8.32	8.61	8.87	9.10	9.30
7	.05	3.34	4.16	4.68	5.06	5.36	5.61	5.82	6.00	6.16	6.30
	.01	4.95	5.92	6.54	7.01	7.37	7.68	7.94	8.17	8.37	8.55
8	.05	3.26	4.04	4.53	4.89	5.17	5.40	5.60	5.77	5.92	6.05
	.01	4.75	5.64	6.20	6.62	6.96	7.24	7.47	7.68	7.86	8.03
9	.05	3.20	3.95	4.41	4.76	5.02	5.24	5.43	5.59	5.74	5.87
	.01	4.60	5.43	5.96	6.35	6.66	6.91	7.13	7.33	7.49	7.65
10	.05	3.15	3.88	4.33	4.65	4.91	5.12	5.30	5.46	5.60	5.72
	.01	4.48	5.27	5.77	6.14	6.43	6.67	6.87	7.05	7.21	7.36
11	.05	3.11	3.82	4.26	4.57	4.82	5.03	5.20	5.35	5.49	5.61
	.01	4.39	5.15	5.62	5.97	6.25	6.48	6.67	6.84	6.99	7.13
12	.05	3.08	3.77	4.20	4.51	4.75	4.95	5.12	5.27	5.39	5.51
	.01	4.32	5.05	5.50	5.84	6.10	6.32	6.51	6.67	6.81	6.94
13	.05	3.06	3.73	4.15	4.45	4.69	4.88	5.05	5.19	5.32	5.43
	.01	4.26	4.96	5.40	5.73	5.98	6.19	6.37	6.53	6.67	6.79
14	.05	3.03	3.70	4.11	4.41	4.64	4.83	4.99	5.13	5.25	5.36
	.01	4.21	4.89	5.32	5.63	5.88	6.08	6.26	6.41	6.54	6.66
15	.05	3.01	3.67	4.08	4.37	4.59	4.78	4.94	5.08	5.20	5.31
	.01	4.17	4.84	5.25	5.56	5.80	5.99	6.16	6.31	6.44	6.55
16	.05	3.00	3.65	4.05	4.33	4.56	4.74	4.90	5.03	5.15	5.26
	.01	4.13	4.79	5.19	5.49	5.72	5.92	6.08	6.22	6.35	6.46
17	.05	2.98	3.63	4.02	4.30	4.52	4.70	4.86	4.99	5.11	5.21
	.01	4.10	4.74	5.14	5.43	5.66	5.85	6.01	6.15	6.27	6.38
18	.05	2.97	3.61	4.00	4.28	4.49	4.67	4.82	4.96	5.07	5.17
	.01	4.07	4.70	5.09	5.38	5.60	5.79	5.94	6.08	6.20	6.31
19	.05	2.96	3.59	3.98	4.25	4.47	4.65	4.79	4.92	5.04	5.14
	.01	4.05	4.67	5.05	5.33	5.55	5.73	5.89	6.02	6.14	6.25
20	.05	2.95	3.58	3.96	4.23	4.45	4.62	4.77	4.90	5.01	5.11
	.01	4.02	4.64	5.02	5.29	5.51	5.69	5.84	5.97	6.09	6.19
24	.05	2.92	3.53	3.90	4.17	4.37	4.54	4.68	4.81	4.92	5.01
	.01	3.96	4.55	4.91	5.17	5.37	5.54	5.69	5.81	5.92	6.02
30	.05	2.89	3.49	3.85	4.10	4.30	4.46	4.60	4.72	4.82	4.92
	.01	3.89	4.45	4.80	5.05	5.24	5.40	5.54	5.65	5.76	5.85
40	.05	2.86	3.44	3.79	4.04	4.23	4.39	4.52	4.63	4.73	4.82
	.01	3.82	4.37	4.70	4.93	5.11	5.26	5.39	5.50	5.60	5.69
60	.05	2.83	3.40	3.74	3.98	4.16	4.31	4.44	4.55	4.65	4.73
	.01	3.76	4.28	4.59	4.82	4.99	5.13	5.25	5.36	5.45	5.53
120	.05	2.80	3.36	3.68	3.92	4.10	4.24	4.36	4.47	4.56	4.64
	.01	3.70	4.20	4.50	4.71	4.87	5.01	5.12	5.21	5.30	5.37
∞	.05	2.77	3.31	3.63	3.86	4.03	4.17	4.29	4.39	4.47	4.55
	.01	3.64	4.12	4.40	4.60	4.76	4.88	4.99	5.08	5.16	5.23

RANDOM DIGITS

Table B.5
Random digits

Row number										
00000	10097	32533	76520	13586	34673	54876	80959	09117	39292	74945
00001	37542	04805	64894	74296	24805	24037	20636	10402	00822	91665
00002	08422	68953	19645	09303	23209	02560	15953	34764	35080	33606
00003	99019	02529	09376	70715	38311	31165	88676	74397	04436	27659
00004	12807	99970	80157	36147	64032	36653	98951	16877	12171	76833
00005	66065	74717	34072	76850	36697	36170	65813	39885	11199	29170
00006	31060	10805	45571	82406	35303	42614	86799	07439	23403	09732
00007	85269	77602	02051	65692	68665	74818	73053	85247	18623	88579
00008	63573	32135	05325	47048	90553	57548	28468	28709	83491	25624
00009	73796	45753	03529	64778	35808	34282	60935	20344	35273	88435
00010	98520	17767	14905	68607	22109	40558	60970	93433	50500	73998
00011	11805	05431	39808	27732	50725	68248	29405	24201	52775	67851
00012	83452	99634	06288	98033	13746	70078	18475	40610	68711	77817
00013	88685	40200	86507	58401	36766	67951	90364	76493	29609	11062
00014	99594	67348	87517	64969	91826	08928	93785	61368	23478	34113
00015	65481	17674	17468	50950	58047	76974	73039	57186	40218	16544
00016	80124	35635	17777	08015	45318	22374	21115	78253	14385	53763
00017	74350	99817	77402	77214	43236	00210	45521	64237	96286	02655
00018	69916	26803	66252	29148	36936	87203	76621	13990	94400	56418
00019	09893	20505	14225	68514	46427	56788	96297	78822	54382	14598
00020	91499	14523	68479	27686	46162	83554	94750	89923	37089	20048
00021	80336	94598	26940	36858	70297	34135	53140	33340	42050	82341
00022	44104	81949	85157	47954	32979	26575	57600	40881	22222	06413
00023	12550	73742	11100	02040	12860	74697	96644	89439	28707	25815
00024	63606	49329	16505	34484	40219	52563	43651	77082	07207	31790
00025	61196	90446	26457	47774	51924	33729	65394	59593	42582	60527
00026	15474	45266	95270	79953	59367	83848	82396	10118	33211	59466
00027	94557	28573	67897	54387	54622	44431	91190	42592	92927	45973
00028	42481	16213	97344	08721	16868	48767	03071	12059	25701	46670
00029	23523	78317	73208	89837	68935	91416	26252	29663	05522	82562
00030	04493	52494	75246	33824	45862	51025	61962	79335	65337	12472
00031	00549	97654	64051	88159	96119	63896	54692	82391	23287	29529
00032	35963	15307	26898	09354	33351	35462	77974	50024	90103	39333
00033	59808	08391	45427	26842	83609	49700	13021	24892	78565	20106
00034	46058	85236	01390	92286	77281	44077	93910	83647	70617	42941
00035	32179	00597	87379	25241	05567	07007	86743	17157	85394	11838
00036	69234	61406	20117	45204	15956	60000	18743	92423	97118	96338
00037	19565	41430	01758	75379	40419	21585	66674	36806	84962	85207
00038	45155	14938	19476	07246	43667	94543	59047	90033	20826	69541
00039	94864	31994	36168	10851	34888	81553	01540	35456	05014	51176
00040	98086	24826	45240	28404	44999	08896	39094	73407	35441	31880
00041	33185	16232	41941	50949	89435	48581	88695	41994	37548	73043
00042	80951	00406	96382	70774	20151	23387	25016	25298	94624	61171
00043	79752	49140	71961	28296	69861	02591	74852	20539	00387	59579
00044	18633	32537	98145	06571	31010	24674	05455	61427	77938	91936
00045	74029	43902	77557	32270	97790	17119	52527	58021	80814	51748
00046	54178	45611	80993	37143	05335	12969	56127	19255	36040	90324
00047	11664	49883	52079	84827	59381	71539	09973	33440	88461	23356
00048	48324	77928	31249	64710	02295	36870	32307	57546	15020	09994
00049	69074	94138	87637	91976	35584	04401	10518	21615	01848	76938

Table B.5
(continued)

Row number										
00050	09188	20097	32825	39527	04220	86304	83389	87374	64278	58044
00051	90045	85497	51981	50654	94938	81997	91870	76150	68476	64659
00052	73189	50207	47677	26269	62290	64464	27124	67018	41361	82760
00053	75768	76490	20971	87749	90429	12272	95375	05871	93823	43178
00054	54016	44056	66281	31003	00682	27398	20714	53295	07706	17813
00055	08358	69910	78542	42785	13661	58873	04618	97553	31223	08420
00056	28306	03264	81333	10591	40510	07893	32604	60475	94119	01840
00057	53840	86233	81594	13628	51215	90290	28466	68795	77762	20791
00058	91757	53741	61613	62669	50263	90212	55781	76514	83483	47055
00059	89415	92694	00397	58391	12607	17646	48949	72306	94541	37408
00060	77513	03820	86864	29901	68414	82774	51908	13980	72893	55507
00061	19502	37174	69979	20288	55210	29773	74287	75251	65344	67415
00062	21818	59313	93278	81757	05686	73156	07082	85046	31853	38452
00063	51474	66499	68107	23621	94049	91345	42836	09191	08007	45449
00064	99559	68331	62535	24170	69777	12830	74819	78142	43860	72834
00065	33713	48007	93584	72869	51926	64721	58303	29822	93174	93972
00066	85274	86893	11303	22970	28834	34137	73515	90400	71148	43643
00067	84133	89640	44035	52166	73852	70091	61222	60561	62327	18423
00068	56732	16234	17395	96131	10123	91622	85496	57560	81604	18880
00069	65138	56806	87648	85261	34313	65861	45875	21069	85644	47277
00070	38001	02176	81719	11711	71602	92937	74219	64049	65584	49698
00071	37402	96397	01304	77586	56271	10086	47324	62605	40030	37438
00072	97125	40348	87083	31417	21815	39250	75237	62047	15501	29578
00073	21826	41134	47143	34072	64638	85902	49139	06441	03856	54552
00074	73135	42742	95719	09035	85794	74296	08789	88156	64691	19202
00075	07638	77929	03061	18072	96207	44156	23821	99538	04713	66994
00076	60528	83441	07954	19814	59175	20695	05533	52139	61212	06455
00077	83596	35655	06958	92983	05128	09719	77433	53783	92301	50498
00078	10850	62746	99599	10507	13499	06319	53075	71839	06410	19362
00079	39820	98952	43622	63147	64421	80814	43800	09351	31024	73167
00080	59580	06478	75569	78800	88835	54486	23768	06156	04111	08408
00081	38508	07341	23793	48763	90822	97022	17719	04207	95954	49953
00082	30692	70668	94688	16127	56196	80091	82067	63400	05462	69200
00083	65443	95659	18238	27437	49632	24041	08337	65676	96299	90836
00084	27267	50264	13192	72294	07477	44606	17985	48911	97341	30358
00085	91307	06991	19072	24210	36699	53728	28825	35793	28976	66252
00086	68434	94688	84473	13622	62126	98408	12843	82590	09815	93146
00087	48908	15877	54745	24591	35700	04754	83824	52692	54130	55160
00088	06913	45197	42672	78601	11883	09528	63011	98901	14974	40344
00089	10455	16019	14210	33712	91342	37821	88325	80851	43667	70883
00090	12883	97343	65027	61184	04285	01392	17974	15077	90712	26769
00091	21778	30976	38807	36961	31649	42096	63281	02023	08816	47449
00092	19523	59515	65122	59659	86283	68258	69572	13798	16435	91529
00093	67245	52670	35583	16563	79246	86686	76463	34222	26655	90802
00094	60584	47377	07500	37992	45134	26529	26760	83637	41326	44344
00095	53853	41377	36066	94850	58838	73859	49364	73331	96240	43642
00096	24637	38736	74384	89342	52623	07992	12369	18601	03742	83873
00097	83080	12451	38992	22815	07759	51777	97377	27585	51972	37867
00098	16444	24334	36151	99073	27493	70939	85130	32552	54846	54759
00099	60790	18157	57178	65762	11161	78576	45819	52979	65130	04860
00100	03991	10461	93716	16894	66083	24653	84609	58232	88618	19161
00101	38555	95554	32886	59780	08355	60860	29735	47762	71299	23853
00102	17546	73704	92052	46215	55121	29281	59076	07936	27954	58909
00103	32643	52861	95819	06831	00911	98936	76355	93779	80863	00514
00104	69572	68777	39510	35905	14060	40619	29549	69616	33564	60780
00105	24122	66591	27699	06494	14845	46672	61958	77100	90899	75754
00106	61196	30231	92962	61773	41839	55382	17267	70943	78038	70267
00107	30532	21704	10274	12202	39685	23309	10061	68829	55986	66485
00108	03788	97599	75867	20717	74416	53166	35208	33374	87539	08823
00109	48228	63379	85783	47619	53152	67433	35663	52972	16818	60311

Table B.5
(continued)

Row number										
00110	60365	94653	35075	33949	42614	29297	01918	28316	98953	73231
00111	83799	42402	56623	34442	34994	41374	70071	14736	09958	18065
00112	32960	07405	36409	83232	99385	41600	11133	07586	15917	06253
00113	19322	53845	57620	52606	66497	68646	78138	66559	19640	99413
00114	11220	94747	07399	37408	48509	23929	27482	45476	85244	35159
00115	31751	57260	68980	05339	15470	48355	88651	22596	03152	19121
00116	88492	99382	14454	04504	20094	98977	74843	93413	22109	78508
00117	30934	47744	07481	83828	73788	06533	28597	20405	94205	20380
00118	22888	48893	27499	98748	60530	45128	74022	84617	82037	10268
00119	78212	16993	35902	91386	44372	15486	65741	14014	87481	37220
00120	41849	84547	46850	52326	34677	58300	74910	64345	19325	81549
00121	46352	33049	69248	93460	45305	07521	61318	31855	14413	70951
00122	11087	96294	14013	31792	59747	67277	76503	34513	39663	77544
00123	52701	08337	56303	87315	16520	69676	11654	99893	02181	68161
00124	57275	36898	81304	48535	68652	27376	92852	55866	88448	03584
00125	20857	73156	70284	24326	79375	95220	01159	63267	10622	48391
00126	15633	84924	90415	93614	33521	26665	55823	47641	86225	31704
00127	92694	48297	39904	02115	59589	49067	66821	41575	49767	04037
00128	77613	19019	88152	00080	20554	91409	96277	48257	50816	97616
00129	38688	32486	45134	63545	59404	72059	43947	51680	43852	59693
00130	25163	01889	70014	15021	41290	67312	71857	15957	68971	11403
00131	65251	07629	37239	33295	05870	01119	92784	26340	18477	65622
00132	36815	43625	18637	37509	82444	99005	04921	73701	14707	93997
00133	64397	11692	05327	82162	20247	81759	45197	25332	83745	22567
00134	04515	25624	95096	67946	48460	85558	15191	18782	16930	33361
00135	83761	60873	43253	84145	60833	25983	01291	41349	20368	07126
00136	14387	06345	80854	09279	43529	06318	38384	74761	41196	37480
00137	51321	92246	80088	77074	88722	56736	66164	49431	66919	31678
00138	72472	00008	80890	18002	94813	31900	54155	83436	35352	54131
00139	05466	55306	93128	18464	74457	90561	72848	11834	79982	68416
00140	39528	72484	82474	25593	48545	35247	18619	13674	18611	19241
00141	81616	18711	53342	44276	75122	11724	74627	73707	58319	15997
00142	07586	16120	82641	22820	92904	13141	32392	19763	61199	67940
00143	90767	04235	13574	17200	69902	63742	78464	22501	18627	90872
00144	40188	28193	29593	88627	94972	11598	62095	36787	00441	58997
00145	34414	82157	86887	55087	19152	00023	12302	80783	32624	68691
00146	63439	75363	44989	16822	36024	00867	76378	41605	65961	73488
00147	67049	09070	93399	45547	94458	74284	05041	49807	20288	34060
00148	79495	04146	52162	90286	54158	34243	46978	35482	59362	95938
00149	91704	30552	04737	21031	75051	93029	47665	64382	99782	93478
00150	94015	46874	32444	48277	59820	96163	64654	25843	41145	42820
00151	74108	88222	88570	74015	25704	91035	01755	14750	48968	38603
00152	62880	87873	95160	59221	22304	90314	72877	17334	39283	04149
00153	11748	12102	80580	41867	17710	59621	06554	07850	73950	79552
00154	17944	05600	60478	03343	25852	58905	57216	39618	49856	99326
00155	66067	42792	95043	52680	46780	56487	09971	59481	37006	22186
00156	54244	91030	45547	70818	59849	96169	61459	21647	87417	17198
00157	30945	57589	31732	57260	47670	07654	46376	25366	94746	49580
00158	69170	37403	86995	90307	94304	71803	26825	05511	12459	91314
00159	08345	88975	35841	85771	08105	59987	87112	21476	14713	71181
00160	27767	43584	85301	88977	29490	69714	73035	41207	74699	09310
00161	13025	14338	54066	15243	47724	66733	47431	43905	31048	56699
00162	80217	36292	98525	24335	24432	24896	43277	58874	11466	16082
00163	10875	62004	90391	61105	57411	06368	53856	30743	08670	84741
00164	54127	57326	26629	19087	24472	88779	30540	27886	61732	75454
00165	60311	42824	37301	42678	45990	43242	17374	52003	70707	70214
00166	49739	71484	92003	98086	76668	73209	59202	11973	02902	33250
00167	78626	51594	16453	94614	39014	97066	83012	09832	25571	77628
00168	66692	13986	99837	00582	81232	44987	09504	96412	90193	79568
00169	44071	28091	07362	97703	76447	42537	98524	97831	65704	09514

Table B.5
(concluded)

Row number										
00170	41468	85149	49554	17994	14924	39650	95294	00556	70481	06905
00171	94559	37559	49678	53119	70312	05682	66986	34099	74474	20740
00172	41615	70360	64114	58660	90850	64618	80620	51790	11436	38072
00173	50273	93113	41794	86861	24781	89683	55411	85667	77535	99892
00174	41396	80504	90670	08289	40902	05069	95083	06783	28102	57816
00175	25807	24260	71529	78920	72682	07385	90726	57166	98884	08583
00176	06170	97965	88302	98041	21443	41808	68984	83620	89747	98882
00177	60808	54444	74412	81105	01176	28838	36421	16489	18059	51061
00178	80940	44893	10408	36222	80582	71944	92638	40333	67054	16067
00179	19516	90120	46759	71643	13177	55292	21036	82808	77501	97427
00180	49386	54480	23604	23554	21785	41101	91178	10174	29420	90438
00181	06312	88940	15995	69321	47458	64809	98189	81851	29651	84215
00182	60942	00307	11897	92674	40405	68032	96717	54244	10701	41393
00183	92329	98932	78284	46347	71209	92061	39448	93136	25722	08564
00184	77936	63574	31384	51924	85561	29671	58137	17820	22751	36518
00185	38101	77756	11657	13897	95889	57067	47648	13885	70669	93406
00186	39641	69457	91339	22502	92613	89719	11947	56203	19324	20504
00187	84054	40455	99396	63680	67667	60631	69181	96845	38525	11600
00188	47468	03577	57649	63266	24700	71594	14004	23153	69249	05747
00189	43321	31370	28977	23896	76479	68562	62342	07589	08899	05985
00190	64281	61826	18555	64937	13173	33365	78851	16499	87064	13075
00191	66847	70495	32350	02985	86716	38746	26313	77463	55387	72681
00192	72461	33230	21529	53424	92581	02262	78438	66276	18396	73538
00193	21032	91050	13058	16218	12470	56500	15292	76139	59526	52113
00194	95362	67011	06651	16136	01016	00857	55018	56374	35824	71708
00195	49712	97380	10404	55452	34030	60726	75211	10271	36633	68424
00196	58275	61764	97586	54716	50259	46345	87195	46092	26787	60939
00197	89514	11788	68224	23417	73959	76145	30342	40277	11049	72049
00198	15472	50669	48139	36732	46874	37088	63465	09819	58869	35220
00199	12120	86124	51247	44302	60883	52109	21437	36786	49226	77837

WRITING STYLE

Some helpful guidelines concerning writing style are described in the *APA Publication Manual,* © 1974 by the American Psychology Association. Pages 25–28 from this manual follow below. Reprinted by permission.

WRITING STYLE

Teaching the art of writing is beyond the scope of the *Publication Manual.* Instead, this chapter provides some general guidelines on effective writing, points out frequent faults, and suggests ways to assess and improve writing style. Mastery of grammar rules is not enough for good communication; craftsmanship in the use of language is also necessary. These guidelines are not intended to be so rigid that personal style is overly constrained, nor do they suggest the same style for all audiences.

To achieve clarity, good writing must be precise in its words, free of ambiguity, orderly in its presentation of ideas, economical in expression, smooth in flow, and considerate of its readers. A successful writer invites readers to read, encourages them to continue, and makes their task agreeable by leading them from thought to thought in a manner that evolves from clear thinking and logical development. The references in section 6.3 elaborate on these ideas.

Using the Precise Word

Make certain that every word used means exactly what it is intended to mean. Any writer, sooner or later, will discover that his own use of a word may not agree entirely with the definition in a standard dictionary. Prefixes are frequent troublemakers and require careful checking. For example, *disinterested* means impartial; *uninterested* means apathetic. Qualifiers are almost always a source of imprecision. Almost always? How much of the time is almost always? Expressions such as *quite a large part, practically all, very few,* and the like are interpreted differently by different readers or in different contexts. They weaken statements, especially those dealing with empirical observations.

Fortunately, choosing the precise word or phrase is easier for technical than for nontechnical concepts, where the choice is wider. The wider the choice, the greater the difficulty in selecting the exact word. Even the literate reader may be uncertain of the meaning of a rare or unfamiliar word.

Do not use words incorrectly (when you mean *think,* do not write *feel*); avoid colloquial expressions (use *insert,* not *put in; report* not *write up*), and avoid coined terms (use *concept,* not *conceptuum*).

Avoiding Ambiguity

The referent for each term should be so apparent that the reader will not have to search over prior material. The simplest referents are the most troublesome: *which, this, that, these,* and *those.* If you include the referent every time you use *this, that, these,* and *those* (e.g., *this test* and *that trial*), you can avoid ambiguity. Avoid overuse of *this,* even with the referent. Also, make certain that the first sentence of a paragraph is comprehensible by itself; do not depend on a vague reference to earlier statements.

The editorial *we* is not used in scientific writing because it is often ambiguous. *We* means two or more authors or experimenters, including yourself. Use *I* when that is what you mean.

An awkward and often ambiguous construction results when a long string of modifiers is placed before the noun modified, especially when the modifiers are themselves nouns used as adjectives. For example, *a new performance test of motor skills used in colleges* is better than *a new motor skills performance college test.*

When writing about experimental groups, label them carefully. Using only numerals or letters can create ambiguity for the reader. Instead, whenever possible, use a key word to designate the treatment of each group. Remember that no reader is as familiar with your research as you are.

Orderly Presentation of Ideas

Thought units and sequences must be orderly. The reader expects continuity in words, concepts, and thematic development from opening statement to final conclusion, and is troubled by an author who misplaces words in sentences, abandons familiar syntax, shifts the criterion for items in a series, or clutters the sequence of ideas with irrelevancies. Reread the manuscript for coherence some time after the original writing and remove any barriers to an even progression.

Punctuation marks contribute to continuity by providing transitions between ideas. They cue the reader to the pauses, inflections, and pacing normally heard in speech, although punctuaton differs in speech and writing. Some writers tend to overuse commas; other are too frugal with them. Overuse may annoy the reader; underuse can confuse him. Use punctuation to support meaning.

Although transitional words are sometimes used as a crutch, they can aid the reader attempting to follow a complex experimental design or an abstract theoretical development. Some transitional words are frequently misused. *While* does not mean *whereas* or *although; due to* and *since* do not mean *because.*

Economy of Expression

Short words are easier to comprehend than long words. However, the experienced writer will know when a long technical term should be selected for precision or when one long unusual word expresses an idea better than several short ones. The space necessary to express an idea lies somewhere between the terseness of telegraphic style and the circumlocution, excessive qualification, and verbiage of artificial scientific style. Authors in science are more often guilty of the latter than the former. Wordiness, redundancy, evasiveness, and clumsiness characterize unprofessional writing.

By the same token, writing only in short, simple sentences produces choppy prose; but writing exclusively in long, involved sentences creates difficult if not unreadable material. Varying sentence length gives writing relief and interest. When involved concepts require long sentences, the components should march along like a parade, not dodge about like a broken-field runner.

The same cautions apply to paragraph length. Some writers construct paragraphs that are too long. On the other hand, many authorities on writing warn against short single-sentence paragraphs. Long material that does not break easily into paragraphs may need reorganization for clarity and logic. Even if reorganization is not necessary, consider breaking long paragraphs for visual relief.

Smoothness of Expression

Some linguistic situations can distract the reader: contradictions (real or inferred), insertion of the unexpected, omission of the expected, and sudden shifts. An author can usually catch real contradictions by reading a paper once for this fault alone. Inferred contradictions are more likely to surface if someone else reads the manuscript.

Do not introduce a topic abruptly. If the reader is likely to ask "How does that fit in?" more transition is necessary. This fault is common in literature reviews by graduate students, but it is not unknown among their mentors. Similarly, do not abandon an argument or development of a theme suddenly. If a reader feels "left hanging," the discussion needs a concluding statement.

Sudden shifts in tense should be avoided. Do not move capriciously between past and present tense within the same paragraph or successive paragraphs. Past tense is usually appropriate for a literature review *(Smith reported)* or the experimental design or procedure *(the judges were told),* inasmuch as it is a historical account. Use present tense to describe and discuss the results that are literally there before the reader *(shows auditory stimuli are more effective).* The present tense suggests a dialogue between author and reader, appropriate at that point of the paper. Future tense is rarely needed.

Obviously, verbs must agree with their subjects, and pronouns with the nouns to which they refer. This simple rule is usually not troublesome except with plural words of Latin or Greek origin that end in *a. Data, criteria,* and *phenomena* are plural, the high frequency of misuse notwithstanding. Check use of collective nouns; be certain that *faculty* or *staff,* for example, really refers to the collective group when using the singular verb or pronoun.

Frequently an author uses synonyms or near-synonyms to avoid repetition of a term. Although this intention is laudatory, the result may seriously detract from the flow of the paper. Learn to use a thesaurus, but with constraint. When a synonym is used, the reader cannot know if you intend to convey the *same* meaning as the first term or if a subtle difference in meaning is your intent. If monotony occurs, it may be from repeating ideas as well as words.

Consideration of the Reader

In scientific writing, devices that attract attention to words, sounds, or other embellishments, instead of ideas, are inappropriate. Heavy alliteration, accidental rhymes, poetic expressions, and clichés are suspect. They are unsuitable in scientific writing because they lead the reader, who is looking for information, away from the theme of the paper. Metaphors are sometimes helpful, but use them sparingly. Avoid mixed metaphors: Literal and figurative usages mix badly, to the detriment of communication; for example, "During the interview, the client sat with her head in her hands and her eyes on the floor."

Absolute insistence on the third person and the passive voice has been a strong tradition in scientific writing. Authorities on style and readability have clearly shown that this practice results in the deadliness of pomposity they call "scientificese." Some scientists maintain that this style preserves objectivity, but the validity of this assertion is suspect. Now, reputable journals are breaking the tradition with notable success, and writing manuals are recommending a more personal style. The *American National Standard for the Preparation of Scientific Papers* (1972) gives the following guideline:

> *Authors should not always use verbs in the third person, passive voice. When a verb concerns the interaction of inanimate objects ("the membrane is acted upon by the drug"), the active voice is usually preferable ("the drug acts on the membrane") because it is more direct and concise.*

> *When a verb concerns an author's belief or conjecture, use of the imper-sonal passive ("it is thought" or "it is suggested") is highly inappropri-ate. When a verb concerns action by the author, he should use the first person, especially in matters of experimental design ("to eliminate this possibility, I did the following experiment"). Constant use of the first person is not advisable, however, since it may distract the reader from the subject of the paper. (p. 13)*

An experienced writer can use the first person and the active voice without dominating the communication and without sacrificing the objectivity of the research. If any discipline should appreciate the value of personal communication, it should be psychology.

Finally, as a matter of consideration to readers, writers should be aware of the current move to avoid generic use of male nouns and pronouns when content refers to both sexes, and may wish to use alternatives to words such as *chairman* and to avoid overuse of the pronoun *he* when *she* or *they* is equally appropriate.

Criticism, Assistance, and Improvement

For many able researchers, writing is a difficult and irksome task, but writing, after all, is the expression of thinking. It is better to seek advice from others before submitting a manuscript than to hope that the editor will overlook faults. Choose a critic from outside your specialized research area. A spouse or close friend is usually not a good critic; enemies are better. If they do a good job, they may become friends. If material does not read well to an intelligent person who knows little of your area, it is probably presented poorly. Psychologists who communicate with only the dozen or so experts in their narrow specialties are not contributing significantly to the literature.

GUIDELINES FOR NONSEXIST LANGUAGE

The *Publication Manual* of the American Psychological Association (1974, p.28) suggest that journal authors "be aware of the current move to avoid generic use of male nouns and pronouns when content refers to both sexes . . . (and) avoid overuse of the pronoun *he* when *she* or *they* is equally appropriate." The first change sheet to the *Publication Manual* (1975, p.2) says: "For some specific suggestions on how to avoid such language, see Guidelines for Nonsexist Use of Language, which was prepared by the APA Task Force on Issues of Sexual Bias in Graduate Education and published in the June 1975 *American Psychologist* (pp.682–684)." Those guidelines, while helpful, are not specific to journal articles.

This second change sheet states the policy on sexist language in APA journals, offers some general principles for journal authors to consider, and suggests some ways to avoid sexist language.

To obtain single copies of this change sheet, send a stamped, self-addressed envelope to Publication Manual, Change Sheet 2, American Psychological Association, 1200 Seventeenth Street, N.W., Washington, D.C. 20036.

POLICY STATEMENT

APA as a publisher accepts journal authors' word choices unless those choices are inaccurate, unclear, or ungrammatical. However, because APA as an organization is committed to both science and the fair treatment of individuals and groups, authors of journal articles are expected to avoid writing in a manner that reinforces questionable attitudes and assumptions about people and sex roles.

Language that reinforces sexism can spring from subtle errors in research design, inaccurate interpretation, or imprecise word choices. Faulty logic in design, for example, may lead an investigator to report sex differences when the stimulus materials and materials and measures used give one sex an unwarranted advantage over the other. Or, in interpretation, an investigator may make unwarranted generalizations about all people from data about one sex. Imprecise word choices, which occur frequently in journal writing, may be interpreted as biased, discriminatory, or demeaning even if they are not intended to be.

Advice on research design and interpretation is beyond the scope of the APA *Publication Manual*. However, in the spirit of the guidelines on writing style in Chapter 2, the following guidelines on nonsexist language are intended to help authors recognize and change instances where word choices may be inaccurate, misleading, or discriminatory.

GUIDELINES

Sexism in journal writing may be classified into two categories that are conceptually different: problems of *designation* and problems of *evaluation.*

Problems of Designation

An author must use care in choosing words to ensure accuracy, clarity, and freedom from bias. In the case of sexism, long-established cultural practice can exert a powerful insidious influence over even the most conscientious author. Nouns, pronouns, and adjectives that designate persons can be chosen to eliminate, or at least to minimize, the possibility of ambiguity in sex identity or sex role. In the following examples, problems of designation are divided into two subcategories: *ambiguity of referent,* where it is unclear whether the author means one or both sexes, and *stereotyping,* where the writing conveys unsupported or biased connotations about sex roles and identity.

Problems of Evaluation

By definition, scientific writing should be free of implied or irrelevant evaluation of the sexes. Difficulties may derive from the habitual use of clichés, or familiar expressions, such as "man and wife." The use of "man and wife" together implies differences in the freedom and activities of each, and evaluation of roles can occur. Thus, *husband and wife* are parallel, *man and wife* are not. In the examples that follow, problems of evaluation, like problems of designation, are divided into *ambiguity of referent* and *stereotyping.*

I. PROBLEMS OF DESIGNATION

Examples of common usage	Consider meaning. An alternative may be better	Comment
A. Ambiguity of Referent		
1. The client is usually the best judge of the value of *his* counseling.	The *client* is usually the best judge of the value of counseling.	*His* deleted.
	Clients are usually the best judges of the value of the counseling they receive.	Change to plural.
	The best judge of the value of counseling is usually *the client.*	Rephrased.
2. *Man's search* for knowledge has led *him* into ways of learning that bear examination.	*The search* for knowledge has led us into ways of learning that bear examination.	Rephrased, using first person.
	People have continually sought knowledge. The search has led them, etc. . . .	Rewritten in two sentences.
3. Man, mankind	people, humanity, human beings, humankind, human species	In this group of examples, a variety of terms may be substituted.
man's achievements	human achievements, achievements of the human species	
the average man	the average person, people in general	
man a project	staff a project, hire personnel, employ staff	
manpower	work force, personnel, workers	
Department of Manpower	(no alternative)	Official titles should not be changed.

Examples of common usage	Consider meaning. An alternative may be better	Comment
4. The use of experiments in psychology presupposes the mechanistic nature of *man*.	The use of experiments in psychology presupposes the mechanistic nature of the *human being*.	Noun substituted.
5. This interference phenomenon, called learned helplessness, has been demonstrated in rats, cats, fish, dogs, monkeys, and *men*.	This interference phenomenon, called learned helplessness, has been demonstrated in rats, cats, fish, dogs, monkeys, and *humans*.	Noun substituted.
6. Issues raised were whether the lack of cardiac responsivity in the premature *infant* is secondary to *his* heightened level of autonomic arousal . . .	. . . responsivity in the premature *infant* is secondary to *the* heightened level . . . . . . responsivity in premature *infants* is secondary to *their* heightened levels . . .	*His* changed to *the*. Rewritten in plural.
7. First the individual becomes aroused by violations of *his* personal space, and then *he* attributes the cause of this arousal to other people in *his* environment.	First *we* become aroused by violations of *our* personal space, and then *we* attribute the cause of this arousal to other people in *the* environment.	Pronouns substituted, *he* and *his* omitted.
8. Much has been written about the effect that a child's position among *his* siblings has on *his* intellectual development.	Much has been written about the relationship between sibling position and intellectual development in *children*.	Rewritten, plural introduced.

Examples of common usage	Consider meaning. An alternative may be better	Comment
9. Subjects were 16 girls and 16 boys. Each *child* was to place a car on *his* board so that two cars and boards looked alike.	Each child was to place a car on his or her board so that two cars and boards looked alike.	Changed *his* to *his or her;* however, use sparingly to avoid monotonous repetition. *Her or his* may also be used, but it sounds awkward. In either case, keep pronoun order consistent to avoid ambiguity.
10. Each person's alertness was measured by the difference between *his* obtained relaxation score and *his* obtained arousal score.	Each person's alertness was measured by the difference between *the* obtained relaxation and arousal scores.	*His* deleted, plural introduced.
11. The client's husband *lets* her teach part-time.	The client's husband *"lets"* her teach part-time. The husband says he *"lets"* the client teach part-time. The client *says her husband "lets"* her teach part-time.	Punctuation added to clarify location of the bias, that is, with husband and wife, not with author. If necessary, rewrite to clarify as allegation. See Example 24.

B. Stereotyping

Examples of common usage	Consider meaning. An alternative may be better	Comment
12. males, females	men, women, boys, girls, adults, children, adolescents.	Specific nouns reduce possibility of stereotypic bias and often clarify discussion. Use *male* and *female* as adjectives where appropriate and relevant (female experimenter, male subject). Avoid unparallel usages such as 10 *men* and 16 *females.*

Examples of common usage	*Consider meaning. An alternative may be better*	*Comment*
13. Research scientists often neglect their *wives* and *children*.	Research scientists often neglect their *families*.	Alternative wording acknowledges that women as well as men are research scientists.
14. When a test developer or test user fails to satisfy these requirements, *he* should . . .	When *test developers* or *test users* fail to satisfy these requirements, *they* should . . .	Same as Example 13.
15. the psychologist . . . *he*	psychologists . . . *they;* the psychologist . . . she	Be specific or change to plural if discussing women as well as men.
the therapist . . . he	therapists . . . they; the therapist . . . she	
the nurse . . . she	nurses . . . *they;* nurse . . . *he*	
the teacher . . . she	teachers . . . they; teacher . . . he	
16. woman doctor, lady lawyer, male nurse	doctor, physician, lawyer, nurse	Specify sex if it is a variable or if sex designation is necessary to the discussion ("13 female doctors and 22 male doctors").
17. mothering	parenting, nurturing, (or specify exact behavior)	Noun substituted.
18. chairman (of an academic department)	Use *chairperson* or *chair* if it is known that the institution has established either form as an official title. Otherwise, use *chairman*.	*Department head* may be appropriate, but the term is not synonymous with *chairman* and *chairperson* at all institutions.
chairman (presiding officer of a committee or meeting)	chairperson, moderator, discussion leader	In parliamentary usage *chairman* is the official term. Alternatives are acceptable in most writing.

Examples of common usage	Consider meaning. An alternative may be better	Comment
19. Only *freshmen* were eligible for the project.	(No alternative if academic standing is meant.)	First-year student is often an acceptable alternative to *freshman* but in these cases, *freshmen* is used for accuracy.
20. foreman, policeman, stewardess, mailman	supervisor, police officer, flight attendant, postal worker or letter carrier	Noun substituted.

II. PROBLEMS OF EVALUATION

A. Ambiguity of Referent

21. The authors acknowledge the assistance of *Mrs. John Smith.*	The authors acknowledge the assistance of *Jane Smith.*	Use given names in author acknowledgments. When forms of address are used in text, use the appropriate form: Mr., Mrs., Miss, or Ms.
22. men and women, sons and daughters, boys and girls, husbands and wives	women and men, daughters and sons, girls and boys, wives and husbands	Vary the order if content does not require traditional order.

B. Stereotyping

men and girls	men and women, women and men	Use parallel terms. Of course, use *men* and *girls* if that is literally what is meant.

Examples of common usage	Consider meaning. An alternative may be better	Comment
24. The client's husband lets her teach part-time.	The client teaches part-time.	The author of this example intended to communicate the working status of the woman but inadvertently revealed a stereotype about husband-wife relationships; see Example 11.
25. ambitious men and aggressive women.	ambitious women and men or ambitious people aggressive men and women or aggressive people	Some adjectives, depending on whether the person described is a man or a woman, connote bias. The examples illustrate some common usages that may not always convey exact meaning, especially when paired, as in column 1.
26. The boys chose typically male toys. The client's behavior was typically female.	The boys chose (specify) The client's behavior was (specify)	Being specific reduces possibility of stereotypic bias.
27. woman driver	driver	If specifying sex is necessary, use *female driver*.
28. The *girls* in the office greeted all clients.	secretaries, office assistants	Noun substituted.
29. coed	female student	Noun substituted.
30. women's lib, women's libber.	women's movement, feminist, support of women's movement	Noun substituted.

Examples of common usage	Consider meaning. An alternative may be better	Comment
31. Subjects were 16 men and 4 women. The *women were housewives.*	The men were (specify) and the women were (specify).	Describe women and men in parallel terms. *Housewife* indicates sex, marital status, and occupation, and excludes men. *Homemaker* indicates occupation, and includes men.

A FINAL WORD

Attempting to introduce nonsexist language at the cost of awkwardness, obscurity, or euphemistic praising does not improve scientific communication. An author should make clear that both sexes are under discussion when they are and should indicate sex when only one sex is discussed. Under no circumstances should an author hide sex identity in an attempt to be unbiased, if knowledge of sex may be important to the reader.

Any endeavor to change the language is an awesome task at best. Some aspects of our language that may be considered sexist are firmly embedded in our culture, and we presently have no acceptable substitutes. In English, the use of third-person singular pronouns is one example: the generic use of *he* is misleading, *it* is inaccurate, *one* conveys a different meaning, and *he or she* can become an annoying repetition. Nevertheless, with some rephrasing and careful attention to meaning, even the generic *he* can be avoided most of the time. The result of such efforts is accurate, unbiased communication, the purpose of these guidelines.

SUGGESTED READING

APA Task Force on Issues of Sexual Bias in Graduate Education. Guidelines for non-sexist use of language. *American Psychologist,* 1975, 30, 682–684.

Burr, E., Dunn, S., and Farquhar, N. *Guidelines for equal treatment of the sexes in social studies textbooks.* Los Angeles: Westside Women's Committee, 1973. (Available from Westside Women's Committee P. O. Box 24D20, Los Angeles, California 90024.)

DeBoard, D., Fisher, A. M., Moran, M. C., and Zawodny, L. *Guidelines to promote the awareness of human potential.* Philadelphia, Pa.: Lippincott, undated.

Harper & Row. *Harper & Row guidelines on equal treatment of the sexes in textbooks.* New York. 1976.

Henley, N., and Thorne, B. *She said/he said: An annotated bibliography of sex differences in language, speech, and nonverbal communication.* Pittsburgh, Pa.: Know, 1975. (Available from Know, Inc., P.O. Box 86031, Pittsburgh, Pennsylvania 15221.)

Holt, Rinehart & Winston (College Department). *The treatment of sex roles and minorities*. New York. 1976.

Lakoff, R. *Language and woman's place*. New York: Harper & Row, 1975.

Lerner, H. E. Girls, ladies, or women? The unconscious dynamics of language choice. *Comprehensive Psychiatry,* 1976, 17, 295–299.

McGraw-Hill. *Guidelines for equal treatment of the sexes in McGraw-Hill Book Company publications*. New York. Undated.

Miller, C., and Swift, K. *Words and women*. Garden City, N.Y.: Anchor Press/Doubleday, 1976.

Prentice-Hall. *Prentice-Hall author's guide* (5th ed.). Englewood Cliffs, N.J. 1975.

Random House. *Guidelines for multiethnic/nonsexist survey*. New York. 1975.

Scott, Foresman. *Guidelines for improving the image of women in textbooks*. Glenview, Ill. 1974.

John Wiley & Sons. *Wiley guidelines on sexism in language*. New York. 1977.

This change sheet was prepared by the APA Publication Manual Task Force. Members of the task force are Charles N. Cofer (Chairperson), Robert S. Daniel, Frances Y. Dunham, and Walter I. Heimer. Ellen Kimmel served as liaison from the Committee on Women in Psychology, and Anita DeVivo as APA staff liaison. This material may be reproduced in whole or in part without permission, provided that acknowledgment is made to the American Psychological Association © 1974.

RESEARCH REPORT: EXAMPLE OF AN "A" PAPER

Effect of Delay on the

Serial Position Curve in Free Recall

Brenda Brilliante

Bowling Green State University

The present paper describes the first experiment conducted by members of a course in human learning at Bowling Green State University, April, 1979, under the supervision of Kirk Smith and Laura Wallrabenstein.

Running head: Delay and the Serial Position Curve

Abstract

The usual serial position curve was found in immediate free recall whereas the recency effect was absent when recall followed 30 seconds of arithmetic. A final recall of all lists produced lowered recall and a flat serial position curve beyond the first few positions. The results are interpreted as support for a distinction between a short term store responsible for the recency effect and long term store responsible for the remainder of the serial position curve. The fact that no relationship between probability of initial and final recall of recency items was found is discussed as evidence against the hypothesis that initial recall of these items weakens their representation in long term store.

Effect of Delay on the Serial Position

Curve in Free Recall

In the experimental procedure known as free recall, a subject tries to recall a list of words in any order. The subject's ability to recall a given word has generally been found to be a U-shaped function of its serial position in the list. Subjects tend to recall more words from the beginning and end of the list than from the middle. The heightened recall of the first few words in the list is known as the primacy effect. The somewhat greater enhancement of recall for words in the last several positions of the list is known as the recency effect. The ''duplex,'' or twostore, theory of memory (Klatzky, 1975) attributes the two effects to different storage mechanisms. The

---

The format used in these two sample research reports differs from the APA guidelines in order to conserve space. Arrangement of the manuscript should follow the APA guidelines and the suggestions given in this text (abstracts and charts/figures should appear on separate pages).

recency effect is explained by retrieval of words from a short term store that is easy to access but of limited capacity and short duration. The primacy effect, on the other hand, is attributed to the operation of a long term store that has a greater capacity and longer duration but is less easily accessed.

Glanzer and Cunitz (1966) presented evidence for the foregoing interpretation of the serial position curve in free recall. They argued that performance based on short term storage should, by definition, be affected primarily by the amount of time that elapses between presentation and recall. It follows that delay should have an effect only on the recency portion of the curve. To test this hypothesis, Glanzer and Cunitz tested subjects under three conditions—immediate recall, 10-second delay and 30-second delay. In the delay conditions, subjects were shown a digit after the last word in the list and then counted aloud from that number until stopped by the experimenter. The purpose of the counting task during the delay period was to prevent rehearsal of the list. The 10-second delay was found to remove most of the end peak of the curve, and with a 30-second delay the recency portion of the curve was flattened to the level of the middle section of the curve.

Another finding often cited in support of the duplex theory was first reported by Craik (1970). Subjects were given 10 lists of words for immediate recall, one after the other. After recalling the 10th list, they were instructed to recall as many words as they could from all 10 lists (in any order). The serial position curve for this final recall failed to show the typical recency effect. The usual explanation derived from the duplex theory is that final recall performance in Craik's experiment reflects retention after a somewhat longer delay, and therefore represents the same long term storage mechanisms observed after brief delays.

In fact, Craik actually reported that the last few words in each list showed the lowest probability of recall, compared to other serial positions Craik referred to this result as the ''negative recency effect'' to contrast it with the usual ''positive'' recency effect obtained in immediate recall, where the last one or two words show the highest probability of recall. The negative recency effect can be explained by the duplex theory with the additional assumption that registration in long term store depends on the length of time an item resides in short term storage during input. This time period is a rough measure of the amount of coding and elaboration the item receives, and toward the end of the list, items receive progressively less processing of this kind. (Rundus, 1971, has provided evidence for this view.)

The difficulty with the foregoing view is that there is a negative correlation between probability of initial, immediate recall and final recall for words in the recency region of the curve. It is possible that items at the end of the list are retrieved during initial recall by a process that reduces the strength of these items for subsequent recall. Although the exact nature of this process is not clear, the foregoing hypothesis can be ruled out by a simple empirical test. If a difference in initial recall of the last few items can be produced by some manipulation, the hypothesis predicts a corresponding difference in the opposite direction during final recall.

The present experiment tested the foregoing hypothesis in the following way. There were two conditions of initial recall, immediate and delayed. In the latter condition, recall followed a 30-second period of mental arithmetic. It was expected on the basis of Glanzer and

Cunitz's (1966) findings that the recency effect would be eliminated by the filled delay. A final recall of all lists was expected to produce a lower overall level of recall. The reduction would be consistent with Craik's (1970) findings. If the negative recency effect is due to some destructive aspect of initial recall of items in the recency portion of the curve, then a greater negative recency effect in final recall should occur for lists recalled immediately as compared to lists recalled initially after a 30-second delay.

Method

Subjects

   The subjects were 18 students between the ages of 19 and 25 enrolled in an undergraduate psychology class on human learning. The subjects were tested as a group in their regular classroom during a laboratory meeting of the course.

Materials

   The words were 180 AA nouns, 4 to 6 letters long, drawn from the Thorndike-Lorge list (1944). They were displayed on a screen with an automatic slide projector. Each word was printed in black on a white background. Order of words in the lists was random.

Procedure

   Four conditions were generated by two experimental variables--immediate vs. delayed and initial vs. final recall. Each subject was run in all four experimental conditions and all subjects were presented with the same lists in the same order.

   Subjects were first asked to number and initial 12 blank sheets of paper. They were then presented with two 15-word practice lists, each representing one of the initial recall conditions.

On Trial 1, subjects were instructed that 15 words would be shown at a rate of about one every 4 seconds. When the list was over, the word ''Recall'' appeared and subjects wrote down as many of these words as they could in any order on Sheet No. 1. Subjects were allowed 60 seconds following exposure of the list for recall.

Subjects were told that Trial 2 would consist of a new list of words and that this time, when the last word of the list appeared, the experimenter would call out a 3-digit number. Subjects were to write down the number on the left side of Sheet No. 2 and subtract three, write down the answer, subtract three again, continuing until the experimenter said ''Stop.'' Following this, subjects were to write down as many words from this list as they could in any order. The delay interval, during which subjects performed the arithmetic task, lasted 30 seconds. The recall period was again 60 seconds.

After allowing time for questions and clarification of the procedure, the 10 experimental trials were run with 15-word lists. Five trials were run for each initial condition in counterbalanced order.

Following the experimental trials, subjects were instructed to initial and number a 13th sheet of paper. They were then instructed to recall as many words as they could remember from all 12 lists. The final recall period was 5 minutes.

Results

The results are presented in Figure 1. Each curve represents one of the four experimental conditions. It can be seen that the 30-second delay in initial recall was sufficient to remove the recency effect. In addition, final recall was lower than initial recall.

Effect of Delay

6

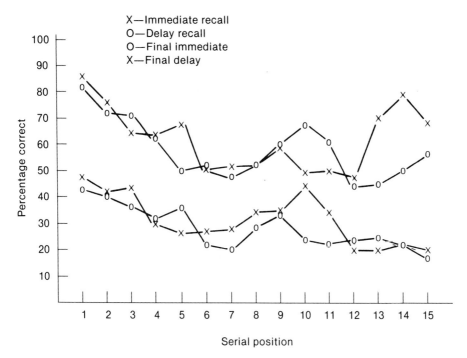

Fig. 1. Percent of words correctly recalled as a function of serial position in the list for lists recalled initially after no delay (immediate) or 30-seconds of delay and for final recall at the end of the session for the same lists.

A series of t tests was carried out on the number of words recalled from the last three serial positions, which constitute the recency effect. Recall from these terminal positions was significantly higher in initial as opposed to final recall, t (17)=3.98, p<.01. In addition, within the initial condition, performance was significantly reduced by the 30-second delay, t (17)=3.15, p<.01. During final recall, the immediate and delay condition did not differ in the recency region, t (17)<1.

Discussion

The results not only replicate previous findings but also are inconsistent with an explanation of the negative recency effect by a destructive mechanism associated with the immediate recall of the last two or three words in the list. In the initial immediate condition, the usual serial position curve was found. A 30-second period of counting backwards by three's eliminated the recency effect as predicted by the duplex theory. The latter result also replicates the findings of Glanzer and Cunitz (1970). As expected, final recall was generally lower than initial recall. There was no evidence that the higher recall of the last few words of a list in the initial immediate condition was reflected in lower recall in the final immediate condition. However, there was no obvious negative recency effect in either final recall condition. The latter is at odds with the findings reported by Craik (1970).

The results of the present study should be treated with some caution. The absence of a clear negative recency effect may have been due to the relatively long presentation interval, which permitted time for adequate encoding of all words in the list. The failure to find a difference in final recall between the two conditions of initial recall could also reflect inadequate control of important variables such as list composition. It should be noted that all subjects received the same assignment of particular lists to experimental conditions; the results may reflect this confounding by reducing a true difference.

Given the critical importance of presentation rate, the present experiment needs to be repeated using a faster rate, e,g., 1 or 2 seconds per word. Such a study should also be designed to sample several random assignments of words to lists with perhaps some effort made to counterbalance this variable.

One criticism of the present study from a conceptual point of view is that a delay period might also have a destructive effect on information in memory about the last few items on the list, although the effect could be due to a different process such as interference from counting backwards. A possible method of exploring this explanation would be to identify the last 3 to 5 words in each list (for example, by printing them in red ink) and then signalling recall selectively at the end of the list in one of three ways, as follows: (a) Recall all words (both red and black) after the last one is presented. This condition provides a standard against which the other would be compared. It is crucial that this condition show the negative recency effect reported by Craik (1970). (b) Recall only the first 10 to 12 words (black items). Because the subject cannot anticipate when this condition will occur, all words should be processed in the usual way, but words in the recency region would not be exposed to the hypothesized destructive processes connected with recall. Thus, there should be no negative recency effect. (c) Recall only the last 3 to 5 words (red items). This condition should display a negative recency effect similar to condition (a) above. The purpose of including condition (c) is to ascertain whether the effect of processing but not recalling a word is similar for all words or whether, as proposed in the introduction, the destructive effects of recall operate selectively on the last few words in the list.

References

Craik, F.I. The fate of primary memory items in free recall. Journal of Verbal Learning and Verbal Behavior, 1970, 9, 143-148.

Glanzer, M., & Cunitz, A.R. Two storage mechanisms in free recall. Journal of Verbal Learning and Verbal Behavior, 1966, 5, 351-360.

Klatzky, R.L. Human memory: Structures and processes. San Francisco: Freeman, 1975.

Rundus, D. Analysis of rehearsal processes in free recall. Journal of Experimental Psychology, 1971, 89, 63-77.

Thorndike, E.L. & Lorge, I. The teacher's word book of 30,000 words. New York: University Press, 1944.

RESEARCH REPORT: EXAMPLE OF A "C" PAPER

MANIPULATION OF SHORT TERM MEMORY

IN LIST LEARNING PROCEDURES

Evelyn Everett

Department of Psychology, Bowling Green State University

Bowling Green, Ohio 43403

Running head: Everett

Abstract

Using list-learning procedures in a memory recall task of 15 words per trial there was no statistical significant difference between immediate recall and delayed recall conditions. Nineteen male and female college students between the ages of 19 and 22 were tested for memory recall immediately after being presented the words in five trials (immediate condition). The subjects were also tested for memory recall after a 30 sec delay of counting backwards by threes in five other trials (delayed condition). A serial position curve was obtained from the data and analysis was done on the primacy and recency portions of the curve. The recency portion of the curve is thought to be representative of short-term memory (STM) and was affected by the delayed conditions but not significantly when compared to the immediate condition, perhaps due to the small subject size.

Short-term memory Delayed recall Serial position curve

MANIPULATION OF SHORT TERM MEMORY
IN LIST LEARNING PROCEDURES

Human memory is an intriguing phenomena which has astonished mankind for many years. The questions of how memories are processed, stored, and retrieved in the physical brain and mental mind has plagued researchers for many years, and only in the last century have the answers to many of these questions started to become more clearly understood. There have been many experiments designed to try and break memory down into smaller units or single step processes which fit into the working system of an operational memory as we know it. From all of this research have come several different theories and models of the memory system.

When discussing theories involving memory processes there are several different aspects that are responsible for the memory system. Perhaps the most reputable of these models is the one involving immediate, short-term, and long-term memory (Glanzer and Cunitz, 1966). Immediate memory which is characterized by an instantaneous representation of a stimuli in a person's senses or sensory registers will not be examined in this experiment, but both short-term memory (STM) and long-term memory (LTM) processes will. In the experimental paradigm that will be used for this experiment the process of STM will be studied most extensively.

Past research has shown that there can be many different ways to interpret an experimental result, with many ambiguities stemming from inconsistent methods and inappropriate control devices. The model design of the experiment is a simple modification of the ''list-learning'' procedures first employed by Herman Ebbinghaus in 1885 (Ebbinghaus, 1885). Ebbinghaus used himself as a subject in trying to understand memory in its capacities by learning lists of nonsense syllables and then recalling what he could of these syllables. From this research came a more thorough investigation of serial positions in list learning and what is known today as the ''serial position curve.'' The serial position curve is simply the percentage of correct recalls of items at each serial position. The curve is often broken up into three parts when analyzing the data it is referring to. The first part is known as the primacy effect which is thought to be the result of

LTM (Craik, 1970). When a subject is to learn a list of words the first few have a better chance to be rehearsed because there is nothing else to interfer with these words. These words are then thought to be put into LTM. As more words are introduced the subject cannot keep rehearsing all of the words so that a large percentage of words in the middle of the curve are often forgotten. As the final few words are presented the subject once again has a chance to rehearse the last words and if he is to recall them immediately he will often dump these last words out quickly. These last words or the recency effect, is thought to be representative of STM. One basic point that must be understood for this working model to be correct is the limits of STM. It has been shown that STM only has a capacity of 7±2 items. This short-term memory span is present but without continuing rehearsal the items in STM will soon be forgotten and if they are continually rehearsed they will soon be transferred to LTM.

Since words that are presented near the end of a list seem to be stored in STM and dumped immediately upon recall, an experiment designed to manipulate the results of STM could be performed by not allowing the subjects to recall immediately, or not rehearse the last few words. In the present experiment this is what was done by presenting two conditions, immediate and delayed recall, with the delayed condition having a 30 sec delay in which the subjects were to direct their attention to a different task of counting backwards by threes. From these two conditions we expected to get a normal serial position curve from the immediate condition, and a lower percentage of recall in the recency portion of the serial position curve in the delayed condition. The delayed condition result would be due to the fact that the last words would not be continually rehearsed or immediately recalled and would be lost resulting in a lower than normal recall effect for STM.

Method

Subjects

Nineteen subjects between ages of 19 and 22 were seated in a small classroom. The subjects consisted of both males and females who are attending Bowling Green State University, enrolled in a Learning and Memory psychology course. Each of the subjects has been through approximately two years of post-high school studies including an introductory psychology course and possibly one or two higher level psychology courses.

Materials

The 150 words that were presented to the subjects to recall were AA, high frequency nouns, and consisted of four, five, and six letters in length (Thorndike and Lorge, 1944). Each of the words were presented from a circular, rotating slide projector onto a movie screen approximately 15 to 25 ft.(4.5 to 7.5 m) away from the subjects (the subjects were seated in three rows). The words were presented with dark lettering on a light background while the room was normally illuminated. The subjcts were asked to recall by writing on half sheets of notebook paper.

Procedure

All subjects were seated and then were read the instructions by the experimenter along with several examples of what was to be done. The subjects were shown 15 consecutive slides of words in each trial, with ten scoring trials and two practice trials. Each of the 15 words were presented on the screen for approximately four sec with the next word being presented immediatly afte the preceding word was removed from the screen.

The experiment was conducted with two conditions in mind for testing memory recall. The two conditions were immediate and delayed recall. The immediate condition was characterized by an immediate recall of the 15 words that were presented, with no specific order of recall required. The subjects were to write down as many words that they could remember in the specific trial in no particular order upon viewing the last slide with ''recall'' marked on it. The subjects had to do this with the next trial starting soon afterwards. The delayed condition was characterized by the same procedure as the immediate condition except that following the last word (15th) of the trial, a blank slide was shown and the experimenter then wrote an arbitrary three-digit number on the chalkboard and asked each of the subjects to count backwards by threes from that number for 30 sec. The subjects were asked to write the counting numbers on each of the trial sheets in the delayed condition to assure the experimenter that the subjects were counting and not rehearsing the words. After 30 sec of counting the subjects were then allowed 60 sec to recall the words in any desirable order. When all 12 trials were complete including the practice trials, the subjects were then allowed 5 min to try and recall any word that was presented to them in the trials. These words were then scored in the final recall.

Of the ten scoring trials that were used there were an equal number of immediate and delay trails. The immediate condition was represented by trials 3, 6, 7, 10, and 11, while the delayed condition

6

was represented by trials 4, 5, 8, 9, and 12. Trials one and two were
the practice trials and were not scored.

Results

The 15-word serial position curves were analyized in groups of
three serial positions creating five groups. The recency effect means
in the three group sets in both immediate and delayed conditions were
compared using the Student t̲-test for dependant means. Comparing the
mean recency effects of the two conditions there was no significance,
t̲(2)= 3.91,p̲>.05. Figure 1. is a graph showing serial position curves
including the recency effects. Likewise in the final recall
comparison between the mean recency effects of the two conditions
there was no significance, t(2) = .486, p>.05. Figure 2. is a graph
showing final recall serial position curves for both conditions.

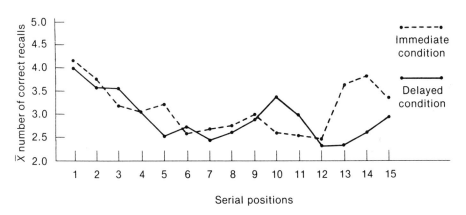

Fig. 1. Serial position curve of means

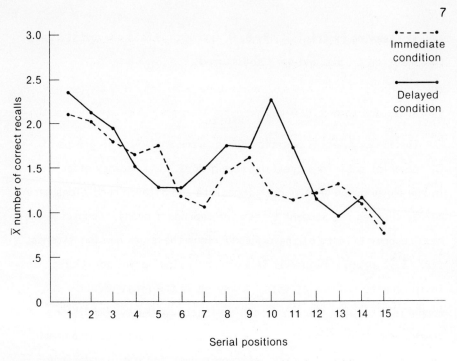

Fig. 2. Serial position curve of means for final recall

Discussion

The results for this experiment were close to what was expected, but perhaps due to the small subject size statistical significance was not obtained in the difference between the recency portions of the curves. But by examining the graphs drawn there was clearly a manipulation of STM in the delayed condition.

Subjects in this experiment may not have been representative of a population because of their exposure to mnemonic techniques uncovered in the book Improving Your Memory by Laird Cermak. The book has several aids to improve your memory and if the subjects had a chance to look through it they could pick up a few memory aids such as word associations.

8

The last factor that may have had an affect on the curves was the rate of presentation of the words to be remembered. The words were on the screen for approximately four sec each and that was long enough to rehearse each word or perhaps store it with some already known sequence of items. If the presentation rate of each word was decreased to one or two sec there could have been lower recall scores, perhaps increasing the difference between the recency effects of the two conditions.

References

1. Craik. The fate of primacy memory items in free recall. JVLVB 9: 143, 1970.

2. Ebbinghaus, H. Uber das Gedachtnis. Leipzig: Duncker and Humblot, 1885.

3. Glanzer and Cunitz. Two storage mechanisms in free recall. JVLVB 5: 351, 1966.

4. Thorndike, E.L. and I. Lorge. The teachers word book of 30,000 words. New York: Columbia University Press, 1944.

GUIDE FOR ASSESSING RESEARCH REPORTS

GUIDE FOR ASSESSING RESEARCH REPORTS

The following guidelines were taken from an article by Brendan A. Maher which appeared in a special issue of an APA journal entitled *Journal of Consulting and Clinical Psychology,* 1978, *46,* 595–838. The entire issue was devoted to methodological problems. Drafts of the article were reviewed by a large number of researchers. Although the guidelines were intended primarily for clinical type research, they are applicable to most other kinds of research. Most of the guidelines contained in the article are included here. We want to acknowledge both Brendan A. Maher and APA for making them available.

INTRODUCTION

1. Are all the citations correct and necessary, or is there padding? Are important citations missing? Has the author been careful to cite prior reports contrary to the current hypothesis?

2. Is there an explicit hypothesis?

3. Has the origin of the hypothesis been made explicit?

4. Was the hypothesis correctly derived from the theory that has been cited? Are other, contrary hypotheses compatible with the same theory?

5. Is there an explicit rationale for the selection of measures, and was it derived logically from the hypothesis?

METHOD

1. Is the method so described that replication is possible without further information?

2. Subjects: Were they sampled randomly from the population to which the results will be generalized?

3. Under what circumstances was informed consent obtained?

4. Are there probable biases in sampling (e.g., volunteers, high refusal rates, institution population atypical for the country at large, etc.)?

5. What was the "set" given to subjects? Was there deception? Was there control for experimenter influence and expectancy effects?

6. How were subjects debriefed?

7. Were subjects (patients) led to believe that they were receiving "treatment"?

8. Were there special variables affecting the subjects, such as medication, fatigue, and threat that were not part of the experimental manipulation? In clinical samples, was "organicity measured and/or eliminated?

9. Controls: Were there appropriate control groups? What was being controlled for?

10. When more than one measure was used, was the order counterbalanced? If so, were order effects actually analyzed statistically?

11. Was there a control task(s) to confirm specificity of results?

12. Measures: For both dependent and independent variable measures—was validity and reliability established and reported? When a measure is tailor-made for a study, this is very important. When validities and reliabilities are already available in the literature, it is less important.

13. Is there adequate description of tasks, materials, apparatus, and so forth?

14. Is there discriminant validity of the measures?

15. Are distributions of scores on measures typical of scores that have been reported for similar samples in previous literature?

16. Are measures free from biases such as
    a. Social desirability?
    b. Yeasaying and naysaying?
    c. Correlations with general responsivity?
    d. Verbal ability, intelligence?

17. If measures are scored by observers using categories or codes, what is the interrater reliability?

18. Was administration and scoring of the measures done blind?

19. If short versions, foreign-language translations, and so forth, of common measures are used, has the validity and reliability of these been established?

20. In correlational designs, do the two measures have theoretical and/or methodological independence?

REPRESENTATIVE DESIGN

1. When the stimulus is a human (e.g., in clinical judgments of clients of differing race, sex, etc.), is there a sample of stimuli (e.g., more than one client of each race or each sex)?

2. When only one stimulus or a few human stimuli were used, was an adequate explanation of the failure to sample given?

STATISTICS

1. Were the statistics used with appropriate assumptions fulfilled by the data (e.g., normalcy of distributions for parametric techniques)? Where necessary, have scores been transformed appropriately?

2. Were tests of significance properly used and reported? For example, did the author use the p value of a correlation to justify conclusions when the actual size of the correlation suggests little common variance betwen two measures?

3. Have statistical significance levels been accompanied by an analysis of practical significance levels?

4. Has the author considered the effects of a limited range of scores, and so forth, in using correlations?

5. Is the basic statistical strategy that of a "fishing expedition"; that is, if many comparisons are made, were the obtained significance levels predicted in advance? Consider the number of significance levels as a function of the total number of comparisons made.

FIGURES AND TABLES

1. Are the figures and tables (a) necessary and (b) self-explanatory? Large tables of nonsignificant differences, for example, should be eliminated if the few obtained significances can be reported in a sentence or two in the text. Could several tables be combined into a smaller number?

2. Are the axes of figures identified clearly?

3. Do graphs correspond logically to the textual argument of the article? (E.g., if the text states that a certain technique leads to an increment of mental health and the accompanying graph shows a decline in symptoms, the point is not as clear to the reader as it would be if the text or the graph were amended to achieve visual and verbal congruence.)

DISCUSSION AND CONCLUSION

1. Is the discussion properly confined to the findings or is it digressive, including new post hoc speculations?

2. Has the author explicity considered and discussed viable alternative explanations of the findings?

3. Have nonsignificant trends in the data been promoted to "findings"?

4. Are the limits of the generalizations possible from the data made clear? Has the author identified his/her own methodological difficulties in the study?

5. Has the author "accepted" the null hypothesis?

6. Has the author considered the possible methodological bases for discrepancies between the results reported and other findings in the literature?

REFERENCES

Abelson, R. P., and Miller, J. C. Negative persuasion via personal insult. *Journal of Experimental Social Psychology,* 1967, *3,* 321–333.

Badia, P., Harsh, J., and Abbott, B. Choosing between predictable and unpredictable shock conditions: Data and theory. *Psychological Bulletin,* 1979, *86,* 1107–1131.

Baker, S. *The practical stylist.* New York: Thomas Y. Cromwell Co., 1973.

Baker, J. P., and Crist, J. L. Teacher expectancies: A review of the literature. In J. D. Elashoff and R. E. Snow (Eds.). *Pygmalion reconsidered.* Worthington, Ohio: Charles A. Jones, 1971.

Barber, T. X., and Silver, M. J. Fact, fiction, and the experimenter bias effect. *Psychological Bulletin Monographs,* 1968, *70,* 1–29. (a)

Barber, T. X., and Silver, M. J. Pitfalls in data analysis and interpretation: A reply to Rosenthal. *Psychological Bulletin Monograph,* 1968, *70,* 48–62. (b)

Barton, E. S., Guess, D., Garcia, E., and Baer, D. M. Improvement of retardates' mealtime behaviors by timeout procedures using multiple baseline techniques. *Journal of Applied Behavior Analysis,* 1970, *3,* 77–84.

Bensen, H. *The relaxation response.* New York: Morrow, 1975.

Bickman, L., and Henchy, T. (Eds.) *Beyond the laboratory: Field research in social psychology.* New York: McGraw-Hill, 1972.

Badia, P., Haber, A., and Runyon, R. *Research Problems in Psychology.* Reading, Massachusetts: Addison-Wesley, 1970.

Berscheid, E., Baron, R. S., Dermer, M., and Libman, M. Anticipating informed consent: An empirical approach. *American Psychologist,* 1973, *28,* 913–925.

Black, A. H. A comment on yoked control designs (Tech. Rep. 11). Hamilton, Ontario: McMaster University, Department of Psychology, 1967.

Blehar, M. C., Lieberman, A. F., and Ainsworth, M. D. S. Early face-to-face interaction and its relation to later infant-mother attachment. *Child Development,* 1977, *48,* 182–194.

Botwinick, J. *Aging and Behavior.* New York: Springer Publishing Co., 1978.

Brady, J. V. Ulcers in "executive" monkeys. *Scientific American,* 1958, *199* (4), 95–100.

Brehm, J. W. *A theory of psychological reactance.* New York: Academic Press, 1966.

Buros, O. K. (Ed.) *The seventh mental measurements yearbook.* Highland Park, New Jersey: Gryphon Press, 1972.

Buros, O. K. (Ed.) *Personality tests and reviews: II.* Highland Park, New Jersey: Gryphon Press, 1974.

Campbell, D. T., and Erlebacher, A. How regression artifacts in quasi-experimental evaluation can mistakenly make compensatory education look harmful. In E. L. Struening and M. Guttentag (Eds.). *Handbook of Evaluation Research.* Beverly Hills-London: Sage Publications, 1975.

Campbell, D. T., and Stanley, J. C. *Experimental and quasi-experimental designs for research.* New York: Rand McNally, 1963.

Chapin, F. S. *Experimental designs in sociological research.* New York: Harper & Row, 1955.

Church, R. M. Systematic effect of random error in the yoked control design. *Psychological Bulletin,* 1964, *62,* 122–131.

Comroe, J. H., Jr. and Dripps, R. D. Scientific basis for the support of biomedical science. *Science,* 1976, *192,* 105–111.

Cook, T. D., and Campbell, D. T. *Quasi-experimentation: Design and analysis issues for field settings.* New York: Rand McNally College Publishing Co., 1979.

Cronbach, L. J., and Meehl, P. E. Construct validity in psychological tests. *Psychological Bulletin,* 1955, *52,* 281–302.

Doob, A. N., and Gross, A. E. Status of frustrator as an inhibitor of horn honking responses. *Journal of Social Psychology,* 1968, *76,* 213–218.

Elashoff, J. D., and Snow, R. E. *Pygmalion reconsidered.* Worthington, Ohio: Charles A. Jones, 1971.

Erlebacher, A. Design and analysis of experiments contrasting the within- and between-subjects manipulation of the independent variable. *Psychological Bulletin,* 1977, *84,* 212–219.

Freedman, J. L., and Fraser, S. C. Compliance without pressure: The foot-in-the-door technique. *Journal of Personality and Social Psychology,* 1966, *4,* 195–202.

Frey, P. W. Within-subject analysis of the CS-US interval in rabbit eyelid conditioning. *Learning and Motivation,* 1970, *1,* 337–345.

Gallup, G. G., and Suarez, S. D. On the use of animals in psychological research. *Psychological Record,* 1980, *30,* 211–218.

Gelfand, D. M., and Hartmann, D. P. *Child Behavior.* New York: Pergamon Press Inc., 1975.

Glass, D. C., and Singer, J. E. *Urban Stress.* New York: Academic Press, 1972.

Greenwald, A. G. Within-subjects designs: To use or not to use? *Psychological Bulletin,* 1976, *83,* 314–320.

Grice, R. G. Dependence of empirical laws upon the source of experimental variation. *Psychological Bulletin,* 1966, *66,* 488–498.

Hartmann, D. P. Considerations in the choice of interobserver reliability estimates. *Journal of Applied Behavior Analysis,* 1977, *10,* 103–116.

Hastorf, A., and Cantril, H. They saw a game: A case study. *Journal of Abnormal and Social Psychology,* 1954, *49,* 129–134.

Hersen, M., and Barlow, D. H. *Single case experimental designs.* New York: Pergamon Press, 1976.

Hopkins, R. H., and Edwards, R. E. Pronunciation effects in recognition memory. *Journal of Verbal Learning and Verbal Behavior,* 1972, *11,* 534–537.

Hunt, M. *Sexual behavior in the 1970s.* Chicago: Playboy Press, 1974.

Jones, P. D., and Holding, D. H. Extremely long-term persistence of the McCollough effect. *Journal of Experimental Psychology: Human Perception and Performance,* 1975, *1,* 323–327.

Kahneman, D., and Tversky, A. On the psychology of prediction. *Psychological Review,* 1973, *80,* 237–251.

Kenny, D. A. *Correlation and causality.* New York: John Wiley & Sons, 1979.

Keppel, G. *Design and analysis: A researcher's handbook.* Englewood Cliffs, New Jersey: Prentice-Hall Inc., 1973.

Kimmel, H. D., and Terrant, F. R. Bias due to individual differences in yoked control designs. *Behavior Research Methods and Instrumentation,* 1968, *1,* 11–14.

Kinsey, A. C., Pomeroy, W. B., and Martin, C. E. *Sexual behavior in the human male.* Philadelphia: Sanders, 1948.

Kinsey, A. C., Pomeroy, W. B., Martin, C. E., and Gebhard, P. H. *Sexual behavior in the human female.* Philadelphia: Saunders, 1953.

Latané, B. Field studies of altruistic compliance. *Representative Research in Social Psychology,* 1970, *1,* 49–60.

Leitenberg, H. The use of single-case methodology in psychotherapy research. *Journal of Abnormal Psychology,* 1973, *82,* 87–101.

Levenson, H., Gray, M., and Ingram, A. Current research methods in personality: Five years after Carlson's survey. American Psychological Association Meetings, Chicago, 1975.

Lykken, D. T. Statistical significance in psychological research. *Psychological Bulletin,* 1968, *70,* 151–159.

Maher, B. A. A reader's, writer's and reviewer's guide to assessing research reports in clinical psychology. *Journal of Consulting and Clinical Psychology,* 1978, *46,* 835–838.

Mahoney, M. J. *Scientist as subject.* Cambridge, Massachusetts: Ballinger Press, 1976.

McNemar, Q. *Psychological statistics* (4th ed.). New York: John Wiley & Sons, 1969.

Meehl, P. E. Nuisance variables and the ex post facto design. In M. Radner and S. Winokur (Eds.). *Minnesota studies in philosophy of science.* Minneapolis: University of Minnesota Press, 1970.

Milgram, S. Some conditions of obedience and disobedience to authority. *Human Relations,* 1965, *18,* 57–76.

Milgram, S. The lost-letter technique. *Psychology Today,* June, 1969, 30–33, 66.

Milgram, S. The experience of living in cities. *Science,* 1970, *167,* 1461–1468.

Mitchell, S. K. Interobserver agreement, reliability, and generalizability of data collected in observational studies. *Psychological Bulletin,* 1979, *86,* 376–390.

Nunnally, J. C. *Psychometric theory.* New York: McGraw-Hill, 1967.

Nunnally, J. C., and Durham, R. L. Validity, reliability, and special problems of measurement in evaluation research. In E. L. Struening and M. Guttentag (Eds.) *Handbook of Evaluation Research.* Beverly Hills-London: Sage Publications, 1975.

Orne, M. T., On the social psychology of the psychological experiment: With particular references to demand characteristics and their implications. *American Psychologist,* 1962, *17,* 776–784.

Orne, M. T. and Schiebe, K. E. The contribution of non-deprivation factors in the production of sensory deprivation effects: The psychology of the panic button. *Journal of Abnormal and Social Psychology,* 1964, *68,* 3–12.

Penner, L. *Social Psychology: A contemporary approach.* New York: Oxford University Press, 1978.

Piliavin, J. A., and Piliavin, I. M. Effect of blood on reactions to a victim. *Journal of Personality and Social Psychology,* 1972, *23,* 353–361.

Poor, D. D. S. Analysis of variance for repeated measures designs: Two approaches. *Psychological Bulletin,* 1973, *80,* 204–209.

Poulton, E. C. Unwanted range effects from using within-subjects experimental designs. *Psychological Bulletin,* 1973, *80,* 113–121.

Publication Manual of the American Psychological Association, Second Edition, Washington, D.C., 1974.

Rabkin, J. G., and Struening, E. L. Life events, stress, and illness. *Science,* 1976, *194,* 1013–1020.

Rosenberg, M. J. The conditions and consequences of evaluation apprehension. In R. Rosenthal and R. L. Rosnow (Eds.). *Artifact in Behavioral Research.* New York: Academic Press, 1969.

Rosenthal, R., and Jacobson, L. *Pygmalion in the classroom.* New York: Holt, Rinehart & Winston, 1968.

Rosenthal, R., and Rosnow, R. L. *Experimenter effects in behavioral research.* New York: Appleton-Century-Crofts, 1966.

Rosenthal, R., and Rosnow, R. L. *The volunteer subject.* New York: John Wiley, 1975.

Rothstein, L. D. Reply to Poulton. *Psychological Bulletin,* 1974, *81,* 199–200.

Rubin, Z. Designing honest experiments. *American Psychologist,* 1973, *28,* 445–448.

Runyon, R. P. *Non-parametric statistics: A contemporary approach.* Reading, Massachusetts: Addison-Wesley Publishing Co., 1977.

Runyon, R. P., and Haber, A. *Fundamentals of Behavioral Statistics.* Reading, Massachusetts: Addison-Wesley Publishing Co., 1980.

Schaller, G. B. *The Mountain Gorilla.* Chicago: University of Chicago Press, 1963.

Schaps, E. Cost, dependency and helping. *Journal of Personality and Social Psychology,* 1972, *21,* 74–78.

Schulz, S. C., van Kammen, D. P., Balow, J. E., Flye, M. W. and Bunney, Jr., W. E. Dialysis in schizophrenia: A double blind evaluation, *Science,* 1981, *211,* 1066–1068.

Seeman, J. Deception in psychological research. *American Psychologist,* 1969, *24,* 1025–1028.

Sellitz, C., Wrightsman, L. S., and Cook. S. W. *Research Methods in Social Relations,* New York: Holt, Rinehart, & Winston, 1976.

Shapiro, A. K., and Morris. L. A. The placebo effect in medical and psychological therapies. In S. L. Garfield and A. E. Bergin (Eds.) *Handbook of Psychotherapy and Behavior Change.* New York: John Wiley & Sons, 1978.

Sherrod, D. R. Crowding, perceived control, and behavioral aftereffects. *Journal of Applied Social Psychology,* 1974, *4,* 171–186.

Sidman, M. *Tactics of Scientific Research*. New York: Basic Books, 1960.

Siegel, S. *Non-parametric statistics*. New York: McGraw-Hill, 1956.

Silverman, I. Nonreactive methods and the law. *American Psychologist, 1975, 30*, 764–769.

Sudman, S. *Applied Sampling*. New York: Academic Press, Inc., 1976.

Taylor, J. A. The relationship of anxiety to the conditioned eyelid response. *Journal of Experimental Psychology, 1951, 41*, 81–92.

Tichy, H. J. *Effective writing for engineers, managers, scientists*. New York: John Wiley & Sons, Inc., 1966.

TRACES: Basic research links to technology appraised. *Science, 1969, 163*, 374–375. (Technology in retrospect and critical events in science.)

Wason, P. C. On the failure to eliminate hypotheses in a conceptual task. Quarterly *Journal of Experimental Psychology, 1960, 12*, 129–140.

Wason, P. C., and Johnson-Laird, P. M. *Psychology of Reasoning* Cambridge: Harvard University Press, 1972.

Webb, E. J., Campbell, D. T., Schwartz, R. D., Sechrest, L., and Grove, J. B. *Non-reactive Measures in the Social Sciences*. Chicago: Rand McNally & Company, 1981.

Weber, S. J., and Cook, T. D. Subject effects in laboratory research: An extension of subject roles, demand characteristics, and valid inference. *Psychological Bulletin*, 1972, *77*, 273–295.

Weiss, J. M., Effects of coping response on stress. *Journal of Comparative and Physiological Psychology, 1968, 65*, 251–260.

Weiss, J. M. Effects of coping behavior in different warning signal conditions on stress pathology in rats. *Journal of Comparative and Physiological Psychology, 1971, 77*, 1–13 (a).

Weiss, J. M. Effects of punishing the coping response (conflict) on stress pathology in rats. *Journal of Comparative and Physiological Psychology, 1971, 77*, 14–21 (b).

Weiss, J. M. Effects of coping behavior with and without a feedback signal on stress pathology in rats. *Journal of Comparative and Physiological Psychology, 1971, 77*, 22–30 (c).

Weisskopf, V. F. The significance of science. *Science, 1972, 176*, 138–146.

Wilson, D. W., and Donnerstein, E. Legal and ethical aspects of nonreactive social psychological research. *American Psychologist, 1976, 31*, 765–773.

Winer, B. J. *Statistical Principles in Experimental Design*. New York: McGraw-Hill Book Company, 1971.

Yerkes, R. M., and Dodson, J. D. The relation of strength of stimulus to rapidity of habit formation. *Journal of Comparative and Neurological Psychology, 1908, 18*, 459–482.

Zimbardo, P. The human choice: Individuation, reason, and order versus deindividuation, impulse and chaos. In W. J. Arnold and D. Levine (Eds.). *Nebraska Symposium on Motivation* (Vol. 17). Lincoln: University of Nebraska Press, 1969.

Zimbardo, P. G. *Psychology and Life,* Tenth Edition. Glenview, Illinois: Scott, Foresman and Company, 1979.

INDEX

INDEX